THE HANDBOOK OF COMMERCIAL REAL ESTATE INVESTING

The Handbook of
Commercial Real Estate Investing

John McMahan

McGraw-Hill

New York   Chicago   San Francisco   Lisbon   London   Madrid
Mexico City   Milan   New Delhi   San Juan   Seoul
Singapore   Sydney   Toronto

1 2 3 4 5 6 7 8 9 0 DOC/DOC 0 9 8 7 6

ISBN 0-07-146865-X

This publication is designed to provide accurate and authoritative information in regard to the subject matter covered. It is sold with the understanding that the publisher is not engaged in rendering legal, accounting, or other professional service. If legal advice or other expert assistance is required, the services of a competent professional person should be sought.

—From a Declaration of Principles Jointly Adopted by a Committee of the American Bar Association and a Committee of Publishers and Associations

McGraw-Hill books are available at special discounts to use as premiums and sales promotions, or for use in corporate training programs. For more information, please write to the Director of Special Sales, Professional Publishing, McGraw-Hill, Two Penn Plaza, New York, NY 10121-2298. Or contact your local bookstore.

 This book is printed on recycled, acid-free paper containing a minimum of 50% recycled de-inked paper.

Library of Congress Cataloging-in-Publication Data

McMahan, John, 1937-
   The handbook of commercial real estate investing / by John McMahan.
     p. cm.
   Includes index.
   ISBN 0-07-146865-X (alk. paper)
   1. Commercial real estate. 2. Real estate investment.   I. Title.
HD1393.55.M384   2006
332.63'24—dc22
                                       2005035415

CONTENTS

INTRODUCTION   1

PART I

REAL ESTATE INVESTMENT PROCESS   3

CHAPTER 1

How Value Is Created in Real Estate   5

Value cycle of real estate . . . How investors participate in the value creation process . . . Role of synergy in creating value . . . Role of location in enhancing value . . . Land use regulation . . . Submarket location factors . . . Property factors . . . Market timing . . . Asset management

CHAPTER 2

Market Demand Drivers   23

Economics . . . Technology . . . Demographics . . . Business organization . . . Physical workplace . . . Workplace location

CHAPTER 3

Property Type Characteristics   37

Apartments . . . Retail . . . Office . . . Industrial . . . Hotels

CHAPTER 4

Major Players   59

Life insurance companies . . . Foreign investors . . . Real Estate Investment Trusts (REITs) . . . Pension funds

CHAPTER 5

Understanding Investor Objectives   71

Pension funds ... Individual investors . . . Foreign investors . . . Differing investor objectives . . . Reconciling investment focus with portfolio diversification

PART II

TRANSACTION MANAGEMENT   83

CHAPTER 6
Sourcing, Screening, and Preliminary Underwriting   85
Property sourcing . . . Property screening . . . Preliminary underwriting

CHAPTER 7
Preliminary Approvals and Negotiation   103
Preliminary approvals . . . Negotiations

CHAPTER 8
Due Diligence   111
Role of due diligence . . . Managing the process . . .Physical due diligence . . . Legal due diligence . . .Business due diligence

CHAPTER 9
Final Underwriting and Closing   137
Final underwriting . . . Final approvals . . .Closing documents . . . Title holding entity . . . Waive and closing . . . Transition to asset management

CHAPTER 10
Disposition   147
Targeting buyers . . . Broker selection . . . Listing agreement . . . Confidentiality agreement . . . Offering memorandum . . . Property reports . . . Disposition alternatives . . . Transaction documents . . . Due diligence . . . Transition to buyer's asset management staff

PART III

ASSET MANAGEMENT   161

CHAPTER 11
Role of Asset Manager   163
The modern asset manager . . . Asset versus property management . . . Asset manager's responsibilities

CHAPTER 12
Role in Investment Transactions   173
Acquisitions . . . Transition to asset management . . . Dispositions

CHAPTER 13

Tenant Relations   183

Know the tenant's business . . . Understanding the tenant's financial condition . . . Tenant's view of the building and management . . . Renewing leases . . . New Leases

CHAPTER 14

Building Operations   191

Maintenance . . . Construction management . . . Security . . . Disaster planning

CHAPTER 15

Financial Reporting   201

Financial statements . . . Federal tax reporting . . . Comparative analysis

PART IV

ENTERPRISE MANAGEMENT   211

CHAPTER 16

Leadership   213

Why has it been so difficult? . . . How real estate is changing . . . What is leadership? . . . Qualities of a good leader . . . How leadership skills can be improved . . . Establishing a nurturing work environment . . . Allow broader participation in decision making

CHAPTER 17

Strategic Planning   229

Strategic planning process . . . Evaluating alternatives . . . Formulating the final plan . . . Implementation . . . Summary

CHAPTER 18

Market Positioning   247

Identifying the target market . . . Refining the target market . . . Competitive environment . . . Battlefield mapping . . . Proposed fund features . . . A learning process

CHAPTER 19

Risk Management   263

Managing risk in a mixed asset portfolio . . . Managing real estate portfolio risks . . . Managing real estate enterprise risks

CHAPTER 20

Governance   279

Collapse of Enron . . . Legislative and regulatory reform . . . Reaction to governance reforms: public firms . . . Public real estate companies and corporate governance . . . Board of directors governance guidelines . . . Continuing corporate governance . . .Current situation

APPENDIX A

Technology and the Due Diligence Process   303

APPENDIX B

Legal Documents   315

Glossary   373
Index   385

John McMahan has enjoyed a professional career in real estate as a consultant; investment manager; public board member; educator and writer; and industry and community leader.

Real Estate Consultant: In 1963 John cofounded Development Research Associates (DRA), a market research, financial analysis, and appraisal firm which became one of the nation's major real estate consulting firms. In 1970, DRA was acquired by Booze, Allen & Hamilton, with John heading DRA as well as serving as Vice President, Real Estate, for the parent firm.

Investment Manager: In 1973 he established John McMahan Associates (JMA), which acquired several hundred million in U.S. properties for foreign investors. In 1980 JMA became McMahan Real Estate Advisors, a Registered Investment Advisor, shifting its focus to investing pension capital in real estate. In 1990 the firm merged with a subsidiary of Mellon Bank to form Mellon/ McMahan Real Estate Advisors, with John as CEO. By 1994, Mellon/McMahan managed $2.2 billion in assets and was the nation's sixteenth largest pension real estate advisory firm.

Public Board Member: As part of the Mellon relationship, John assumed responsibility for turning around Mellon Participating Mortgage Trust, Inc., a troubled mortgage REIT. In 1994 John left Mellon/McMahan becoming chairman of BRE Properties, Inc. and led its restructuring into one of the leading apartment REITs in the nation. He also has served as chairman of two additional public REITs and as a board member of a public REIT and two private corporations.

Educator and Writer: Throughout his career, John has been involved in real estate education. For 17 years he taught "Managing the Real Estate Enterprise" as a Senior Lecturer at the Stanford Graduate School of Business. More recently he taught "Institutional Real Estate Investment" at the Haas School of Business, Univerisity of Califronia at Berkeley.

John's first book, *Property Development,* was published in 1976 (and 1989) by McGraw-Hill with *The McGraw-Hill Real Estate Pocket Guide* following in 1979. He also has written 40 professional articles and over 20 cases on real estate management, which became the focus of his latest book *Cases in Commercial Real Estate Investing,* published in July 2005.

He has been awarded The Louise L. and Y. T. Lum Award for Excellence in Teaching and the William S. Ballard Award for writing, as well as Certificates of Commendation from the California Assembly and the Los Angeles City Council. He is a Registered Investment Advisor and a California licensed real estate broker.

Industry and Community Service: John has served on the governing boards of the National Association of Real Estate Investment Managers (Chairman), Association of Foreign Investors in US Real Estate (Secretary General), the Urban Land Institute (Council Chairman), Counselors of Real Estate (Board Member), Lambda Alpha International (Chapter President), San Francisco Architectural Heritage (President), and the Trust for Public Land (Advisory Board). He is also a member of the Aspen Group, the Real Estate Round Table, and the Anglo-American Real Property Institute.

A graduate of the University of Southern California and the Harvard Business School, John has four grown children and lives in San Francisco with his wife of thirty-two years, Jacqueline.

ACKNOWLEDGMENTS

In order to provide the reader a current and practical framework of reference, the book was reviewed by professional managers in the investment management industry. Some of the more technical chapters also were reviewed by specialists in related areas.

Part I, Real Estate Investment Process, was reviewed by Steve Laposa, Director of Real Estate Research for PricewaterhouseCoopers, LLP (PwC), and Geoffrey Dohrmann, Chairman and CEO of Institutional Real Estate, Inc.

Part II, Transaction Management, required multiple views since so many professions are involved in the acquisition and disposition process. Noel Nellis, Esq., Chair of the Global Real Estate Practice for Orrick, Harrington & Sutcliffe, LLP, looked at the process from the legal perspective and provided the documents that appear in Appendix B. Phillip Helms-Cook, Senior Vice President of Marx/Okubo, provided the physical due diligence perspective as well as several photos and plans used as exhibits.

Since Part II is fundamentally about managing transactions, Jeffrey Congdon, Executive Director of the Financial Services Group of Cushman & Wakefield, supplied the professional broker's point of view. Craig Severance, former Head of Acquisitions for AMB Properties, contributed insights throughout the section, and also authored Appendix A on the use of technology in the due diligence process. Bradley Griggs, EVP and Chief Investment Officer of BRE Properties, Inc., also reviewed Section II, providing the apartment investment perspective.

Part III, Asset Management, turned out to be more process oriented and therefore required a review by individuals currently managing asset management operations. Preston Sargent, Executive Vice President of Kennedy Associates Real Estate Counsel, brought the viewpoint of managing office, industrial, and retail properties; and Deirdre Kuring, Executive Vice President of BRE Properties, provided the apartment management perspective. Jeff Kiley, a Real Estate Audit Partner in PwC's Boston office, provided the financial reporting and tax examples and wrote much of the text describing these subjects in Chapter 15.

A research approach was taken in developing Part IV, Enterprise Management, since it required a senior manager's perspective from a broad range of firms. The CEOs who contributed to this section include Hamid

Moghadam, AMB Corporation; Terry Dickens, Bixby Land Company; Connie Moore, BRE Properties; Bob Zerbst, CB Richard Ellis Investors, LLC; Claude Zinngrabe, Fremont Realty Capital LP; Gene Sanger, Hunt Realty Corporation; Al Galpern, Sarofim Realty Advisors Co.; and Scott Urdang, Urdang & Associates Real Estate Advisors, Inc. Also Jeff Pero, Esq., of Latham & Watkins, who brought his usual thoroughness and wise counsel in his review of the corporate governance material in Chapter 20.

A special note of thanks to Bill Croteau, U.S. Real Estate Industry Leader for PwC, for coordinating the overall effort by members of his firm.

Also, I'm in deep gratitude to Lena Sloan for her work in proofing and producing the draft manuscript, as well as assistance in developing many of the exhibits and the Glossary.

I would also like to thank my wife Jacqueline, who worked on my first book, *Property Development,* over 30 years ago and keeps wondering when I will ever tire of writing and talking about real estate. Also my children—Cathy, Jason, Justin, and Vanessa—who provide great joy to their father and are in his heart and mind always.

John McMahan
San Francisco
2005

THE HANDBOOK OF COMMERCIAL REAL ESTATE INVESTING

INTRODUCTION

The *Handbook of Commercial Real Estate Investing* is about investing in one of America's largest industries—commercial real estate—and how to manage the process more effectively and efficiently. Commercial real estate is defined as including office buildings, shopping centers, industrial buildings, apartments, and hotels.

The overall viewpoint of the book is that of the professional investment manager who represents the interests of other investors. This may be a manager of a public real estate investment trust (REIT), an investment advisor to pension funds, a general partner in an investment partnership, or an advisor to foreign investors through any one of a number of investment vehicles.

In so doing, the investment manager is a fiduciary to his or her investors, requiring a high level of professional care by placing the interests of the investor(s) foremost in any management decision.

In most cases, the investment manager is also a beneficiary of the success of investment decisions, either directly—as is the case with a general partner—or indirectly through stock ownership or other management incentive programs

The reader should note that this book provides somewhat of a personal view of the industry, based on the author's 45 years of involvement as an entrepreneur, professional manager, board member, educator, consultant, management trainer, and personal investor. It is hoped that this background will provide a "real world" perspective, and as a result be meaningful in conveying how the real estate investment process actually operates.

The book also reflects a career personal involvement with a wide variety of real estate investors, including pension funds, public real estate companies, corporate real estate managers, foreign investors, family companies, and wealthy individual investors. To be effective, it is essential that the investment manager get into the mind-set of his or her investors by fully understanding their investment objectives and concerns.

The book has, to some extent, an institutional slant, since the author spent much of his professional career working for and with financial institutions, including an early involvement in assisting pension funds and foreign investors with their real estate investment programs. Some of these programs have grown over the years to the point where their sponsors now comprise some of the largest and most influential real estate investors in the industry.

The book can be read from several levels.

From 30,000 feet it is meant to serve as a strategic guide to managing a real estate investment management firm.

At a finer grain, the middle sections are meant to serve as a "best practice" guide to the management of functional operating areas. Part II, Transaction Management, is directed at managers involved in investment transactions such as acquisitions and dispositions. Part III, Asset Management, deals with the increasingly critical role of the asset manager, who has responsibility for ownership issues during the investment holding period.

Senior managers and board members will find Part IV, Enterprise Management, responsive to concerns about enterprise issues such as building leadership, strategic planning, market positioning, risk management, and corporate governance.

For those entering the industry—graduate students in real estate and career-changing employees coming from other industries—this *Handbook of Commercial Real Estate Investing* seeks to provide a realistic view of today's real estate investment business.

The reader may note some redundancy between chapters since each chapter is designed to be read independently, as well as a part of a section or the entire book. Where appropriate, references between chapters are provided.

There are two appendices: Appendix A describes the problems and opportunities of applying technology to the real estate investment process, particularly due diligence on prospective investment assets. Appendix B is a sample of the various legal documents associated with real estate investment.

Finally, a glossary and index provide a definition of terms used in the book as well as rapid access to the discussion of specific issues.

PART I

Real Estate Investment Process

CHAPTER 1

How Value Is Created in Real Estate

Welcome to the wonderful world of commercial real estate, where values are created intentionally and unintentionally every day. Some investors are astute enough to anticipate trends and changes in property characteristics that can lead to value creation and profit from effective investment strategies. Other investors profit in some cases, but then lose in others because they're rolling the dice with each property investment, never understanding what worked and what didn't. Still other investors, perhaps the majority, never play at all in the property market, preferring instead the stock or bond markets, mutual funds, or other non-real-estate investments.

The purpose of this book is to demystify the commercial real estate investment process in order to understand how values are created and to develop the tools necessary to be a successful real estate investor.[1] The lessons are basic and apply to most investors, whether institutional, corporate, or individuals, and whether they're taking the investment risk themselves or serving as advisors to those who are.

VALUE CYCLE OF REAL ESTATE

The ultimate time horizon for real estate is generally longer than other asset classes. This is because it is a "hard" asset, fixed in location and subject to regulation by federal, state, and local governmental agencies.

---

[1] This book focuses almost exclusively on traditional commercial real estate property types—retail, office, industrial, hotels, and apartments. It is not concerned with single family housing except by reference where necessary.

FIGURE 1-1

Life Cycle of Real Estate

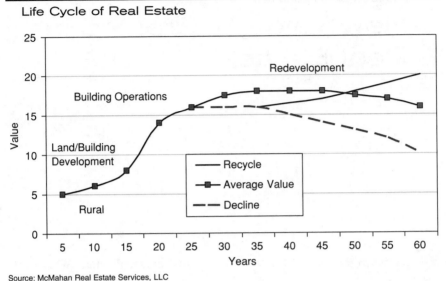

Source: McMahan Real Estate Services, LLC

Figure 1-1 is a stylized representation of the life cycle of a property over a period of 60 years from being a parcel of rural land to a redeveloped building in an urban neighborhood.

Conversion of Rural Land

Most urban land begins as rural land, often on the edge of an existing urban area. As the urban area grows in population and economic activity, land within its existing boundaries becomes less available and more expensive.

Seeking lower costs and greater profits, new development begins leapfrogging outward to rural areas, generally along existing highway arterials or other transportation corridors. As the price of land increases, farmers find it attractive to sell, and move their agriculture operations still farther out to lower cost land areas or simply retire.

There are many players involved in transforming rural land to real estate opportunities. As stated, for example, in a recent *New York Times* article: "KB Home has 483 communities under development in 13 states and expects to complete more than 40,000 new homes this year. Yet it is just one of about two dozen such corporate giants fiercely competing for land and customers at the edge of America's suburban expanse."[2]

---

2 *New York Times,* August 15, 2005.

In most cases, local governmental agencies accommodate this transformation process. This is accomplished through the rezoning of former agriculture areas, construction of new or upgrading of existing arterials, construction of sewer systems, provisions for water and other utilities, construction of new schools, and other steps to provide the urban infrastructure necessary to encourage this sprawling pattern of urban growth.[3]

Generally, it is not lost on most civic leaders that these new growth patterns, while costing money in both capital and servicing costs, create higher levels of tax revenue for local government coffers.

Land investors are usually quick to take advantage of these situations, often buying up farmland by the acre and selling residential home sites by the lot. In many cases these investors lobby their government representatives to rezone the properties and approve new infrastructure improvements.

In some cases investors take the lead in getting the property rezoned by financing a portion (if not all) of the improvements. The rewards to land investors are often huge—ranging from 20 to 50 percent annually—creating enormous wealth for those who are successful.

However, the risks are huge as well, as less fortunate land investors find their investments bypassed by new urban infrastructure, with development opportunities postponed for many years. This substantially reduces, if not eliminates, any opportunity for investment returns commensurate with the risk taken.

Building Development

As the necessary infrastructure is established and rural areas urbanize to the point of establishing a critical mass of residential development, many land investors begin investing in buildings as well. Building developers from other cities and towns, noting the growth of these new areas, establish local operations to take advantage of the opportunities.

Building development is much more complex, however, involving planning and design, gaining necessary governmental entitlements, securing long-term financing, leasing tenant spaces, construction, and, finally, building operations and management. It's also very competitive: Developers with experience and larger staffs, such as KB Home,[4] are often able to provide all of these services in a fully integrated package.

---

3 In recent years several local and state governments have attempted to redirect new growth into established urban growth areas in order to concentrate growth and better utilize existing infrastructure, thereby reducing the loss of productive farmland. An example is the state of Oregon's "urban growth boundary" program.

4 In 2004, KB Home had $7 billion in sales, making it sixth among all Standard & Poor's 500 companies in total revenues. (*New York Times,* August 15, 2005.)

Decline and Renewal

As urban areas grow larger and become more complex, it is inevitable that some areas will fare worse than others. Generally these are older neighborhoods, usually in downtown areas, with serious building deficiencies or areas where certain land uses—such as older industrial—have moved on to more functional areas, generally in the outlying suburbs.

Over time, some of these declining areas begin to recycle either privately or through the efforts of government action, such as capital improvement programs and/or urban renewal projects. In some cases these areas take on an aura of their own, with recycled residential units as well as new restaurants, tourist attractions, and other commercial uses.[5]

This process of urban growth, decline, and renewal goes on in most American and some foreign cities on a continuous basis, creating a wide range of investment opportunities for an increasing diverse group of operating companies and potential investors.

HOW INVESTORS PARTICIPATE IN THE VALUE CREATION PROCESS

As urban areas grow and buildings become more complex, portions of the process are increasingly contracted out to specialists in various building types or development processes, and they perform one or more of the required steps, assuming a portion of the risk with the master developer.

Figure 1-2 indicates how investor risk and return is reduced as a building project moves closer to successful completion.

In many cases the building developer is also the investor, ultimately taking title to the building upon completion. As urban areas grow and building projects become more complex, the amount of capital required becomes larger and developers seek investment partners.

Investors evaluating investment in building development projects soon discover that, as the building moves toward completion and lease-up, risk is reduced and so are returns. This is a sorting out process with investors able to invest in elements of projects that suit their own risk/return profiles.

In fact it is not unusual to find different types of investors with different risk/return profiles, investing in different stages of a project. Developers also have discovered that the longer they can self-finance a project, the higher return they can capture for themselves—but also at a higher risk.

---

5 An example is the LoDo District in Denver, Colorado.

FIGURE 1-2

Real Estate Risk and Return

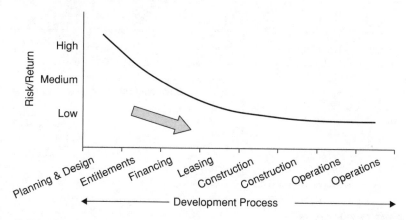

Source: McMahan Real Estate Services, LLC

In time, the lines between developers and investors may become blurred, with some developers becoming investors and some investors becoming developers.[6]

ROLE OF SYNERGY IN CREATING VALUE

One of the reasons so many players are interested in participating in the real estate value creation process is the role played by synergy in making it happen. Figure 1-3 indicates how synergy creates value by systematically reducing the level of risk in the final building product.

As indicated in the figure, each of the individual cost items in the development process adds up to a total of $25 million, but an investor might pay $30 million for the rights to own the building, assuming it is sufficiently leased, generating a profit of $5 million to the developer for putting all of the pieces together.

This is not too different than investing in common stocks, as indicated in Figure 1-4. The real estate example is the same as in Figure 1-3. The stock example uses different terms to describe the steps in the valuation creation process but is essentially the same as that in real estate.

---

6 From time to time mortgage lenders also become interested in enhancing investment returns through special arrangements in mortgage instruments that allow them to "participate" in a project's equity returns.

FIGURE 1-3

The Role of Synergy in Creating Property Value

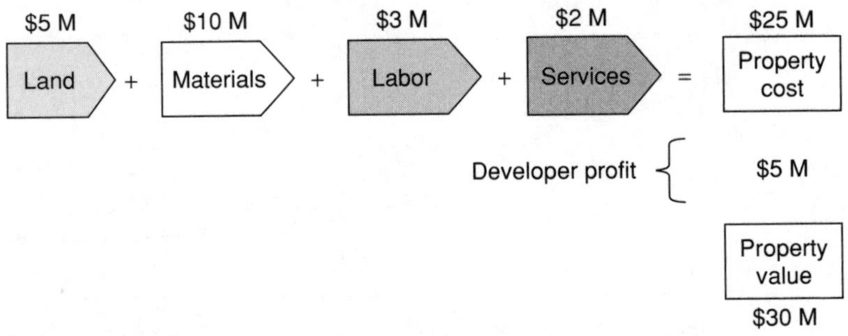

$5 M		$10 M		$3 M		$2 M		$25 M
Land	+	Materials	+	Labor	+	Services	=	Property cost

Developer profit { $5 M

Property value

$30 M

Source: McMahan Real Estate Services, LLC

FIGURE 1-4

The Value Creation Process: Common Stocks and Real Estate

	Common Stocks	Real Estate
Cost to create		
Book value (development cost)	$20.0 M	$20.0 M
Earnings (NOI)	$2.5 M	$2.5 M
P/E (cap rate)	8×	12.5%
Value to investors		
P/E (cap rate)	10×	10.0%
Market value	$25.0 M	$25.0 M
Entrepreneurial profit	$5.0 M	$5.0 M

Source: McMahan Real Estate Services, LLC

The book value of the firm is $20 million, which is the same as the cost of creating the real estate project. Earnings are the same in both cases: $2.5 million annually.

The stock investor utilizes a price earnings ratio (PE) of 10 times earnings to arrive at a value of the company of $25 million. The real estate investor divides by the reciprocal of the PE ratio (10 percent) to arrive at the same $25 million in value.

In both approaches the annual earnings are equal, the capitalization process essentially similar, and the final estimated value the same. More important to the entrepreneurs in both cases, the profit in creating the investment opportunity is identical.

ROLE OF LOCATION IN ENHANCING VALUE

There's an old adage in real estate that the three major factors in real estate value creation are (1) location, (2) location, and (3) location. While it would be easy to dismiss this homily as being too simple, no experienced real estate investor can overlook the importance of location in influencing the value creation process.

Metro Area Competition

Not only is the United States growing faster than other industrial countries, but some American metro areas are growing much faster than others. Much of this growth is tied directly to job creation. While technology-oriented metros dominated job growth in past years, the momentum has shifted to cities with low costs, growing populations, and reliable and stable sectors such as health care and government. Tourism and new housing construction jobs are also magnets for many job seekers.

The Milken Institute of Los Angeles ranks the largest 200 metro areas in the United States each year by a series of job-creating factors that include new job formation, growth in salary and wages, and annual increases in Gross Domestic Product.

Figure 1-5 illustrates Milken's ranking of the top 10 job-creating metro areas out of the top 200 in the United States as of November 2004.

Since the Milken Index measures annual growth, it tends to favor smaller metro areas with smaller statistical bases. Of the largest U.S. metros, Washington, D.C., scored highest, placing eleventh, followed by Atlanta

FIGURE 1-5

Rank of Leading Job-Creating Metro Areas, November 2004

2004 Rank	Metro Area	2003 Rank
1	Fort Myers-Cape Coral, FL	3
2	Las Vegas, NV	2
3	Phoenix-Mesa, AZ	43
4	West Palm Beach-Boca Raton, FL	4
5	Daytona Beach, FL	116
6	Sarasota-Bradenton, FL	41
7	Fayetteville-Springdale-Rogers, Ark. (1)	1
8	Riverside-San Bernardino, CA	20
9	Fort Lauderdale, FL	29
10	Monmouth-Ocean, NJ	10

Source: Milken Institute, "Best Performing Cities"

(72), Philadelphia (84), Houston (104), Dallas (114), New York, (139), Los Angeles (140), Boston (144), San Francisco (152), and Chicago (166).

Role of Entrepreneurship

The Milken report also comments on the role of entrepreneurs in determining which metro areas will have the highest growth rates:

> Entrepreneurs are necessary visionaries of the economic potential of new technologies and how to apply them to business concept innovations. Fast-growing, entrepreneurial companies epitomize regional economic dynamism. For a metro area to be a successful over the long haul, it has to have capable entrepreneurs. Over the long term, cities with strength in entrepreneurship will be among our Best Performing Cities.[7]

The report goes on to define the qualities of these entrepreneurial people:

> A region's most important source of competitive advantage is the knowledge embedded in its people. In the past, firms attracted people; in the current, increasingly intangible economy, concentrations of talent are attracting firms. The knowledge, skills, experience, and innovative potential of talented individuals have greater value than capital equipment. A successful enterprise accesses, creates, and utilizes knowledge to sustain competitive advantage.

LAND USE REGULATION

A metro area may be rapidly growing in population but might not necessarily be a good target for real estate investors. It is important, therefore, to also understand the land use policies of local government agencies.

In terms of land use, metro markets in the United States can be divided into "commodity" and "constrained" markets.

Commodity Markets

In commodity markets the emphasis is on job formation, with real estate viewed largely as a factor of production. As a result, commodity markets generally reflect a strong progrowth and projobs philosophy. In fact, the often stated public objective of these policies is to keep land costs and building rents low so that the area continues to be attractive to new firms and existing firms don't leave.

---

7 Milken Institute, op. cit.

These policies are accomplished by a very general plan: relatively lenient zoning restrictions, largely nonunion labor, and an expedited entitlement process. The result is real estate markets with relatively low rents and high vacancy rates. This situation also encourages a considerable amount of shifting between urban nodes as new product becomes available, often at lower costs. Examples of commodity markets include Atlanta, Austin, Charlotte, Dallas, Houston, Memphis, Orlando, and Phoenix.

Many institutional real estate investors believe that the public policy creating commodity markets implicitly favors real estate speculators at the expense of long-term investors. As a result, of the top 10 target markets identified by institutional investors in 2005, *none were commodity markets.*[8]

Constrained Markets

In constrained markets, real estate supply is restricted as an integral part of public policy. This is accomplished through a strong general land use plan and a rigorous process by which new projects are approved. By limiting supply, this process allows rents to seek market levels and, in most cases, results in appreciation in real property assets. Constrained markets include Boston, Chicago, Los Angeles, Miami, New York City, Philadelphia, San Francisco, San Diego, Seattle, and Washington, D.C.

The intuition of institutional investors is supported by a certain amount of research. Figure 1-6 is based on a study by the Johnson/Souza

FIGURE 1-6

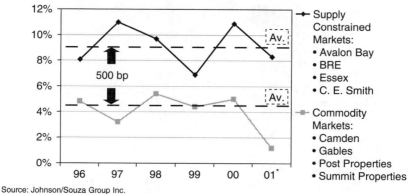

Supply Constrained vs. Commodity Markets (Same-Store NOI Growth)

Source: Johnson/Souza Group Inc.

---

8 Pension Real Estate Association, 2005.

Group Inc. of the same-store Net Operating Income (NOI) of selected multifamily real estate investment trusts between 1996 and 2001.[9] The REITs
were grouped into constrained and commodity categories, based on the
geographical location of the majority of their portfolio.

The Souza study concluded that multifamily REITs operating in constrained markets generated annual NOI returns averaging approximately
500 basis points higher than REITs operating in commodity markets.[10]

SUBMARKET LOCATION FACTORS

Each regional market is generally broken down into a series of submarkets, based on local real estate factors. Figure 1-7 shows a stylized version
of key factors affecting location decisions at this finer grain of analysis.

In most regional areas there are one or more growth corridors that
influence urban growth over the medium term (five to 10 years). These
corridors may reflect the development of new arterials or the upgrading of
existing ones. In some areas the development of high-speed or light-rail
service also may influence growth patterns.

Transportation is not the only growth inducer. Higher density rezoning, urban renewal projects, new sewer lines, and neighborhood revital-

FIGURE 1-7

Submarket Analysis

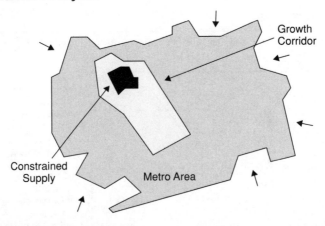

Source: McMahan Real Estate Services, LLC

---

9 The Johnson/Souza Group Inc.
10 The Souza study is based on real estate returns, independent of stock values.

ization programs are just some of the changes in urban living and working patterns that can represent new real estate investment opportunities.

Since these changes generally span a number of years, the key issue for the real estate investor is one of timing: You don't want to be too early or too late to benefit from the increase in real estate values that generally accompanies this type of change in the urban fabric.

Since zoning is usually a province of local government, it is also possible to find submarkets that are constrained more than others, reflecting local voter preferences. Beverly Hills, California (Wilshire Boulevard); Scottsdale, Arizona (Camelback Road); Buckhead, Georgia (Peachtree Street); and Tyson Corner, Virginia (Dulles Airport corridor)—all are examples of classic real estate investment situations in which a constrained submarket is located in the path of an economic growth corridor, creating upward pressure on land and building values.

PROPERTY FACTORS

At the property level, a wide variety of factors influence future value enhancement. With today's emphasis on good site planning, the sheer size of a parcel can influence the ability to create a good site development plan and phase development over time. Soil conditions can also be a factor in the ability to build down (parking) and up (building size). In earthquake-prone areas it may be the dominant factor.

A "perfect storm" of factors contributing to property value appreciation is a parcel or improved property located in a constrained local jurisdiction, in the path of a growth corridor, and in a regional constrained market. Unfortunately, most of the existing opportunities have already been captured—the challenge is to find or create the next perfect storm!

MARKET TIMING

Many successful real estate investors, when queried about their investment strategy, reply that they are "market timers," deciding when to enter or leave a given market.

While this strategy may work when investors are "insiders" presented with truly unique one-off situations, it's usually hard for noninsiders to replicate these situations or to form the basis for a systematic, long-term strategy for successful real estate investing.

It's also hard to continually be involved in seeing new property investment deals unless the investor is in the deal business as a broker or investment banker. Even in these situations it is often difficult to take advantage of insider knowledge in an increasingly transparent and increasingly regulated business environment where conflicts of interest require disclosure, thereby undermining some portion of insider advantage. This is not to say that investors should be unaware of the importance of timing in decision making, just that they shouldn't depend on it as a fundamental investment strategy.

An example is the knowledge of real estate cycles. Glenn Mueller, formerly of Johns Hopkins University and Legg Mason,[11] has done extensive research on real estate cycles and provided a long-term view of the cyclical effects of real estate markets. Figure 1-8 is a graphic representation of some of his observations.

Mueller's research is based on the interaction of two types of cycles: (1) the *physical cycle* reflecting the interaction of demand and supply, which drives rental rates; and (2) the financial cycle, which reflects capital flows and primarily impacts property prices. (These two cycles may not necessarily move together.)

FIGURE 1-8

Real Estate Cycle

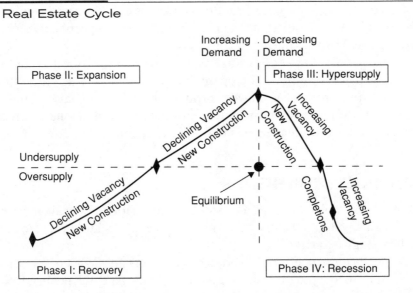

Source: Glenn Mueller, Ph.D., Colorado State University

---

11 Now Loveland Commercial Endowed Chair of Real Estate and Director of the Everitt Real Estate Center at Colorado State University.

Phase I: Recovery

Beginning at the market low (lower left side of Figure 1-8), the market-place is in a state of oversupply from previous new construction or nega-tive demand growth. At this bottom point occupancy is at its trough. Typically, the market bottom occurs when excess construction from the previous cycle stops.

As the cycle bottom is passed, demand growth begins to slowly absorb the existing oversupply, and supply growth is nonexistent or very low. As excess space is absorbed, vacancy rates fall, allowing rental rates to stabilize and even begin to increase.

As the recovery continues, positive expectations about the market allow landlords to increase rents at a slow pace (at or below inflation). Eventually, the market reaches its long-term occupancy average when rental growth is equal to inflation.

Phase II: Expansion

As the market moves through equilibrium, it continues to tighten with rents rising rapidly, until they reach a "cost-feasible" level that allows new construction to occur. In this period of tight supply, rapid rental growth may occur, creating rent "spikes."

Once cost-feasible rents are achieved, demand growth continues to lead supply growth (due to construction lag times) and long expansionary periods are possible. As long as demand growth rates are higher than supply growth rates, vacancy rates will continue to fall. The cycle peaks when demand and supply are growing at the same rate. Before this point, demand grows faster than supply; after equilibrium, supply grows faster than demand.

Phase III: Hypersupply

Most real estate players do not recognize the point of equilibrium because it occurs in what appears to be a strong market. In reality, supply growth is now higher than demand growth, causing vacancy rates to rise back toward the long-term occupancy average.

While there is no painful oversupply during this period, new supply completions now compete for tenants in the marketplace. As more space comes into the market, rental growth slows.

Eventually the players realize that the market has turned down, and commitments to new construction slow and ultimately stop. Once the long-term occupancy average is passed, if new supply continues to grow faster than demand, the market moves into Phase IV.

Phase IV: Recession

The extent of the market downturn will be determined by the difference (excess) between demand growth, and the growth in market supply. In the past, massive oversupply coupled with negative demand growth has resulted in some of the worst markets the United States has experienced; for example, 1984–1990.

During this phase, landlords realize that their rental rates must be competitive in order to retain existing tenants and to attract new ones. They therefore begin lowering rates, sometimes to a level just enough to cover fixed expenses.

Property market liquidity is low or nonexistent in this phase, as the bid-ask spread in property prices is too wide. The cycle eventually reaches bottom as existing construction is completed and new buildings are put on hold. The cycle moves back to Phase I when demand growth turns up and begins to grow at a higher rate than new supply.

It should be noted that each metro area has its own cycle, and it may vary considerably from other areas and from an overall national average. Generally, markets located in metropolitan areas with constrained growth policies will be less volatile than those in commodity markets.

Also, the real estate cycle varies between property types. Generally, office, industrial, and hotel markets are more susceptible to cyclical extremes than retail or apartment markets. It's necessary, therefore, to view the dynamics of each local market and property life independently.

Figure 1-9 indicates how an investor might use real estate cycle knowledge as a foundation for a "market timing" investment strategy.

An immediate reaction to Figure 1-9 might be: "Why not buy or sell at the peak or trough of the cycle?" The problem is twofold: First, it's very difficult to tell in advance when the peak or trough of a cycle is going to be reached, let alone to put together a marketing or acquisition plan to maximize value (minimize cost). Second, buying or selling before the peak ensures less competition in the marketplace. It's better to be a leader on the upside and leave profits to others who will discover that their precise timing was diluted by intense market competition to get into or out of the market.

ASSET MANAGEMENT

Regardless of where a property is located, it still has to be managed, and in some cases effective asset management can make a difference in investment value. Unfortunately, many investors are oriented to reducing and maintaining the lowest building operating costs possible. This is not always the best way to optimize value.

FIGURE 1-9

Real Estate Cycle Investment Strategy

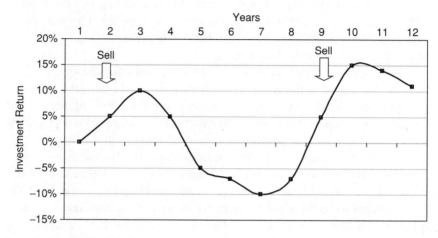

Source: McMahan Real Estate Services, LLC

The major reason is that most real estate operating costs are relatively fixed in nature, and there's little that managers can do about it. Property taxes can be protested, insurance coverage can be negotiated, janitorial and other service contracts can be put out to bid, repairs can be postponed, and some building service costs can even be passed on to tenants.

All of these steps can and should be considered, but they have to be weighed against their impact on tenants; that is, how the tenants view the building, and their willingness to consider other buildings when their lease comes up for renewal.

The bottom line is that a building's location is fixed, but the tenant's location isn't, or at least not when the lease comes up for renewal. Tenants who believe they are receiving "fair value" are more likely to stay or consider other locations in the building, provided their space requirements can be met.

As real estate markets become more fluid and large multibuilding companies emphasize good landlord-tenant relations, building managers are under increasing market pressure to treat their tenants fairly if they wish to retain them.

A focus on retention can also be profitable. As discussed in greater detail in Chapter 13, "A survey of a 12 million square foot portfolio with a 6 percent rollover indicated that $900,000 per year could be added to the bottom line for every 10 percent of expiring space that was renewed rather than retenanted."

The move to recognize tenants as "customers" has other ramifications as well. One is the strategy of approaching tenants about renewing before the lease term is up. This not only demonstrates a willingness on the part of the landlord to negotiate new terms before being forced to, but also a willingness to work with tenants in understanding and attempting to meet their space needs over the longer term.

This approach also has certain downside risks for the investor. An obvious one is that if the market rate is lower than the rent the tenant is currently paying, the investor will have several months of less rental income from this particular tenant. Another is that the tenant will tell other tenants, who will ask for similar concessions. Still another is that the tenant will shop the offer with other buildings to get the best deal.

Each of these risks, as well as others, has to be weighed carefully before proceeding with an aggressive re-leasing program, but at least the alternative has to be weighed, particularly in weak rental markets. Losing a tenant and not being able to re-lease the space is not a good alternative either.

It also allows the landlord to "spread" tenant leases on a more staggered basis, thereby reducing the "bunching" of lease turns and the tendency of one or a few tenant decisions to influence the behavior of others.[12] Figure 1-10 is a graphic representation of how a lease term spreading program might operate.

FIGURE 1-10

Lease Spreading Strategy

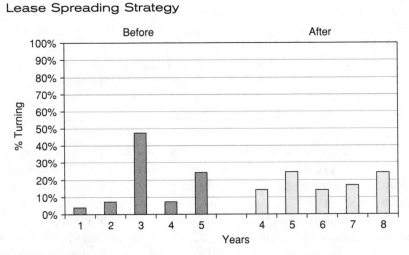

Source: McMahan Real Estate Services, LLC

12 Lease terms are often "bunched" because leasing occurs in anticipation of building completion and, unless this pattern is changed by the landlord, may continue at five- and 10-year intervals.

In the remainder of Part I, we will discuss the nature and character of real estate market demand, the difference and similarities between the major commercial property types, who the major players are, and what they are seeking from the asset class. We will then look at how to implement a successful real estate investment program incorporating some of the strategies we have discussed.

CHAPTER 2

Market Demand Drivers

We begin our exploration by examining major market demand drivers of real estate. Figure 2-1 graphically describes how these forces can interact with real estate supply. We will explore each of these to determine what role they play in making real estate an attractive investment.

ECONOMICS

As illustrated in Figure 2-2, the relative proportion of all real estate as a share of private fixed investment has been steadily declining since 1958, with the exception of the last few years, because of the increase in single family housing purchases.

A large part of this relative decline has been in the growth of other sectors, particularly in the business sector, where financial assets have replaced structural assets as the major component of U.S. business (see Figure 2-3).

TECHNOLOGY

Another factor in the relative decline in real estate has been the influence of technology in our nation's economy. With the exponential growth of computer hardware, software, and of telecommunications, technology[1] is now the largest employer in the country, larger than housing, automobiles, or food. The technology sector now employs one out of two workers in the labor force.[2]

---

1 Includes hardware, software, and telecommunications.
2 U.S. Department of Commerce.

FIGURE 2-1

Major Real Estate Market Drivers

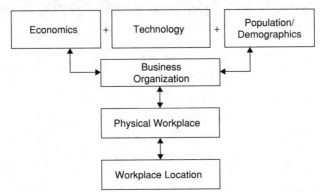

Source: McMahan Real Estate Services, LLC

FIGURE 2-2

Real Estate Share of Private Fixed Investment

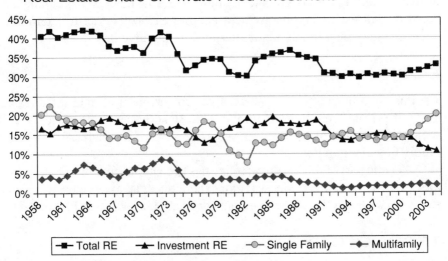

Source: U.S. Department of Commerce, Bureau of Economic Affairs

As illustrated in the bar graph in Figure 2-4, technology has also had a major impact on productivity.

E-Commerce

Not only has technology become the major source of employment and productivity in the United States, but the phenomenon of electronic com-

FIGURE 2-3

Changing Importance of Business Assets

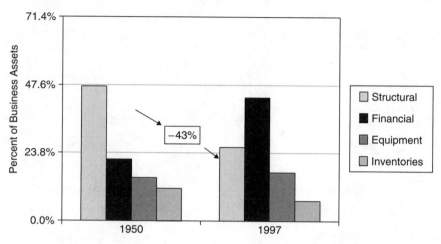

Source: Federal Reserve System, Prudential Real Estate Investors

FIGURE 2-4

Productivity

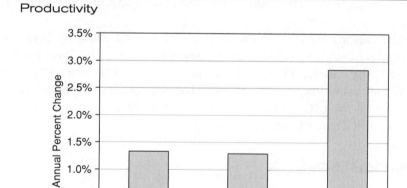

Source: U.S. Department of Labor

merce, or "e-commerce," has influenced the way most firms and many individuals operate in their day-to-day lives. Figure 2-5 illustrates how e-commerce has assumed such a major presence in our lives in a relatively short period of time.

FIGURE 2-5

Components of e-Commerce

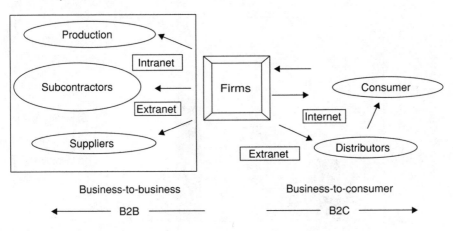

Source: McMahan Real Estate Services, LLC

E-commerce interfaces with both individual consumers (B2C) and business firms (B2B). B2C's major interface is the ubiquitous Internet, through which firms sell products and services to customers around the world.

The major interfaces in the B2B sector are the *extranet* (between firms) and the *intranet* (within a firm). The extranet is used in contacts with subcontractors and suppliers, and the intranet is used by firms to better control internal business functions. B2B has had a major impact on office and industrial uses; B2C has had some impact on retailing and hotel uses, which we will discuss in the next chapter.

DEMOGRAPHICS

The United States has a unique position among industrialized nations in that it is still growing in population. An important reason is that approximately 40 percent of the nation's population growth in the 1990s was a result of new immigration.[3] This is expected to be an even more significant factor in the future—it is expected to account for about 63 percent of population growth over the next 50 years.[4]

---

3 Center for Immigration Studies, "The Impact of Immigration on U.S. Population Growth," August 21, 2001. Testimony before Congress by Steven Camarota, Director of Research.
4 Center for Immigration Studies, ibid.

The bar graph in Figure 2-6 shows the absolute population change for each of the past four decades as well as projections for the current decade.

As you can see in the chart, the major U.S. population surge came in the 1960s with the rise of the generation now commonly referred to as the "Baby Boomers," with other booms in the 1990s and the current decade.

The chart in Figure 2-7 translates population growth into generations. Each of these generations are having and will continue to have an impact on U.S. real estate for some years to come.

In the descriptions of these generations that follow, the ages we cite for each are as of 2005. The categories are generalized to provide a context. Obviously there are individuals in every generation who do not reflect the traits and beliefs of their peers.

Silent Generation: 63 to 80

This generation had about 60.8 million people as of 2000 and will decline through death to approximately 40.8 million by 2010. The Great Depression and World War II heavily influenced this generation. The experience of

FIGURE 2-6

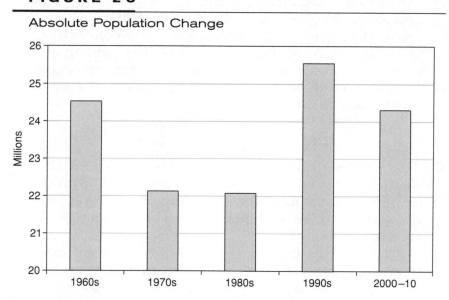

Absolute Population Change

Source: U.S. Census Bureau

FIGURE 2-7

Generation Cohorts

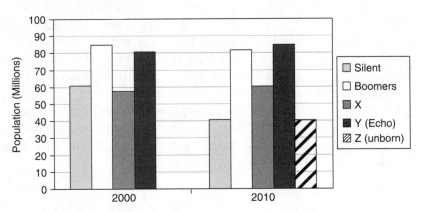

Source: U.S. Census Bureau

seeing their parents out of work and having difficulty in finding new jobs resulted in a great respect for the security of employment. As a result, college majors tended to be practical in nature, such as engineering and business.

The experience of World War II provided this generation with respect for authority and decisive leadership. Roosevelt, Eisenhower, and Truman were all "top down" leaders of large enterprises. This same view permeated postwar business organizations, resulting in large, hierarchical organizations run according to "command and control" management systems.

Such offices were generally enclosed, with corner offices taking on special significance. Business dress consisted of white shirts, tie, and possibly a hat. Coats usually were worn in the office, even when sitting at a desk. Not surprisingly, the best-selling business book for this generation was *The Organization Man*.

Baby Boomers: 41 to 62

The Baby Boomers constituted the largest generation in American history, with approximately 84.8 people as of 2000, declining slightly to 81.8 by 2010. Growing up, this generation was influenced by the Vietnam War, the civil rights movement, Watergate, television, and the birth control pill, not necessarily in that order.

In coming of age, Boomers were exposed to contrasting leadership styles, ranging from idealistic leaders such as John Kennedy and Martin Luther King, Jr. to so-called "realpolitik" leaders such as Richard Nixon and Lyndon Johnson.

Over time, Boomers became cynical about leadership and began questioning authority. They were also turned off to business as a future career, and more commonly majored in liberal arts. As it turned out, many ended up in business anyway, and modifications in personal appearance, as well as the liberalized dress codes within firms, can be ascribed to their values. The best-selling business book of the period was *The Dilbert Principal.*

Sometimes called yuppies, a term coined from the phrase "young urban professionals"—and often characterized in the media as self-indulgent—Boomers nevertheless made a break with their parents' concept of leadership and the role of authority. As *Fortune* magazine put it:

> As managers they espouse values that any progressive organization would endorse: lots of communication, sharing of responsibility, respect for each other's autonomy.
>
> They are also thoroughly uncomfortable with much of what has traditionally ... been thought of as the leader's role. They don't like telling others what to do any more than they like being told.[5]

In retrospect, this generation has been pivotal in laying the groundwork for a completely new view of U.S. business organization and management.

Generation X: 29 to 40

The Boomers were followed by a much smaller generation called, for lack of a better name, the "X generation." As of 2000, this generation had 57.4 million people and is expected to grow slightly, to 60.1 million by 2010.

In growing up, attitudes of Xers were influenced by the Ronald Reagan presidency, the personal computer, and AIDS, among other things. In terms of careers and the workplace, they were the first generation living in a world in which both parents worked full-time outside the home. It was also the period in which divorce rates peaked, which meant for some of them moving back and forth between two homes.

Growing up in broken families or at least families in which parents often were not home, some within this generation would have felt deprived of their parents' company and decided not to repeat their parents' lives. This might be a factor explaining why many Xers seem to want stable marriages in order to build traditional families, and why they plan to be more available to their children as they grow up.

---

5 *Fortune,* April 10, 1989

In essence, many Xers are "working to live rather than living to work." They value interesting work and want their organizations to help them find ways to integrate family life into their demanding careers. An example is the move toward incorporating child care facilities in business complexes.

In their formative years the Xers were no doubt influenced by the massive layoffs of the early 1990s (43 million middle management people), as American industry outsourced work and moved to become "leaner" in order to better compete with the Japanese and other foreign firms. Perhaps this contributes to the attitude of Xers who do not trust organizations and instead value independence. However, this generation cannot be characterized as antibusiness, and many among this group have majored in business and engineering.

In fact, Generation X generally has strong capitalist ideals and is entrepreneurial. A recent study by the IBM Corporation indicated that one in five small business owners is now under 35 years old.[6] Another study finds that 24- to 35-year-olds are starting businesses at a higher rate than the rate of Baby Boomers.[7] The University of Michigan concludes that "becoming wealthy" is considered important to 46 percent of Xers, versus only 37 percent of Baby Boomers.[8]

Xers generally believe they must construct their own future, independent of business organizations, being loyal only to themselves and their peers. They view job loss as a real possibility and so want a "mix" of skills to help them move on if they don't like where they are.

In essence, many Xers move up by moving to another firm. The trade-off with their employers is that they are willing to work long hours while training for their next job. They want to be informed and involved, and seek work experiences that best fit their career aspirations. Many also believe that business firms should be organized differently.

This view of the world is possible because they are members of a relatively small generation and, to date, finding a job has not been a problem. Xers are also the first generation to be raised on computers on a personal level. This gives them certain advantages, such as accessing and manipulating information better than an older employee, which in essence provides another lever over the organization. It's not just a coincidence that Xers often mentor older employees in tasks involving technology.

---

6 IBM Corporation.
7 Kaufman Index of Entrepreneurial Activity: Ewing Marion Kauffman Foundation, September 22, 2005. The study also found that "immigrants have substantially higher rates of entrepreneurship than native-born individuals."
8 University of Michigan.

The Xers linkage with technology was perhaps most evident in the dot-com boom of the mid- to late-1990s, when they were in positions within tech organizations, and in some cases in leadership roles. Some of them made phenomenal fortunes while still in their 20s, and looked forward to retiring in their 30s to begin raising a family.

With the collapse of the dot-coms and the onset of a recession, however, many found their hopes dashed as reality set in, and were thankful just to have a job. Subsequently, some Xers who were involved in the dot-com boom have become senior executives of technology firms, which, as pointed out earlier, is now America's leading industry.

Echo Boomers: One to 28

The sons and daughters of the Boomers, known in media parlance as the "Y generation," and more recently as "Echo Boomers," belong to a generation even larger than that of their parents. As of 2000, according to the U.S. Census Bureau, these Echo Boomers numbered 80.7 million, and are expected to grow to 84.9 million by 2010.[9]

Among the influential events of this generation were the first Gulf war, the stock market boom and bust of the late 1990s, the impeachment trial of President Clinton, the impact of the coming of the millennium, the events of September 11, the resultant war on terrorism, and the war in Iraq.

Many of the Echo Boomers are entering the labor force now, so it's too early to ascertain what their preferences will be in terms of a work environment. Having been "raised" on the Web, so to speak, they are even more technologically proficient than the Xers, and have many of the same work habits and clothing preferences. No book has yet emerged as a defining piece of business literature for this generation, although several books have been written about them, among them, *The Mentoring Advantage: Creating the Next Generation of Leaders* and *Managing Generation Y.*

BUSINESS ORGANIZATION

The Echo Boomers will find a much different workplace than that of their parents, largely through the pioneering efforts of Generation X. Successful firms today are highly focused on customers as well as the production process. Employees are expected to do everything humanly possible to attract and retain customers. This "customer facing" culture is now becoming deeply institutionalized within most American firms.

---

9 U.S. Census Bureau.

Today, successful firms are managed by business models that are keyed to achieving the firm's business goals and interests. Organizational structures are less hierarchical and more horizontal, with employees connected by technology into a series of high performance "project" teams focused on product/service tasks. Each project team contains its own marketing and financial personnel reporting directly to the project manager and indirectly to the corporate marketing and finance functional managers.[10]

Increased immigration and higher educational achievements by minorities mean that the workplace is becoming ethnically and racially more diverse. There are also more women in middle and senior management.

In some respects, this new approach to organization is an assault on tradition, overturning established relationships and reengineering markets. It attacks long established price points, deconstructing and reconstructing value chains. More than ever it affects longstanding institutions and forces organizational change in order to survive.

Figure 2-8 illustrates the emerging "project" organizational format in contrast to the traditional "silo" format.

FIGURE 2-8

Contrasting Organizational Formats

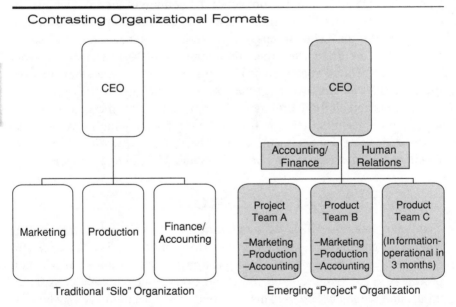

Source: McMahan Real Estate Services, LLC

---

10 Some firms reverse this reporting relationship.

A new business culture appears to be emerging in which openness is encouraged and people are expected to help each other. Learning is becoming more institutionalized so that people can acquire the skills necessary to do their jobs. Old systems are "deconstructed" in order to provide a new foundation for creative change.

In this environment, almost everyone is a leader in some way, and the challenge is to create an environment for team and individual success. Authority is delegated; collaboration expected. Leaders evangelize, generating a positive "buzz" about the organization and its future. Risk taking is encouraged, and everyone—including the boss—is expected to roll up his or her sleeves and work incredibly long hours.

This revolution in the workplace has major implications for real estate not only in terms of building design and the tenant's use of space, but the economies and growth of American cities and towns.

PHYSICAL WORKPLACE

Because of these organizational changes, the physical work environment is becoming increasingly "open" to accommodate the forming and reforming of project teams. Buildings are often two or three story "walk-up" facilities, because horizontal movement offers less impediment to information sharing than vertical, elevator-served space. These facilities also provide exercise for overworked employees.

Within the building, larger floor plates with fewer columns and movable partitioning support new organizational formats. Floor-to-ceiling partitioning is utilized primarily for conference rooms and "war rooms" to meet the meeting requirements of high performance project teams.

Many firms are also extending work hours in order to facilitate flextime schedules and late night sessions. Given the 24/7 work environment, common areas are necessary to provide employee services such as day care, food service, exercise, dry cleaning, etc. In some cases, satellite offices are built within 60 miles of headquarters or a large regional office in order to reduce commute time. In a tight labor market, the physical environment is increasingly important in attracting and retaining key employees.

Office-related employment is also increasing. In 1970 it was 12.4 percent of total nonfarm employment; by 2003 it had increased to 18.4 percent.[11] With business profits increasingly driven by investment in intellectual

---

11 Steven Laposa, Director of Global Strategic Real Estate, PricewaterhouseCoopers, in a presentation to the CREW Network, September 2005. Based on data provided by Economy.com.

capital—where knowledge workers are a key ingredient for business success—the cost of losing good employees is usually much greater than the cost of creating adequate work space.

In many industries there also has been a move in recent years to *reduce individual employee work areas* through open space plans and shared facility programs such as "hoteling."[12] This not only applies to engineers and technology personnel, but to support employees and even senior management. Figure 2-9 illustrates the decline in office space per employee.

While any one firm's space reduction efforts may not be important, the collective action of many firms increasing employee density could ultimately mean lower rates of growth in the demand for total work space. This may in part explain how new jobs were added over the last several years without adding a significant amount of new work space.

One of the reasons some employees appear willing to accept higher densities in their office environment is that in many cases they are spending less time there. With the mobility offered by the personal computer, cell phones, and e-mail, people are increasingly working in other venues, such as their homes, second homes, hotels, client offices, and airplanes. As some managers put it in a survey a few years back:

FIGURE 2-9

Square Feet per Office Worker

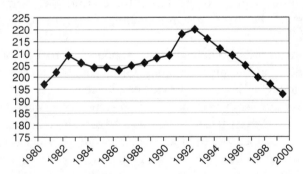

Source: Prudential Real Estate Investors

---

12 This is a concept in which employees do not have a regular office but rather a "locker" in which they store their personal effects. They are then assigned a work space for a day or as long as they will be in that office. Used primarily by accounting and other professional firms with multiof-fice locations.

Five years ago the office was a pretty big part of my life; now it's just another place to go. I don't have to be here to get my work done.

People can work out of the office or in Timbuktu. It's never going back the way it was.

The empire of your own box isn't relevant anymore. Work is mobile— the cell phone, e-mail, and your computer. It's not just technology, it's a mind-set—like casual clothes. What's going on is a convergence of life, work, and home.[13]

In addition, the drive to lower real estate costs has led many corporate real estate managers to locate office functions in other property types, most notably industrial buildings. Industrial construction is not only cheaper, but facilities can be located closer to reasonably priced residential areas and designed in an "open space" manner that allows more flexibility in creating and disbanding task force and project teams. Figure 2-10 is a sales brochure describing one of three such buildings in the Dallas suburbs.

Individual buildings also provide external firm identification that may be lost in a multitenant building. Often located on fiber-optic trunk lines, this type of facility increasingly offers employers attractive alternatives to high-rise space in the Central Business District (CBD) and midrise suburban office space.

WORKPLACE LOCATION

Technology permits the dispersal of economic activity in a manner not possible before. Recognizing the importance of knowledge employees as a critical firm resource, business managers now are locating operations in areas attractive to key employees. With half of the workforce now in technology-related industries, there is increasing importance on locating in areas with strong technology infrastructure (e.g., universities, training, etc.) in order to provide opportunities for employees to keep their knowledge base current.

Positive changes are also occurring in office employment in many CBDs, much of it in culturally attractive older office and industrial buildings. High technology metros such as San Francisco, New York, and Seattle have reduced their vacancy levels, and even cities like Houston and Baltimore have made impressive gains.

We can conclude that, driven largely by technology and generational change, the American workplace is going through major changes in organization, culture, philosophy, and leadership. This, in turn, influences building type, space planning, location selection, and, ultimately, real estate values.

---

13 Lend Lease Corporation, *Emerging Trends in Real Estate,* 2000.

F I G U R E   2-10

Office Use in Industrial Space

Freeport III
Dallas, TX

Two-story, 151,200
SF office building
1/8 mile from
Freeport I & II,
with similar
amenities.

• Large floor plates
  (flexibility in
  40,000 SF
  increments)
• 24-hour HVAC/
  digital VVT
  system
• Fiber-optics

Tenants include
document
management and
insurance firms.

Source: Kennedy & Associates

CHAPTER 3

Property Type Characteristics

People tend to talk about real estate in somewhat monolithic terms such as "real estate industry," "real estate field," and "real estate finance." In fact, "real estate" is a collection of disparate subsets that are alike in the fundamental sense of usually being attached to land. But these subsets are quite different in character, sources of demand, and investment opportunity.

One of these, of course, is location, which we touched on in Chapter 1. We also discussed property types in the previous chapter, particularly ways in which demand for each property type is influenced by changes in demographics and technology. In this chapter we will delve deeper to determine the market demand drivers for each of the major property types and how they interact with other factors, such as location, to create investment value.

Figure 3-1 is a graphic representation of how demand for each of the major property types is created in the American economy.

Demand drivers can be divided into two broad categories: (1) Those dependent primarily upon households, and (2) those dependent upon firms. The link between the two is employment, which generates income for households and, along with capital, profits for firms. Both groups then make expenditures for real estate—households for housing, and retail and firms for office and industrial operating facilities. Both households and firms support hotels and other lodging facilities.

We noted in Chapter 2 that one of the three major demand drivers for real estate is changes in population growth and demographic profiles. We also noted the impact of demographics on the way in which business and governmental organizations are reorganizing how they operate.

F I G U R E   3-1

Sources of Demand for Property Types

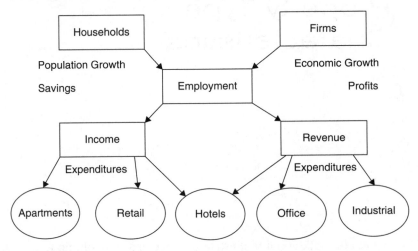

Source: McMahan Real Estate Services, LLC

The most direct impact of changes in population growth and demographic profiles is on single family homes, apartments, and other housing needs. Our focus is on apartments, the most common form of income housing.[1]

APARTMENTS

The link between overall population growth and the demand for apartments can occur as a result of demographic change and/or shifts in the choices people make about where they want to live. It also can be impacted by supply constraints such as zoning or improvement districts, as well as outright discriminatory restrictions on apartment development.

Population Growth

As we noted earlier, the United States is one of the few major industrial countries whose population is increasing (more new people are being added

---

1 As noted in Chapter 1, this book focuses on only those land uses that are income generating in the normal course of their use. In terms of residential uses, our discussion involves only apartments, although single family homes may be rented occasionally by owner-dwellers and most recently have been utilized as a way to offset operating costs in houses purchased for speculative resale. There also are certain location factors between rental and ownership housing that may be similar.

than are leaving). This is the result of the interaction of two forces: (1) a greater number of births than deaths, and (2) net immigration.

Births have been relatively high as a result of the Baby Boomers and their gift to our country—the Echo Boomers, many of whom are just now starting to have their own offspring, repeating the cycle. Deaths have been lower as a result of people living longer, made possible by major break-throughs in medical research and a strong economy.[2]

Net migration is also running at higher rates, largely as a result of migration from Mexico, Central America, Asia, and Eastern Europe. In some border states, such as California, Texas, Arizona, and New Mexico, immigration is the dominant growth factor, increasing the demand for education, jobs, and, of course, housing.

Propensity to Rent

Since our main focus is rental housing, the next step is to establish the portion of the market that is more likely to rent rather than own. Economists refer to this as the "propensity to rent."

Historically, the general assumption has been that, all other factors being equal, Americans would prefer to own rather than rent their housing requirements. This assumption has been reenforced in recent years by low mortgage rates and a general view that housing is a good investment opportunity. The expanded development of condominiums, which allows ownership of smaller units with "worry-free" communal facilities and services, has only served to enhance this view.

Unfortunately, for less affluent Americans—particularly those living at or below the poverty line—rental housing may be the only realistic alternative they have. Because of the increasing costs of developing new housing, the rental housing market for low-income residents, particularly in the inner city, is often left by default to public agencies and slumlords.

In some high-priced housing areas such as New York, Washington, D.C., Chicago, and San Francisco many residents are forced to rent despite personal resources or preferences. This is magnified by the increasing tran-sitory nature of American business and the sense that the next job may be in another metro area and it's only pragmatic to "remain flexible."

In the broader scope of the American housing market, however, rental housing increasingly is influenced by demographics rather than individual preferences.

---

2 This may change somewhat in the future as a result of increasing levels of obesity among young Americans.

Demographics

We've noted that a combination of an older generation retiring at the same time their children are coming of age has created the greatest potential demand for multifamily residential housing that we've seen in years.

Not that the generations have the same multifamily housing needs or preferences. Aging Boomers are more affluent, and generally seeking upscale apartments with large rooms, high ceilings, two parking stalls, and lots of storage. Perhaps this reflects the desire of those who had a single family housing experience to replicate that without the extra bedrooms or headaches of maintaining a lawn or swimming pool.

In retirement situations, they may be looking to relocate to a more urban setting, in the Central Business District or near a university. Others may feel more comfortable living in or near the same neighborhoods in which their single family house is located and many of their friends remain. Still others may wish to retire to a favorite vacation locale, perhaps in a more favorable climate such as Florida, Arizona, or Hawaii.

Many in this generation have the financial resources to afford ownership housing, including second homes, so this market is susceptible to condos and other ownership schemes.[3]

The Echo Boomers, however, more closely resemble traditional apartment dwellers, and they represent the largest potential rental housing market for the next decade.

Generally, Echo Boomers want to live in metro areas with entry level employment opportunities where they can land their first job or change to another one if they become dissatisfied or opportunity beckons. They also prefer an urban location, where they can be near entertainment opportunities as well as other young people.

Further, they are willing to move into transitional neighborhoods going through the revitalization process. In areas with good public transportation systems, they may find it desirable to locate near a transit station or well-serviced transfer point. Many believe that the money they save in commuting costs can be traded off against higher rent.

Having less financial resources than their parents, they're used to smaller living spaces and higher tenant densities. For those coming from college, the experience is not too different than that of the dormitories or fraternity/sorority houses they have left behind. A major generational difference from their parent's apartment living experience, however, is that

---

3 U.S. tax policy also encourages this by allowing a taxpayer to postpone capital gains taxes on the sale of a personal residence if they reinvest the proceeds in another home within a certain timeframe.

both sexes now often share living space, which again is not too dissimilar from their college experiences.

Location Factors

Once an investor targets a metro area, the next step is to identify desirable residential neighborhoods within that area. Figure 3-2 is a graphic representation identifying the major favorable location factors for apartment investment.

The first location issue concerning most apartment investors is the neighborhood in which the investment is located. This may be an established residential neighborhood or a recently built suburban subdivision. Generally this is an area within a five to 15 minute drive.

If the tenants have children, the desirable supporting educational facilities include elementary and middle schools and possibly a high school. Ideally, schools for the younger children will be located within walking distance of the property, and high schools a relatively short carpool or bus ride away. It is also desirable to have a neighborhood shopping center close by, as well as churches and synagogues.

Regional location considerations are facilities and services located within a 20 to 90 minute drive from the apartment project. These include employment centers and entertainment nodes as well as community or

FIGURE 3-2

Apartment Location Factors

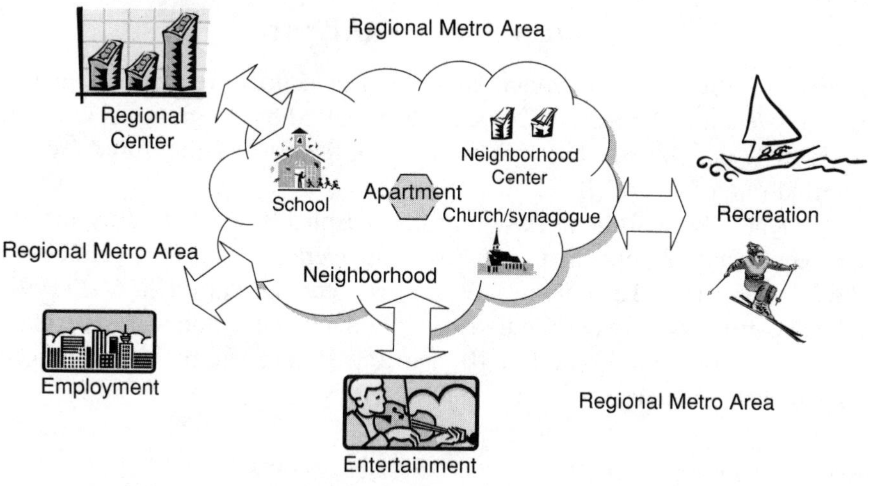

Source: McMahan Real Estate Services, LLC

regional shopping centers. Nighttime entertainment facilities such as movie theaters, restaurants, and night clubs also may be within this area, as well as recreational facilities such as golf courses, ballparks, beaches, sailing, etc.

Other Criteria

In terms of potential market demand, important statistical criteria include jobs located within a reasonable commute time, public institutions, shopping centers, industrial complexes; unemployment data; and the median income of existing residents in the market area.

Market supply concerns include the number and quality of existing units; units under construction and planned; current and historical occupancy rate (five mile radius); competitive rents, barriers to future apartment development (e.g., land availability, zoning, political attitudes, etc.).

Major competitive projects—also referred to as a property's "peer group"—should be shopped in order to obtain a detailed view of their strengths and weaknesses in regard to the investment.

Site criteria include visibility and access from major roads, crime and level of public safety, day and nighttime noise levels, views and natural amenities, and the quality and character of nearby single family neighborhoods.

Building criteria include the mix of units (as related to potential demand generators), unit size, room furniture layout potential, tenant communal facilities (e.g., swimming pool, health club, fire pit, video theater).

Investment Returns

Figure 3-3 illustrates the annual apartment investment returns[4] to institutional investors over the last 20 years, as reported by the National Council of Real Estate Investment Fiduciaries (NCREIF) and measured by the internal rate of return (IRR).

Generally, apartments have returned reasonably steady returns, mostly between 7 and 12 percent annually, with an average IRR of 9.4 percent for the 20-year period. The only negative or low returns occurred in 1991–1992, when apartments were substantially overbuilt and the nation was experiencing a recession. During the last 10 years, apartment returns have averaged 11.9 percent annually.

---

4 Investment returns for all property types are "total returns," including annual cash flow plus appreciation (depreciation) in value.

FIGURE 3-3

Apartment Investment Returns

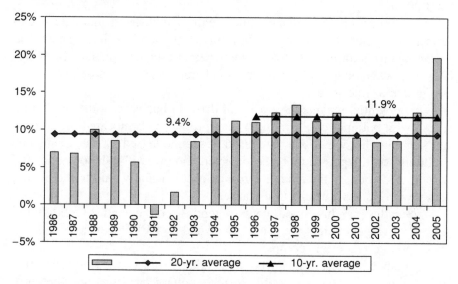

Source: National Council of Real Estate Investment Fiduciaries (NCREIF)

RETAIL

The second major income property type supported largely by households is retail, primarily located in shopping centers, Central Business Districts, and strip commercial. Some purchases for goods and services come from business firms, but the vast majority is made by individual households. Our focus is on shopping centers, the primary type of retail of interest to most potential investors. The major types of shopping centers are neighborhood centers, community centers, power centers, regional centers, and super regional centers.

Neighborhood Centers

Usually located within 15 minutes driving time of most of its shoppers, this most common type of shopping center provides customers with the necessities, such as food, drugs, and personal services, as well as fast food restaurants. It does this primarily through anchor tenants such as large food and drug chains. Neighborhood centers range from 30,000 to 100,000 square feet of gross leasable area (GLA), and they average about 60,000 SF.[5]

Nonanchor in-line tenants are usually small, local merchants who generally do not have strong credit ratings, may tend to "hide" sales, and often require a lot of TLC from a management standpoint. This is changing somewhat, however, as more national credit tenants choose to (or have to) utilize in-line space.

If potential tenants have a lot of drive-in business, some (including those with national credit ratings) may prefer "pads" located in the center's parking lot, which are purchased or ground leased by the tenant. The buildings on the pads may be constructed and owned by the owner or the tenant. If owned by the tenant, a ground rent is usually paid to the owner, often with a sales participation clause.

Smaller neighborhood centers tend to be owned by individual investors; larger centers are generally owned by REITs, pension funds, or large private real estate companies.

From an investor's viewpoint, neighborhood centers are attractive because they are less susceptible to recessionary pressures and therefore usually have steadier cash flow. The advantage is also the major drawback: Large food and drug anchor tenants usually have very tough lease requirements and pay relatively low rent, with most of the upside coming from participating in their sales successes through percentage rent.

Community Centers

A community center serves customers within a market radius of approximately 30 minutes driving time. In addition to providing the same retail goods and services as a neighborhood center, most community centers also feature tenants selling hard lines such as appliances and hardware, as well as soft good merchants handling men's, women's, and children's apparel.

Community centers have a wide size range, with some as small as 100,000 SF and some 250,000 SF or even larger.

Power Centers

Basically these centers are a collection of "big box" buildings, containing at least 20,000 SF each and leased to major (usually discount) retailers

---

[5] The source for this and most of the other shopping center statistical data is *The Dollars and Cents of Shopping Centers,* published by the Urban Land Institute (ULI).

specializing in bulk foods, drugs, toys, home furnishings, sporting goods, consumer electronics, computers, office supplies, and home improvement goods and services. Generally, a center needs at least four of these retailers (called "category killers") to provide critical mass. In some situations, anchors may occupy 80 to 90 percent of the total center.

In the last several years these power centers have emerged as a major competitive threat to community centers and, in some cases, regional centers.

Regional Centers

Serving a market area of up to 45 minutes driving time, the regional center was for many years what most people thought of for their "big purchase" needs, including general merchandise, apparel, furniture, and home furnishings.

A regional center ranges in size from 500,000 to 900,000 SF. Most are anchored by one or two full-line department stores (each averaging around 50,000 SF). A regional center may also have tenants such as travel agencies, home services, restaurants, entertainment, banks, and other personal and business services.

Super Regional Centers

This center has the same merchandise mix as the regional center, only in greater quantity and diversity. Anchored by three or more department stores (generally averaging 75,000 SF each), the super regional center ranges in size from 500,000 to 1.5 million SF and serves a market area of up to 60 minutes driving time. The super regional center also may have a sizable office employment center and entertainment complex on or adjacent to its site. In essence, it is more similar to a CBD than any of the other centers.

Location Factors

Figure 3-4 is a graphic representation of the location factors associated with shopping centers of various sizes.

Since most shoppers drive to a center, there is usually a direct relationship between the size of the center and the size of the road or highway serving it. Neighborhood centers, as an example, tend to be located on an arterial or large public street serving the neighborhood in which it is located. Community centers also may locate on arterials, but generally prefer expressways or even smaller freeways. Regional and super regional centers almost always are located on or near freeways or expressways.

FIGURE 3-4

Retail Location Factors

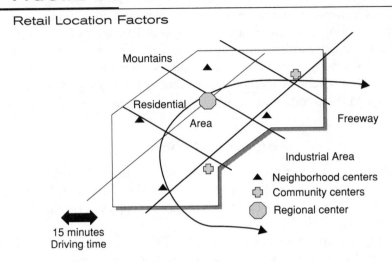

Source: McMahan Real Estate Services, LLC

The overall size of the center's gross leasable area will mainly be determined by: the number of households in the market area and their income level; the future growth prospects for this market; the size, type, and retailing prowess of the competition; and the strength of the anchor tenants in their respective markets.

For each type of center, the footprint of the land area also must be large enough to accommodate tenant space, public spaces, service facilities (e.g., maintenance, restrooms, equipment), access and internal road systems, and approximately five to 5.25 parking spaces per SF of GLA.[6]

Investment Returns

As illustrated in Figure 3-5, retail investment returns have averaged 9.3 percent over the past 20 years, only slightly lower than apartments. The years 1991 and 1992 were negative, however, for the same reasons affecting apartment returns and reflecting the dependency of both property types on household expenditures.

OFFICE

In the previous chapter we noted that the demand for office space is directly related to the expansion or relocation of business firms, which results from the demand for office jobs brought about by the economy.

---

6 Urban Land Institute, op. cit.

FIGURE 3-5

Retail Investment Returns

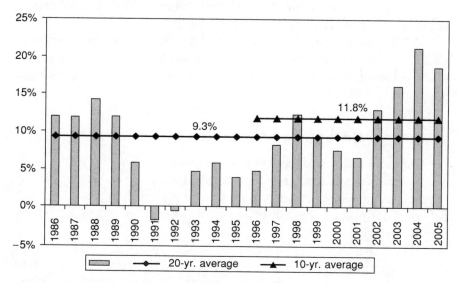

Source: National Council of Real Estate Investment Fiduciaries (NCREIF)

For investors, this primarily applies to space created for service jobs as opposed to jobs related to a manufacturing operation in an industrial facility. In fact, many of these operations are owned by the firms utilizing the space. The major business operations that provide most of the service jobs that utilize office space are finance, insurance, real estate, professional services, business services, and technology (primarily software firms).

In Chapter 2 we also noted the significant impact that technology has had on the use of office space, mainly due to the development of personal computers and the Internet, which permits individuals to function in their homes, hotels, and other nonoffice environments. As noted in Chapter 1, industrial buildings are increasingly meeting the needs of firms seeking more flexible office space configurations and/or lower rents as a result of lower construction costs. This tendency has been particularly noteworthy among firms employing a primarily younger labor force.

Generally, office space has not fared well in terms of the business cycle. During the rapid expansion of the technology sector in the late 1990s, a considerable amount of new office space was built in many cities, some of it largely on a speculative basis. While office occupancy rates in most mar-

kets improved subsequently, most of the space was leased at below pro-
forma rates, and portions of it have yet to be absorbed. This overhang in
available space created a highly competitive office market, with a dampen-
ing impact on rents and investment returns.[7]

This combination of structural and cyclical forces has served to
dampen the demand for office space in most cities across the country. As a
result, construction of new office space in recent years peaked in 2000 and
has declined every year since.

Selecting Metro Area Markets

In Chapter 1 we discussed the demand/supply characteristics of "constrained"
and "commodity markets." In constrained markets, office buildings generally
require a longer time to gain approval, but once approved, they face less competition from new competitive buildings, which also must face a stringent
approval process.

This environment is particularly suitable to office building investment, which usually involves longer term leases. When these leases turn
over, building management has a better chance of maintaining or improving future cash flow generation because there is generally less vacant space
competing for tenants.

Office leases also lend themselves to staggering as a further way to
assist in maintaining a steady earnings flow. Despite the deterioration in
the national office market in the early part of this decade, there is a positive absorption of approximately 140 million SF in the United States since
2003.[8] The recent competition of investors for quality office buildings in
New York City and Washington, D.C., illustrates that some investors will
"pay up" for well-seasoned, credit-quality office building cash flows.[9]

Investing within Metro Areas

In Chapter 1 we discussed investing in smaller political jurisdictions that
have tougher development standards in the path of metro area growth.
Office investment is particularly attractive in these areas, again because

---

7 Office operating costs have remained largely fixed or increased in cost, thereby also squeezing
  investment returns.
8 Torto Wheaton Research.
9 Washington, D.C., and New York City have tended to avoid the full impact of these forces in part
  due to the presence of government, multinational corporations, and institutional space users with
  long-term leases signed in the 1990s.

of the long-term nature of lease obligations and the need to effectively manage tenant lease turns. As noted, Buckhead, Arizona, Beverly Hills, California, and Scottsdale, Arizona, are good examples of this type of investment situation.

Location Factors
The location of office buildings tends to be associated with "nodes" of business and community activity. Figure 3-6 indicates some of the nodes that are particularly effective in attracting office buildings and related activity.

Downtown Areas
Office uses have traditionally been the dominant land use in the downtown areas, or Central Business Districts, of most American cities, Generally, the space is occupied by financial institutions, legal and accounting firms, governmental agencies, and the headquarters of major corporations.

In recent years residential and specialized retail uses, as well as convention and sporting facilities, have been developed in the downtowns of many cities (e.g., Denver, Atlanta, Houston), helping to revitalize the local economy and bringing people, particularly the young, back into the CBD, perhaps for the first time in many years.

FIGURE 3-6

Office "Nodes"

Source: McMahan Real Estate Services, LLC

Uptown Commercial Nodes

In past years, tenants leaving deteriorating downtown areas often located along major arterials passing through older, usually affluent areas of the city. This formed a linear-shaped node generally referred to as an "uptown" area, as can be seen above in Figure 3-6.

Office uses in these areas can vary, often depending upon the "prestige" of the older residential area. Office buildings are typically medium rise in size, appealing primarily to business services, legal, and accounting tenants.

Office Parks

A large part of new office development has been in office park locations in various parts of American metro areas. Originally located primarily in industrial areas, office parks have become nodes and destination points of their own. The parks themselves have also expanded to include other uses, such as restaurants, retail services, and, in some cases, residential. Recognizing the peak hour traffic that develops to and from these employment centers, and their proximity to major freeways and expressways, is considered essential.

Specialized Nodes

Office development also occurs within or near nonoffice nodes. Office buildings serving private physicians, drug companies, and health organizations are often located near hospitals; research and development tenants are drawn to office locations near universities; firms dependent upon frequent air service may tenant office buildings near airports; and firms providing services to households may have an office in or near regional and superregional shopping centers.

Investment Returns

Figure 3-7 illustrates investment returns from office building investments over the last 20 years, which has averaged 6.1 percent. This dismal performance is a direct reflection of the demand and supply forces discussed above.

As can be seen in the chart, office investment returns in the years 1990 through and 1993 were negative. This was the result of overbuilding office space in the 1980s and the recessionary environment of the early 1990s that followed.

Investment returns increased to more acceptable levels in the later half of the 1990s but dipped to subpar levels again (though not negative) in the dot-com bust in early 2000. Returns during 2004 and the first half of 2005 began returning to more favorable levels.

FIGURE 3-7

Office Investment Returns

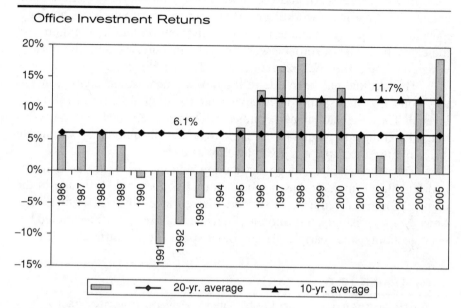

Source: National Council of Real Estate Investment Fiduciaries (NCREIF)

If we recalculate the average return for the last 10 years (1996–2005), we find it is 11.3 percent—much improved, but still slightly less than apartment and retail returns for the same period. It should be noted, however, that office returns are more volatile than either apartments or retail returns, reflecting higher risk levels in the ownership of office buildings.

INDUSTRIAL

Similar to office uses, industrial demand is driven by the decisions of business firms. Industrial demand generally falls into one of three categories: (1) manufacturing, (2) light manufacturing and assembly, and (3) distribution. Manufacturing and assembly facilities are usually owned by corporate tenants; the primary focus of investors, therefore, is on distribution facilities, primarily warehouses and office-oriented uses located in industrial buildings.[10]

---

10 There are two thoughts on this: (1) These are office investments that just happen to be hosted in industrial buildings, or (2) these are industrial investments that just happened to have office tenants.

In Chapter 2 we noted the impact of technology and generational change on America's workplace. These forces, particularly technology, have had an equally dramatic impact on distribution facilities. Figure 3-8 indicates the relationship between private inventories and final sales, which declined over 57.2 percent during the last 55 years.

This decline has been due to the development of bar coding, inventory control systems, and other devices and systems to control inventory levels.[11] These developments, coupled with improved stacking and warehouse handling equipment, have served to reduce the amount of warehouse space required to support a given level of sales.[12]

The net result is, although distribution buildings have increased in area and height, the increase has not been sufficient to avoid shrinkage in the demand for space required to support a given level of distribution operations. Not surprisingly, the amount of new warehouse space constructed has been declining since early 2001 and older space is often difficult to lease.

FIGURE 3-8

Technology Impact on Distribution: Private Inventories to Final Sales

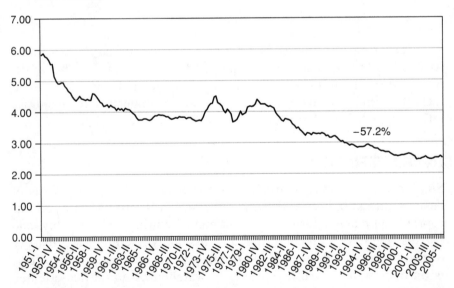

Source: Bureau of Economic Analysis

---

11 Some argue that it is also partially due to the interstate deregulations in the early 1980s and the deregulation of intrastate regulation in the early 1990s.

12 In addition, several large retailers, such as Wal-Mart, have begun utilizing trucks as storage units for goods. This increases the amount of paved storage area but, unfortunately for real estate investors, reduces the amount of building required.

Location Factors

While there are industrial investment opportunities in almost every metro-politan area, the major opportunities are concentrated in a few major trans-portation hubs that have emerged during the last several years.

These include port cities such as Los Angeles, New York/New Jersey, San Francisco, Seattle, and Miami, as well as air and ground transportation centers such as Atlanta, Dallas, Chicago, and Memphis.[13] Metro areas that combine both air and shipping and also serve large regional populations, such as New York and Los Angeles,[14] are in a particularly good position to compete for distribution facilities.

Within metropolitan areas, it's critical to be as close as possible to transportation facilities since shipping time means money, and the ability to get goods in and out of storage can often be critical to both the shipper and receiver of the goods.[15]

Having good access to major highways is also important since most of the goods will leave the warehouse by truck for distribution either within the metro area or to smaller cities. Proximity to rail transportation is desir-able in port locations and other areas where large, heavy items are being forwarded to other destinations.

Building Factors

Most new industrial buildings are built to meet prospective tenants' oper-ating requirements, which have been impacted by the technological inno-vations mentioned above.

Most are "big boxes" with 24- to 30-foot heights[16] as well as room for the circulation of forklifts and other vehicles required to move storage boxes around. Most space is air-conditioned or at least air-cooled to main-tain relatively constant temperatures.

The site should contain adequate room for truck and trailer turning and parking, as well as automobile parking for building employees and visitors.

Figure 3-9 is a schematic representation of the relationship between shipping and storage and how this has changed during the last decade.

---

13 Notably absent from the list of port cities is New Orleans, which recently was hit by a devastating hurricane and whose future as a major port was not entirely clear at the time of this writing.

14 In the case of Los Angeles, this is increasingly due to major distribution facilities located in the Riverside–San Bernardino area, which are connected to Los Angeles–Long Beach ports through a dedicated rail link.

15 Inventory velocity (the time to order and deliver a good) has decreased over the last decade due to improved use of technology in inventory management and logistic supply management.

16 The 30-foot height allows tenants to stack goods five pallets high, which is necessary for build-ings located in transportation hubs. Generally, a 24-foot-height (four pallets) is sufficient for most local markets.

FIGURE 3-9

Types of Warehouse Layouts

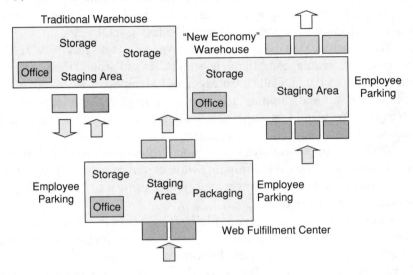

Source: McMahan Real Estate Services, LLC

In the traditional building warehouse layout shown in the upper left-hand corner, incoming and outgoing goods arrive and depart through the same overhead doors and may even use the same docks.

More commonly today, as more warehouse facilities are used to "break down" larger shipments into smaller ones, the incoming and outgoing functions are separated, usually at opposite sides of the building, with a "staging area" to unpackage and repackage stored goods, generally from larger packages to smaller ones. Parking is usually provided for truck trailers, which may park overnight and load outgoing shipments early the next morning. More commonly, outgoing goods are handled by smaller trucks serving the local metro area or nearby destinations.

If the warehouse is utilized as a Web fulfillment center, the packaging may become more complex (smaller and with a greater variety of packaging), and a portion of the warehouse is devoted exclusively to packaging.

As additional employees are added to perform functions within the warehouse, more of the site is utilized for parking, generally requiring a larger land parcel. The area set aside for office functions gets larger as the role of the warehouse becomes more complex.

Investment Returns

Figure 3-10 indicates industrial investment returns for the last 15 years. You will note that industrial uses had a small negative dip during the 1991–1992 recessions but recovered until the dot-com bust of 2001–2002, when returns dropped but did not turn negative.

The average return over the 20-year period has been 8.5 percent, but for the last 10 years improved to 12.2 percent, higher than office, apartments and retail.

FIGURE 3-10

Industrial Investment Returns

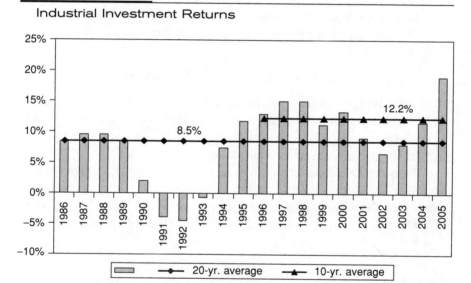

Source: National Council of Real Estate Investment Fiduciaries (NCREIF)

HOTELS

Hotels and other transient commercial facilities are the only type of real estate that derives its demand from both business firms and individual households.[17] Furthermore, hotels have several additional characteristics that differentiate them from other types of real estate:

---

17 All types of real estate get some demand from both households and business firms, but one or the other is significantly dominant as indicated by our discussion throughout this chapter. In the case of hotels and other transient commercial facilities, however, demand from these sources can be equal or nearly equal, depending upon the type of facility and the management strategy of the operator.

- Successful room rental is the key to success of a hotel project. Other income sources, such as restaurants, bars, and conference facilities, are important but the margins are much smaller. When room occupancy is above break-even, virtually all of the funds flow to service debt and provide returns to investors.
- Maximizing room revenue requires a balancing act between pricing policy and occupancy. Nothing is as unprofitable as a vacant hotel room.
- As a result, hands-on management plays a much more critical role than with other types of real estate. Hotels basically provide services, and the quality of the services is a function of the quality of management. Fortunately, the industry now has a stable of professional hotel managers, many of whom excel in this role.

Sources of Hotel Demand

Figure 3-11 is a graphic representation of the sources of hotel demand. As can be seen, the sources break into two categories: individuals and groups. These categories also break into two subcategories: pleasure and business travelers as well as conventions and tours.

Pleasure travelers are individuals traveling alone or as a family. They require lodging en route, and in some cases after they arrive at their destination. They are generally very price-sensitive, and the emphasis should be on a no-frills approach that meets their overnight needs. Since

FIGURE 3-11

Sources of Hotel Demand

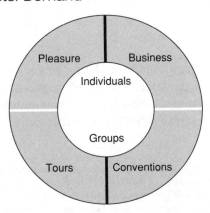

Source: McMahan Real Estate Services, LLC

the stay is usually only for one night, beds and showers are particularly important. Swimming pools also are desirable when traveling with children, particularly in warmer climates. An on-premises restaurant is desirable but not essential.

Business travelers, intent on accomplishing a specific purpose, generally stay two to three days. Since the hotel room is usually a base of operations for them, proximity to business centers and services is essential, as are room amenities such as a desk and Internet connection services. Good telephone service is also a critical part of the hotel selection decision, though to some extent this requirement is becoming less critical as more business travelers rely on cell phones rather than landline connections. Pricing is less important than for pleasure travelers, but still can be critical if the traveler is paid on a commission basis or is on a "per diem" expense account.

Conventioneers have an average stay of two to four days, depending upon the length of the conference or convention meeting. Proximity to the convention or conference facility is essential since guests may wish to go to their rooms at breaks in the meeting. An on-premises restaurant and bar is also essential, particularly one with room service. A swimming pool and workout facility are desirable supplements (essential to some guests). Price is important, but less critical than for pleasure or business travelers, and is usually negotiated in advance as part of the conference package.

Tours are usually organized by travel agents, airlines, and special tour management firms. Price is usually critical since the organizer's profits come from the spread between the hotel costs and the tour price. The room is the same as for the business traveler, unless in-room entertaining is desired. Tours are usually given favorable pricing since the revenue is guaranteed. Tour groups also may be given less desirable rooms, which otherwise would have remained unsold.

Types of Lodging Facilities

Hotels provide a full range of services, including rooms, restaurant and bar, and room service, plus retail facilities such as a barbershop, beauty salon, magazine and book shop, office service center, and in some cases a clothing store. Hotels are usually located in major commercial centers such as CBDs, regional shopping centers, or at transportation centers such as airports. The major customers are business travelers, either as individuals or participants in a convention or other type of group activity.

Resort hotels provide most of the services of a hotel but are located in resort areas and emphasize recreational facilities such as golf, tennis, beach areas, walking and hiking, etc. Proximity to a major natural or artificial amenity and favorable weather will generally play a major role in the success of the facility.

Motels are basically sleeping room operations oriented to guests arriving by car. Check-in may occur at any time of the day or night, with guests usually parking near their room. Pleasure travelers and some budget-oriented business travelers comprise the major source of demand for this type of facility.

Motor hotels are basically motels with certain types of hotel services and facilities, including a restaurant, bar, and small banquet rooms. Pleasure and business travelers constitute the main source of demand, often for extended stays. In recent years some motor hotel chains have developed new products, such as an all-suite operation with guest rooms containing a bedroom, kitchen, bar, and in some cases a desk with computer network connections. These products appeal particularly to business travelers planning an extended stay and families traveling for pleasure.

Investment Returns

Hotels are generally not institutional investments, so there is no NCREIF return data available. Hotel ownership also tends to be concentrated in corporations, which own and operate hotel chains.

Individuals can invest in hotels by buying stock in public operating companies, participating in private ownership syndicates that contract with operating companies, or by buying a smaller motor hotel or motel facility. Investment returns should be higher for hotels than other real estate investments in order to compensate for the greater risks involved.

CHAPTER 4

Major Players

In 2005 institutional investors, who have always dominated real estate debt markets, became the largest investors in equity real estate as well.[1] Figure 4-1 reflects the growth in the investment portfolios of the major players in institutional real estate equity investments over the last decade.

Figure 4-2 is a snapshot of institutional equity real estate investment as of mid-2005. A discussion of each of the major players follows.[2]

LIFE INSURANCE COMPANIES

World War II was financed largely through debt sold by the U.S. government to America's financial institutions, primarily life insurance companies. Following the war, as this debt matured, insurance companies utilized the proceeds to invest in real estate mortgages, attempting to satisfy the nation's pent-up demand for real estate of all types.

In order to support this investment program, many insurance companies established regional offices to make and manage their mortgage and equity real estate investments. This "on the ground" asset management infrastructure enabled them to become investment managers for other, more passive institutional investors, primarily pension funds.

---

1 This chapter focuses exclusively on institutional investors, not because there aren't sizable individual investors engaged in real estate investing, but because they often team up with institutions, which have the capital and set most of the ground rules for the investment program.
2 Commercial banks and savings associations have $3.2 billion in real estate equities and are not considered major players for the purposes of this discussion.

FIGURE 4-1

Major Institutional Equity Players

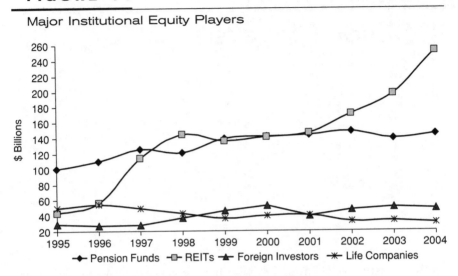

Source: Emerging Trends 2005—ULI and PricewaterhouseCoopers

FIGURE 4-2

Equity Investment

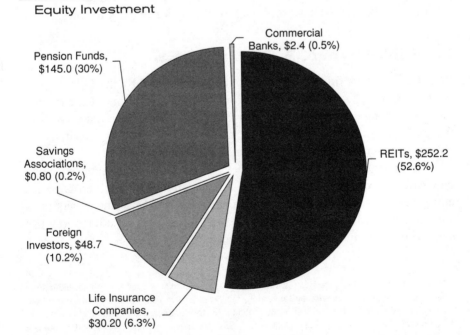

Source: Emerging Trends 2005—ULI and PricewaterhouseCoopers

FOREIGN INVESTORS

Individuals and institutions from other nations were some of the original investors in the United States. Most of these investments were in the form of land, often large tracts syndicated for broad investment by European and other foreign investors. British investors, in particular, have a long record of U.S. land investing.

More recently, foreign investment has taken the form of both land and buildings, beginning with the OPEC oil embargo of 1973, which demonstrated the need to recycle accumulated funds into U.S. investments. This led to considerable investment by Arabs and Iranians in U.S. cites such as Atlanta, Houston, Salt Lake City, and throughout California. During this period, Canadian developers purchased extensive land holdings in California, Arizona, and Texas for often ill-fated development projects.

Dutch investors were active in Atlanta, New York, Washington, D.C., and other eastern U.S. cities. Australian development and investment companies initiated operations in the western states, particularly California. Individual investors from Hong Kong, Singapore, and Latin America bought properties in Florida, Texas, and California. Japanese investors, buoyed by a large trade surplus with the United States, increased their investments in the mid-1980s, primarily in trophy office buildings in major cities.

European banks and pension funds also have invested large amounts of capital in projects throughout America. During the last decade, German investors have been major investors through bank-sponsored investment funds freed to invest overseas through changes in German banking laws.

Figure 4-3 illustrates the status of foreign real estate investment as of December 31, 2003. Japan is still by far the largest holder of U.S. real estate assets, followed by Germany, Great Britain, the Netherlands, Canada, and Australia. The remainder of the investment capital is spread over other European countries, Latin America, Asia (except Japan), and Africa and the Middle East.

REAL ESTATE INVESTMENT TRUSTS (REITS)

REITs were originally organized by Congress in 1960 as a means of allowing greater individual participation in real estate on a tax "pass-through" basis. The legal entity is a corporation or trust managed by a board of directors or trustees. Here the resemblance to other public companies ends, however, reflecting the special nature of REITs.

FIGURE 4-3

Foreign Investment in U.S. Real Estate

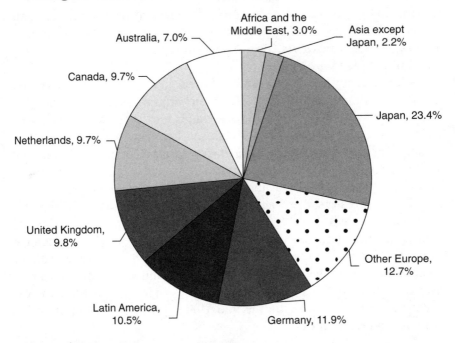

Source: Emerging Trends 2005—ULI and PricewaterhouseCoopers

REITs are required to have at least 100 shareholders, no five of which can own more then 50 percent of the stock (the 5/50 rule).[3] REITs also must hold 75 percent of their assets in real estate equity, mortgages, shares in other REITs, cash, and certain other securities. Seventy-five percent of the income must consist of rents or mortgage interest payments. Ninety-five percent must be "passive," and 95 percent of taxable income must be distributed currently. REITs also cannot act as "dealers," must be integrated, and their shares must be transferable.

Brief History

At first, most REITs were small, passive, and managed externally. There was little management ownership, analyst coverage, or market activity.

In the late 1960s several financial institutions created new REITs as a vehicle to underwrite and fund mortgage loans that were too risky for

---

3 The effect of this rule was modified to allow pension funds to invest by considering individual plan beneficiaries as REIT shareholders (the "look through" rule).

their traditional portfolios. These were largely construction loans, often secured by speculative projects located in secondary markets.

Ultimately, REITs were the largest source of mortgage financing for the 1971–1975 real estate boom. Most of these REITs collapsed in the mid-1970s, however, leading to a 75 percent loss in REIT market value. This gave REITs a negative image in the investment community for at least the next 10 years.

Largely as a result, REITs did not attract any significant new capital and, luckily, missed the real estate "bubble" of the 1980s. In the subsequent collapse of real estate markets at the end of the decade, all forms of capital for real estate evaporated.

Developers and investors found themselves with highly leveraged properties, often built with short-term financing, and no source of refinancing. With interest rates falling and real estate at bargain basement prices, Wall Street saw an opportunity to arbitrage private and public markets.

The Kimco offering in late 1991 was the first sign that REITs could play a major role in financing real estate and, more important, real estate operating companies (REOCs). During 1991 eight REIT IPOs raised $808 million. A similar number were completed in 1992, raising $919 million.[4]

While this was meaningful investment activity, particularly in a capital-starved real estate market, 1993 proved to be a real turning point, with 75 equity IPOs raising $11.1 billion.

Excluding placements of less than $50 million, 39 IPOs were completed, raising $8.2 billion, approximately 14 percent of total IPO activity in the entire securities market for the year. More real estate capital was generated by these 39 IPOs than by any other source.[5]

More significantly, the character of the 1993 IPOs was dramatically different. Most of the new REITs were organized as vertically integrated REOC companies specializing by property type.

They were also significantly larger: 10 equity REITs had market capitalization of over $500 million (versus two at the end of 1991), and 40 had capitalization exceeding $200 million (versus 10 in 1991).[6]

Almost two-thirds of new REITs were structured as Umbrella Partnership REITs (UPREITs). Under this structure, the REIT and the original investors each owned an interest in an Operating Partnership (OP), an approach designed to reduce the tax impact on selling private investors.

Most of the 1993 IPOs were internally managed, and in most cases management had significant equity positions, thus minimizing conflicts

---

4 National Association of Real Estate Investment Trusts (NAREIT).
5 NAREIT, ibid.
6 NAREIT, op. cit.

and enhancing the congruency of objectives with investors. Many of the management groups had been specializing in a particular property type and had effectively worked together as a team for several years, through at least one full real estate cycle.

The difference between the "old" and the "new" REITs could be summarized as follows:

Old vs. New REITS	
Old REITs	**New REITs**
1960–1992	1992–2005
Passive investments	Operating company
External administered	Self-administered
Institutional sponsors	Entrepreneur sponsors
Small management ownership	Large management ownership
Diversified portfolio	Focused portfolio
Small capital base	Large capital base
Little analyst coverage	Extensive analyst coverage

At the end of 1993 the REIT market was thriving. The total market capitalization of all REITs increased to $31.6 billion. The 30 largest REITs represented $15.1 billion, versus $8.6 billion at the beginning of the year.[7]

Over the next 20 years REITs continued to grow and prosper, and today are the major source of real estate capital, with over half of equity real estate investments (52.6 percent). If pension capital is deducted, the nonpension capital in REITs is $232.7 billion, still a sizable force in real estate investing.

REITs invest across the entire spectrum of the real estate industry. Figure 4-4 indicates the current assets that REITs hold, broken out by property type.

PENSION FUNDS

As noted in Figure 4-2 at the beginning of this chapter, U.S. pension funds currently have approximately $145 billion invested in U.S. real estate equities, second only to REITs, with $252.2 billion. Since pension funds are also major investors in REITs, we will review their investment history

---

7 NAREIT, op. cit.

FIGURE 4-4

REIT Investment by Property Type, 2005

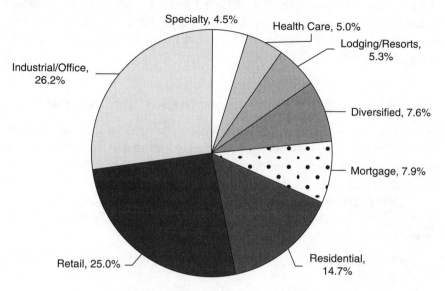

Source: Emerging Trends 2005—ULI and PricewaterhouseCoopers

in some detail. (For the purpose of this discussion "pension funds" include foundations and endowments as well.)

Early History

Pension funds were established in the 1950s by corporations such as General Motors to supplement Social Security and attract and retain key employees. The investment objectives of these early pension funds were relatively modest: to preserve accumulated capital, achieve sufficient returns to meet beneficiary liabilities, and maintain sufficient liquidity to pay the funds' operating expenses.

Pension Managers Avoid Real Estate

Most pension fund managers avoided real estate equity investment on any scale until 1975.[8] This hesitancy was based primarily on concerns about

---

8 Prior to this time, insurance companies and bank trust departments did invest pension capital in whole loan mortgages and net leased properties on a fully discretionary basis, using insured accounts.

real estate's nonfungibility, market fragmentation, infrequent pricing, lack of an auction market, and general lack of information about the asset class. Many fund managers also believed that real estate favored taxable, rather than tax-exempt, investors. As a result of these and other concerns, real estate was perceived to be riskier than financial investments such as stocks and bonds.[9]

ERISA Sets New Investment Standards

In 1974, Congress passed the Employment Retirement Income Security Act (ERISA). This legislation was directed primarily at preventing a repeat of pension abuses related to corporate bankruptcy (Studebaker) and union graft and corruption (Teamsters).

ERISA established tough new fiduciary standards for the management of pension plans. Henceforth, managers of pension fund capital were expected to:

- Discharge their duties solely in the interests of participants and beneficiaries
- Demonstrate "prudence" in all investment decisions
- Diversify plan investments to minimize the risks of large losses

Penalties for violating ERISA standards became "personal and criminal," to drive home to individual trustees the serious consequences of violating the provisions of the new legislation. ERISA also established the obligation of pension sponsors to look at the total spectrum of investment opportunities. This opened up consideration of nonfinancial assets such as real estate.

Open-End Funds

The primary investment vehicle in the early years was open-end funds sponsored by insurance companies and banks ("open end" because investors could withdraw on a periodic basis.) These funds represented large pools of capital, reflecting a diverse investor base in which pension funds believed they could safely participate. Through a periodic withdrawal device, open-end funds also provided investors with a measure of liquidity.

---

9 In fairness, many pension decision makers had been trained in the management of financial assets and had little previous exposure to commercial real estate as an investment.

Disadvantages included the fact that investors were buying and selling on appraised values rather than actual market transactions. Also, the "queue" to take investment capital out was not always viewed as fair to all investors.[10] This could be a particular concern if the fund sponsor were forced to liquidate properties in order to meet redemption requests.

Closed-End Funds

Observing the success of financial institutions in attracting large sums of capital from pension funds, Coldwell Banker and several other large entrepreneurial real estate firms began sponsoring closed-end funds, which they believed were more reflective of the true nature of real estate as a relatively illiquid asset.[11]

The holding entity is a unit trust, but here the similarity to open-end funds ends. Closed-end funds have a finite life, usually 10 years. Investor dollars are "called for" to fund properties as they are acquired. Investors establish the maximum amount of capital they wish to invest in the fund and capital is drawn against this commitment until the maximum is reached.

Closed-end funds also are more focused in terms of investment strategy, investing in properties of a particular type, in a certain geographical area, or that have other distinguishing characteristics.

There are several disadvantages of closed-end funds. They generally invest in smaller properties, there is less diversification within the funds, and fund sponsors are perceived to be under greater pressure to invest. They also are highly illiquid, with investors unable to reclaim cash until the fund is liquidated. A major concern was that liquidation might come at the wrong time in the real estate cycle, forcing investors to accept lower returns or, in some cases, a possible loss of capital value.[12]

---

10 The problem wasn't so much the "queue," per se, but the way it was administered, namely on a first-in first-out rather than a pro-rata basis. This forced pension managers to notify the fund sponsor of its desire to liquidate if others were doing so, creating somewhat of a "run on the bank" mentality.

11 Coldwell Banker utilized a limited partnership format as the investment entity. Subsequent closed-end funds sponsored by RREEF, Heitman, LaSalle, and AEW used a group trust format, which was closer to being a true commingled fund.

12 Although closed-end funds didn't use appraisals for liquidation purposes, they were used in determining annual fees. This created what many investors viewed as a conflict of interest because the manager was perceived to be less interested in selling when portfolio assets were highly valued, as this would reduce the manager's fee income.

Qualified Plan Asset Manager (QPAM) Legislation

In the early 1980s, Congress clarified ERISA requirements regarding the hiring of real estate managers.[13] The role of a Qualified Plan Asset Manager (QPAM) was established to allow plan sponsors to escape direct responsibility for the management of real estate assets in their portfolios.

To qualify, a manager had to (1) have the power to acquire, manage, and dispose of any real estate assets in its portfolio; (2) be registered as an investment advisor under the Investment Advisors Act of 1940 (or a bank or insurance company as defined by ERISA); and (3) acknowledge in writing that it was a fiduciary of the plan.[14]

Not only did this legislation lessen the liability of plan sponsors for actions of its managers, but managers who qualified were given more flexibility in the management of portfolio assets, particularly in terms of transaction approvals, management deployment, asset operating decisions, etc.

Concentration of Capital and Management

Today, the pension real estate industry is concentrating at a rapid pace. As of 2004, the 10 largest pension investors in real estate held $48 billion in assets, representing 44.9 percent of the funds supplied by the 200 largest pension funds investing in real estate equities. Nine of the 10 are public employee plans, three located in California.[15]

The 10 largest pension plans have $10.8 billion invested in REITs. Two are corporate plans; the rest are public plans. These 10 plans represent 56 percent of the total capital supplied by the top 200 funds investing in REITs.[16]

In terms of pension real estate investment managers, the top 10 control $144 billion in pension assets. Nine of these firms are now owned or controlled by financial institutions (including three foreign institutions), and one is a major corporation. Two of the firms were initially entrepreneurial companies but subsequently have been acquired by financial insti-

---

13 The term "investment manager" is used generically throughout this book to include registered investment advisors, managers of Real Estate Investment Trusts (REITs), general partners, and any other individuals or firms who serve as a fiduciary to real estate investors.

14 Natalie A. McKelvy, Pension Fund Investments in Real Estate, 1983.

15 Pensions & Investments, January 24, 2005.

16 Pensions & Investments, ibid.

tutions. These 10 firms represent 56.2 percent of the total capital managed by the 50 largest firms.[17]

Today, most pension plans have a positive view of real estate as an investment class. Most plan trustees are aware of real estate's lower volatility, portfolio diversification benefits, and ability to generate cash flow. Unfortunately, pension real estate investment in the near term may be constrained due to the difficulty of increasing target allocations since it means lower allocations to other, more established, asset classes.

17 Pensions & Investments, op. cit.

CHAPTER 5

Understanding Investor Objectives

It is essential for investment managers to be aware of the differing interests of the various types of investors, and to be certain their interests are considered in making investment and management decisions.

PENSION FUNDS

As noted in Chapter 4, pension funds are the major institutional investors in real estate today. It is particularly important to understand their broader portfolio objectives and how they view real estate in a portfolio context.

Today, most medium to large pension funds are faced with the following challenges and opportunities when considering real estate as an asset class:

The Plan Funding Obligations

Historically, most pension managers have been oriented to investing plan assets in traditional financial investments, primarily stocks and bonds. Part of this bias is because managers have been trained in corporate finance, and thus feel more comfortable with this asset class. (This is particularly true of corporate plans.)

Financial managers also have tended historically to emphasize cash flow generated from asset appreciation (increases in stock price) over cash flow from the periodic income stream generated by the asset itself (dividends).

It should also be noted that the financial services industry is a powerful "lobby" that has often (correctly) viewed investments in other asset classes as eroding their investment base, with a resultant decrease in income generated for those individuals and firms who manage the investment process.

Recent demographic changes in the mix of plan participants toward proportionally more retirees and longer retiree lives, however, has forced plans to rethink the mix of assets that should be in plan portfolios. As a result, many pension managers' attitudes are now changing to include at least some assets (such as real estate) that generate current income.

Today, more plans appear to be evolving toward a more balanced approach to portfolio building, which increasingly includes real estate in the mix of acceptable investment assets.

Portfolio Risk Diversification

Modern Portfolio Theory (MPT) maintains that one of the best ways to increase overall portfolio return is to reduce total portfolio risk. This is particularly relevant to pension funds since they pay for plan obligations out of *total portfolio* income, not that of an individual asset or asset class.

It has become increasingly clear that, if total portfolio income is the goal, then a mix of assets with complimentary risk characteristics will reduce overall portfolio risk and increase the dependability of the future portfolio income stream. It is important, therefore, to understand how various investments interact when they are in a portfolio environment.

Using computer modeling techniques, pension funds and their consultants have come up with a mix of assets reflecting the lowest overall portfolio risk exposure and therefore the highest potential risk-adjusted income for the plan. Most of the modeling indicates that including real estate in a mixed asset portfolio increases risk-adjusted investment returns.

Cash Generation

Many pension funds today face an emerging problem in funding their plan liabilities. This has been brought about by the demographics of plan participant populations in which Boomers are beginning to retire in ever increasing numbers. At the same time, most are expected to live longer, increasing the overall liability of the plan to fund retirement benefits.

For public plans, the problem is compounded by the policies of many plans to provide for early retirement to employees in their late 50s and early

60s. Reportedly, some public employee retirees begin collecting a retirement check at the same time they begin a second career in another field.

The situation is further compounded by the fact that the other widely used traditional portfolio financial instruments—bonds—have been generating less income over the last several years due to lower interest rates.

In contrast, commercial real estate historically has had a reputation as a "cash generator" investment with a steady cash return to investors. This appeal has been enhanced in recent years, with real estate gaining favor as an appreciating asset as well.

For these and other reasons, pension funds have become major investors in real estate, and thus it is important to understand the nature of their existing real estate portfolios and their strategy for future investing.

In order to gain an understanding of current pension real estate investments, Figure 5-1 breaks down pension real estate investments in 2004 by type of pension plan.

Investment Vehicles

Note that commingled funds, direct investment, and public securities (mostly REITs) consistently comprise 72 to 80 percent of total pension real estate investment activity, regardless of the type of pension fund investor.

The interest in pooled accounts and public securities (REITs) has grown dramatically since 2000. There are several reasons for this:

FIGURE 5-1
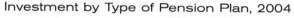

Investment by Type of Pension Plan, 2004

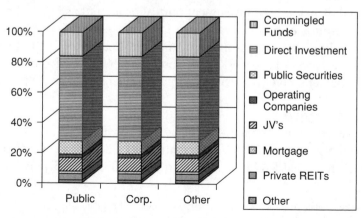

Source: Pension Real Estate Associates

1. Large pension investors are committing a sizable amount of new capital to opportunity funds and offshore pooled investments, in order to share risks with other investors.
2. For smaller plans, pooled accounts enable more efficient deployment of capital, enabling them to achieve portfolio diversification earlier.
3. Managers are marketing more pooled accounts today since they cannot enter the bidding for many major asset disposition programs unless they can prove to the seller that they have investment discretion, which investment pools usually provide.

Public pension plans are the major direct investors in real estate, largely because of the cash flow characteristics of the asset class, as noted above. An increasing proportion of this is in the form of joint venture limited partnerships with experienced private investors, REITs, and selected investment managers.

Also, it should be noted that pension funds hold $18.9 billion in public REITs and $3.6 billion in private REITs. This combined total is the equivalent of 7.7 percent of total REIT assets as of February 2005.[1]

Investment Characteristics

In 2004 the Pension Real Estate Association (PREA) conducted a survey of pension plan managers regarding other characteristics of their real estate investment portfolios.[2] The following is a summary of what the PREA discovered.

Leverage

In general, pension fund investment portfolios are not as highly leveraged as the portfolios of private real estate investors. Only 5.3 percent of pension portfolios have greater than a 75 percent Loan-to-Value (LTV) ratio. Forty-three percent have a 31 to 50 percent LTV ratio, 38.6 percent have 51 to 75 percent, and 10.5 percent of portfolios have 11 to 30 percent.

Property Type

Office was the most popular type of property investment in pension portfolios (34.5 percent), followed by apartments (20.4 percent), retail (18.7 percent), industrial/R&D (13.5 percent), and hotels (3.5 percent).[3] The

---

1 Pension Real Estate Association and National Association of Real Estate Investment Trusts.
2 Pension Real Estate Association, Plan Sponsor Research Report, March 2004.
3 Pension Real Estate Association, op. cit.

remaining 9.4 percent was primarily invested in land/timber, senior housing, mixed use, and self-storage facilities.

Geography

The largest percentage of pension investments by region were in the West (36.4 percent), followed by the East (27.8 percent), the South (22.0 percent), and the Midwest (13.8 percent). Generally, corporate plans were more apt to hold investments in the East and Midwest, while public and other plans focused on investing in the West and South. Also, there was not a large difference in geographical preference between smaller plans and those over $25 billion.[4]

Multiasset Portfolios

Pension investors typically have many assets in their portfolios—stocks, bonds, money market funds, venture capital, hedge funds, international funds, etc. Real estate is often selected as an investment not only because of its intrinsic values, but also how it relates to other investment classes in a multiasset portfolio.

As an example, pension investors may wish to include real estate investments in their portfolios because it compliments other assets (such as stocks and bonds) in terms of investment return, cyclical timing, cash generation, volatility, and risk.

Institutional investors also may have different investment objectives from each other, not dissimilar to individual investors. As noted, some pension funds are now projecting negative cash flows and may be more interested in cash generation. Other institutional investors, such as foundations, may be more interested in asset appreciation.

Investment Managers

Pension investors select investment advisors and partner with operating companies because they believe the firm's investment strategy is consistent with their overall investment objectives and that the advisor/partner can find, acquire, manage, and dispose of properties that fulfill their investment needs.

In the case of investment partnerships, this strategic approach to real estate investing is encapsulated in the joint-venture agreement and other investment documents that comprise the contract between the parties.

---

4 Pension Real Estate Association, op. cit.

Investment Strategies

Most current pension real estate investment strategies can be organized along the real estate risk/return curve, as illustrated in Figure 5-2.

While definitions are not always consistent, most pension plans and investment managers currently view the various levels of risk and return somewhat as follows:

Core

Investments in office, industrial, retail, and apartment properties built with quality construction and located in major metropolitan areas of the United States. Leverage is generally not used, with most properties having a stabilized income stream at the time of purchase. Total investment return expectations are generally in the 8 to 10 percent IRR range.

Enhanced Core

Generally, core-quality properties with some type of problem that needs to be "enhanced" before the properties can produce stabilized income at acceptable yield levels. This enhancement may take the form of redevelopment, retenanting, refinancing, or some other form of problem mitigation. This category also includes the development of new core properties,

FIGURE 5-2

Real Estate Investment Strategies

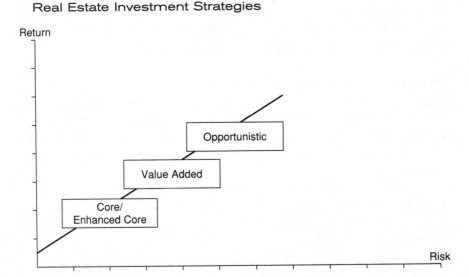

Source: McMahan Real Estate Services, LLC

with the use of leverage to enhance returns. Investment return expectations vary, but are generally in the 10 to 12 percent range.

Value-Added

This category consists of properties that do not meet core quality standards but can add value to the overall portfolio. These investments generally involve a higher level of risk and include properties such as hotels, restaurants, entertainment complexes, factory outlets, and business showrooms. Often, these value-added investments also involve a higher level of financial leverage. Expected investment returns are generally in the 12 to 15 percent range.

Opportunistic

Investment situations that involve some form of value arbitrage arising from disequilibrium in the marketplace. The classic situation was the Resolution Trust Corporation (RTC) marketing of deeply discounted properties in the mid-1990s, followed by the subsequent recovery of the real estate market, producing significantly above-average returns for those investors who participated.

Opportunities of this scale are often difficult to find, requiring more of a niche approach. As a result, today's opportunity programs often focus on land investment, infill development, foreign properties, and real estate enterprise investment. Opportunistic investments usually involve higher levels of leverage, with most sponsors investing "side by side" with pension investors.[5] Total returns are sometimes in the 20 percent plus range, but most are less, generally 15 to 18 percent for domestic investments.

Risk Diversification

The need to have a focused investment program is balanced by the need to diversify risks within each investment portfolio.

Real estate is quite different than stocks, bonds, and other financial investments that can be bought and sold readily to balance and rebalance portfolio risk. Financial investments also have an advantage in that they can be purchased in small increments, enabling an investment portfolio to be diversified almost regardless of how little investment capital is involved.

Real estate portfolios are diversified by spreading potential risk, that is, not concentrating investments in a single property type, geographical

---

5 In many cases, sponsor returns are subordinated to pension investor returns until certain predetermined return thresholds are reached.

submarket, tenant business, or ownership vehicle. Since most portfolios are built "one property at a time," an individual portfolio may not be diversified until several properties have been acquired.

This places an obligation on the investment manager to be conscious of the portfolio risks that are being assumed as properties are added to the portfolio, and to be certain that the overall direction of the investment activities are moving toward portfolio diversification rather than concentration.[6]

Institutional Partnerships

From time to time private investors coinvest in partnership with institutional investors such as pension funds or real estate operating companies such as REITs.

The preferred vehicle for this form of investing is a joint-venture investment partnership that is focused on an investment strategy attractive to both groups of investors.

The private investment manager is typically the general partner of the investment partnership, although, in most cases, the financial partner will be investing the majority of funds required and may receive preferences in the sequencing of investment returns.

INDIVIDUAL INVESTORS

Most noninstitutional real estate investors are high net worth (HNW) individuals who generally invest through one or more limited partnerships. In this situation, investment in real property is evidenced by ownership of partnership interests.

The main method of receiving investment returns for these investors is through quarterly cash flow payments, the refinancing of properties, and/or the ultimate disposition of the asset(s). As a result, there is a strong emphasis among most HNW investors on the investment program's proposed refinancing or exit strategy. Not all HNW investors have the same investment objectives. Older investors, for example, may be more interested in the level of cash payments, while younger investors may be more concerned with potential appreciation in the value of the properties in the portfolio, with cash being realized upon refinancing or disposition. Still other individuals may be

---

6 The exception would be pension funds with large real estate portfolios that engage an investment manager to "focus" on a single property type, geographical area, or investment strategy. In this situation, the pension plan is taking the diversification risk. This fact should be clearly acknowledged by both parties in the investment plan and management contract.

interested in sheltering income from taxes through depreciation, interest, and other deductions available to the real estate investor.

FOREIGN INVESTORS

It's dangerous to generalize about foreign investors since they come from such diverse countries and cultures. In some cases, individual investors are represented by institutions such as banks, insurance companies, or other intermediaries; in other situations, they are investing through a U.S. broker or personally. Each of these situations should be handled in a different manner.

Investing Through an Intermediary

Foreign investors may choose to work through an investment intermediary based in the United States or a foreign country (which may not be necessarily the home country of the investor). If an institution is involved, it's important to see the investment contract to determine what their arrangement is with the actual investor. The major clauses of importance are the sections containing the investment criteria and the level of discretion the intermediary poses.[7]

If there is no contract with the investor, this may not be a situation to be pursued because, without discretion, it is difficult to get good investments under control, let alone close them.

In other situations, a foreign investor may be dependent upon a fellow countryman or relative living in the United States. The best way for these investors to be effective is to meet their representatives and establish the level of discretion they have been given by the investor. Again, if they do not have discretion, it may not be an opportunity worth pursuing.

Representing the Investor Directly

A preferred approach is to represent the investor directly, not only to better understand the investor's personal objectives but to also shorten the communications and decision-making loop.

This has become a much easier task in recent years as a result of dramatic improvements in electronic communications. A note of caution: Use of these communication tools should be considered a supplement to,

---

7 If the intermediary objects, the financial arrangements are less consequential, so this portion of the agreement can be omitted.

and not a substitute for, a trip to the United States to survey selected metro area markets and the types of real estate investments that can be acquired to satisfy the investor's portfolio objectives.

DIFFERING INVESTOR OBJECTIVES

As with most business situations, not all real estate investors have the same investment objectives. In the case of individual foreign investors, as noted above, older investors may be more interested in the level of cash flow, while younger investors may be more concerned with potential appreciation in the value of properties in their portfolio.

Types of properties also may serve different roles at different phases in their ownership cycle. For example, a parcel of land may serve portfolio appreciation objectives in the early years of ownership and then be transformed into a cash generator at some point in the investment cycle through the development process.

Institutional investors attempt to mirror the interests of their constituents. Thus, pension funds with an older participant profile may be more interested in investments that generate cash flow to pay retirement benefits, while those with younger participants may desire investments that are expected to demonstrate greater appreciation in value, but have little interim cash flow.

These differing investor objectives are managed by having focused investment strategies that carefully match the nature of the assets with the interests of the investor(s). Large investment managers may have a variety of investment products in which investors self-select the product that matches their investment interests. Smaller firms are faced with a more difficult problem of matching investors with available opportunities, which may mean a more limited approach to the market and even turning down investment opportunities that are otherwise attractive.

In order to maintain market creditability (and continue to receive investment opportunities), it is important for the investment manager to have a clear statement to the marketplace as to the type of investment properties currently desired, and to be willing to only pursue investments that reflect potential investor interests.

RECONCILING INVESTMENT FOCUS WITH PORTFOLIO DIVERSIFICATION

Investors select an investment manager because they believe that the manager's strategy is consistent with their overall investment objectives and that the manager can find, acquire, manage, and dispose of properties that fulfill their investment needs. This strategic approach to real estate investing is encapsulated in the Investment Management Agreement, or in the case of individual investors, the Private Placement Memoranda (PPM), or other investment documents that comprise the investment manager's contract with investor clients.

It should be noted that it is generally impossible to reconcile all investor objectives and create an investment vehicle that pleases everyone. To some extent, differing investment objectives are managed by having a diversified property portfolio in which different properties are acquired or developed for different purposes.

Individual properties also may serve different roles at different phases in their ownership cycle. Portfolio diversification also serves to spread potential investor risk by not concentrating investments in a single geographical area or property type.

It should be noted that investment managers are not expected to diversify away all investment risk. Through documents such as a PPM, investor partners are made aware of the targeted investment strategy for a specific investment offering that draws on the specific experience and skills of the investment manager.

This targeted strategy, by its nature, involves a certain degree of portfolio concentration, usually by certain types of properties in certain geographical market areas.

Potential investors are attracted to these investment offerings *because of this concentration, but expect to find property level diversification within this targeted strategy* (e.g., economic location, lease expiration, tenant credit, etc.).

It is therefore important to understand the strategic objectives of each investor and continually keep in mind how assets under management continue to meet or diverge from the stated investment objectives.

PART II
Transaction Management

CHAPTER 6

Sourcing, Screening, and Preliminary Underwriting

The first step in the investment process is finding the right potential investment. A successful acquisition sourcing program must be rigorously systematic and yet sufficiently flexible to capture opportunities as they arise. It must be capable of reviewing many opportunities simultaneously and rejecting those that do not meet the investment criteria or that have a minimal chance of being closed. A successful program continues to focus and refocus on its goals and on ways in which it can operate most efficiently.

Unfortunately, all of this must be accomplished within a relatively short period of time, and often in competition with other active buyers in the marketplace, some with greater resources. This situation can be compounded when multiple investment opportunities are pursued simultaneously. This means that, to be successful in sourcing superior investments, the investment manager must seek continually to build strong relationships with key players in the targeted real estate markets *before* pursuing a specific transaction.

Real estate is very much a people business in which individuals help people whom they like, trust, and know can perform. Often the strength of personal and firm relationships gives one buyer an advantage over another in discovering an investment opportunity or helps ease the way in a difficult negotiating situation. It is also a major way to develop repeat business, with all of the efficiencies that this can represent.

Figure 6-1 represents a flow chart of the property acquisition process.

FIGURE 6-1

Property Acquisition Process

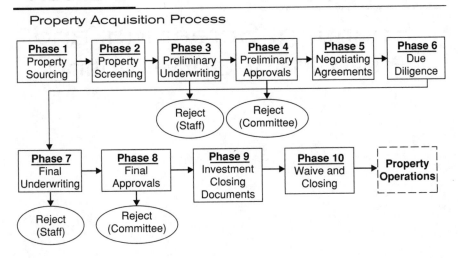

PROPERTY SOURCING

The first phase of this process is the investment search. In this part we will go into the major sources of investment opportunities.

Property Owners

The decision to sell a property and whom to sell it to ultimately resides with the property owner. In today's world, however, property owners are often financial institutions or corporations where final decisions are made or approved by top executives and/or committees and it is not always possible to single out an individual as the "key" decision maker. It is important, therefore, to identify people who will heavily influence the decision to sell.

In the case of investment properties managed or owned by *investment advisors* or *REITs,* the key "influencer" is often the head of asset management, and the asset manager responsible for managing the property.

If a *corporation* is the owner, there usually will be a person in the corporate real estate department responsible for managing the property. In some cases this person will be situated in the headquarters or regional office of the corporation, which may be located in another city.

In addition, individuals employed by the local third-party property or facility management firm may have an influence on the sales decision. In some cases this person may be an employee of the same brokerage firm that has the sales listing agreement.

Acquisitions from *developers* may be quite different since many of them presell properties under construction or upon completion. In these situations it is important to have a continuing relationship with development firms and to keep abreast of their schedule of future building completions. In some cases this may create an opportunity to tie up a property while still under construction, subject to final approval of due diligence and closing upon completion.

Maintaining relationships with *property owners who are not actively marketing their properties* may also provide a good source of potential acquisitions. In some instances a property owner (usually private) might prefer to forego an active marketing process and avoid unwanted publicity or additional cost. These property owners usually prefer to sell in a highly personalized, strictly confidential manner.

A property owner who has confidence in an investment manager's ability to perform and to keep the terms of the transaction confidential can be very valuable. By purchasing property in this manner, the acquirer foregoes a highly competitive multibidder sales process, in effect controlling the acquisition process without interference from other prospective buyers.

Brokers

Relationships with brokers also are important in the success of an acquisition program. A *listing broker* who has been retained by a seller to market a property may have considerable influence over the ultimate sales decision. Also, brokers who have been utilized in the past to dispose of assets for firm investors should be contacted since they "owe a favor" and may be interested in returning it.

A *tenant representative* or *leasing broker* also may be valuable in uncovering a property that will be coming on the market in the near future.

Since brokers usually are paid a "performance based" commission, they are particularly interested in the ability of an investment manager to successfully consummate a transaction. Brokers also are interested in the reputation of such companies in respecting and supporting brokers and not trying to make the broker's commission the final "squeeze" in the negotiating process.

Effective investment managers are proud of their ability to close transactions successfully and efficiently. It is therefore important to bring this record of accomplishment to the attention of brokers whenever the opportunity arises.

Tenants

Tenants in an investment manager's existing portfolio can be a valuable source of new acquisition leads. Understanding a tenant's expansion needs and potential can lead to potential build-to-suit opportunities and/or leasing candidates for buildings that are being marketed without tenants.

A good way to find out more about tenant requirements is to stay in close contact with the corporate real estate representative responsible for properties in the investment manager's portfolio(s). Maintaining such a dialogue may result in a "home grown" tenant, ultimately leading to a potential acquisition.

Others

Long-term private owners of older properties are often good leads for possible sale. These individuals can be accessed directly or through their professional advisors (accountants, attorneys, trust banks, estate planners, etc.).

Other members of the real estate community that may be able to provide leads to potential acquisitions include lending institutions, mortgage bankers, construction loan managers, title company employees, appraisers, and market research professionals, among others.

In summary, the key to a successful property sourcing program is to (1) identify players in organizations who might influence property sales decisions and (2) build personal relationships that may lead to a competitive advantage over other potential buyers.[1] This can best be accomplished by (3) knowing their objectives, both professionally and personally, and (4) building confidence that the investment manager can analyze and close a transaction in an expeditious manner at a competitive price.

PROPERTY SCREENING

The screening process compares potential acquisitions against criteria "screens" to determine which submissions best measure up to a set of preestablished investment criteria. This process assists investment managers in continuing to focus on acquiring properties that are consistent with their investor's investment strategy.

It does not do any good to acquire properties that don't meet investment objectives, regardless of how good the "deal" may be from a classic real estate point of view. It's even worse to compound the prob-

---

1 In situations where competitive marketing is unavoidable, good relationships help ensure that the investment manager at least will be allowed to compete for a property when it comes to market.

lem by trying to rationalize the investment criteria to fit the characteristics of a property.

Most investment managers have limited operating resources, and pursuing a property that does not reflect investor requirements may keep the firm from pursuing another. This is not only a waste of time and money, but may lead to "opportunity costs" that ultimately can be much greater.

The first step is for the investment manager to alert potential sources of the types of properties the firm is in the market to acquire. This is accomplished by an investment criteria sheet for each search.[2]

Investment Criteria Sheet

Investment criteria sheets are established by the acquisition management group and usually approved by the Investment Committee.[3] Generally, these criteria are derived from the investment objectives of the firm's investors as expressed in various investment documents.

Examples of investment criteria include targeted geographical markets, property type(s), parcel size, building size and age, tenant mix and credit quality, lease turn characteristics, funds required, photos of the property, key tenants (by SF, if available), price, and the contact person for the transaction. Figure 6-2 is an example of an Investment Criteria Sheet.

Property Submittals

Once the investment criteria sheet has been distributed to prospective leads, submissions should begin arriving in a variety of formats (e-mail, fax, telephone, letter, etc.).[4]

When this information is received, the submission is registered temporarily (date and time stamped) and held for a stated period (generally 36 to 48 hours), pending receipt of additional information, which generally includes a rent roll, property financial statement (preferably for the last two years), and proposed purchase terms.

---

2 Some firms with large amounts of uninvested capital and continuing requirements for similar properties may distribute criteria sheets that reflect their "standing" criteria for certain types of properties.

3 Throughout this book, the term "Investment Committee" is used to represent a formal or informal group of the firm's owners and/or managers who establish and monitor the firm's investment policy.

4 Some property owners may utilize an Offering Memorandum (OM), which is a formal description of the property being offered for sale and the terms of the prospective transaction. This is most commonly used in a competitive bidding situation.

F I G U R E 6-2

Investment Criteria Sheet, Western Commercial Property
Fund, October 3, 2005

Property Type	Light Industrial; flex office
Metro Area	Bay Area (8 counties) Denver Inland Empire (Riverside–San Bernardino) Los Angeles County Orange County Phoenix Portland San Diego Seattle
Building(s) Age Floors Construction Size Land Area Parking Loading Power Water Data Area (30 minutes)	 Under 10 years 1 or 2 Light steel or tilt-up concrete 100,000 SF–200,000 SF 3–10 Acres 3 spaces/1,000 SF floor area Minimum 2 docks High capacity Potable Fiber-optic Medium priced housing, shopping; restaurants, hotels, etc.
Desirable features Minimum Leased Lease Term Years Remaining Tenant Credit(s) Target Tenants Tenant Exclusions:	 50% NNN 5 years B+ or better Technology; financial services; business services Retail, medical office
Send submissions to: (Letter, fax, or e-mail)	Charles Fisher Acquisition Director Western Commercial Property Fund, Ltd. 4619 Flower Street Los Angeles CA Phone: 415 659 4327 Fax: 415 549 4328 Cfisher@westernfund.com

Source: McMahan Real Estate Services, LLC

Following receipt of this additional information, the registration is complete and the submitting broker(s) acknowledged as the procuring agent(s) for the transaction, should it occur.[5]

Early Warning on Pursuit Costs

At this stage the investment manager begins spending "real money," in terms of the allocation of staff resources and, if the process proceeds, in the cost of due diligence resources such as consultants, lawyers, travel, etc. While this is part of doing business, an investment manager must be continually conscious of the cost of the sourcing and acquisition process and strive to utilize resources as efficiently as possible.

In each potential transaction, pursuit costs should be budgeted accurately and every attempt made to manage these costs as close to budget as possible.

This log-in process is necessary in order to avoid broker disputes over potential commissions that can delay the acquisition process and may result in time wasting and possibly adverse litigation for the investment manager.[6]

Figure 6-3 is an example of an entry in an investment log.

PRELIMINARY UNDERWRITING

As properties are submitted or uncovered through the investment manager's proactive initiatives, the immediate task is to quickly develop the facts about a property in order to compare it to the investment criteria sheet. This is generally a one- or two-page underwriting analysis.

In some cases the investment manager may not have all the information necessary to make effective comparisons and must immediately take steps to get the required information from the broker, owner, or other submission source.

The objective of the screening program is to eliminate properties that, for one reason or another, do not meet investment criteria before a lot of time is spent on a site visit and/or further analytical work. Too often a

---

5 Brokers are usually "protected" for a period (generally two to three months), provided they keep in touch and notify the investment manager of any change in the status of the property.

6 Ideally, the submission is entered on a database (rather than on an Excel or Word program), which not only expedites the review but makes it easier to allocate deal reviews among the acquisition team, retrieve data on deals marked as good "comps," and autogenerate rejection letters.

FIGURE 6-3

Investment Log Entry, Western Commercial Property Fund, October 7, 2005

Property Location

Property	Multimetric Building
Address	1474 Mountain Flower Avenue
City & State	Centennial, CO
Zip Code	80237

Property Description

Year Built	2001	
Construction	Light steel frame	
Rentable Area	1 floor 124,800	SF
Land Area	7.0	acres
Parking	482	spaces

Tenant

Property Use	Flex Office	
Tenant	Multimetric Technology, Inc.	
Credit	B+	
Lease	10 years; NNN	$14.50
Operating Exp.		$5.25
Remaining Lease Term	6	Years

Other: Located in relatively new, well-planned
R&D park near Denver Tech Center

Seller Information

Owner	Morgan Company
Broker	Sloan Realty
Phone	303 568 1224
E-mail	lena@sloanre.com

Negotiation Schedule

Offering Received	10/07/05
Preliminary IC Approval	10/14/05
LOI Submitted	10/17/05
LOI Executed	10/19/05
Purchase Contract Executed	10/28/05

Due Diligence Schedule

Due Diligence Begins	11/01/05
Tenant Interview	11/03/05
Due Diligence Complete	11/16/05
Final IC Approval	11/18/05
Remove All Conditions	11/21/05
Close of Escrow	11/23/05

Price	$22,000,000
Price/SF	$176.28
Initial Cap Rate	8.2%

Note: Exhibit based on actual building; details disguised.

Source: McMahan Real Estate Services, LLC

lot of time is burned off chasing deals that will ultimately prove unsuitable for the investment manager's investors.

Preliminary Site Visit

In some cases the investment manager may have tracked a property before it comes to market and may have a good idea of its location, key tenants, building quality, surrounding land uses, and market area.[7]

If the property is unfamiliar, a quick site visit will be necessary to establish a "visceral" understanding of the property's features. This visit can be undertaken by a member of the acquisition or asset management team, depending upon individual availability. In certain situations, a trusted local contact may be utilized. An external survey is generally sufficient, although gaining access to the building (if security permits) can often provide a better understanding of the features of the property (e.g., floor plan, design features, tenant diversity, building maintenance standards). It also is important to drive the neighborhood to review surrounding land uses, competing properties, etc. Photographs and/or videos of the property and the surrounding area should be taken, if possible.

If the property survives initial screening and a site visit, it is time to consider it as a prospective acquisition target and begin a preliminary underwriting of its investment potential. This effort does not replace a rigorous due diligence process (discussed in Chapter 8), but rather, allows for a preliminary understanding of the target asset to determine if an offer is warranted.

In the interests of time, the information and data submitted by the seller are deemed to be reasonably accurate, subject to final verification through the due diligence process. In fact, one of the roles of the preliminary underwriting is to identify risk issues that *must* be addressed during the due diligence phase.

Preliminary Title Report

One of the early steps is to order a preliminary title report from the local office of a national title company. This report will pinpoint the general history of the property's ownership and any liens that may have been placed by other parties. Liens or other encumbrances may indicate parties who may have a claim to a security interest in the title. Typical liens and encumbrances include:

---

7 Asset managers are often a good source of information on properties coming to market in areas in which they are active.

- Monetary liens
- Property tax liens
- Mechanics liens
- Financial liens
- Judgment liens
- Easements
- CC&Rs (Covenants, Conditions, and Restrictions)
- Leases
- Equipment liens (UCC filings)

A review of the preliminary title report also may indicate additional title research that needs to be undertaken in the due diligence phase. Figure 6-4 is an example of a preliminary title report.

Metro Area Analysis

The purpose of the metro area analysis is to develop a general understanding of socioeconomic trends that may affect the economic health of targeted submarkets in which the firm is active and prospective property acquisitions are located.

The metropolitan boundaries of most urban areas are well defined by federal governmental agencies (particularly the U.S. Census Bureau), local planning agencies, and private market research firms.

In order to study past trends and project future growth patterns, data should be collected on an annual basis over a five- to 10-year period. This data should be maintained for each Metropolitan Statistical Area (MSA) in which the investment manager is operating or plans to invest and operate in the future. It should be continually updated so it is immediately available for due diligence and other purposes. State and national data in each of the categories also should be accessible for comparative purposes.

Key data to be collected and maintained includes:

- Demographic data
  □ Population growth
  □ Demographic breakdown of population (age, gender, etc.)

- Number of households
- General educational level (if available)
- Growth in household income
- Employment/firm data

FIGURE 6-4

Preliminary Title Report, Western Commercial Property Fund

Issued for the sole use of:
Western Commercial Property Fund, Ltd.
4619 Flower Street
Los Angeles CA
Phone: 415 659 4327
Fax: 415 549 4328

Property Address:
Multimetric Building
1475 Mountain Road
Centennial, CO 80237

Dated as of: October 12, 2005

Title Vested in:
Morgan Property Partnership, LLC

Property Description:
Parcel 2 of Parcel Map No. 193 in the County of Denver. State of Colorado, as per Map recorded in Book 4, page 55 of Parcel Maps, in the Office of County Recorder of said County.

Exceptions and Exclusions:
1. Taxes and assessments, general and special, for the fiscal year 2005–2006, a lien, but not yet due or payable.
2. Water rights, claims or title to water, whether or not shown by the public records.
3. A certified copy of a copy of Limited Partnership filed in the office of the Secretary of State for Colorado, dated January 15, 2001, disclosing the general partner as being the Morgan Company, Inc.
4. We find no open Deeds of Trust of record.
5. Any environmental issues related to the Property.
6. Rights and claims of parties in possession.
7. Any unrecorded and subsisting leases.
8. The requirement that this Company be provided with an opportunity to inspect the land (the Company reserves the right to make additional exceptions and/or requirements upon completion of its inspection).

Should you have any questions, please contact your title officer immediately.
Note: Exhibit based on preliminary title report, disguised

Source: McMahan Real Estate Services, LLC

- Employment growth by Standard Industrial Code (SIC) code
- Number of firms (offices)
- Number of patents (if available)
- Retail sales (shopping centers)

- Real estate market data related to the property type being considered (as available)
  □ Construction
  □ Vacancy rate
  □ Rental rates
  □ Sales comps

Submarket Data

Data on targeted submarkets are more difficult to generate but often more meaningful in understanding demand and supply trends and overall market conditions.

In most metro areas, public agencies and private firms such as brokers maintain data by generally acceptable submarket definitions. In other words, these are market areas that buyers/sellers and landlords/tenants would recognize as having relatively similar characteristics.[8]

A preliminary understanding of local submarket conditions is a vital component of the preliminary underwriting, since it is necessary to understand how a potential acquisition property competes within its market area. To do so, it is essential to identify which properties compete directly or indirectly with the subject property and what level of competition they represent.

Significant new supply coming into a market has the potential to have a disruptive effect on market conditions. It is important, therefore, to identify other sites where new building construction is likely to occur. An understanding as to whether and when these sites may be developed can also be helpful in better understanding the dynamics of the local market.

Other submarket factors to consider are market rental trends, gentrification of market area (primarily apartments), local government attitudes toward new supply, etc.

Competitive Survey

Within the submarket, specific buildings will compete directly with the subject property for tenants. In order to evaluate a potential property, it is necessary to have an understanding of the competitive advantages and disadvantages of the property vis-à-vis existing properties as well as new ones that are in the development pipeline. Important factors to consider

---

8 In some instances it is helpful not only to analyze broker-generated data, but to interview two or three individual brokers active in the submarket. Key questions include free rent and other concessions, TI allowances, leasing commissions, and broker commission splits.

include property location, accessibility, infrastructure, building(s) size and configuration, key tenants, and a ranking of the property as compared with the potential acquisition property.

Important factors to consider include:

- Location
  - Proximity to residential areas
  - Proximity to employment centers
  - Proximity to public facilities
  - Location profile (prestige of neighborhood, visibility from highway, signage, etc.)
- Accessibility
  - Traffic circulation
  - Public transportation
- Infrastructure
  - Utilities
  - Parking
- Building(s)
  - Size
  - Approximate age
  - Construction quality
  - Availability of parking
- Tenants
  - Major tenants (office or industrial); anchor tenants (shopping centers)[9]
  - Other tenants
  - Pad tenants (shopping centers)
  - Image in marketplace
  - Estimated occupancy
  - Rent roll (if available)
  - Lease rollovers (if available)

Figure 6-5 is an example of a Competitive Properties Survey.

Cash Flow Analysis

With an understanding of the leases in place as well as the physical aspects of the property and its surroundings, a cash flow analysis can be

---

9 A "major" tenant in an office or industrial building occupies a high percentage of space in the building; an "anchor" tenant in a shopping center generates shopper traffic for other, usually smaller, tenants.

FIGURE 6-5

Competitive Properties Survey, Western Commercial Property Fund Multimetric Building Underwriting, Denver Tech Area, October 13, 2005

Property	Location	Built	SF	Floors	Average Rents Gross	Average Rents Net	Average Rents Op. Exp.	Comments
Subject								
Multimetric Building	1475 Mountain Road Englewood, CO	2001	124,800	1	$19.75(a)	$14.50	$5.25	Single tenant with six years remaining; NNN lease; no renewal clauses Potential upgrade to full office?
Flex/Office Buildings								
Mountain Financial Ctr.	5470 Willow Drive Englewood, CO	1995	47,443	3	$21.75			Mountain views; near hotels, retail, clubs, and light rail station
Aspen Office Plaza	7340 Tucson Way Centennial, CO	1997	20,000	2	$18.15(a)	$12.50	$5.65	Parklike setting; new security system
Mile High Office Center	7740 Holly St. Centennial, CO	1996	24,000	2	$20.50			Upscale neighborhood
	Average		30,481		$20.63(b)			
Industrial Buildings (with office uses)								
Technology Center	8865 Orchard Road Englewood, CO	1999	90,000	1.5	$15.75(a)	$12.50	$3.25	Mostly technology firms
7010 Alton Way	7010 Alton Way Englewood, CO	1986	45,000	1	$17.10(a)	$13.00	$4.10	40% office uses
Bolder Creek Bus. Park	7350 Alton Way Englewood, CO	1987	60,000	1.5	$16.20(a)	$12.25	$3.95	50% office uses
	Average		65,000		$16.20(b)			

(a) Gross Equivalent (net rent + operating expense)
(b) Weighted by amount of square footage
Note: Exhibit based on actual buildings; details disguised

Source: McMahan Real Estate Services, LLC

completed. The projection period is generally 10 years, although this may vary, depending upon the circumstances of the property and/or the investors targeted for potential investment.

The pro-forma cash flow analysis (usually an Argus or Excel model) forms the backbone of the preliminary underwriting of the investment opportunity. The analysis forecasts anticipated revenue and expenses over a projected holding period. It incorporates items such as tenant lease obligations and other leasing and market assumptions as well as anticipated expenses from property operations and tenant improvements, leasing commissions, and capital expenditures.

In the final year of the analysis, the property is assumed to be sold for cash. The combined net cash flow over the holding period is then compared to the acquisition costs of the property to determine whether the investment will meet investor return expectations. This is accomplished through discounted cash flow analysis.

Discounted Cash Flow Analysis

Since the cash flow occurs in different amounts in varying years, it is necessary to discount the flows to the present in order to measure them in meaningful terms.

Two relatively similar analytical techniques are commonly used in discounting the cash flows: *internal rate of return* (IRR) and *net present value* (NPV). The IRR is important in determining the overall return on the investment, comparing it to the target investment return of the investor(s). The NPV is helpful as a pricing tool to establish a range of possible offering and ceiling prices for negotiations.[10]

Examples of a cash flow, IRR, and NPV analysis of a prospective office building investment are illustrated in Figure 6-6.

Sensitivity Analysis

The analytical program should also facilitate "what if" questions by means of sensitivity analysis. The analyst should be able to plug in varying

---

10 A note of caution: All of these analytical techniques are subject to manipulation to obtain favorable outcomes. It is therefore critical for the investment manager to have standards as to how these techniques are developed and interpreted. It is also important to be certain that these techniques are consistent with industry standards and fully understood by the investor or shareholder. Industry groups such as NCREIF and NAREIT have been involved in developing such standards, as well as other industry organizations and academic groups. There are also package analytical programs available that are consistent with industry standards.

FIGURE 6-6

Preliminary Cash Flow Analysis, Western Commercial Property Fund Multimedia Building

Year	0 Investment	1 Operations	2 Operations	3 Operations	4 Operations	5 Operations	6 Operations Sale
Investment	($21,000,000)						
Rentable SF		124,900					
Annual Rent/SF (NNN)		$14.50					
Inflation 3.0%							
Annual Rent		1,811,050	1,865,382	1,921,343	1,978,983	2,038,353	2,099,503
Disposition Cap Rate							8.5%
Disposition Price							24,831,500
Selling Costs	5.0%						1,241,575
Disposition Proceeds							23,589,925
Annual Cash Flow	($21,000,000)	1,811,050	1,865,382	1,921,343	1,978,983	2,038,353	25,689,428

Internal Rate of Return (IRR)							10.8%

(Annual cash flows; discounted by guess of 10%)

PV Factor @ 10.0%		0.9093	0.8264	0.7513	0.6830	0.6209	0.5645
	(21,000,000)	1,646,771	1,541,637	1,443,536	1,351,673	1,265,656	14,501,682

Net Present Value (NPV)							21,750,956

Source: McMahan Real Estate Services, LLC

assumptions regarding price, postclosing improvement costs, annual rent and operating costs, and, if utilized, mortgage financing. The sensitivity analysis also may be useful in answering questions from the Investment Committee and, if required, potential investors.

This information also may prove valuable in the Letter of Intent (LOI) negotiations, as well as establishing which of the underlying assumptions need to be tested in greater depth during the due diligence phase. In the case of investment partnerships, to be certain that investment partners will receive targeted returns the analysis can be expanded to include distribution flows.

Preliminary Investment Underwriting

Based on the information generated by the cash flow analysis and preliminary due diligence activities, a summary of anticipated risks associated with the investment should be outlined, as well as preliminary thoughts regarding possible mitigation steps that might be employed to reduce or eliminate identified risks.

The magnitude of each risk and its potential negative impact on the success of the investment can then be tested in the due diligence phase, as well as the probabilities of success of planned mitigation measures.

Figure 6-7 is a preliminary investment underwriting of the submittal outlined in Figure 6-3 and analyzed in Figure 6-6.

At this stage the acquisition staff should evaluate whether they want to recommend the investment to the Investment Committee. If the IRR analysis indicates that the investment return will be marginal (as measured against targeted investment returns), or there is substantial risk in the investment that can't be readily mitigated, it may be desirable to terminate the acquisition at this point and move on to other prospects.

No matter how much pressure (internal and external) is placed on the acquisition team to find investment opportunities, it is very important to maintain personal and firm integrity—there will always be another day and another deal.

Preliminary Investment Underwriting, Western Commerical Property Fund Multimetric Office Building, October 14, 2005

Comparison to Investment Criteria

❑ Suburban Denver ranked first in SF office leasing among WCPF's regional target markets for first three quarters of 2005; sixth nationally (Source: Cushman & Wakefield Research)

❑ DTC area one of strongest tech office nodes in Denver Metro

❑ Building well designed; appears to be of good construction quality

❑ Located near fiber-optic line

❑ Single tenant; limited ongoing asset management requirements

❑ Tenant has B+ credit rating

❑ Remaining lease term greater than five years

❑ Near medium priced residential areas

❑ Near hotels, retail, and restaurants

❑ Going in Cap Rate of 7.5% or greater; preliminary IRR in excess of 10.0% (at offering price)

Upside Potential

❑ Denver Metro and DTC area continue to strengthen in attraction to office tenants

❑ Possible upgrade to office use; building design flexible in terms of redesign (e.g., partial second level)

❑ Excess land for new building addition(s)

Exit Strategy

❑ Existing tenant has no renewal clause

❑ If strategy to keep tenant, negotiate rent increase to market levels 12 months prior to lease expiration

❑ If strategy to change tenant, consider one or a combination of the following:

  ○ Lease to new tenant

  ○ Upgrade building to exclusively office use

  ○ Expand building design (partial second floor; first floor extension; second building; etc.)

Downside Risks

❑ Denver metro area loses its attraction to business firms

❑ New competitive nodes introduced through urban renewal or zoning/land use conversion

❑ Single tenant; no opportunity to hedge leasing risk

❑ Credit exposure: if tenant has financial problems; possible loss of income for period of time

Recommendations

❑ Proceed with offer of $20 million; willing to go to $21 million

❑ Evaluate tenant's future rental plans in tenant interview

❑ Evaluate tenant's credit thoroughly; if desirable, seek credit enhancement in final negotiations

❑ Evaluate postexpiration expansion and/or reuse possibilities in due diligence phase

Source: McMahan Real Estate Services, LLC

CHAPTER 7

Preliminary Approvals and Negotiations

PRELIMINARY APPROVALS

Investment Committee

In most investment management firms, the Investment Committee is comprised of the senior officers or partners of the organization.

These individuals usually have many years of experience in each of the major disciplines required to successfully invest in real estate: acquisitions, dispositions, asset management, and financial reporting. Some Investment Committees also have client-oriented members representing one or more investor clients of the firm (often referred to as "portfolio managers").

The purpose of the Investment Committee is to govern the investment practices and procedures of the investment manager to assure investors their interests are being protected and enhanced at all times. This generally includes approval of property acquisitions, dispositions, debt encumbrances, asset management business plans and budgets, significant property improvements, investment restructurings, rehabs, due diligence budgets and contractors, and other major property and portfolio decisions.[1]

The Investment Committee also is responsible for monitoring markets and trends in the real estate industry in order to establish and modify the firm's investment policies as well as to provide leadership regarding new investment programs to be developed for investor consideration.

---

1 Since a large portion of potentially adverse litigation focuses on decisions made by the Investment Committee, it is usually comprised largely of "stakeholders" in the firm either as officers, partners, or shareholders. In public real estate companies, final approval of investment decisions may be reserved for the board of directors or a special committee of the board.

103

Each member of the Investment Committee usually has a single vote on any action item. Generally, a majority of members must approve a transaction involving the acquisition or disposition of any property in the firm's investment portfolios. Some investment managers require a super majority or even unanimous approval in order to proceed with certain transactions.[2]

Most Investment Committees are "on call" to meet every week or two to review potential transactions (often via telephone) and at least once a quarter to monitor the performance of the firm's investment portfolio (usually in person).

The acquisition information summary and related detailed analytical material developed by the acquisition staff is transmitted to the Investment Committee for a preliminary decision as to whether to pursue a recommended investment opportunity.[3]

Employees involved in the preparation and evaluation of the opportunity are expected to be available to explain and defend their recommendations, as well as discuss future courses of action if the investment is approved on a preliminary basis.

Due Diligence Budget

A due diligence budget generally is developed by the acquisition staff for each potential acquisition, including anticipated costs as well as direct payments to third-party contractors and the services they will provide.

The due diligence budget is usually approved by the Investment Committee or an officer or partner of the investment manager before any costs are incurred. In some cases proposed diligence contractors not on the firm's approved list also must be approved.

---

2 A major objective of the Investment Committee is to allocate potential investment opportunities fairly and diversify investment risk in each investor's portfolio. In order to accomplish this objective, some investment managers are organized so that members of the Investment Committee include senior asset managers representing "assets" based on geography and/or property type, as well as senior portfolio managers representing "investor clients" whose portfolios may cut across several geographical areas or property types. In some instances portfolio managers have a veto on new investments in client portfolios.

3 Most Investment Committees meet at least twice to consider each potential acquisition: (1) to give preliminary approval of the transaction and the due diligence budget, and (2) to provide final approval or rejection of the deal upon completion of the due diligence process. Most of them have busy schedules, so it is critical that the acquisition staff get information regarding recommended acquisitions into their hands as soon as possible.

Acquisition Timeline

A timeline is recommended for most acquisitions. The acquisition timeline details critical events during the acquisition process, including:

- Confidentiality Agreement executed (bid situations)
- Offering Memorandum received (bid situations)
- Letter of Intent delivered, negotiated, and (hopefully) executed
- Preliminary Investment Committee approval
- Purchase Agreement negotiated and executed
- Cash deposit posted (beginning of due diligence)
- Delivery dates of key due diligence materials
- Approval from debt sources (if utilized)
- Approval from equity investors (if required)
- Final Investment Committee approval
- Waiver of Conditions ("going hard" on deposit)
- Investor Memorandum delivered
- Call for funds
- Close of escrow (COE)

Acquisition timelines are entered in the investment manager's main computer calendar so interested parties can be aware of critical dates, possible conflicts in scheduling, the flow of cash deposits, etc. Timelines are recognized to be somewhat flexible and subject to change as circumstances warrant and provided the change is approved by both the buyer and seller.

NEGOTIATIONS

Once an investment opportunity has received preliminary approval from the Investment Committee, the next step is to negotiate a series of written agreements with the seller. This includes legal instruments such as a Confidentiality Agreement (C/A) and Purchase Agreement (competitive bidding situation), as well as more informal agreements such as a Letter of Intent (LOI), which establishes business guidelines for reaching agreement on key issues prior to entering into legally binding contracts.

Letter of Intent

A Letter of Intent (LOI) is used by the potential buyer to make an offer on a potential property acquisition. (In noncompetitive bidding situations the acquisitions process generally begins with the LOI.) The LOI is a nonlegal term sheet that sets forth certain basic business parameters regarding a potential acquisition.[4]

An LOI is also useful in "setting up" subsequent negotiations. The document lists prospective data to be provided by the seller (or agent), on which the buyer's price and terms are based. To the extent that due diligence uncovers deviations from seller-provided information, the LOI also can define a pricing mechanism that adjusts the final price based on the amount of the deviation. Inclusion of this type of language can preempt "brinkmanship" or "take it or leave it" negotiating "in the rush to close." (An example of an LOI is shown in Appendix B-1.)

Terms usually covered by an LOI include, but are not limited to:

- Offering price
- Conditions, if any
- Amount and form of deposit, holder of deposit and its use if the transaction proceeds or does not proceed
- Terms regarding the assumption of existing debt (if utilized)
- Description and timing of due diligence documents to be provided by the seller
- Critical points (dates or elapsed time) when documents and/or actions have to be completed and/or approved by each party
- Length of due diligence and closing periods
- Warranties (if any)
- Prorations of and credits between the parties
- Real estate brokers and finders who are exclusively entitled to a commission or finder's fee
- Confidentiality
- Terms of acceptance

In most firms, an LOI can only be executed by a senior officer or partner of the investment management firm.

While neither party is legally bound by an LOI,[5] the concise document is critical in serving to reduce confusion and provide clarity

---

4 The LOI is a "business document" and should not indicate an attorney as the contact. It's a good idea, however, to have the format of a standard LOI reviewed by an attorney before utilizing it.

5 It is important that the LOI expressly provides that it is not intended to be a legally binding agreement and that the parties will not be bound unless and until a complete Purchase Agreement has been negotiated and signed. Unless the parties make this entirely clear, there can be some risk that a court might hold that the LOI has become a legally binding document.

about the business terms of an acquisition before legal documents are negotiated.

In most cases, the LOI serves to temporarily remove the property from market competition and focuses the attention of the seller on the firm offering the LOI as the potential "buyer" of the property.

The LOI also serves as a road map of the business terms of the agreement for attorneys subsequently involved in preparing the Purchase Agreement. The process generally excludes attorneys from negotiations until the respective business representatives of each firm can reach agreement on fundamental transaction terms.

Purchase Agreement

Once an LOI has been negotiated and executed by the businesspeople, a Purchase Agreement is negotiated by attorneys representing each side (or multiple sides, if a lender is involved or the offer involves multiple investor groups). The Purchase Agreement translates the business terms of the LOI into a binding and legally enforceable contract between the parties. Appendix B-2 is an example of a Purchase Agreement.

In addition to the terms outlined in the LOI, the Purchase Agreement contains legal representations by the seller regarding the condition and legal status of the property and the fact that all documents and other materials will be provided to the buyer and are—to the seller's knowledge— complete and accurate. Other standard provisions include the timing and conditions of the due diligence review, assignability rights, default provisions, and casualty and condemnation clauses.[6]

In some cases, buyers are able to negotiate certain warranties from the seller regarding the physical quality of the property and the performance of equipment such as HVAC, electrical, plumbing, and other critical systems. A big issue usually is the length of the warranty period, which has tended to be shorter in the last few years.

Closing documents (bill of sale, warranty or grant deed, assignment of contracts, assignments of leases, etc.) should also be negotiated at this time and attached as exhibits to the Purchase Agreement. This is important to avoid panic negotiations just before closing, which often can be detrimental to the buyer.

The Purchase Agreement is usually executed by a senior officer or partner representing both the buying and selling firms.

---

6 If possible, it's important to control the drafting rights of the Purchase Agreement. The extra legal costs usually are more than made up through better control of the form and language used in preparing the documents.

Escrow

Today, most real estate transactions utilize an escrow to collect and disburse documents, funds, and other items required by the Purchase Agreement. Deposit receipts are generally in the form of an earnest money deposit (EMD) placed in escrow by the buyer.[7]

Funds can be either in the form of cash or a Letter of Credit (LOC) from a financial institution. If earnest money funds are not delivered into escrow by the date specified in the Purchase Agreement, the buyer may be in default under the contract. It is desirable, therefore, to arrange for the transfer of funds well in advance of the specified date. If the deposit is in the form of an LOC, it is important to monitor the expiration date carefully to make sure it does not expire if the due diligence period is extended. If cash is utilized, the escrow holder should be given a Form W-9 and investment instructions to make sure that the deposit is earning interest until it is cashed.

If the buyer cancels the transaction due to failure of the seller to satisfy the conditions of the Purchase Agreement (failure to provide diligence material, failure to meet time deadlines, etc.), the EMD is usually returned to the buyer. If the buyer breeches the terms of the Purchase Agreement by failing to close after removing conditions (i.e., "going hard"), the seller retains the deposit as liquidated damages.

Once a Purchase Agreement has been negotiated and executed by the parties, the EMD is posted and the due diligence process begins.[8]

Negotiating Strategies

There are probably as many negotiating strategies as there are experienced "deal" people. It is not the purpose of this book to cover all of them, but there are some important themes with which the reader should be familiar:

- The LOI should be considered an important tool in getting the seller to view the investment firm as the "favored" buyer for the property. As such, it should include favorable background information regarding the investment management firm, including size, operating philosophy, level of investment discretion, investor clients (if not confidential), existing portfolio characteristics,

---

7 In today's world, the EMD is much more common than cash. It is almost always a part of transaction negotiations and, when negotiated, incorporated directly into the Purchase Agreement.

8 In some cases the beginning of the due diligence period is tied to an event such as receipt of specified due diligence information required to conduct due diligence. This helps to keep the seller's eye on the ball.

amount of funds available for new properties, investment closing batting average, policy regarding brokers, etc.

- The LOI should be hand-delivered by a senior officer of the investment management firm who is proficient at personal negotiations and has sufficient discretion to modify the LOI, if required.

- In essence, the seller's representative should be allowed sufficient time to consider the offer, but not enough time to "shop" it extensively with the buyer's competitors or have uncontested "second thoughts" regarding proceeding with the transaction.

- If the seller is located in another metro area and wants some time to consider the offer or discuss it with others, the acquisition officer should allow sufficient travel time to return to the seller's offices in a few hours or overnight to complete negotiations.

- The legal firm utilized by the potential buyer should be experienced in working with LOIs and in completing the transaction. Some attorneys view preparation of the Purchase Agreement as an opportunity to reopen negotiations rather than convert what has been negotiated by principals into final legal form.

- It is also helpful if the buyer's attorney is familiar with the seller's legal firm, and ideally has experience in negotiating real estate agreements with them.

- In negotiating both the LOI and Purchase Agreement, the buyer and the buyer's attorneys should be careful to allow sufficient time to successfully complete due diligence activities. Sellers and/or their legal representatives often try to shorten the diligence period and/or limit the items covered. Agreeing to this may end up costing the investment manager and its investor(s) as a result of adverse litigation following the close.

- The method of handling the cash deposit and its intended use as liquidated damages should be carefully spelled out in the purchase agreement.

CHAPTER 8

Due Diligence

Once a Purchase Agreement has been negotiated and executed by the parties, the initial cash deposit is posted and the due diligence process begins.

As noted in Chapters 4 and 5, commercial real estate investment in the United States has been increasingly influenced by financial institutions, primarily pension funds.

These investors are fiduciaries to their various constituents, and as such, concerned that their investment managers follow "best practice" standards in order to avoid lawsuits or other adverse consequences once the transaction has been completed. It also helps to minimize expensive mistakes in pricing (e.g., higher capital costs), which investors ultimately pay for in diminished returns.

As a result, most commercial real estate transactions today require a "due diligence" evaluation on behalf of the investor in order to decide whether to finalize the investment process. Generally, the acquiring investor undertakes these evaluations in a relatively short period of time (30 to 60 days) in an atmosphere of extreme pressure. Due diligence participants attempt to be thorough in considering all aspects of the property, both positive and negative.

It is important that aspects of future property ownership considered negative can be mitigated in some fashion, either before or after closing of the transaction. Having such a strategy *prior to close* is an important factor in the acquisition process.

From a fiduciary liability perspective, due diligence is the most critical period in terms of adverse legal exposure, and one that requires the utmost attention of everyone involved.

This legal exposure is compounded by the fact that the time allowed for due diligence is relatively short (usually 30 to 60 days), and receipt and evaluation of due diligence materials requires the simultaneous involvement of a variety of technical specialists. In some cases there may be additional pressure to approve the transaction due to a "backup buyer" waiting in the wings.

ROLE OF DUE DILIGENCE

The major objective of due diligence is to "prove the lie" by finding worst-case problems with the acquisition property, and if discovered, develop a strategy to mitigate any significant negative aspects that might adversely affect the investment. It is not enough to discover problems; there also have to be solutions. If there are no solutions, or they are inadequate, then the transaction should be terminated.

The due diligence process also involves verifying previously disclosed information and testing the assumptions that formed the basis of the preliminary analysis presented to the Investment Committee (see Chapter 7). It also may involve discovering new information from in-depth investigations that the seller would not permit until he or she knows that the terms of the transaction are legally binding, subject to satisfactory completion of buyer due diligence.

MANAGING THE PROCESS

Most due diligence activities are performed by independent, third-party contractors. Potential problem areas may be analyzed by different contractors, requiring a final reconciliation by a master contractor or manager of the due diligence team.

In some cases the terms of the Purchase Agreement can be negotiated to compensate the buyer for problems unearthed by the diligence process. This might be in the form of a lower price, a holdback of a portion of purchase funds until a problem can be corrected, a guarantee or warranty by the seller, or some other provision outlined in the Purchase Agreement. Changes in the Purchase Agreement obviously require approval of the seller, so it becomes entirely a negotiated situation.

If the problems are relatively minor, the buyer may decide to "waive" the deposit and proceed to close the transaction. If the buyer waives, the deposit becomes nonrefundable and a closing occurs shortly thereafter (usually 30 days).

Transaction litigation often centers around due diligence activities, with major emphasis on the "process" that is followed by the investment manager. It is essential to make certain that the due diligence process is systematic, well documented, and carefully managed.

Selecting Contractors

It is particularly important that *independent, third-party contractors retained by the buyer* be utilized for the technical portion of the due diligence process. While engineering, environmental, and other reports prepared by seller contractors can be utilized as historic information and points of reference, these reports must be reviewed and validated by the buyer's contractors, utilizing their own testing procedures. Figure 8-1 on the following page is a chart illustrating the organizational relationship of the major due diligence contractors.

Contractor Coordination

In order to reduce the number of individual contractors, it is common to have a master contractor (usually an architectural or engineering firm) with more specialized firms serving as subcontractors.[1] This also helps put the total physical situation in perspective as well as reducing professional fees. Some professional firms specialize exclusively in performing due diligence activities.

Budget and Timeline Update

Once the due diligence contracts are in place it is timely to update the due diligence budget and acquisition timeline (Chapter 7) in order to reflect the specific delivery dates and costs of contracted work.

Checklist

In order to ensure that the acquisition team performs all the due diligence tasks that follow, a due diligence checklist should be completed for each potential acquisition. A copy of such a checklist is included as Figure 8-2.

Steps Prior to Proceeding

As noted previously, in the last few years the time allowed for due diligence has steadily been reduced. This has placed an immense amount of

---

1 The master contractor may perform some of the specialized tasks directly.

FIGURE 8-1

Organization of Due Diligence Contractors

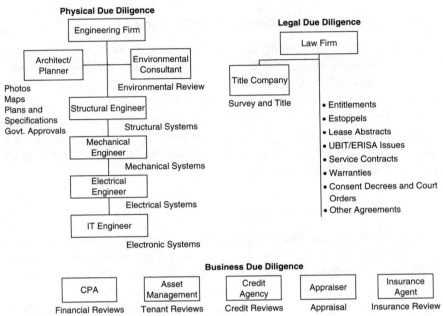

pressure on managing the due diligence process, and this factor, coupled with litigation associated with due diligence mistakes, makes it very important to have as much as possible in place prior to the beginning of the diligence time period.

There are several steps that can be taken to get ready:

- Have the diligence team selected and under contract with an approximate date for beginning work. Generally it's best to have the date tied to gaining access to the property (e.g., within one or two days thereafter), which is usually spelled out in the Purchase Agreement.
- Have a due diligence "kickoff" meeting with your key consultants to review critical issues, schedules, and specific roles and responsibilities. Communication is very important in running any successful due diligence program.
- Obtain from the seller all of the information and data that has been accumulated to date. (Note: this should be negotiated in the Purchase Agreement.)

- Have the selected environmental consultants order the databases from the various regulatory bodies that govern use of the property. (Be willing to pay for any costs associated with this if the sale falls through.)
- Explore with the insurance agent any risk-management tools he or she can deliver if adverse environmental conditions are discovered.
- Explore with the legal consultant the possible use of an additional escrow for use in handling environmental mitigation measures.
- Identify a postclosing remediation team (management and consultants) that will be responsible for monitoring any environmental remediation, if required.

FIGURE 8-2

Due Diligence Checklist

Review Code			
A	Appraiser	I	Insurance Agent
AF	Acquiring Firm	L	Lawyer
AP	Architect Planner	ME	Mechanical Engr.
C	Consultant	NE	Environmental Engr.
CA	Credit Agency	S	Seller
EE	Electrical Engineer	SE	Structural Engr.
G	Government	T	Title Company

	Source	Review	✓
Physical Due Diligence			
Photos			
Property	S	AP/SE/NE	
Aerial	S	AP/SE/NE	
Maps			
Metro area	S/G	AP/EE	
Submarket	S/G	AP/EE	
Plans and Specifications			
Land use and circulation	S	AP/SE	
Site plans	S	AP/SE	
Building plans & specs	S	AP/SE	
Tenant floor plans	S	AP/SE	
Construction documents	S	AP/SE	
Reports			
Phase I Environmental	S	NE	
Phase II Environmental	S	NE	
Governmental Approvals			
Building permits	S	AP/L	
Zoning	S	AP/L	
Zoning variances	S	AP/L	
Certificates of occupancy	S	AP/L	
Licenses	S	AP/L	

F I G U R E   8-2

Due Diligence Checklist (*Continued*)

Warranties

Roof	S	
HVAC	S	
Paving	S	

Service Contracts   S

Existing Condition Survey   S

Structural systems

Foundation	SE	
Load bearing	SE	
Exterior building shell	SE	
Floor system	SE	
Roofing system	SE	
Seismic	SE/NE	

Mechanical systems

Plumbing	ME	
HVAC	ME	
Vertical transportation	ME	

Electrical systems

Main system	EE	
Emergency power	EE	

Electronic systems

Fiber-optic capacity	EE	
Raised floors	EE	
Phone demarcation	EE	
Phone & server closets	EE	

Repair History   S

Environmental review

Hazardous substances		
Asbestos	NE	
Radon gas	NE	
Lead paint	NE	
Sick building syndrome	NE	
Soil conditions		
Geological	NE/SE	
Hydro geological	NE	
Protected biological	NE	
Catastrophic risk exposure		
Flood Hazard Zone	NE	
Flooding Hazard	NE	
Fire Hazard	NE	
Wildland	NE	
Earthquake	NE	
Seismic Hazard Zone	NE	

FIGURE 8-2

Due Diligence Checklist (*Continued*)

Legal Due Diligence
Survey

Physical boundaries	L/T/S	
Easements	L/T/S	
CC&R's	L/T/S	
Rights of way	L/T/S	
Zoning violations	L/T/AP	

Title

Form of ownership	L/T	
ALTA Title Insurance	L/T	
Assignment of project	L/T	

Escrow

Buyer's Closing Statement	AC	
Supplemental Instructions	AC	
Amendments to Close	AC	

Entitlements

Zoning	AP/L/S	
Zoning variances	AP/L/S	
Buliding codes	AP/L/S	
Utility permits	AP/L/S	
Special District Permits	AP/L/S	
Local Improvement Districts	AP/L/S	

Tenant Estoppels Certificates

Location of space	L/AF	
Size of space (SF)	L/AF	
Parking spaces	L/AF	
Term of lease	L/AF	
Starting date	L/AF	
Rent	L/AF	
Expense recovery	L/AF	
Tenant options	L/AF	

Lease Abstracts — L/AF
Service Contracts — L

Warranties	L	
Consent decrees and court orders	L	
Assignment of Project Documents	L/AC	
UBIT/ERISA Issues	L	
Tax Withholding	L/AC	
1031 Status	L/AC	

F I G U R E   8-2

Due Diligence Checklist (*Continued*)

Business Due Dilligence

Market analysis	AF/C	
Financial analysis	AF	
Tenant interviews	L/AF	
Tenant Financial Review	AF	
Tenant Credit Review	AF/CA	
Appraisal (Optional)	L/AF/A	
Insurance review		
Existing coverage	L/AF/I	
New coverage	L/AF/I	

Source: McMahan Real Estate Services, LLC

PHYSICAL DUE DILIGENCE

Most people think of physical due diligence as *being due diligence.* Certainly this is the area of greatest diligence focus, as well it should be, since mistakes in this area are the most costly to remediate and, if unsuccessful, the most damaging to long-term asset value.[2] This is reinforced by relatively strict government rules and regulations in the area and the fact that, once proven, courts have tended to readily approve most damage claims.

This is one area, therefore, where a seller is most likely to agree to pay for remediation (or adjust the sale price), since they know they will have to do it at some point in the future, if they want to sell to another potential buyer.

In the following paragraphs, the most commonly used contractor(s) for the task to be performed is identified in parentheses. These tasks may be performed by other contractors as well.

Photos (Architect/Planner)

Property photos should include not only the subject property, but surrounding land uses as well. Attention should be paid to power lines, pooled water, parking congestion, etc. The seller may have photos of the

---

2 Although this discussion focuses primarily on property acquisition, many of the comments in this chapter apply to commercial leases, mortgage transactions, and company acquisitions.

buildings under construction, which might prove helpful to the engineering contractors.

Aerial photos are helpful in describing the neighborhood and the relationship of the property to major arterials, freeways, residential districts, etc. Historic aerial photos can be utilized in spotting previous uses of the property that might influence the environmental analysis.

Maps (Architect/Planner)

Maps are generally collected during preliminary underwriting (Chapter 7). There may be some specialized maps, however, that need to be located in order to round out a picture of the property and the surrounding neighborhood (Figures 8-3 and 8-4). For example, there may be specialized maps such as income, households, business taxes paid, etc., that might be helpful in updating the market analysis.

Local, state, and federal government agencies are usually the best sources for maps. City planners also should be interviewed regarding neighborhood characteristics, problem areas, future public works projects, public finances, etc.

FIGURE 8-3

Photo Showing Possible Underground Gasoline Storage Tanks

Source: Marx Okubo, San Francisco

FIGURE 8-4

Aerial Photo Map Showing Shopping Center and Its
Relationship to the Neighborhood

Source: Marx Okubo, San Francisco

Plans and Specifications (Architect/Planner)

Plans and specifications of the property should include:

- Land use and circulation plan
- Site plans
- As-built building plans and specifications (if available)
- Floor plans showing tenant improvements (space plans)
- Construction documents (new buildings)

Figure 8-5 is an example.

Governmental Approvals (Architect/Planner)

Copies of the following government approval documents should be obtained
and reviewed[3]:

- Building permits
- Zoning (planning entitlements)
- Zoning variances

---

3 It should be noted that governmental approvals apply to the present use of the property only. If a
change in use is contemplated postclosing, the requirements for this new use should be investigated
to be certain that the property will be able to conform.

FIGURE 8-5

Office Park Land Use and Circulation

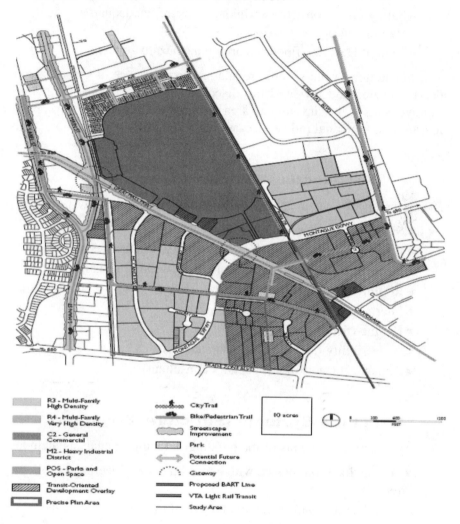

- Land use and circulation (traffic studies)
- Parking
- Life safety codes
- Certificates of occupancy (CO)
- Licenses
- Americans with Disabilities (ADA) compliance reports
- Compliance with FHA requirements (apartments)

- Federal Aviation Administration (FAA) airspace restrictions
- Water, petroleum, and timber rights (including access rights)
- Safety infractions (fire sprinkler pressure, inadequate traffic signing, etc.)
- Natural Hazards (flood or earthquake hazard zones)

In addition to site-specific regulatory conformance, it's also a good idea to develop and review data related to government plans for public improvements in the surrounding area (utilities, roads and highways, public transit, commercial rail service, water or petroleum wells, etc.).

Architectural Systems (Architect)

The key architectural elements of the building(s) requiring analysis include:

- Site improvements (functional adequacy)
- Envelope (material suitability, durability, weather resistivity)
- Doors and windows (functional utility, weather resistivity)
- Roofing (drainage, remaining service life)
- Interiors (service life, code compliance)
- Exiting (fire and life/safety)
- Accessibility (ADA, FFHA, state codes)[4]
- Acoustical (typically a specialty consultant)

Structural Systems (Structural Engineer)

The key structural elements of the building(s) requiring analysis include:

- Foundation (compliance with geotechnical engineering or soil reports)
- Load bearing walls (gravity and lateral loads)
- Exterior building shell (settlement, movement)
- Floor system (allowable floor loading capacity)
- Roof structure (equipment loading, deflection)
- Earthquake (Seismic Risk Assessment)

Figure 8-6 is an example.

---

4 ADA is American with Disabilities Act; FFHA is Federal Fair Housing Act.

FIGURE 8-6

Engineering Drawing Showing
Linkage Between Industrial
Building Foundation and
Load-Bearing Walls

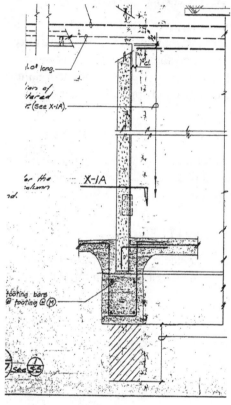

Source: Marx Okubo, San Francisco

Common structural problems encountered include cracks in the foundation, roofing that needs full or partial replacement, or certain structural elements that do not meet current building codes. There also may be deterioration in the building shell.

If deficiencies are discovered, the architectural and structural system analysis allows the buyer to seek a credit from the seller for any deficiencies that were not disclosed when the parties agreed to the purchase price. If the deficiencies were disclosed, the analysis provides a budgeted amount to correct the problem following close of escrow, usually at the expense of the buyer.

Mechanical Systems (Mechanical Engineer)

The mechanical engineer reviews the building in terms of two major areas: (1) plumbing (tenant areas, sprinklers, etc.); and (2) heating, ventilation, and air-conditioning (HVAC). The latter review may also be undertaken by an HVAC contractor.

A building's HVAC system is generally the major source of mechanical deficiencies. Typical problems include too much or too little heat/air between seasons and/or between different locations in the building(s). If the capacity of the system is sufficient, then the issue may be one of balancing the distribution of air. This is also a good area to explore in the tenant interviews.

Figure 8-7 diagrams an apartment building's HVAC system.

Electrical Systems (Electrical Engineer)

Electrical systems that generally require analysis are the main power system and, if applicable, the emergency power system. It also is important to check lighting in exterior common areas, parking, and pedestrian walkways. In more complex or larger scale buildings, it may be necessary to retain a fire/life safety consultant to review fire alarm and sprinkler systems.

Vertical Transportation (Elevator Consultant)

Passenger and freight elevators, escalators, etc., are typically reviewed for operational performance and system maintenance. Areas of concern are modernization of control systems and remaining service life.

Electronic Systems (IT Engineer)

As more and more buildings utilize built-in electronic transmission systems, Information Technology (IT) becomes an increasingly important item of

FIGURE 8-7

Mechanical Drawings Indicating Apartment Building HVAC System

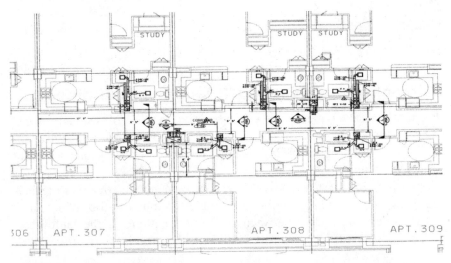

Source: Marx Okubo, San Francisco

due diligence review. Areas of particular concern include fiber-optic cabling capacity, availability and flexibility of raised floor distribution systems, location of phone demarcation points—where the phone service enters the building(s), location of phone and server closets, etc.

Service contracts should be reviewed in cases where the electronic distribution system is controlled by an independent service provider.

Figure 8-8 shows a sample drawing.

Environmental Review (Environmental and Other Consultants)

The environmental review is the longest in duration and may be the most critical element of the due diligence process. The ultimate cost of not investigating a potential environmental problem could exceed the purchase price of the property as well as impose a potential remediation liability, exposing the investment manager and possibly its investment partners to a sizable adverse legal judgment.[5]

Lenders also are highly sensitive to a property's environmental condition and may not finance a property if they are dissatisfied with the

FIGURE 8-8

Engineering Drawing Illustrating a Building's Fiber-Optic System, Keaukaha Elementary Fiber-Optic Backbone Plan

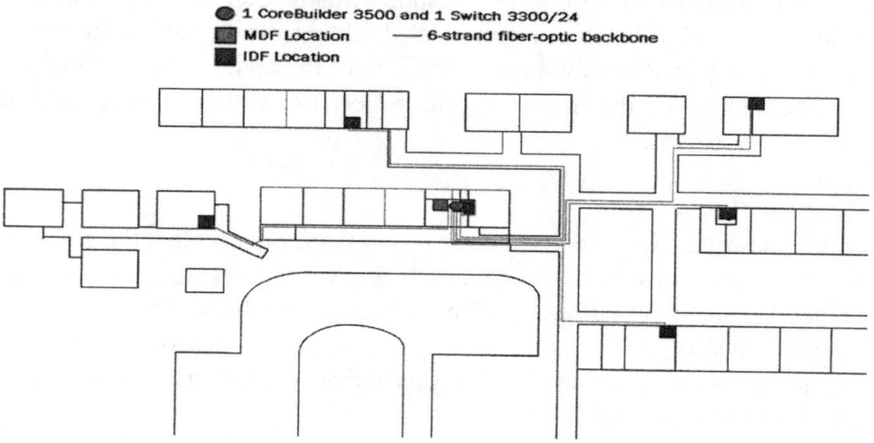

Source: Marx Okubo, San Francisco

---

5 For practical purposes, it's wise to assume that the investment manager will pay for its due diligence mistakes one way or the other.

environmental review. For all concerned, this step in the due diligence process requires a high level of care to make certain that unwarranted and unknown environmental liabilities are not unwittingly assumed. It is critical, therefore, for the investment manager to thoroughly understand and follow through with the following steps involved in the environmental review process.

Phase I

All acquisitions require a Phase I Environmental Site Assessment (ESA). The process is largely an evaluation of the property's environmental history as discerned from an initial inspection of the site, historical records, and governmental regulatory data sources. Generally, no on-site testing occurs in this phase.

The Phase I analysis examines historic property use as well as that of the surrounding area, identifying possible on-site or off-site environmental problems.

One environmental problem that may be identified is underground storage tanks (UST) utilized in the past for gasoline or other petroleum products. If the tank still exists, the regulatory authorities most likely will require removal. If the tank has been removed, the seller should establish that proper procedures were followed and completed in the process.

Depending upon the age of the building, the Phase I analysis also may identify asbestos-containing materials that could be present,[6] as well as early signs of potential soil or groundwater contamination.

Additional areas of concern include investigation for the presence of radon gas, lead paint, mold,[7] and sick building syndrome. In situations involving new construction in open land areas, the review also may include an examination of the impact of the project on wetlands and protected biological systems.

Phase II

If the Phase I analysis indicates that possible problems exist, the environmental consultant usually recommends that further investigation be conducted pursuant to a Phase II Environmental Analysis. This is a more extensive investigation of the property that generally involves on-site testing, providing a higher level of analysis and accuracy from which to draw more precise conclusions.

---

6 In its heyday, asbestos was not only used for the insulation and fireproofing of buildings, but in the manufacture and application of floor tiles, plaster, roofing, and other building materials.

7 Lead paint and mold problems are primarily associated with the acquisition of apartment properties.

A Phase II negative finding does not necessarily disqualify a property from being purchased, provided adequate remediation measures can be realistically adopted. The costs of remediation measures are usually an obligation of the seller. In terms of scheduling, a Phase II analysis usually requires a legal extension of the due diligence period.[8]

Litigation Alert

In some situations, expert witnesses have opined that an investment manager is negligent if a transaction is closed without ordering a Phase II evaluation when recommended by the Phase I environmental consultant.

Environmental Insurance

In addition to conducting an environmental review, investment managers should consider environmental insurance coverage. An environmental insurance policy usually covers costs associated with environmental cleanup when ordered by a governmental authority. Environmental insurance coverage can also be extended to lenders, who may accept this coverage in lieu of a recourse guarantee for environmental protection. In some situations environmental insurance may be assigned to successors in interest.

LEGAL DUE DILIGENCE

The second major area of due diligence concerns the myriad of legal considerations involved in a property acquisition. Generally this due diligence is undertaken by a single law firm, aided by legal research resources and the assistance of an experienced title company. The law firm should have a background in hazard liability and environmental law in order to interpret the legal considerations of any pertinent physical due diligence findings.

Survey and Title

A survey depicts not only the physical boundaries and dimensions of the improvements, but also certain other legal rights, including easements, encroachments, covenants, and rights of way.[9]

---

8 It's important to receive all Phase II reports in draft form so that the environmental counsel can review for proper compliance and to avoid potential future liability.

9 The title survey should be consistent with the requirements of the American Land Title Association (ALTA) and the American Congress on Surveying and Mapping (ACSM).

From a due diligence perspective, the survey and title review:

- Determine that the title description shown on the survey is the same as that shown in the title report.
- Confirm exactly what real property is being acquired.
- Establish all easements, Reciprocal Easement Agreements (REAs), Covenants, Conditions, and Restrictions (CC&Rs), and encroachments affecting the use of the property (some if not all of these may have been established in the preliminary title report).

Once the subject property's survey and title situation is understood, there may be several steps that should be requested of the seller to "clean up" the title situation prior to close.

Perhaps the most important concern is to see if there are any liens that should be discharged and released or CC&R violations that need to be cleaned up. It is also important to determine if there are any zoning violations. Finally, any easements or encroachments that, if activated, would materially affect operation of the property. An example would be the need to tear up a floor slab to repair underground utilities running under a building.

Since these actions will require negotiation and execution prior to close, discussions with the seller's counsel should begin as soon as possible.

Entitlements

Most properties are located in political jurisdictions that limit in some way the use of the property by the owner. Through the legal process, these jurisdictions establish the uses of a property to which an owner is "entitled."

Common entitlements include:

- Zoning
- Zoning variances
- Building codes
- Utility permits
- Special District permits
- Local Improvement Districts (LID)

Entitlement due diligence consists of a review of the applicable zoning ordinances affecting the subject property and that of the surrounding area. Discussions also should be held with the local planning, zoning, and building departments to understand any contemplated changes that might affect the future entitled status of the property.

The main purpose of this review is to determine (1) whether the property complies with the applicable zoning ordinances and building codes, including setback, parking,[10] height, and coverage limitations (floor/area ratio, or FAR), and (2) whether there have been any zoning or building code violations, particularly any life/safety violations. The review also analyzes the consequences of a "nonconforming structure" being destroyed or damaged by a casualty event.

Attempts also should be made to obtain the following from the local jurisdiction:

- Certificate of Occupancy
- Zoning Compliance letter
- Building Code Compliance letter

Although a prospective buyer cannot legally rely on these documents, they do provide an added measure of assurance that no major land use/zoning issues exist.

Tenant Estoppel Certificates

Tenant Estoppel Certificates are documents that verify certain lease information. Tenants are required in most leases to execute estoppels. (Estoppels forms may be negotiated in the Purchase Agreement.) In general, it is the seller's responsibility to circulate and retrieve the estoppels. The estoppels process may take several weeks to complete, so it should be initiated early in the due diligence process.

Items usually covered in the estoppels include:

- Location of space
- Size of space (square feet)
- Parking spaces
- Terms of lease
  □ Starting date
  □ Rent
  □ Base rent
  □ Future escalations
  □ Percentage rent

---

10 For example, the zoning ordinance may require more parking than is currently provided on the property.

□ Method and timing of expense recovery
□ Calculation of pro-rata share
□ Base year
□ Exclusions
□ Tenant options
□ Renewal
□ Expansion
□ Termination

- Absence of any option to purchase the property
- Security deposit
- Outstanding improvement allowances due tenant
- Subleasing arrangements
- Any known tenant or landlord defaults under the lease
- Side letters or other documents beyond the lease
- Ability of landlord to relocate tenants within the building (used primarily with shopping center acquisitions)
- Tenant's comments and complaints

Estoppels allow the buyer to rely on certain lease facts that may have been critical in the original decision to purchase the property. They also usually bring any conflicts or misunderstandings between the landlord and the tenant to the surface.[11]

Once estoppels have been received by the buyer, they should be compared with the lease abstracts developed by the attorneys. Any changes or discrepancies should be noted.

An example of a Tenant Estoppels Certificate is outlined in Appendix B-3.

Lease Abstracts

Concurrently with the estoppels process, the legal advisor summarizes the key elements of each of the tenant leases. Attorneys familiar with leasing issues and their structure generally develop abstracts that accurately and succinctly set forth the obligations of each tenant. The lease abstract usually covers much of the same information as the estoppels.[12]

---

11 An estoppel also can be used to remedy a difference of opinion between the buyer and the seller. For example, if it is discovered that the seller has been overbilling a tenant for CAM, the buyer might accept a well-worded estoppel as an alternative to an indemnity from the seller.

12 It's important that the Purchase Agreement restricts the ability of the seller to modify or terminate existing leases or enter into new leases without the specific written consent of the buyer.

The results of the lease abstract are then compared to the pro-forma rent roll and financial analysis furnished by the seller as well as the executed tenant estoppels to determine any inconsistencies.[13]

Appendix B-4 is an example of a lease abstract.

UBIT/ERISA Issues

If one or more of the equity investors are pension fund investors, there may be Unrelated Business Income Tax (UBIT) or Employee's Retirement Income Security Act (ERISA) issues that need to be considered. Examples include:

- An affiliate of one of the pension fund investors is also a tenant in the building(s)
- Future earn-outs of leveraged properties
- Parking income
- Cable television contract

Any of these may possibly trigger undesirable consequences for pension fund investors, including possible loss of tax-exempt status or violation of ERISA regulations. It is important, therefore, that the due diligence attorney and tax accountant review all legal documents for possible UBIT and/or ERISA problems.

Warranties

The attorneys also should review warranties and guaranties to make certain they are transferable to the buyer. If the contracts require transfer fees, these should be arranged by the seller before close. The closing documents should identify service contracts that the buyer wishes to retain and warranties that he or she wishes transferred.

Service Contracts

Purchase Agreements usually stipulate that the buyer has the right to assume or reject contracts for services such as trash removal, fire alarm monitoring, building security, landscaping, and janitorial services. Many of these contracts contain clauses that the buyer may find unacceptable, such as non-market rates, poor service response, or use of outdated equipment.

---

13 Increasingly, lease abstracting is being outsourced (often offshore) to achieve lower costs, higher quality, and faster turnaround.

In addition, the buyer may simply want to use another service provider that he or she is using in other buildings in their portfolio.

As a result, the terms of the service contracts need to be reviewed during the due diligence phase. If the buyer does not like the terms of the contract(s) or wishes to change a service provider, they can do so after close, provided the contracts are cancelable in 30 days. (Contracts not cancelable in 30 days may constitute ERISA violations.) If they are not cancelable, the buyer should attempt to have them canceled by the seller or set aside holdbacks to cover the possible cost of liquidated damages.

Consent Decrees and Court Orders

While not common in most real estate transactions, the legal research should include consent decrees and/or court orders that might affect the property.

Other Agreements

Other agreements that should be included in the legal due diligence include partnership and joint venture agreements, agreements requiring third-party consent, and broker/finder agreements.

BUSINESS DUE DILIGENCE

Tenant Interviews (Asset Management Staff)

During the due diligence process, the buyer is usually permitted to interview a representative of each tenant. The tenant interview should be conducted by a member of the asset management team, preferably the individual who will be assigned to the property if the acquisition proceeds.

This interview is designed to accomplish the following:

- Provide an introduction to the investment manager as the new landlord
- Better understand tenant's business operations
- Description of tenant's organizational structure (sole proprietor, corporation, subsidiary of public company, etc.)
- Business background of interviewee
- Determine tenant's current use of the space (tour of the space)
  □ Business offices
  □ Lavatory space

□ Manufacturing operations (industrial)
□ Residential living space (apartments)
□ Storage
□ Shipping and receiving (loading dock)
□ Parking
□ Other
- Establish tenant's current view of the property
  □ Tenant space
  □ Parking
  □ Circulation
  □ Operating equipment (HVAC, plumbing, electricity, public space, etc.)
  □ Signage (off-site, monument, store, etc.)
- Tenant's observations about the management of the building(s)
  □ Janitorial
  □ Security
  □ Billing and collections
  □ Marketing and promotion (retail)
- Estimate future space needs
- Probability of lease renewal

Utilizing the asset management staff to conduct the interview can provide a good beginning for a solid landlord-tenant relationship. This is reinforced if, after the transaction is closed, the asset manager assigned to the property calls on each of the tenants with a checklist and timetable to correct the problems mentioned during the interview.

A suggested Company-Tenant Interview Questionnaire is included in Figure 8-9.

In addition to the tenant interviews, there may be other areas of business due diligence that the investment manager should consider.

Financial Review (CPA Firm)

A financial review confirms the historic property operating statements and other financial statements concerning the property's operation. The financial audit provides a third-party independent validation of the assumptions used in the pro-forma cash flow analysis, which is relied upon by the Investment Committee, investment partners, and possible lenders.

Appraisal (MAI or SRA Appraiser)

An appraisal may be necessary if lender financing is to be utilized to close the transaction. Many lenders require an appraisal before they will approve a loan.

Insurance Review
(Insurance Agent or Consultant)

Review by an insurance company, agent, or consultant regarding the adequacy of existing coverage and unique problems the property may encounter in obtaining adequate coverage.

FIGURE 8-9

Company-Tenant Interview Questionnaire, Western Commercial Property Fund (Office-Industrial)

Property Name:_____ Building/Suite No.:_____
Interviewee:_____ Position:_____
Please describe your business operation? (history, strategy, clients, sales trends, viability):_____
_____

Number of employees:_____ Location of headquarters:_____
Other locations and operations:_____
_____
What were your key determinant(s) in selecting this location?_____
_____
What do you consider the strengths in this location?_____
_____
Weakness of this location:_____
_____
Who handles your real estate needs, nationally? _____
_____
Let's discuss any physical issues that you may have with the building:

OK

Visibility/Signage	□	_____
Roof	□	_____
HVAC	□	_____
Sprinkler Capacity	□	_____
Space Configuration	□	_____
Clear Height	□	_____
Security/Crime	□	_____
Truck Maneuvering Room	□	_____
Parking	□	_____

Company-Tenant Interview Questionnaire, Western Commercial Property Fund (Office-Industrial) (*Continued*)

Any environmental issues (underground storage tanks, hazardous waste, etc.)?_____

_____

Describe your future space needs (expected expansion or contraction)_____

_____

What is your assessment of the current property management of the building?_____

_____

Open Issues: (Please be clear and specific in your description, if applicable):
1. Any additional TIs or building improvements required at rollover?:_____

_____

2. Due diligence open issues (Issues to follow up on):_____

_____

3. Are there any other issues you would like to mention?_____

_____

_____

4. Any issues we should follow up with after the acquisition is closed?

_____

_____

_____

Estimated Renewal Probability: <50%□   50/50%□   >50%□
Recommendations:_____

_____

_____

Interviewer:_____Date:_____

CHAPTER 9

Final Underwriting and Closing

FINAL UNDERWRITING

As noted, the assumptions and conclusions of the preliminary underwriting (Chapter 6) should be continually updated over the life of the due diligence period. There are several tasks that need to be completed prior to the final Investment Committee decision to proceed with (or reject) the investment.

Reconciling Due Diligence Findings

As the output from due diligence activities begins arriving, the acquisition team should begin reconciling the findings of the various contractors. They should then be reconciled with the preliminary underwriting that was utilized to gain preliminary approval of the transaction by the Investment Committee.

One of the objectives of the due diligence process is to approach certain critical issues from several independent viewpoints. For example, the property's entitlements are reviewed by the architectural contractor, the legal consultant, and, if utilized, an appraiser. Further, seismic risk exposure may be reviewed by both the structural engineer and the environmental consultant.

Problems with the building's electrical, mechanical, and electronic systems are covered by the engineering consultants, legal consultants, and tenant interviews. Critical factors in tenant leases are reviewed by the legal consultant, the tenant interviews, and, if utilized, an appraiser.

The findings of each of these contractors must be compared to each other to see if there are any significant differences in facts or opinions. If so, a member of the acquisition team must contact each of the involved parties and satisfactorily resolve these differences.

This seeming duplication of effort is an attempt to get several perspectives on major potential problem areas. It is usually the problems that haven't been identified by previous owners that prove to be the most expensive to mitigate following closing. It is better to know these costs in advance and have the seller bear (share) in the cost of resolution. The ultimate operating and capital savings should more than compensate for the incremental professional fees.

Next, the reconciled due diligence findings should be matched with the preliminary underwriting previously presented to the Investment Committee. In many cases discrepancies arise from misstated or inaccurate facts contained in the seller's offering memorandum. In other words, new information becomes available through the due diligence process, which was unknown to the seller or, if known, not disclosed.

A memo is prepared for the Investment Committee outlining the material changes that have occurred since the preliminary underwriting. The DCF analysis should be rerun to see the impact, if any, of these changes on the cash flow projections and the anticipated success of the investment.

Final DCF Analysis

The DCF analysis, which has been continually updated throughout the acquisition process, should now be put into final form.

Figure 9-1 is an example of a final DCF analysis. [1]

Final Risk Underwriting

Each of the major risks associated with the proposed investment is then matched with the proposed underwriting mitigation.

Mitigation costs are usually estimated by the due diligence contractors. These costs are then summarized and, depending upon their magnitude, discussed with the seller. Generally, minor costs are traded off if the seller accepts responsibility for the major items. This is often the case since in most situations the seller will have to pay these costs in the event of another buyer and "a bird in hand may be worth more than one in the bush."

---

1 It's generally not necessary to develop an NPV analysis since the actual price has been established.

FIGURE 9-1

Final DCF Analysis, Multimedia Building, Denver, CO, November 17, 2005

Year	0	1	2	3	4	5	6	7	8	9	10	11	12	13
	Investment	Operations	Operations	Operations	Operations	Operations	Operations	Remodeling Re-leasing	Operations	Operations	Operations	Operations	Operations	Disposition
Investment	($21,000,000)													
Rentable SF		124,900						150,000						
Annual Rent/SF (NNN) [Inflation 3.0%]		$14.50	$14.94	$15.38	$15.84	$16.32	$16.81	($15.00)	$20.00	$20.60	$21.22	$21.85	$22.51	
Annual Rent		$1,811,050	$1,865,382	$1,921,343	$1,978,983	$2,038,353	$2,099,503	($2,250,000)	$3,000,000	$3,090,000	$3,182,700	$3,278,181	$3,376,526	
Disposition Cap Rate														7.5%
Disposition Price														$45,000,000
Brokerage Fees (5%)								(750,000)						(2,250,000)
Annual Cash Flow	($21,000,000)	1,811,050	1,865,382	1,921,343	1,978,983	2,038,353	2,099,503	(3,000,000)	2,498,000	2,572,940	2,650,128	2,729,632	2,811,521	42,750,000
Internal Rate of Return (IRR)														11.8%

Remodeling: 25,100 SF added to second floor, existing space upgraded, 75 new parking spaces; existing restriped; landscaping replanted. Cost $15/SF

Note: Exhibit based on actual building, disguised

Source: McMahan Real Estate Services, LLC

139

In most cases the terms of the Purchase Agreement can be altered to compensate the buyer for problems unearthed by the due diligence process. This might take the form of a lower price, a holdback of a portion of purchase funds until a problem can be corrected, a guarantee or warranty by the seller, or some other aspect of the Purchase Agreement.

Obviously, changes in the Purchase Agreement require approval of the seller so it is entirely a negotiated solution. It is also a critical negotiation, particularly if the mitigation costs are significant. If too much is demanded, the buyer risks (1) losing the transaction or (2) being forced to perform and absorb the costs after closing.

A copy of a Final Investment Underwriting based on the property introduced in Chapter 6 is included as Figure 9-2 on the following page.

If the problem(s) is relatively minor, the buyer may decide to "waive" the deposit and proceed to close the transaction. If the buyer waives, the deposit becomes nonrefundable and a closing occurs shortly thereafter.

FINAL APPROVALS

With all of the information provided by the Final Investment Underwriting, the Investment Committee is ready to make a decision regarding whether to proceed with the acquisition. This decision is usually a choice between three outcomes:

1. Approve the transaction as originally negotiated with the seller.
2. Approve the transaction with some final conditions imposed by the Investment Committee, subject to seller approval.[2]
3. Reject the transaction.

Outcomes 1 and 3 are relatively straightforward. If the transaction is approved, the buyer waives his or her rights to the earnest money deposit and proceeds to close. If the transaction is rejected, the earnest money deposit is returned and the amount of pursuit costs tallied, with "lessons learned" from the experience hopefully applied to a future transaction.

Outcome 2 is more complex. If the conditions are relatively minor, the seller will most likely approve and proceed to close. If the conditions are significant, the seller should question the wisdom of agreeing to the changes.

A lot will depend upon whether there are "backup" buyers waiting in the wings to step into the original buyer's position. Usually, the Investment

---

2 At this point, having the conditions come from the Investment Committee rather than the acquisition team usually improves the chances of seller agreement.

Final Investment Underwriting, Western Commercial Property Fund, Multimetric Office Building, November 17, 2005

Comparison to Investment Criteria

- ❏ Suburban Denver ranked first in SF office leasing among WCPF's regional target markets for first three quarters of 2005; sixth nationally (Source: Cushman & Wakefield Research)
- ❏ DTC area one of strongest tech office nodes in Denver Metro (supported by diligence research)
- ❏ Building well designed (use of excess land required for new parking spaces)
- ❏ Located near fiber-optic line
- ❏ Single tenant; limited ongoing asset management requirements
- ❏ Multimedia has B+ credit rating
- ❏ Remaining lease term of six years (tenant has indicated little interest in releasing)
- ❏ Near medium priced residential areas
- ❏ Near hotels, retail, and restaurants
- ❏ Going in Cap Rate of 7.5%; projected IRR of 10.8%

Upside Potential

- ❏ Multimedia indicated in tenant interview they most likely will not release at end of lease (six years)
- ❏ As noted in Preliminary Underwriting, Denver Metro and DTC area continue to strengthen in attraction to office tenants (this view was strengthened during due diligence)
- ❏ Preliminary discussions with architects indicate that approximately 25,000 SF can be built on second floor; existing space also can be ungraded to office space to create 150,000 SF of total office space; new space would require 75 new parking stalls; these improvements plus landscaping upgrade would cost approximately $15.00/SF or approximately $2,250,000; if held for five additional years, total IRR. would increase from 10.8% to 11.8%; this program would use all excess land. (see Final Cash Flow Analysis)

Exit Strategy

- ❏ Multimedia has no renewal clause and has indicated at this point they will not release
- ❏ If strategy to keep tenant, negotiate new lease at market levels at least one year prior to expiration
- ❏ If strategy to change tenant, consider one or a combination of the following:
  - ○ Lease to new tenant on "as is" basis or minor improvements
  - ○ Upgrade building to exclusively office use
  - ○ Expand building design (partial second floor; best alternative)

Downside Risk Mitigation

- ❏ **Denver metro area loses its attraction to business firms**; additional research during diligence indicates this is not occuring; in fact, just the opposite, strong market growth indications; important to monitor after COE
- ❏ **New competitive nodes introduced through urban renewal or zoning/land use conversion**; no indications of this during diligence; requires long lead time, however, allowing time to sell if becomes problem
- ❏ **Tenant credit risk:** unable to obtain personal lease guarantee from owner; additional credit checks during dilligence, however, indicates Multimedia has strong credit history and good reputation in local business community

Final Recommendations

- ❏ Proceed to close deal at negotiated price of $21 million
- ❏ Monitor office space situation; move to finalize plans for conversion at beginning of fifth year if supported by market

Source: McMahan Real Estate Services, LLC

Committee should be made aware of the level of competition and proceed cautiously in making major last minute changes in the deal.

There also may be broader considerations, such as whether future seller dispositions will be brought to the investment manager's attention if the seller has a reputation for changing the transaction at the last minute. Since the real estate investment community is relatively small and close-knit, it is also possible that the investment manager may be taken off potential buyer lists by other sellers as well.

Finally, it may have been a long time since a transaction has been made for an investor. As a result, some investors may pressure the investment manager to "make a deal" as quickly as possible.[3]

Clearly, the Investment Committee is ultimately responsible for the fiduciary behavior of the investment manager, and facing tough decisions is part of their overall governance responsibilities. This is why the committee must have the full support of all employees in reaching well-reasoned decisions, based on the best possible information available, and in a timely fashion.

CLOSING DOCUMENTS

Once the Management Investment Committee approves the final transaction and the seller agrees, a series of legal documents are finalized.

Financing Memorandum

A Financing Memorandum is required for all transactions involving debt financing utilized as a part of the closing process. The document permits lenders to quickly review a potential acquisition and prepare a term sheet detailing the terms and conditions of their loan. The Financing Memorandum generally includes a property description, pro-forma cash flow, market analysis, and lease comparables.

Investor Memorandum

Some acquisitions require an Investor Memorandum. If the investment manager does not have full discretion to invest, this document allows investors to review a potential acquisition to determine if an investment

---

3 Interestingly, these may be the same investors who sue the investment manager for fiduciary neglect a few years later.

is desirable and should be approved. The Investor Memorandum includes the same basic items as the Financing Memorandum as well as any management comments regarding possible areas of risk mitigation to be undertaken and a final investment return analysis. Some managers include comments regarding the future operating strategy for the property once it is in the portfolio.

Acquisition Report

All of the information collected during the due diligence and analytical processes is now compiled and included in the Acquisition Report, which should reflect all work performed by the acquisition team and its contractors. This report is an internal document reflecting the official record of the transaction. In addition, this document is helpful to the asset manager in preparing the property's first-year business plan.

TITLE HOLDING ENTITY

The new title holding entity also has to be thought through carefully. In order to reduce liability exposure, many institutional investors insist on having a single entity established for each asset. In the case of pension funds, this holding entity is usually a Limited Liability Corporation (LLC) or a 501C(25) corporation, limited to holding real estate assets exclusively.

Care must be taken to be certain that the new entity is enabled to transact business in the state in which the property is located. These organizational documents must be delivered to the title company in order to establish the buyer's "existence and authority."

Bank accounts for the new holding entity also should be established in advance. Some states require an owner to hold security deposits in a separate account in order to avoid commingling funds with property operations. In other situations, investors may require a lockbox for tenant rental payments. Care must be taken that sufficient time is allowed to handle these situations, which might place pension investors in danger of violating ERISA or other statutes.

WAIVE AND CLOSING

Waiving contingencies and putting the cash deposit at risk of forfeiture usually requires approval of the Investment Committee. It also may be a policy of the investment manager that all due diligence has been completed and there are no outstanding items whatsoever before a transaction can close. In transactions involving financing prior to close, there must be a binding commitment from a lender to provide acceptable financing.

The waiver should be considered the final and definitive moment in which all things that can be known or discovered about the acquisition have occurred. Thereafter, the closing process becomes more of an administrative procedure whereby funds are placed into escrow and the title of the property passes to the new owner.

The closing process is generally divided into the following categories:

Pro-Rations

Pro-rations involve the apportionment of property revenues and expenses consistent with the time period in which they are earned or incurred. Information derived from the pro-rations is, in turn, incorporated into the Closing Statement.

Closing Statement

The Closing Statement is a "sources and uses" statement prepared by the title company from the perspective of both the buyer and seller. Appendix B-5 is an example of a Closing Statement.

The Closing Statement details the purchase price, loans that are paid off (seller) or originated (buyer), and transaction costs such as title and escrow fees, loan fees, legal fees, etc. Prior to closing, a Closing Statement must be approved by both the buyer and the seller. Usually, it can only be approved by the Investment Committee or its representative.

TRANSITION TO ASSET MANAGEMENT

It is important to effect a smooth and efficient transition of the new investment from seller to buyer. A smooth transition will appear seamless to the tenants and provides an excellent opportunity for a strong first impression by the new owner.

It's important for the asset manager and transaction person to sit down and review specific contractual, title restrictions, postclosing requirements from the sale, and any other information pertinent to the management of the asset.

As discussed in Chapter 8, it is most effective if the asset manager who is going to be responsible for the property is the same person who has conducted the tenant interview in the due diligence process. This not only provides a continuity of a personal relationship, but allows the asset manager to present the tenant with a timetable to deal with any complaints pointed out in the interview.

CHAPTER 10

Disposition

$\mathbf{A}$s noted in Chapter 1, a large amount of anticipated investor return—original investment plus asset appreciation—is realized upon sale of the asset. This underscores the importance of timing and successful disposition execution of the investment manager's program on behalf of its investors.[1]

It should be noted that disposition is not the opposite of acquisition, although there are quite a few similarities. The major difference is the seller's enhanced control of the transaction's timing. Aside from forced liquidations, most disposition transactions occur at the seller's discretion and are directed at harvesting the greatest value possible from the asset. The seller sets the method of sale, price, terms of the transaction, and the timing when the property comes to market.

Furthermore, the seller has an opportunity to target and market to the most likely group of potential buyers, focusing on those attributes of the property with the greatest appeal. Clearly, a well-planned and carefully orchestrated disposition strategy is an important ingredient in capturing the greatest amount of value in a property or a portfolio of properties.

Once the Investment Committee has approved a property for sale, premarketing activities can be initiated.[2] Proper planning and execution of premarketing activities helps ensure a smooth and timely disposition process.

---

1 In real estate investments held for 10 years, disposition cash flow can be as much as one-half of total IRR.

2 See Chapter 12 for a discussion of property disposition decisions, including how to perform a hold–sell analysis.

TARGETING BUYERS

Types of Buyers

In today's market, it is anticipated that larger commercial properties will be marketed to institutional investors, the group that comprises the largest and most active seekers of quality properties. Most institutional buyers tend to align themselves along the same risk/return curve that pension funds use to plot their investment strategies, namely: core and enhanced core; value added (core plus); and opportunistic. (See Chapter 5 for a discussion on the differences and similarities of these strategies.)

Sellers into this market in essence arbitrage the capitalized value of the spread in investment returns as payment for their efforts in reducing investment risk through property development, restructuring, and repositioning. Institutional investors also may enter the market as sellers when they decide to restructure portfolios.

These investors are typically represented by professional investment managers/advisors (and their brokers), which are responsible for acquiring properties for their clients' portfolios.

Properties also may be acquired by real estate operating companies, including REITs, REOCs, and private operating companies. From time to time foreign investors can be formidable buying competitors as well, with sizable amounts of capital and, often, lower expectations on investment return.

It's also possible that partnerships, Tenants in Common (TIC) funds, and other investment firms representing high net worth individual investors will be active buyers, though they may not be willing to pay institutional prices since it will make it difficult, if not impossible, to meet targeted investment returns.[3]

Targeted Geographical Areas

Institutional investors usually have a set of metropolitan areas to which they restrict their real estate investments. Factors influencing investor preferences and/or exclusions for properties include:

- The Public policy that frames the real estate entitlement process (e.g., most institutional investors generally prefer metro areas where the supply of real estate is constrained).

---

3 Many of these firms are more apt to be sellers into this market, in some cases to capture "success" fees triggered by meeting IRR targets.

- The Rate of economic growth (employment, new company formation, patents issued, etc.).
- A well-functioning physical infrastructure (highways, utilities, etc.).
- Avoidance or mitigation of physical risk factors (seismic, flooding, etc.).
- In the case of shopping centers, growth in disposable income and retail sales are important factors in selecting geographical market areas.

Properties in most quality portfolios will meet most if not all of these targeted criteria.

Property Criteria

Potential investors also may have property-specific investment criteria, such as location, "street appeal," building design and construction quality, vehicular circulation and parking, building amenities, proximity to public transit, etc.

Tenant Criteria

Buyers are usually interested in a property's rent roll, related to:

- Tenant mix
- Tenant credit quality
- Lease roll-over schedule
- Average rent per SF (over or below current market)

Weighing the investment style preferences of potential buyers against the characteristics of the disposition property enables the investment manager to establish a list of targeted buyers who will have a high probability of being seriously interested in selected disposition opportunities.[4]

BROKER SELECTION

In most cases, targeted buyers are accessed through the real estate brokerage community. Although "principal-to-principal" transactions may occur, they are rare.

---

4 In many cases brokers or individuals involved in placing investment capital can be helpful in identifying the investment requirements of institutional investors currently active in the marketplace, and their investment manager representatives.

More important, the investment manager has a fiduciary responsibility to its beneficiaries, shareholders, and investment partners to expose properties to as extensive a market as possible, and may assume some degree of liability by not doing so.

Therefore, most institutional sellers have a policy to utilize the brokerage community to market its properties.

Litigation Alert

Sellers of property owned by investor clients can reduce the possibility of adverse investor litigation by initiating and documenting attempts to reach as broad a universe of credible buyers as possible.

Exclusive Representation

An early decision an investor must make is whether to work with a single brokerage firm on an exclusive basis or have an "open listing." This decision is usually a function of:

- The current market for investment properties.
- The difficulty or ease that the disposition property will face in the current market environment.
- The availability of qualified brokerage firms serving the market in which the disposition property is located.
- The experience of the investment manager with specific brokerage firms or individuals. As noted in Chapter 6, it may be desirable to retain a broker who has presented acquisition opportunities in the past—in order to cement the link between the sales and buy side of the relationship—to increase exposure to new deals in the future.

Identifying Potential Brokerage Firms

Most brokers participate in markets through established relationships with both buyers and sellers. The question is which firm will best be able to reach the key acquisition individuals representing the firms on the targeted buyers list.

This is generally answered by interviewing a short list of prospective brokerage organizations currently active in the institutional market as well as in the metro area where the disposition property is located.[5]

Marketing Presentation

When contacted, brokers typically respond with a marketing presentation outlining their qualifications and a specific sales strategy for the property.

During their presentation, most firms identify their marketing team, present a detailed strategy as to how and why they expect to execute a successful disposition, provide a range of anticipated sales prices, and, last but definitely not least, describe the business aspects of the brokerage listing agreement (commission, listing period, scope of broker's responsibilities, liability of parties, etc.).

An integral part of most brokerage marketing presentations is an analysis of current market conditions in the metro area and submarket where the disposition property is located. Key factors usually covered include:

- Current demand and supply conditions for properties
  - Average rent
  - Vacancy
  - Absorption
  - New construction (i.e., future supply)
- Rent comparables
- Sales comparables
- Competitive properties (existing and anticipated)
- Most effective pricing and selling strategies for the property

In evaluating competing brokers, one of the most important considerations is the firm's knowledge and position in the local marketplace and how the proposed marketing team will match up with the list of targeted buyers.

---

5 Modern communication and transportation systems make it possible for a broker to be located in a different metro area than either the targeted institutional buyer(s) or the disposition property. While this may become necessary when dealing with transactions in smaller markets, it is preferable in larger markets that the selected broker has an operating office in the market in which the disposition property is located.

Broker's Local Market Presence

Key issues in evaluating each broker's position in the local market include:

- Years involved in the market
- Scope and quality of market data
- Number of recent transactions completed similar to the disposition property
- Seller confidential reference checks
  - Were you pleased with the broker's performance?
  - Would you utilize the firm again?
- Number and location of current listings for similar transactions
- Number and location of anticipated listings

The last item is important in establishing if the broker might have an existing or prospective property listing that would compete directly with the disposition property during the listing period. If so, it is probably a good idea to utilize a different brokerage firm.

BROKER'S RELATIONSHIP WITH TARGETED BUYERS

In evaluating the ability of the proposed marketing team to be effective with targeted buyers, the following should be considered:

- Years of experience in the institutional real estate market
- Professionalism and maturity of the proposed marketing team
- Number and value of recent disposition transactions with targeted buyers involving similar properties
- Number and value of recent acquisition transactions (similar properties are relevant)
- Quality of most presentations (submittals to institutional buyers require similar skills and resources)

LISTING AGREEMENT

Once a brokerage firm has been selected, the parties enter into a Listing Agreement, a formal contract appointing the broker as the agent with the exclusive right to market the disposition property. A sample Listing Agreement is outlined in Appendix B-6.

Most Listing Agreements contain the following provisions:

- Empowers the broker to market the property for a specified period.
- Specifically sets forth the commission to be paid the broker upon consummation of a sale.
- Identifies "excluded parties"—potential purchasers who, if they become the buyer, are excluded in determining the broker's fee arrangement. (In some cases, the broker receives a reduced commission.)
- Establishes a schedule for the reporting of broker activity.
- Method of handling seller-agent disputes.
- Attorney's fees.
- Extension of the term of the agreement, if applicable.

The Listing Agreement also may cover the following:

- Specific potential buyers to be marketed.
- Minimum deposit required.
- Identification of seller financing that may be made available.
- Role of broker (if any) in assisting with the due diligence process.

Listing Agreements are usually executed by senior officers or partners of the investment manager.

CONFIDENTIALITY AGREEMENT

Prior to receiving a sales package for the disposition property, a prospective buyer normally executes a Confidentiality Agreement (C/A) and returns it to the listing broker or seller.

The C/A is designed to protect against misuse of certain sensitive information concerning property a competitor might be able to use to the seller's disadvantage. This includes information such as tenant lease terms, property operating data, information on the disposing owner entity, etc. In executing a C/A, the prospective buyer agrees to use this sensitive information exclusively to evaluate a potential purchase of the disposition property. Appendix B-7 is an example of a typical C/A agreement.

OFFERING MEMORANDUM

The Offering Memorandum (O/M) is the sales package used to market the disposition property. The following information is generally included:

Disclaimer

A disclaimer is a clause(s) that puts a potential buyer on notice that he or she is purchasing the disposition property on an "as is" and "where is" basis. Furthermore, the seller makes no representations or warranties whatsoever as to the accuracy or completeness of the information presented in the O/M. It is up to the buyer to undertake and pay for the due diligence necessary to support the final purchase decision.

Executive Summary

The Executive Summary presents the disposition property's attributes in a concise manner to allow for a quick and easy understanding of the proposed transaction.

Property Location and Description

The location of the disposition property is established with maps, along with a brief description of the property to be sold.

Building(s) Description

This includes the size of land parcel(s), the size of building(s), type(s) of construction, net rentable/gross SF, column spacing (mid or high rise), floor height, access, parking, and other salient features.

Market Analysis (Optional)

If utilized, a market analysis contains a discussion of current and historic market conditions, including factors such as:

- Space absorption (demand)
- New construction (supply)
- Market rental rates
- Recent property sales (comps)
- Recent leasing activity (comps)

Since information from the market analysis may be utilized by the buyer to support underwriting assumptions, it may be prudent to have it prepared by the broker in order to avoid the investment manager having direct responsibility for the data utilized.

Sales Underwriting

The sales underwriting is generally prepared by the seller and the listing agent, and it usually includes the property's projected cash flow, generally over a 10-year holding period.

This information will most likely be utilized by a prospective buyer to establish the price he or she is willing to pay for the property. Since the buyer will be verifying the underlying assumptions of the under-writing in their due diligence period, it is critical that this information be as accurate as possible. If it isn't, the buyer may have an opportunity to adjust the price offered. Furthermore, inaccurate information may cause the prospective buyer to lose confidence in the sales process and in the professionalism of the investment manager, its employees, and the list-ing broker.

Photographs and Other Visuals

Today, most O/Ms make extensive use of maps, photographs, building plans, and other visuals to present the property. In some cases a VCR tape, CD, or DVD accompanies the package or appears on a restricted access portion of the broker's or seller's Web site, usually connected through an intranet link limiting access to previously qualified buyers.[6] In some cases it may include a "virtual" tour of the property.

Accuracy of Information

Since the O/M is a "disclosure document," it's critical that all informa-tion be as accurate as possible. It is not the broker's responsibility, how-ever, to make sure that the property information is accurate. In fact, the broker relies on receiving accurate information about a property from the seller. Therefore, the seller must ensure that any information released to a broker has been thoroughly vetted.[7] Both the investment manager and the broker also must be certain that each of the qualified potential buyers receives identical information.

---

6 The use of an intranet link is important to the seller and listing broker as well since it provides proof of the date and time that a prospective buyer received requested information and what they received. This lessens the possibility of the seller and/or the listing broker being subject to litigation over withholding critical information or in having the buyer use it as a wedge to lower the price in final negotiations.

7 A complete record should be kept of the supporting data in the event of a subsequent legal dispute with the actual buyer or a potential buyer not selected.

PROPERTY REPORTS

There may be certain third-party property reports that should be updated prior to actively marketing a property, the two most common being:

- Phase I environmental report
- Physical/structural report

Depending upon the individual circumstances surrounding the disposition property, there may be other reports that should be updated as well. In some cases new reports may be required.

Updating reports is useful because it can identify potential concerns a prospective buyer may discover during their due diligence process. Early discovery allows time to develop and price mitigation alternatives before they become major deal points and possibly scuttle a transaction.[8]

Furthermore, updating reports facilitates a smooth sales process and allows a potential buyer to become familiar with the property at an earlier stage.

It should be noted that, in order to meet fiduciary standards, institutional buyers will generally order their own reports from their own contractors. They then will use these reports in conjunction with the seller's updated reports to reach a final underwriting decision.

It is also appropriate to update the property survey prior to inclusion in the O/M. Since the survey may involve long lead times, particularly during periods of heavy market activity, it is important to order the updated survey early in the disposition process.

DISPOSITION ALTERNATIVES

Competitive Bidding

The competitive bidding process is utilized primarily in the case of a multiproperty portfolio sale or the disposition of a large "landmark" building. When this approach is utilized, the O/M is distributed to prospective buyers, usually for a period of 30 days.[9]

During this period, the broker contacts each of the prospective buyers to answer questions, determine the prospective buyer's level of interest, and solicit offers. At the end of this period, a "call for offers" is relayed

---

8 In some cases a "busted" transaction with environmental overtones may create a "cloud" over the property in terms of sale to future prospects.

9 In a portfolio sale, the listing broker and the seller may decide to also accept bids on individual properties in order to maximize proceeds to the seller.

to prospective buyers who, if interested in bidding, must properly indicate it. This may be followed by a "best and final" round of bidding, which is utilized to get the highest price possible from the final bidders.

Litigation Alert

Whether the disposition process is bid or negotiated, the investment manager and the listing broker should document the fact that they have shown the property to a representative selection of prospective buyers and utilized a systematic process of reaching the most favorable outcome for investors.

Negotiated Sale

The nonbidding, negotiated approach to property disposition is used primarily for the sale of small and medium-size properties on a one-off basis. In contrast with simultaneous bidding, a more informal process is utilized, with the broker playing more of a "finder" role, or in some cases representing the potential buyer. The O/M also is less formal and distributed to a larger group of potential buyers.

Interested buyers submit offers at their own discretion, which are reviewed by the investment manager and/or broker as they are received.

Most offers will be in a Letter of Intent format. The LOI generally establishes a deadline for the acceptance of the offer, and the seller either responds or lets the proposal acceptance period lapse. Competing offers may be compared, and the seller may ask for resubmittals by interested parties and then pursue the one that appears most attractive.

TRANSACTION DOCUMENTS

Letter of Intent

An LOI is used by an interested buyer to make an offer on a potential property acquisition. The LOI is a nonlegal term sheet that sets forth certain basic business parameters regarding a potential acquisition. (See Appendix B-1 for an example of an LOI.)

In a bidding situation, the LOIs from the various bidders are incorporated into a Sales Summary. At this point a meeting is held with the listing broker to determine the best strategy and next steps. Depending on the offers received, it may be appropriate to select a buyer or consider an additional round of bidding.

In a negotiated approach, the seller enters into LOI negotiations with the buyer submitting the most attractive offer. The most attractive offer may not be the highest bid; it could, for instance, be based on other attributes, such as an acquirer's track record for closing acquisitions.

Purchase Agreement

Once an LOI has been negotiated and executed by the businesspeople, a Purchase Agreement can be negotiated by attorneys representing buyer and seller. The Purchase Agreement translates the business terms of the LOI into a binding and legally enforceable contract between the parties.

In addition to the terms outlined in the LOI, the Purchase Agreement contains legal representations by the seller regarding the condition and legal status of the property and the fact that all documents and other materials will be provided to the buyer and are, to the seller's knowledge, complete and accurate.

Other standard provisions include the timing and conditions of the due diligence review, assignable rights, default provisions, casualty and condemnation clauses, deposits, length of the due diligence period, outside date for the buyer to remove purchase conditions, source of financing, phone confirmation numbers, and other provisions negotiated between the buyer and seller.

In some cases buyers can negotiate certain warranties from the seller regarding the physical quality of the property and the performance of equipment such as HVAC, electrical, plumbing, and other critical systems. (This is less common in a hot seller's market.) A big issue usually is the length of the warranty period, which over the last several years has generally become shorter.

Closing documents (bill of sale, warranty or grant deed, assignment of contracts, assignments of leases, etc.) should also be negotiated at this time and attached as exhibits to the Purchase Agreement. This is important to avoid panic negotiations immediately prior to closing.

The Purchase Agreement is usually executed by a member of the buyer's Investment Committee.[10] (See Appendix B-2 for a copy of a Purchase Agreement.)

---

10 The seller and the listing broker also may "interview" the selected buyer to establish a more personal relationship for the due diligence period.

Earnest Money Deposit (EMD)

Most real estate dispositions utilize a third-party escrow service to collect and disburse documents, funds, and other items required by the Purchase Agreement. Funds can be either in the form of cash or a Letter of Credit (LC) from a financial institution. (EMDs are discussed in greater detail in Chapter 7.)

DUE DILIGENCE

Documents Transmitted to Buyer

Once a Purchase Agreement has been executed by the parties and the initial cash deposit posted, the buyer's due diligence phase can begin.

At this point the seller is obligated to provide the buyer with the documents, reports, and other information agreed to in the Purchase Agreement.[11] This provided information generally includes:

- Property survey
- Copies of third-party reports (usually updated)
  - Historic environmental reports
  - Phase I environmental reports
  - Environmental and physical/structural survey
- Rent roll
- Copies of all leases
- Historic operating statements

The prospective buyer will need to inspect the property in person and with his or her third-party contractors. The buyer also may wish to interview some or all of the tenants. It is important, therefore, to coordinate these inspections and interviews with the seller's representatives responsible for the property in order to ensure a smooth and efficient process and minimum amount of tenant disruption.

Tenant Estoppels

As noted in Chapter 8, tenant estoppels are documents that verify certain lease information (a tenant is typically required by the terms of the lease to execute estoppels forms). In general, it is the seller's responsibility to circulate and retrieve estoppels.

---

11 Most sellers do not release certain information related to existing debt and/or selling company ownership, investment structure, or profit participation regarding the subject property.

Pro-Rations

Pro-rations involve the allocation of property revenues and expenses consistent with the time in which they are earned or incurred.

Closing Statement

The Closing Statement is a "sources and uses" statement prepared by the title company from the perspective of both the buyer and seller.

The Closing Statement details the purchase price; loans that are repaid (seller) or originated (buyer), as well as transaction costs such as title and escrow fees, loan fees, legal fees, etc. Prior to closing, both the buyer and the seller must approve the Closing Statement. It is usually approved by a senior officer, generally a member of the Investment Committee. (See Appendix B-5 for an example of a Closing Statement.)

TRANSITION TO BUYER'S ASSET MANAGEMENT STAFF

A smooth transition should appear seamless to the tenants, and it provides an excellent opportunity to leave a good impression of the seller's professionalism. This may be helpful in leading to another, future transaction with the new owner.

PART III

Asset Management

CHAPTER 11

Role of Asset Manager

The role of the asset manager has evolved over the last 50 years, as real estate has gone from individual to institutional ownership and from the management of a few properties in a single market to large portfolios located in often dispersed geographical areas.

THE MODERN ASSET MANAGER

The Institute of Real Estate Management (IREM) defines asset management as: A system that directs and measures the performance of asset groups (in this case, real estate assets) and produces a flow of information needed by ownership to make investment decisions.[1]

IREM goes on to outline how the modern asset manager is involved in the investment process:

> Prior to ownership, the asset manager participates in the acquisition and/or development process, to ensure long-term asset performance in accordance with the investor's objectives. During the holding period, the asset manager directs, measures, and changes asset performance as appropriate. To attain the end of maximizing the value of real estate investments, the asset manager is involved in the process of enhancing value during operations and recommending disposition at the appropriate time.

The modern real estate asset manager is a multidisciplined, highly trained real estate professional who is expected to not only be responsible

---

1 IREM Web site, 2005.

for managing investment assets during the investment holding period, but be an integral part of both the acquisition and disposition process.

The professionalism of today's asset manager reflects the higher fiduciary standards required to manage real estate investment programs in today's litigious business environment. The asset manager must deal with a greater frequency of financial reporting and at much more complex levels— largely a reflection of the movement to bring greater transparency to the management of real estate assets—on both the property and portfolio level.

At its heart, the asset manager is responsible for the overall success of the building during the holding period. Since the manager is generally not on site, however, many of the day-to-day duties are delegated to an experienced property manager, often an employee of a third-party service provider.

ASSET VERSUS PROPERTY MANAGEMENT

Many people confuse asset management and property management, and it is important to understand the difference since both functions are critical to the success of the investment.

Property management is the day-to-day management of individual properties, generally involving responsibility for tenant contact, custodial services, maintenance, supply procurement, security, and disaster plan execution.

Property management services may be provided by third-party property management firms, affiliated property management organizations, or as an internal management function, best characterized by the approach taken by most REITs.

In most cases, the property manager is an employee of an independent property management firm, often located in the metro area in which the property is located.

Asset managers usually have different backgrounds than property managers. Most are college graduates, and many have advanced degrees. Some have come up through the ranks of property management, but most have accounting, finance, development, or transaction management backgrounds.

Asset management is almost always an internal function of the investment firm, but property management can be internally or externally provided, depending upon the location and type of the property, the level of involvement of the investment management firm in the local market, or senior management's view of the most effective delivery system for property management services. Often, this "make or buy" decision is made on an individual property basis.

Although not usually a direct responsibility, the asset manager is usually an important participant in the acquisition and disposition of portfolio assets. (We will discuss this in the next chapter.)

In terms of location, the asset manager is generally an internal employee of the investment manager working at home or it may be a regional office that specializes by property type. In smaller investment management firms, the asset manager may not necessarily specialize by property type.

Figure 11-1 indicates graphically the organizational relationship between asset manager and property managers.

While the asset manager is ultimately responsible for all aspects of the operation of each property in his or her portfolio, activities that are better undertaken at the local level are usually delegated to the local property manager.

The property manager also provides input into most of the activities primarily undertaken by the asset manager. In essence, successful execution of this relationship requires close teamwork and a good working relationship. The experience, knowledge, and workload of both the property and asset manager will influence the degree to which responsibilities are allocated.

While the division of responsibility between the asset manager and the property manager will vary with the circumstances of each situation and the policies of the investment manager, they can generally be summarized as illustrated in Figure 11-2.

FIGURE 11-1

Asset–Property Manager Organizational Relationship

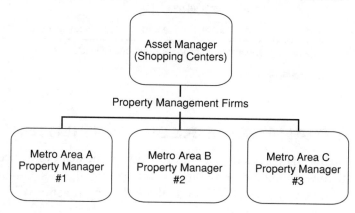

Source: McMahan Real Estate Services, LLC

FIGURE 11-2

Allocation of Management Responsibilities

	Asset Manager	Property Manager
Annual Plan	Prepares	Building input
Diversification Risk	Monitors	Building input
Tenant Relations	Primary responsibility	Day-to-day contact
Insurance	Analyzes, negotiates	Local contact
Building Operations		
Custodial	Approves contractor(s)	Manages contractor(s)
Maintenance	Approves contractor(s)	Manages contractor(s)
Procurement	Approves supplier(s)	Manages suppliers and inventory
Leasing	Negotiates leases	New tenant move-ins
Project Management		
Space Buildouts	Approves design budget and contractor(s)	Coordinates construction
Space Remodeling	Approves design budget and contractor(s)	Coordinates construction Executes (internally or externally)
Building Repairs	Approves budget	
Security	Policy, approves plan	Executes
Disaster Management	Policy, approves plan	Executes
Financial Reporting	Coordinates with Accounting; approves; analyzes	Input
Investor Relations	Participates if requested	Local tours

Generalized representation; specifics of individual situations will vary

Source: McMahan Real Estate Services, LLC

ASSET MANAGER'S RESPONSIBILITIES

While property management is a vital function at the heart of a successful real estate investment program, it is only one of the asset manager's responsibilities, which usually include the following functions.

Tenant Relations

The asset manager's most critical responsibility is maintaining good relations with the building's tenants.

One of the major changes in asset management best practices over the last several years has been the evolving view of the tenant (legal term) to being a "customer" (business term). This is not a distinction without a difference: It represents a fundamental change in attitude on the part of the industry toward recognizing the tenant as the true source of income and cash flow for the property and the key to the ultimate success of an investment.

This makes good sense because real estate is the "residual" of other business activities. If the building is not serving the specific needs of the customer (tenant), ultimately the tenant will be lost to competing buildings.

There also can be an adverse rippling effect. If the tenant is a major regional or national corporation in which the leasing approval process is centralized (common), a negative experience with a property owner with one property can adversely affect decisions regarding other buildings owned or managed by the same firm.

Since tenants also talk to each other through personal relationships and trade organizations, a bad experience could result in the loss of new customers, and over time adversely affect the reputation of the investment manager as an owner and operator of commercial buildings.

This shift in perspective was accelerated by the dot-com and telecom implosion, the recession that began in mid-2000, and the impact and reaction to the events of September 11, 2001.

In addition, the consolidation of ownership in the real estate industry has placed greater emphasis on building strong brand loyalty, which can often make a difference in tenant retention, particularly during economic downturns.

Business Plan

An important part of the asset management process is the development and periodic review (usually annually) of a business plan for each property in the investment portfolio(s).

The business plan describes where the property stands in terms of the original investment underwriting, and the actions that will be taken by the asset and property manager during the coming period to enhance and position the property in the marketplace.

In developing the business plan, the asset manager reviews and may revise the original pro forma cash flow analysis to take into consideration recent events as well as new management initiatives that should be undertaken in the coming year.

The original suite-by-suite cash flow projections are periodically updated by the asset manager. Key elements that usually require updating include:

- Lease rate(s)
- Annual rent increases
- Term
- Commission costs
- Suite improvement costs
- Lease start and end dates
- Vacancy
- Expenses
- Inflation
- Financing terms

These updates are then compared to the original underwriting, in order to determine the effects of any reduction in rental income and/or acceleration of operating costs on future project cash flow.

Utilizing the assumptions of the cash flow analysis, the asset manager develops a current estimate of the value of the property derived from the DCF analysis, based on the property's revised business plan.

The discount factor utilized in the analysis is typically the investor's target return, or in the case of investment partnerships, the return stated in the original partnership agreement.

Diversification Risk

We noted in Chapter 5 that one of the objectives of institutional investors was (1) to increase risk-adjusted investment returns, (2) that real estate portfolios are usually built one property at a time, and (3) that it was the responsibility of the investment manager to be certain the portfolio was "moving toward portfolio diversification rather than concentration."[2]

---

2 The exception is situations in which the investor has directed the investment manager to follow a focused strategy. In this case, the investor takes the responsibility for portfolio diversification, and this should be acknowledged in the investment plan.

Within the investment management firm, asset managers are generally responsible for monitoring portfolio diversification if a nonfocused portfolio is becoming overly concentrated, but in some firms risk diversification is the responsibility of portfolio managers rather than asset managers.

Insurance

A major responsibility of asset managers is to periodically insure properties in their portfolios. Potential losses insured include property loss, property damage, and liability against accidents on the property ("slip and fall" insurance).

In contracting for insurance, the asset manager takes the following into consideration:

- Property risks specific to the geographical area, property type, building location, age, soil conditions, and type of construction
- Liability risks specific to the property such as tenant mix, building materials used in pedestrian areas, parking lot design, traffic flow, and the use of nearby properties
- Insurance carried by major tenants, particularly if a single tenant building
- Major man-made or natural features adjacent to or near the property, such as airports, freeways, stadiums, waterways, forests, etc.
- Special insurance requirements (if any) by clients, lenders, local governmental jurisdictions, etc.

Insurance may be purchased through multiple insurers or a single insurer who insures all properties in all or certain portfolios. For national portfolios, a single insurance policy can produce considerable cost savings because the insurer is able to balance the risks of natural disasters unique to one area against the possible loss from a natural disaster occurring in another area (e.g., earthquakes and hurricanes).

It's generally wise to rebid insurance policies every year or two in order to obtain the best possible rate for the coverage required.

Building Operations

The day-to-day responsibilities of building operations include:

- Custodial
- Maintenance
- Procurement

- New tenant move-ins
- Managing lease delinquencies
- Construction of tenant improvements
- Security
- Disaster planning

While these are the ultimate responsibility of the asset manager, they are usually delegated to the local property manager for execution, discussed in some detail in Chapter 14.

Project Management

The asset manager is usually responsible for procuring and managing construction activities, including building repairs and improvements and customer space build-outs.

Larger investment management firms may have an employee who specializes in construction management, who would report to the asset manager on any projects in his or her asset portfolio. The property manager is usually involved by providing on-site coordination with the contractor.

The projects undertaken can vary, but usually include the following:

Space Build-Outs
The asset manager takes a personal role in tenant space build-outs, since she or he is responsible for maintaining good tenant relations. Usually, there are several occasions for manager-tenant interface, including attendance at meetings with the space planner as well as ongoing discussions with the tenant.

Space Remodeling
When leases turn, the most likely scenario is that a new tenant will move in and some space remodeling will be necessary. If the space is functionally obsolete or the new tenant views the physical environment as an integral part of their business identity (common in retail), then complete remodeling of the space may be required.

Tenant requirements can range in scope from a cosmetic facelift to a full build-out of the space. The importance of the tenant as well as the scope of the project will dictate the continuing involvement required by the asset manager.

Building Repairs
While most repairs to tenant space can be handled directly by the property manager, repairs involving public spaces or building systems should involve the asset manager.

At a minimum, the asset manager should remain abreast of progress on these activities in order to answer tenant and management questions regarding issues such as the scope of the project, its current status, and the anticipated completion date.

Financial Reporting

The asset manager works closely with internal and external accountants in preparing periodic financial reports for investors. He or she is directly responsible for a quarterly review of the assets under his or her management, which then becomes an important supplement to financial reports to the investors. From time to time asset managers may be asked to prepare specialized reports on an asset or real estate market within the scope of their management.

The role of asset managers in financial reporting requires that they be fully aware of several key documents and reports underlying the investment process, including:

Original Underwriting

In order to manage a building successfully, it is important that the asset manager understands the original underwriting assumptions, which include:

- Investment goals of equity investors
- Purchase price (total and per square foot)
- Projected holding period
- Projected exit price
- Amount invested
- Distributions projected during the holding period
- Projected return during the holding period

Loan Agreement

If debt financing is utilized, the asset manager should also understand the essential elements of loan documentation and the terms for each asset in the portfolio that has debt financing. Key components include:

- Loan term
- Interest rate spread (usually stated as being over an index)
- The index utilized to determine the interest rate, usually the London Inter-Bank Offered Rate (LIBOR) or U.S. Treasuries.
- Breakdown between interest and principal amortization
- Required Loan to Value (LTV) ratio

- Required Debt Service Coverage Ratio (DSCR)
- Conditions of default by both borrower and lender
- Reserve requirements (if any)
- Lender participation (if any)
- Property tax and insurance impounds (if any)
- Renewal fee

Schedule of Distributions

In partnership investments, the asset manager should understand the projected underwriting distributions, when they're supposed to occur, any preferences in receiving returns, and the resultant allocations to each investor.

Investor Relations

The asset manager may also be asked to participate in meetings with existing investors or marketing presentations to prospective investors.

Since decisions made during the holding period will directly influence the investor's financial return, and ultimately their level of satisfaction with the investment manager's performance, it is not surprising that good asset managers are becoming one of the most sought after and well-compensated of all investment professionals.

CHAPTER 12

Role in Investment Transactions

Although property transactions are primarily the responsibility of the transactions management group, asset managers play an increasingly important role in developing and implementing a successful acquisition program, establishing and managing the interface with financial reporting, and in evaluating when a property should be sold.

ACQUISITIONS

Today's asset managers are often a vital link between the acquisition of real estate assets and the successful management of these assets over the investment holding period.

Deal Sourcing

Even before an asset has been acquired, the asset manager can be involved in the investment process. At a minimum, the asset manager assists the acquisition team by continually monitoring markets, the success (or failure) of competitive projects, and the future space needs of existing tenants in the investment manager's portfolio(s).

Tenants within the investment manager's portfolio in the local market can be a valuable source of new acquisition leads. Understanding tenants' future space requirements can lead to potential build-to-suit opportunities and/or the identification of leasing candidates for buildings that are being marketed without a strong tenant base.

The asset manager also is in continual contact with other members of the real estate community, who may be able to provide valuable property leads to potential acquisitions. This includes leasing brokers (both project and tenant representatives), mortgage bankers, construction loan officers, title company employees, appraisers, and market research professionals.

Deal Screening

The asset manager usually has a good grasp of the trends and issues in the markets in which the investment manager operates. More important, it's a view established over a period of time as opposed to the "heat of the moment" of an individual transaction.

With this market knowledge, the asset manager can often provide a clear perspective as to how a potential building investment fits into the overall fabric of a local market.

Being in the market over a period of time also gives the asset manager a good perspective regarding the physical characteristics of a building and how attractive or unattractive it may be to tenants in the local market. This knowledge becomes more important as the firm grows, the sourcing process broadens, and new markets are targeted for possible investments.

The asset manager also may be more sensitive to the interrelationships between tenants, and can help avoid a situation in which economic "linking" accelerates the collapse of a tenant base during a declining market.

For example, a building that has financial, legal, brokerage, and investment tenants may appear well-diversified until further analysis establishes that they are all linked to a single industry source of economic stability, such as real estate, financial securities, banking, technology, or other industries. These considerations become particularly important in buildings in which one or a few tenants represent the major portion of the projected rental cash flow from the investment.

Finally, the asset manager is usually better prepared to evaluate the quality of a building's existing property management and to spot opportunities to enhance cash flow through new management initiatives.

These initiatives may involve physical changes in the building (which may require additional capital outlays) or ways in which the building is maintained (more frequent cleaning, parking enhancements, common area and restroom upgrades, additional amenities, improved lighting, better security, etc.).

A question might be: "Why not use local brokers to accomplish these objectives rather than tying up the valuable time of an asset manager?"

While a broker can provide important insights on related transactions, current market pricing, and access to new deals, brokers don't always understand the critical ingredients in the successful management of a building or the importance of longer-term economic and market forces.

Brokers also may not have an understanding of the investment manager's culture or the strategic investment objectives of its investors. Furthermore, brokers' compensation is based on the success of a transaction, rather than the longer-term success of a property investment.

Preliminary Underwriting

In cases where a targeted property survives preliminary screening and a site visit, it is time for the transactions team to consider it as a prospective acquisition and begin a preliminary underwriting of its investment potential.

During this process, the asset manager serves as an "on-call" resource supplying information such as local market data, property type operating characteristics and costs, as well as lease terms prevalent in the local market.

Investment Committees

The asset manager's perspective also can be a vital ingredient in the evaluation of a proposed investment by the firm's Investment Committee. When coupled with the pricing and deal structuring perspective of the acquisition team, the Investment Committee can gain both a short- and longer-term understanding of the potential (or lack or potential) of a proposed transaction.

Investment Agreement Negotiations

Depending upon the nature of the proposed transaction, the asset manager also may be asked to provide information/data for the preparation of the Letter of Intent and the terms of the Purchase Agreement, should the firm decide to make a formal offer.

Due Diligence

The asset manager's most important role in acquisitions is during the due diligence process.

At the beginning of due diligence, there may be some critical questions raised in the preliminary underwriting that need to be evaluated in more detail. Some of these may be market-related, such as evaluating competitive projects more extensively, or analyzing longer-term micro- and macroeconomic factors that may impact demand issues in the local market.

During the due diligence process, the buyer is usually allowed to interview a representative of each tenant. A member of the asset management team—preferably the asset manager who will be assigned to manage the building—should conduct these interviews.

Utilizing the asset manager to conduct the tenant interview can help provide a foundation for a strong, long-term landlord-tenant relationship. This is reinforced significantly if, after the transaction is closed, the asset manager calls on each of the tenants with a checklist and timetable to correct problems mentioned during the interview.

In all these areas, the asset manager brings to the acquisition team skills and resources that are necessary in determining whether to proceed with the transaction or to require modifications in the deal to bring it more in line with investor objectives.

Final Underwriting

In some cases the terms of the Purchase Agreement can be renegotiated to compensate the buyer for problems unearthed by the due diligence process.

This compensation might be in the form of a lower price, a holdback of a portion of purchase funds until a problem can be corrected, a guarantee or warranty by the seller, or some other modification of the transaction. The asset manager can be a valuable resource for the acquisition team in these negotiations.

Waive and Closing

The asset manager to be assigned to the property should become familiar with the Closing Statement as soon as deposits have been waived.

The Closing Statement is prepared by the title company from the perspective of both the buyer and seller. It details the purchase price, loans that are paid off (seller) or originated (buyer), as well as transaction costs, such as title and escrow fees, loan fees, and legal fees. The Closing Statement contains many of the opening entries in the books of account for the new property (or properties) for which the asset manager will become responsible.

TRANSITION TO ASSET MANAGEMENT

A smooth and efficient transition of property from the seller to the buyer will appear seamless to existing tenants and provide an excellent opportunity for a strong first impression of the investment manager as the new owner. There are several steps in a successful ownership transition:

Acquisition Report

All of the information collected in the due diligence and analytical processes should be contained in the Acquisition Report, which is the investment manager's official record of the transaction.

As outlined in Chapter 9, this report provides the background data and blueprint necessary to achieve a successful transition. In addition, the document provides the foundation for the asset manager's first year business plan.

The asset manager should be familiar with the following information from the Acquisition Report:

- Purchase price (both total dollars and on a dollar-per-square-foot basis)
- Projected holding period
- Space absorption projections, if applicable
- Computer model assumptions (suite by suite)
  - Lease rate
  - Annual increases
  - Term
  - Commission cost
  - Tenant improvement cost
  - Lease start dates
  - Concessions
  - Options
  - Special provisions
  - Expense "stops" (if applicable)
- Projected price and dollars per square foot

Investment Partnership Agreement

If the investment is held by a limited partnership, the asset manager should make certain that he or she understands the nature of the agreement and how it might affect ongoing management operations.

Specific information that the asset manager should know from this agreement includes:

- Structure of existing or anticipated debt
- Background and investment objectives of main partners, particularly ones new to the firm.

- Name
- Amount invested
- Real estate investment policy
- Real estate strategy (written statement, if available)
- Nature and amount of distributions to investors
- Conditions necessary to make distributions
- Nominal dollars to investors
- Projected percentage return to investors

Title-Holding Entity

A title-holding entity is usually established prior to close. The asset manager should review the incorporation documents in order to determine the state in which the new entity is domiciled and understand the powers and limitations of the entity.

ERISA and EBIT Issues

As noted in Chapter 8, investing for or with a pension fund, ERISA[1] and UBIT issues may have been identified in the due diligence process. The asset manager should fully understand these issues and be certain to manage the property so they do not become future problems.

Property Accounting

Information from the Acquisition Report and the Closing Statement provide many of the opening entries for the new bank accounts for the new holding entity. The asset manager should discuss these issues with accounting personnel and be certain that he or she fully understands how the bank accounts should be handled.

Cash Management Procedures

If an investment partner (e.g., pension fund) requires a lockbox for tenant rental payments, care must be taken that sufficient time is allowed to handle

---

1 An example of an ERISA-related issue would be a situation in which selection of a property is tied to hiring members of the pension fund to construct or manage the project (problem with union plans in the past). Another example would be having a tenant in a property that is closely linked to the plan sponsor (corporate or public plans).

situations that might place the pension fund in danger of violating ERISA or other statutes.

Mitigation Action Plan

The final underwriting report may include a list of mitigation steps for various risks uncovered in the due diligence process. If so, the asset manager is usually responsible for mitigating most risks assumed by the buyer and should prepare an action plan to accomplish this objective.

Meet with Tenants

Once the asset manager fully understands all aspects of the operation of the property, he or she is ready for kickoff meetings with the existing tenants. Prior to the meetings, the asset manager should review the lease abstract, the tenant's estoppels, and the tenant due diligence interview to be aware of the tenant's existing rights and obligations, as well as the tenant's attitude toward the building and its prior management.

If there are complaints registered in the tenant interview, the asset manager should have an action plan to remedy them (or a good reason for not doing so). If a need for additional space or a desire to relocate within the building was mentioned in the interview, the asset manager should be prepared to discuss in some detail the nature and magnitude of these needs.

DISPOSITIONS

As with the acquisition of assets, the asset manager is an important link between the management of assets and their successful disposition.

Role of an Exit Strategy

During the acquisition process, certain assumptions were made with respect to when a property should be sold and at what price. Collectively, these assumptions are known as an "exit strategy."

The exit strategy is considered one of the most important elements of the investment process because a property sale often represents the liquidity event when the major portion of investment return is generated.

Therefore, it is essential that an exit strategy be formulated and thoroughly understood by the investment manager and its investment partners at the initiation of the investment process.

Unsolicited Offers (Hold–Sell Analysis)

In addition to monitoring the progress of a property in relation to the original exit strategy, the investment manager also must be prepared to respond to unsolicited offers for individual properties in the portfolio. This requires a systematic process by which these offers can be evaluated against the original investment strategy, the current property business plan, and the local market in which the building operates.

NPV analysis provides an effective benchmark against which unsolicited offers can be evaluated. Figure 12-1 presents a sample analysis.

In order to be considered, an all-cash offer should be at least equal to management's estimate of the projected NPV of the property.

This approach is based on two concepts: (1) A property should not be sold in advance of its projected disposition date unless it can meet targeted return levels, and (2) cash in hand today is worth more than cash in the future that is dependent upon the realization of a series of assumptions in the NPV analysis.[2]

There are several reasons why an outside buyer might be willing to pay more for the property:

- The potential buyer has a more optimistic view of the future opportunities for the property than the investment manager.
- The buyer has a noninvestment use for the property that results in a higher valuation.
- The buyer is willing to accept a lower investment return (foreign investor, etc.).
- The buyer has tax objectives that permit paying a higher price.

Regardless of the reason, the investment manager is faced with a decision that has to be made and justified to investors. In reaching this decision, it should be established that:

- The investment manager has held the property for a sufficiently long period to be able to evaluate its future potential (generally at least one year).
- The NPV analysis is reasonably current.
- The offer does not require conditions adverse to the investment manager or its investors.

---

2 The asset manager also may wish to review whether a replacement property can be acquired on equal or more favorable terms.

FIGURE 12-1

Hold-Sell Analysis, ABC Shopping Center

	Purchase $35,000,000	**Current** $46,000,000	**Offer** $50,000,000
Cap Rate	8.6%	6.5%	6.0%

NOI Growth Rates

Year	3.00%	Growth Rate	5.0%	Growth Rate	Variable Growth Rate	
2005		$3,000,000		$3,000,000		3,000,000
2006	103.00	3,090,000	105.00	3,150,000	108.0	3,240,000
2007	103.00	3,182,700	105.00	3,307,500	107.0	3,466,800
2008	103.00	3,278,181	105.00	3,472,875	106.0	3,674,808
2009	103.00	3,376,526	105.00	3,646,519	105.0	3,858,548
2010	103.00	3,477,822	105.00	3,828,845	104.0	4,012,890
2011	103.00	3,582,157	105.00	4,020,287	103.0	4,133,277
2012	103.00	3,689,622	105.00	4,221,301	103.0	4,257,275
2013	103.00	3,800,310	105.00	4,432,366	103.0	4,384,994
2014	103.00	3,914,320	105.00	4,653,985	103.0	4,516,543

NPV Discount Factors

15.0% NPV	51,695,111	52,920,865	53,400,898
12.0% NPV	53,909,830	55,380,265	55,911,591
10.0% NPV	55,651,231	57,319,436	57,888,651

Holding Value (Future Value Less Offer Value)

15% NPV	1,695,111	2,920,865	3,400,898
12% NPV	3,909,830	5,380,265	5,911,591
10% NPV	5,651,231	7,319,436	7,888,651

Allocation to Seller at 12% NPV

50%	2,825,616	3,659,718	3,944,325
25%	977,457	1,829,859	1,972,163

Counteroffer Range

50%	$52,825,616	$53,659,718	$53,944,325
25%	$50,977,457	$51,829,859	$51,972,163
Counteroffer	$53.0 M	$54.0 M	$54.0 M

Source: McMahan Real Estate Services, LLC

- Investors have acknowledged that they are willing to accept cash returns earlier than originally projected.[3]
- If taxable investors, it has been established whether they wish to undertake a 1031 Tax Deferred Exchange.

If the situation meets these criteria, then the sale should be submitted to the Investment Committee for a final decision.

Investment Committee

If a property has achieved its exit strategy assumptions, or, in the case of an unsolicited offer, meets the criteria outlined above, it is presented to the Investment Committee with a recommendation for disposition.

The Investment Committee then proceeds to weigh the factors and implications involved in the sale of the property and vote on a course of action.

Premarketing Activities

Once a property has been approved for sale by the Investment Committee, premarketing activities can be initiated. Proper planning and execution of the premarketing activities will help ensure a smooth and timely disposition process. A well-planned and carefully orchestrated disposition strategy is a direct reflection on the professionalism and industry perception of the investment manager.

Broker Selection

In most cases, targeted buyers are accessed through the real estate brokerage community. Although "principal-to-principal" transactions may occur, they are rare.

More important, the investment manager has a fiduciary responsibility to its investors, shareholders, and investment partners to expose the potential disposition property to as extensive a market as possible, and may assume some degree of liability by not doing so. Therefore, the investment manager should attempt to utilize the brokerage community to market its properties as much as possible.

The asset manager is a vital link between the acquisition and disposition of real estate assets and the successful management of these assets over the investment holding period.

---

3 This should have been established in the partnership agreement or investment plan and subsequently acknowledged by written consent of the investor.

CHAPTER 13

Tenant Relations

As noted in Chapter 11, one of the major changes in asset management best practices over the last several years has been the evolving view of the landlord-tenant relationship as the source of a large portion of the asset's postacquisition increase in value and as one of the keys to success of the overall investment program.

KNOW THE TENANT'S BUSINESS

Maintaining good personal relations with the building's tenants is one of the most important responsibilities of the asset manager. The editor of *Rent & Retain* magazine maintains that about two-thirds of tenants are lost through a lack of personal contact.[1]As a result, more and more asset managers are focusing on good tenant relations as a way to enhance the bottom line.

The way to better understand tenants is through a better understanding of *their* business. In new acquisitions this information generally is provided by the tenant interview, which is conducted by the asset manager, who preferably will be assigned the property once it's acquired (see Chapters 8 and 11). This knowledge can be enhanced by an exploration of the tenant's Web site, news releases, and, if a public company, analyst reports.

For properties that have been in the investment portfolio for some time, it may be necessary for the asset manager to resurvey tenants. Each

---

1 *Journal of Property Management,* September 1, 2002.

of these interviews should be personal, not by mail, e-mail, or telephone. This allows the tenant to expand her or his answers to questions and/or bring up issues that were not considered when the questionnaire was originally conceived. It also helps to build a direct personal relationship between the tenant and the asset manager.

UNDERSTAND THE TENANT'S FINANCIAL CONDITION

Many landlords only check their tenant's financial status when the original lease is negotiated, at the time of subsequent renegotiations, or when rent is in default.

Unfortunately, problems may arise in the intervening period that may lead the tenant to look elsewhere for new space when the lease renewal comes up, or worse, to declare bankruptcy along the way. By keeping in touch with tenants on a regular basis, the asset manager can have a better idea of the current situation of the tenant's operating and financial condition.[2]

Important information to cover includes:

- Revenue growth trends
- Expense trends
- Overall profitability
- Receivables aging
- Vendor credit experience
- Available cash resources

It is also helpful to understand how susceptible the tenant firm is to cyclical and/or seasonal change.

TENANT'S VIEW OF THE BUILDING AND MANAGEMENT

The final step is to gain the tenant's perspective on his or her space, the building, and its management. Areas of concern are:

- What is his or her view toward the property (likes/dislikes)?
  □ Tenant space
  □ Building lobby
  □ Customer parking
  □ Operating equipment (HVAC, plumbing, electricity, etc.)

---

2 Many leases have covenants requiring the submission of periodic financial statements, but these are not always enforced.

- What is his or her view of the management of the property?
  □ Building maintenance
  □ Security
  □ Disaster planning
  □ Property manager

With this base of knowledge, the asset manager can begin building personal relationships with each of the tenants. In order to maintain creditability, problems identified in the interview(s) must be dealt with as soon as possible.

The resolution of complaint(s) provides still another opportunity to expand the asset manager's personal relationship with building tenants while demonstrating that the investment management firm cares about their welfare and operating success.

RENEWING LEASES

A survey of a 12 million SF portfolio with a 6 percent rollover indicated that $900,000 per year could be added to the bottom line for every 10 percent of expiring space that was renewed rather than retenanted.[3] While this was primarily an office building portfolio, the same dynamics apply to other property types as well.

Renewal negotiations are even more critical during economic downturns when additional space is coming on the market and rents are falling. This has been aggravated in recent years by cyclical rent spikes that left many tenants paying overmarket rents.

It's important, therefore, to assess each tenant's situation and have a strategy for dealing with any concerns before they become a serious problem.

Market Conditions

All lease renewal strategies are subject to market conditions in the months leading up to lease expiration/termination.

If vacancies are low and rents rising, the asset manager is in a position to maintain or raise rents, extend the length of the lease, renegotiate terms, or, in some cases, all of the above. This is also a good time to explore an expansion of current space, either in the same building or another in the investment manager's portfolio.

---

3 *Journal of Property Management,* op. cit.

Tenants are faced with a decision of paying increased rent in the future versus the near term costs of relocating, both in terms of monetary costs such as the build-out of new space as well as the cost of staff downtime. Generally, every attempt should be made to treat customers fairly and attempt to retain not only their tenancy, but their goodwill as well.

It should be noted that over the last 20 years, favorable landlord markets have occurred infrequently in the United States and usually in limited locations. More typical is the situation of increasing vacancies, stable or falling rents, and intense competition for new tenants. Under these market conditions, the importance of maintaining good customer relations is more important than ever. It is equally important, however, to make certain that the tenant is worth keeping.

Rights of the Parties

The asset manager should be generally aware of the lease provisions of each tenant in each property in his or her portfolio on a continuing basis, and specifically at least one year prior to lease expiration. The key elements are:

- What are the notification requirements in the lease?
- Does the customer have an option to renew?
- If so, what are the terms and conditions?
- Is the renewal rent at "market" or a stipulated amount?
- Is the renewal conditional on maintaining a financial condition at least as strong as when the initial lease was executed?
- Are there any special conditions in the lease that might impact new lease negotiations?

Although lease renewal provisions do not usually contemplate any modifications in the rights of the parties, it's still wise to contact the tenants and get their views on renewing the lease, preferably at least 12 months in advance of the lease renewal date.

Tenant's Financial Condition

By remaining current on the customer's financial condition, the asset manager should have a good understanding as to the current financial strength of the tenant as well as whether it is going to survive in the longer term.

If there is no renewal option, or the option requires meeting certain financial conditions that are unlikely to be met, it's best to know this as early as possible so marketing efforts to other prospective tenants can begin.

Action Alternatives

Based on this assessment, the asset manager has several alternative courses of action:

Lease Renewal

The simplest action is to renew the lease under its existing terms and conditions. If the tenant's financial condition is healthy and is a strong contributor to the success of the property, but the tenant does not require more space, the asset manager may wish to consider a more aggressive approach and suggest changes in the lease that the tenant may not be contemplating.

Examples include: a reduction in rent in exchange for a longer lease term (in retail, higher percentage rent), refurbishing the tenant's space at a reduced or no cost, an advertising allowance, and removal of onerous lease clauses (perhaps inherited from a prior owner) that do not adversely affect the investment manager's interests.

Since each of these lease modifications generally requires approval of senior management, or in some cases the Investment Committee, it can be more effective if the asset manager has the necessary approvals prior to the meeting.

This approach adds to the image of the asset manager as an important member of the management team, as well as the investment management firm, as a partner in the success of the tenant's business.

Lease Expansion

If the tenant's business operation is expanding and the financial statements are healthy, the tenant may be a good candidate for more space in the building, a move to a better location within the building, or perhaps even a move to another building in the investment manager's portfolio.

Lease Termination

In most cases it's preferable to ask a tenant to leave at the end of the lease term rather than renew a lease with the prospects of bankruptcy during the renewal period.

If there is a renewal option with no minimal financial requirements, there is also the possibility of a negotiated termination of the lease, which may turn out to be better for all concerned.

Reduction in Rent

In situations where the renewal rent is higher than market, a possible way to keep a good tenant is a reduction in rent to bring the rate more in line with the current market and/or the tenant's ability to pay.

In exchange for a rent reduction, the asset manager should ask for an extension in the term of the lease ("blend and extend"), a stipulated step-up in rent at a future date, or, in the case of retail, an increase in percentage rents.

Reduction in Space

Still another alternative to consider is a reduction in space. By keeping abreast of the tenant's business operations and financial condition, the asset manager should have a reasonably good idea as to whether an offer to reduce space is appropriate. This also may be coupled with relocation to a smaller space in the office, industrial building, or shopping center.

In all cases, the asset manager should discuss the situation with the tenant well in advance of lease termination.

NEW LEASES

When a new project is developed or an existing customer decides or is asked to leave a building, the re-leasing process begins.

Internal Candidates

The first step is to find out if the vacant space can be leased to existing tenants in the building for expansion or relocation purposes.

If it is not desirable to relocate tenants within the building, there may be tenants in other buildings in the investment manager's portfolio who might wish to open another or larger operation in the vacant space. The asset manager should have a good understanding of potential candidates for the space within the firm's portfolio.

Even if existing tenants do not want the space, the fact that the investment manager demonstrates an interest in meeting their market needs may strengthen the landlord-tenant relationship and reinforce the tenant's view of the investment manager as being a business partner rather than merely a landlord.

It also demonstrates the importance of the asset management team maintaining contact with their tenants on a continuing basis in order to know the current status of the tenant's operation and their ongoing space requirements well in advance of lease expiration.

External Candidates

If there are no internal candidates, the vacating space goes on the market through the brokerage community. It's important that asset and property

managers maintain good relationships with leasing brokers and tenant representatives in each local market in which they operate.

While the leasing agent is responsible for generating external candidates, the asset manager should take the lead once a prospective new tenant has been identified.

The first step in this process is for the asset manager to begin developing information about the prospective tenant, his or her business operation, and show he or she manages his or her real estate facilities.

A good asset manager also is expected to have a full understanding of the characteristics of the current rental market, competing properties, and the underwriting assumptions of the available space to be leased, including:

- Market
  □ Size and characteristics of market area
  □ Total space available
  □ New leases signed (last six months)
  □ New construction planned
- Competition (major competing buildings)
  □ Market image
  □ Quality of building management
  □ Existing tenant mix
  □ Space on the market
  □ Lease turns (to the extent available)
  □ Lease rate comps (to the extent available)
- Underwriting assumptions
  □ Lease term
  □ Projected rental rate
  □ Tenant finish allowance (if any)
  □ Leasing commission(s)

The asset manager must clearly convey to other members of the listing team his or her expectations for leasing the space. This is accomplished through periodic project meetings where everyone is updated on the current status of the building leasing program as compared to original underwriting protections. At this time the leasing strategy can be adjusted as necessary.

CHAPTER 14

Building Operations

As noted in Chapter 11, the asset manager delegates many of the building operating responsibilities to the property manager (internal or contractor) since these activities require day-to-day involvement and the asset manager may be located in another city.

In this relationship, the property manager is primarily responsible for:

- Maintenance
- Construction management (day-to-day supervision)
- Security
- Disaster planning and execution

The property manager also is expected to attend all tenant meetings, and usually prepares the annual building operations budget, subject to approval by the asset manager.

MAINTENANCE

The proper maintenance of an investment property is probably the most important ongoing concern to tenants and usually the most common complaint they have about their building environment. This applies not only to the space they lease, but to common areas like hallways and building lobbies, as well as exterior facilities such as parking structures, pathways, recreational facilities, and landscaped areas.

This is particularly true with retail tenants whose lifeblood—shoppers—may be the first to complain about a center's appearance, or worse, they simply don't return.

Maintenance concerns range from routine custodial maintenance to longer-term preventive maintenance necessary to facilitate operations and avoid costly repairs.

Custodial Maintenance

The most frequent maintenance work involves vacuuming carpets, washing floors and windows, cleaning around waste receptacle areas, and hosing exterior walkways, driveways, and parking areas.

In larger properties, some or all of these activities may be performed by building employees or by a mix of employees and custodial contractors. In medium and smaller buildings, the work is done mostly by contractors who specialize in one or more functional areas. Some large maintenance companies provide all or most of the necessary services.

The frequency of maintenance is usually a decision of the property and asset manager and is often a balancing act between costs and tenant complaints. A building owner doesn't want to invite tenant complaints but also is aware that custodial maintenance can be costly and is an operating cost that can be reduced through less frequent use. Generally, it takes some time and experimentation to discover the right balance.[1]

Generally, these decisions are made by the property manager, whose on-site knowledge of the building, its tenants, and continuing relationship with local market contractors is essential to a successful yet cost-conscious operation.

Preventive Maintenance

Under the heading of "ounce of prevention" best practices is the scheduling of periodic maintenance surveys of all properties. The objective is to extend the operating life of the building components and equipment as well as avoid the higher costs of nonscheduled, often emergency maintenance.

Preventive maintenance may involve the shutting down of equipment while it is being tested or, at a minimum, turning off power for a period of time. For these reasons, preventive maintenance should be scheduled with affected tenants as far in advance as possible.

---

1 Building maintenance is also a highly competitive industry in which vendors fight to obtain and keep business. Contract bidding can be a very effective tool in reducing operating costs, provided the quality of services is not severely compromised.

Corrective Maintenance

Although many maintenance problems can be avoided through systematic custodial and preventive maintenance programs, there always will be situations where tenants complain about a maintenance problem. It's important that the property manager responds quickly and effectively to these requests.

The traditional way property managers have responded to corrective maintenance requests has been (and still is in some cases) through telephones, pagers, and answering machines.

In recent years, however, technology has dramatically improved response time. The first technology that contributed to this improvement was e-mail, which allowed property managers to respond systematically to service requests without being interrupted by a ringing phone (or worse, not answering it). Tenants also like e-mail because service requests can be sent at times other than business hours since emergencies may occur at any time or on the weekends, with many offices having evolved into a 24/7 work routine.

More recently, several property owners and managers—particularly those with larger properties or portfolios—have begun to utilize the Internet to solve the tenant-manager communication problem. One building owner found that the time needed to submit a service request over the Internet was reduced by one-third.[2] They also found that mistakes in describing the problem were reduced, compared to telephone communication.

Perhaps the most powerful benefit of the Internet handling of service requests, however, has been connecting the customer directly to the person who completes and satisfies the service request, thereby reducing the number of information handlers.

One of the reasons for this benefit is that the system creates a mutual information dependency between the tenant and the person who performs the work. Because tenants have direct access to the completion information, there is heightened accountability among building management employees. Overall, the Internet application appears to have empowered tenants and employees while reducing dependency on others to support the information flow.

Procurement of Building Supplies

Generally, contractors providing maintenance services take responsibility for supplies they use, so the property manager is only responsible for purchasing and storing other maintenance supplies or equipment that might

---

2 Reported experience of Boston Properties over three-year period ending April 29, 2002.

be required. However, the property manager has considerable influence over the quality of supplies selected by the contractor, which is usually part of the periodic contract negotiation between the parties.

CONSTRUCTION MANAGEMENT
Tenant Space Repairs

The property manager generally has responsibility for tenant space repairs and improvements. The asset manager should remain abreast of progress on these activities, however, so that he or she can answer questions posed by tenants, other managers, and investors regarding scope of the project, current status, and anticipated completion date.

Tenant Space Build-Outs

The asset manager generally takes a greater role in customer space build-outs since she or he is responsible for making sure that new tenants' needs are successfully fulfilled. This may include attendance at meetings with the space planner, ongoing discussions with the tenant, and maintaining a current knowledge of the project's progress, including any negative budget variances.

New Construction

The asset manager usually is directly responsible for new construction, such as freestanding pads, additions to in-line shops, new signage, landscaping or parking improvements, and on/off site utilities. This generally includes hiring and supervising the project designer and contractor(s), sometimes subject to Management Committee approvals. Some elements of responsibility may be delegated to the property manager.

SECURITY
Redesign

While many new buildings are now being designed to improved security standards, most existing buildings are difficult to redesign in significant ways to make them more secure. There are, however, some improvements that can be made at the property line and/or in landscape or parking areas.[3]

---

3 Redesign applies mostly to suburban locations. Many buildings, particularly those in CBDs or other urban locations, do not usually have a significant redesign option.

Property Line

At the property line, fences and gates should be redesigned to withstand a breech when the building is not occupied or, if breeched, to set off an alarm that alerts security personnel.

Landscaped Areas

Landscaping should be redesigned to provide a full field of vision for human as well as remote camera surveillance. It is important as well that the landscape plan avoids creating areas that might shelter a potential intruder. Lighting can be utilized to not only provide illumination but also eliminate dark areas where someone might hide.

Parking and Walkways

Protection for tenants or visitors is a major concern, particularly along pedestrian walkways and in parking lots and structures. This is of particular concern in shopping centers, industrial parks, and multifamily projects. Again, lighting and landscaping (or the lack of it) are the major tools to implement security improvements in these areas

Modify Existing Conditions and Operations

While certain features of some properties can be redesigned, most properties must rely on modifications in building access and changes in operating protocols.

Building Exterior

A major line of defense is the walls and roof of the building, as well as areas of potential human penetration such as windows and doors.

While defenses at the property line are meant to be as unobtrusive as possible, here they are expected to be obvious, in the hope that they will become additional deterrents to criminal behavior.

For example, walls and roofs can be designed not only to better withstand natural disasters, but also to deter intruders who are intent upon entering the building by cutting or jackhammering the building surface.

Unapproved entry through skylights, windows, and doors is more likely. Skylights and other penetrations in the roof can be secured by locks, making certain they can be opened from within to permit exiting in times of emergency.[4]

---

4 Unfortunately, in the September 11, 2001, terrorist attack on the World Trade Center, access to the roof was blocked to those trying to exit.

Unauthorized entry through windows can be deterred by reinforcing window frames, installing shatterproof glass, and utilizing window locks.

There are several ways to "harden" doors against unauthorized entry. Locks should be a dead-bolt type to make them difficult to pick. Hollow core doors can be replaced with metal or solid wood doors with attached metal plates. Door frames can be reinforced with metal.

Building Interior

Despite defenses at the property line and the exterior of the building, the working assumption should be that these can be penetrated, requiring an inner level of protection inside the building as well.

Here, the objective is to detect the intruders or, failing this, at least to prevent them from gaining access to anything of great value. Detection is accomplished by the use of motion or infrared detectors, which alert security personnel or activate a closed circuit television recorder. Access to sensitive material is thwarted by dead bolt locks on doors. In open office areas, desks and files should have pick-proof locks. Figure 14-1 shows one of these security measures.

FIGURE 14-1

Photograph of a Hardened Skylight

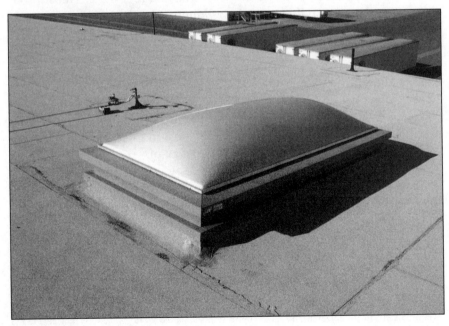

Source: Marx Okubo, San Francisco

Mail Delivery

The use of the mails for terrorist activity was highlighted a few years ago by the delivery of anthrax to congressional and other office buildings. More recently, mailrooms and mail refuse areas have been the focus of efforts to steal monetary and corporate secrets.

To some extent, mailrooms can be secured by having an access control system (both doors and windows) that restricts access to approved personnel and provides detection capabilities during periods when the mailroom is unattended. Undelivered, certified, or registered mail, as well as money, should be stored in locked cabinets when the mailroom is unattended.

"Suspicious packages" are of particular concern and can be identified by being different from other packages in terms of weight, shape, size, or smell. Unfortunately, today's bomb makers are more sophisticated and can disguise bombs to fit into smaller packages or even envelopes or be triggered remotely by electronic devices in the package. More than ever, vigilance is the watchword in mailrooms and throughout the building and its grounds.

DISASTER PLANNING

Since the events of September 11, 2001, billions of dollars and man-hours have been invested in trying to stop another terrorist attack or at least be able to deal with the aftermath more effectively. As of this writing, the United States hasn't had another attack, but that doesn't mean we are necessarily better prepared.

However, there has been some progress. Today, there is better information sharing between governmental agencies and the private sector, particularly in the real estate community since, next to the loss of human life, property value is the major casualty in any catastrophic loss.

While there is usually some advance warning about natural disasters (scientists are even coming up with ways to anticipate earthquakes, previously thought to be the only major natural disaster that can strike without warning), there is little or no warning in connection with a terrorist attack. The only steps asset and property managers realistically can take is to plan and prepare in advance and deal as best they can with whatever circumstances might occur.

Fortunately, there are several major lessons that we have learned from the natural and man-made disasters that have befallen our society over the last few years:

1. There is no cavalry, or if there is, it may arrive late

The recent experience with hurricanes in the Gulf has driven home the fact that building owners and managers have a direct responsibility for the personal safety of their tenants, as well as for the protection of the physical assets under their management.

If property owners don't do the planning necessary to deal with a disaster, the property or properties and tenants under their care suffer, and the property owners may be responsible (if not legally, at least morally) for a sizable portion of adverse consequences.

This means it is necessary to internalize this fact of life and then move on to develop an emergency response plan before the next disaster strikes.[5]

2. An emergency plan has to assume many contingencies

One of the emerging lessons of recent disasters is that we are a highly interdependent society, and a breakdown in one area can quickly lead to a breakdown in another. This means that major adverse events must be identified and planned for in advance.

As an example, who could have anticipated that there would be looting after Katrina or that Americans would shoot at helicopters coming to the rescue of their neighbors? Or that the New York firefighter's response of running up the stairway of a burning World Trade Center (as they had been trained to do) would conflict with civilians tying to escape down the same stairway?

The old adage of "whatever can go wrong, will" is certainly true in a disaster setting, but is compounded by the possible breakdown of federal, state, and local life safety systems that traditionally have been relied upon. Asset and property managers have to rethink the disaster planning process, continually questioning traditional response theories, and ask over and over, "What if this breaks down or fails to materialize?"

3. Tie the plan into public agency planning, but be able to proceed with little or no outside assistance

There is no question that public agencies at all levels of government and in the private sector have learned a lot from recent disasters about how to respond quickly and effectively and also how to avoid the mistakes of the past.

It is incumbent upon and in the self-interest of property owners to support these efforts, both financially and in terms of time and political support.

---

5 Not having a plan would appear to increase the chances of being on the receiving end of adverse litigation.

Building and portfolio disaster plans should tie into and work with public agencies in this effort, but it is also wise to have contingency plans in the event there is a delay or breakdown in the public response process.

4. It's not enough to have an emergency plan; it has to be practiced over and over again

One of the emerging lessons of recent American disasters is that "stuff happens" in the chaos that occurs during and after a disaster that is difficult to anticipate, and it's better to expect the worst and plan for it than to experience it and discover that you are not prepared.

This means drills and more drills in anticipation of not having to use the experience of any of them but gaining a little more knowledge from each of them.

Again, the time to ask the "what if" questions is before the disaster, not after.

5. If a disaster occurs, a good risk management plan can help mitigate financial losses

It's not clear at this writing how insurance claims from recent disasters will be handled or, if necessary, adjudicated by the courts. Suffice to say, it's time for property owners to have sufficient insurance to cover major property and liability risks and be prepared to self-insure for most deficiencies.

In selecting an insurance carrier, it's important to take a look at the company's existing risk exposure profile and experience in paying claims fairly and expeditiously.

A good test is the size and experience of the internal team the company has established to respond to a large number of claims simultaneously. If they don't have such a team, it might be wise to consider moving the policy to a firm that does.

In the case of a large portfolio of buildings, it may be wise to spread insurance coverage over several carriers, in order to minimize the risk of loss exposure to any one carrier. This is particularly true if the portfolio is located in one or a few geographical areas where the risk of loss is concentrated.

In the case of national or regional portfolios, the risk of loss is geographically diversified, and a large carrier may be the best alternative both in terms of risk coverage and premium expense. Acquired properties can also be added to the portfolio without having to review risk issues with each acquisition.

Self-insurance is an option not only due to necessity, but also to reduce insurance premiums. It is also desirable to have analytical programs that continually weigh the trade-offs between making and buying insurance coverage.

Figure 14-2 lists important items that need to be considered in developing a disaster response plan.

F I G U R E   14-2

Disaster Planning Checklist

☐ **Staff**
- O Establish staff person responsible for coordinating emergency response effort. Distribute contact information to other staff, tenants, insurance company, and public agencies.
- O Establish emergency "command center" on site and protocol for its use.
- O Establish tenant, public agency, and media response protocol.
- O Determine which records are to be stored off-site and where and in what manner they are to be stored.
- O Conduct emergency response drills.

☐ **Tenants**
- O Establish with each tenant the responsible person to contact and how to contact him or her.
- O If a larger tenant, understand his or her plans for handling an emergency; suggest changes, coordinate as necessary.
- O If smaller tenant, review building protocol for his or her response (evacuation procedures, fire suppression, etc.).
- O Review tenant insurance policies on equipment, work product, files, etc.; suggest changes as necessary.
- O Establish assembly point in event of evacuation organized by public agencies; establish protocol if direction is to "shelter in place."
- O Identify handicapped or non-English-speaking employees who need extra attention.

☐ **Other Building Users (Shoppers, Visitors, Cleaning Crews, etc.)**
- O Clearly identify how to safely leave the building.
- O Establish assembly points for possible evacuation.

☐ **Public Agencies**
- O Identify "first responder" agencies.
- O Establish person to work with in each agency (usually the property manager).
- O Establish building entrance they will utilize and how they will be identified.
- O Go through a dry run with one of public agency staff to be certain there is a full understanding of the response process.
- O Ask agencies if they have CDs, films, brochure, or other presentations regarding emergency response procedures. If so, set up a method of disseminating information to tenants, visitors, and staff.

CHAPTER 15

Financial Reporting

$\mathbf{T}$he world of commercial real estate accounting is complicated by the varying needs and regulations of different real estate investors.[1] In this chapter we will focus on a particular investment property in order to examine the financial issues of each of the major investor groups—individuals, partnerships, pension funds, and REITs. In this way the differences in current accounting treatment for each group will become apparent.

Before turning to the example, however, it's important to understand some of the fundamentals of financial statement and tax reporting for U.S. tax taxpayers, as well as how each of the investor groups is currently treated under federal tax laws.

FINANCIAL STATEMENTS

Varying needs and regulations lead real estate investors to use one of four common methods of financial statement reporting. An overview of each one is summarized below.

Modified Cash Basis

Under this method of preparing financial statements, rental revenues are recognized when cash is received and operating expenses are recorded when paid.

---

1 The PricewaterhouseCoopers Real Estate Group provided technical support for this chapter.

In addition, the practice of capitalizing the cost of and recording periodic depreciation on real estate assets modifies the pure cash basis of accounting. These financial statements are referred to as OCBOA statements—an acronym for Other Comprehensive Basis of Accounting—because they do not conform with generally accepted accounting principles.

To qualify as OCBOA, a basis of accounting must meet one of the following descriptions cited within generally accepted auditing standards:

- A basis of accounting the reporting entity uses or expects to use to file its income tax return.
- A basis of accounting the reporting entity uses to comply with the requirements or financial reporting provisions of a governmental regulatory agency to whose jurisdiction the reporting entity is subject.
- Using the cash receipts and disbursements basis of accounting, with modifications of the cash basis having substantial support.
- Has a definite set of criteria with substantial support that is applied to all material items appearing in the financial statements, such as the price-level basis of accounting.

The basis of accounting used must be applied to all material financial statement amounts. It would not be acceptable, for example, to use the cash basis for selected amounts and the entity's tax basis for other amounts, assuming the bases are not the same.

Tax Basis

Under the tax basis of accounting, books and records are maintained in a manner consistent with the appropriate provisions of the Internal Revenue Code and support the reporting an entity uses or expects to use to file its federal income tax return.

Tax basis financial statements are usually prepared for the purpose of providing income tax data to the partners in a partnership and qualify as OCBOA. As a result, in practice it is common for partnerships to use the tax basis of accounting for preparing their financial statements.

Fair Value Basis

Many investment entities, including pension plans, insurance company separate accounts, and bank-sponsored real estate trusts invest in real estate for income, capital appreciation, or both.

Under accounting principles generally accepted in the United States (GAAP), real estate investment entities are required to carry their investments at fair value and to report income and appreciation (or depreciation) in the statement of operations.

For real estate as for most operating companies, GAAP is the historical cost model. To arrive at fair value for investment entities, management must estimate the value of the underlying real estate investments and related assets. Usually this value is determined using real estate appraisal techniques often performed by or supported by an independent appraisal.

Historical Cost Basis

This is the traditional accounting model required under GAAP by most operating companies, including real estate operating companies such as REITs.

Under this method, rental revenues are recognized when earned and operating expenses are accrued when incurred. Depreciation expense is also recognized over the useful lives of the related assets. Appreciation is not recognized until a sale occurs.

FEDERAL TAX REPORTING

In addition to the various practices found in financial statement reporting, different real estate investors are also subject to varying federal income tax requirements. The following is an overview of the common federal tax reporting considerations for each of the major real estate investor groups.

Individual Investor

Individuals who invest in real estate are often motivated in part by advantageous tax considerations associated with real estate investments. Investments can be made through a variety of legal forms of ownership, each with its own set of complex tax considerations, and can include partnerships, Limited Liability Corporations (LLCs), and direct ownership.

Most LLCs are usually treated as partnerships for federal income tax purposes, while single member LLCs are usually disregarded as a separate tax entity and treated as a direct ownership interest of its owner.

Individuals are required to report the federal income tax consequences of their real estate investments on their U.S. Form 1040 individual tax filing.

Partnership Investor

As part of its annual U.S. Form 1065 partnership tax filing, a partnership is required to separately allocate to its partners all income and expense items subject to special treatment under the Internal Revenue Code.

Real estate partnerships are required to separately report "passive" net income (or loss) from real estate activities from other items, such as interest income and net short-term and long-term gains (or losses). Each of these items must be reported on a separate line on Form 1065 Schedule K-1 for each partner.

An allocation of income, deductions, credits, etc., will generally be respected for tax purposes if it follows the partnership agreement and the allocation has "substantial economic effect." The allocation cannot distort the economics of the partners' financial arrangements.

To satisfy the "substantial economic effect" standard, the allocation must have "economic effect" and be substantial, according to IRC Section 704(b). To have economic effect, the following requirements must be met:

- Capital accounts must be maintained.
- Liquidating distributions must be made in accordance with positive capital balances.
- A partner with a deficit balance must restore the amount of the deficit by a cash payment to the partnership when the interest in the partnership is terminated.

An economic effect is "substantial" if there is a reasonable possibility that the allocation will substantially affect the dollar amounts to be received by the partners from the partnership, independent of tax consequences.

Pension Investors

Pension plans are generally tax exempt, although they may be subject to an excise tax on unrelated business taxable income (UBTI).

UBTI can arise from "debt financed property" (IRC Section 514) if applicable real estate exceptions do not apply, which are limited to certain pension plans and educational institutions. The portion of income considered to be UBTI is generally calculated based upon the ratio of the debt to the tax basis of the real estate portfolio (see Chapter 8).

It should be noted that UBTI can also result from the receipt of service income and other fees or "bad" income sources considered noninvestor or nontrader income, and from instances where the partnership invests in other pass-through entities that conduct unrelated businesses.

Examples of UBTI activities include the operation of hotels, parking garages, and senior housing with services. UBTI must be reported on a separate line on Form K-1 for each partner in a partnership that generates such income.

In order to protect tax-exempt partners from the receipt of UBTI, partnerships often establish offshore, parallel funds organized as corporations to act as "blockers."

Real Estate Investment Trusts

REITs play an important role as one of the most significant real estate investor groups in the real estate industry.

A REIT would ordinarily be taxed as a corporation, however, once it elects to be taxed as a REIT, and as long as it maintains compliance with REIT tax law requirements, it is permitted a tax deduction for dividends paid. The amounts distributed are generally taxable only to the shareholders. The requirements for REIT status include:

- At least 90 percent of its ordinary taxable income must be distributed to its shareholders.

- At least 100 persons must hold beneficial ownership in a REIT, and five or fewer shareholders may not own more than 50 percent of the REIT shares after the first taxable year in which a REIT election is made.[2]

- At least 75 percent of the value of total assets must be held as real estate assets, including debt and equity interests in real estate, or as cash, trade receivables, and government securities.

- At least 75 percent of total income must be derived from real estate assets or a limited number of other qualified sources, and at least 95 percent of total income must be attributable to those sources or other interest and dividends.

COMPARATIVE ANALYSIS

The property we will use for comparative analysis is a new suburban office building that has just been offered for sale by the developer of the building.

There are four competitors for the investment—an individual investor, a partnership, a pension fund, and a REIT—all willing to pay full price for

---

2 As noted in Chapter 4, this rule was modified to allow for pension fund investment by the "look-through" rule, which considers individual plan beneficiaries as REIT shareholders.

the property. The assumptions, calculations, and financial statements for each of these are outlined in Figures 15-1 and 15-2 on the following pages.

Individual Investors

As noted in Chapter 4, a large amount of real estate is still owned by individual investors. They may have differing objectives in investing in commercial real estate (cash flow, tax shelter, appreciation, etc.) and select the ownership vehicle that provides the most favorable treatment in their current situation and meets their objectives in entering into commercial real estate investments.

FIGURE 15-1

Assumptions and Calculations

	Symbol	Source	
Property			
Completion of Construction			June 1, 2005
Occupied			September 1, 2005
Square Footage	A	Given	100,000
Purchase Price	B	Given	$50,000,000
Allocation to Building	C	(B × 90%)	$45,000,000
Financing			
Mortgage	D	Given	$35,000,000
Equity	E	(B − D)	$15,000,000
Mortgage Term (Years)	F	Given	30
Interest Rate	G	Given	6.0%
Annual Constant	H	Given	7.2%
Annual Debt Service	I	(D × H)	$2,520,000
Balance End of First Year	J	Given	$34,580,000
First-Year Amortization	K	(D − J)	$420,000
Income			
Rental Rate per SF (NNN)	L	Given	$40.00
Annual Rent	M	(A × L)	$4,000,000
Depreciation	N	(C / 40)	$1,125,000
First-Year Interest	O	(I − K)	$2,100,000
Investor Income	P	(M − (N + O))	$775,000
Equity Return	Q	(P / E)	5.2%
Cash at Year End		(M − O)	$1,900,000

FIGURE 15-2

Financial Reporting

Account	Individual (Modified Cash Basis)	Partnership (Tax Basis)	Pension Fund (Fair Value Basis)	REIT (Historical Cost Basis)
Assets				
Cash	$1,813,333	$1,813,333	$1,813,333	$1,813,333
Land	5,000,000	5,000,000	5,000,000	5,000,000
Building	45,000,000	45,000,000	45,000,000	45,000,000
Lease Intangibles				1,000,000
Accum. Dep./Amortization	1,125,000	1,105,750		1,200,000
Accum. Appreciation			1,000,000	
Total Assets	50,688,333	50,707,583	52,813,333	51,613,333
Liabilities				
Mortgage Payable	$34,580,000	$34,580,000	$34,580,000	$34,580,000
Prepaid Rent			333,333	333,333
Equity	16,108,333	16,127,583	17,900,000	15,700,000
Liabilities & Equity	50,688,333	50,707,583	52,813,333	50,613,333
Income Statement				
Rent	$4,333,333	$4,333,333	$4,000,000	$4,000,000
Interest Expense	2,100,000	2,100,000	2,100,000	2,100,000
Depreciation/Amortization	1,125,000	1,105,750		1,200,000
Unrealized Appreciation			−1,000,000	
Net Income	1,108,333	1,127,583	2,900,000	700,000
Beginning Equity	$15,000,000	$15,000,000	$15,000,000	$15,000,000
Ending Equity	16,108,333	16,127,583	17,900,000	15,700,000
Average Equity	15,554,167	15,563,792	16,450,000	15,350,000
Total Returns	7.1%	7.2%	17.6%	4.6%
Notes:				
Building Depreciation	40 Years	39 Years	N/A	40 Years
Lease Amortization				10 Years
Jan. '06 Rent Paid in Dec.'05	333,333	333,333	333,333	333,333

Source: PricewaterhouseCoopers, McMahan Real Estate Services, LLC

As noted in Figure 15-2, an individual investor uses the modified cash basis of accounting for the 2005 financial statements and reports net income of $1,108,333. Using the modified cash basis requires the investor to report as 2005 rent income amounts received in December 2005, which represents the tenant's rent for January 2006. In addition, depreciation expense is recorded using a 40-year life on the building.

For income tax purposes, net taxable income of $1,127,583 is reported, which, in comparison to the modified cash basis, reflects the 39-year life for tax depreciation as well as the midmonth convention for the initial month of depreciation. Rents received in advance are also generally recognized as income for tax purposes.

An individual investor acquiring property through a wholly owned Limited Liability Corporation will report taxable income of $1,127,583 on the 2005 Form 1040 Schedule E, since the LLC is disregarded as a separate tax entity.

Partnership Investor

The situation changes for a partnership investment. In this case, the bidder is a syndicator who has established a partnership of five individuals who will invest $2.5 million each. The syndicator will serve as the general partner of the partnership and contribute $2.5 million to the investment.

In the example, a partnership uses the tax basis of accounting for 2005 financial statements, and reports net income of $1,127,583. Using the tax basis also requires the investor to report as 2005 rent income amounts received in December 2005, which represents the tenant's rent for January 2006.

The tax basis reporting also reflects the 39-year life for tax depreciation as well as the midmonth convention for the initial month of depreciation. A partnership is required to separately report on Schedule K-1 income and expense items that are subject to special treatment under the Internal Revenue Code. For 2005, the partnership will report taxable income of $225,517 on each of the partners' 2005 Form 1065 Schedule K-1, representing each partner's 20 percent ownership interest in the partnership.

Pension Fund Investor

One of the major competitors for the property is an investment advisor representing a large public pension fund. Figure 15-2 indicates the accounting and tax treatment if the pension fund were successful in the bidding.

Pension fund reporting is different from that of other investors primarily because real estate investments are mark-to-market. (GAAP requires pension funds to present investments at fair value.) In this regard, the suburban office property investment experienced market appreciation of 2 percent, or $1 million, during 2005. This amount has been recorded as unrealized appreciation in the fair value basis statement of operations for 2005. No depreciation expense is reported, since such amounts are considered in the mark-to-market category of investments.

In addition, because the fair value basis of accounting utilizes the accrual method of accounting in accordance with GAAP, January 2006 rent paid in 2005 is not recognized as 2005 rental income but is recorded as a prepaid rent liability in the December 31, 2005, balance sheet. For the year ended December 31, 2005, the pension fund reported net income of $2.9 million in connection with its real estate investment.

For income tax reporting purposes, while pension plans are generally tax exempt, the plan may be subject to an excise tax on unrelated business taxable income, particularly in circumstances involving debt-financed income.

Because the pension plan meets the debt-financed real estate exception, no UBTI is generated. No tax is payable by the pension plan for the $1,127,583 of taxable income generated in 2005.

REIT Investor

The fourth competitor for the property is a public office REIT that would like to add the property to its $4 billion portfolio.

The REIT uses historical cost accounting, which is the traditional model used by most operating companies under GAAP, and reported net income of $700,000 for 2005.

As part of GAAP accounting for acquisition costs, the REIT is required to record and amortize the value of the tenant lease that was in place on the January 1, 2005, date of acquisition.

Under historical cost GAAP, REIT management is required to consider the value of costs that were avoided by acquiring a 100 percent occupied property. Such costs would include leasing commissions as well as lost rents and operating expenses such as real estate taxes, insurance, utilities, and other costs required between the time the property is available for occupancy through the date the tenant occupies its space.

REIT management concluded the value of the in-place lease at the date of acquisition was $1 million and is amortizing this intangible asset over the related lease life of 10 years. No appreciation is reported since investments are not allowed to be mark-to-market by the REIT.

Further, because the historical cost basis utilizes the accrual method of accounting in accordance with GAAP, January 2006 rent paid in 2005 is not recognized as 2005 rental income but is recorded as a prepaid rent liability in the December 31, 2005, balance sheet.

For income tax purposes, in order to maintain its REIT status the REIT is required to distribute at least 90 percent of its ordinary taxable income to its shareholders.

Assuming the REIT distributes at least $1,014,824 of the $1,480,000 of cash flow generated in 2005, the REIT will receive a dividends paid deduction that allows for federal taxes to be payable only at the shareholder level on dividends received.

Investment Returns

Figure 15-2 also analyzes the simple investment return to each investor group. The average outstanding equity for the year is calculated and then divided into the total return number to arrive at the average simple return for the year.

The individual and partnership investors have almost similar returns at 7.1 and 7.2 percent respectfully largely because they are treated similarly in terms of tax treatment. The depreciation charge taken by the partnership investor is slightly less, and when added back, results in slightly less cash flow.

The highest return is recorded by the pension investor since it includes $1 million in appreciation and does not take any depreciation because pension funds are tax exempt.

The REIT has a considerably lower simple return of 4.6 percent largely because of lower accrual basis revenues and because management is required to amortize $1 million in lease intangibles.

Enterprise Management

CHAPTER 16

Leadership

This chapter discusses why the real estate industry traditionally has had so much difficulty in adopting many of the management concepts and tools that have been successful in other industries, and why the development of organizational leadership, even today, continues to be elusive.

Despite this, many senior managers of real estate firms are trying to change the ground rules—through a better understanding of the nature of leadership—by identifying potential leadership in others, improving their own ability to lead, and creating a nurturing organizational environment where leadership is encouraged and rewarded.

WHY HAS IT BEEN SO DIFFICULT?

From an organizational perspective, real estate traditionally has been linked to the production of new assets through the development process, with an emphasis on one or a few key individual entrepreneurs in the leadership role.

This doesn't mean that other aspects of real estate—acquisition, asset and property management, brokerage, finance, etc.—weren't important, but it was the developer and the development organization that historically set the leadership tone for the industry.

The historic public image of the developer has often been that of a tenacious individual, overcoming all obstacles—restrictive governmental officials, unimaginative lenders, reluctant tenants, and a continuing shortage of money, in part to satisfy the personal need of the entrepreneur to achieve industry and community recognition and build long-term personal net worth.

In many cases "leadership" was actually defined in terms of "community" or "industry" leadership, rather than building strong, healthy organizations.

It should be noted that this lack of organizational leadership was not the result of entrepreneurship, per se, but other factors that were somewhat unique to real estate—heavy emphasis on the production process, extensive use of outside consultants, high levels of financial leverage, and the tendency to organize firms on a functional basis.

Emphasis on the production of new assets and heavy use of debt financing also contributed to confusion as to who was the real "customer" of the firm. In many cases customers were perceived to be lenders or investors rather than tenants who occupied the buildings and generated the cash flow that ultimately determined building value.[1]

In contrast, the major area of entrepreneurship in America today—the high technology field—has created an environment where teamwork, business alliances, and talent building are generally considered major keys to success.

This is reenforced by financial rewards, which are largely based on organizational rather than individual success, as reflected in the IPO process and its emphasis on the quality of the firm and its leadership, as well as stock options as a major ingredient in individual compensation.

The final irony is that for many young people today, the word "developer" now means someone who develops computer programs and products rather than building real estate projects.

HOW REAL ESTATE IS CHANGING

The traditional view of the real estate leader has changed dramatically in the last 10 years. The emergence of vertically integrated REITs, restructured investment advisory firms, and large real estate service companies has produced a much different real estate organizational environment.

In this environment, the tenant is generally acknowledged to be the "customer," and the organizational focus has shifted from production to successful fulfillment of the value proposition with the customer. In addition, the value proposition itself is under considerable change, as firms experiment with ways in which to add products and services to attract and retain tenants and to expand revenue opportunities.

---

1 Following a 1997 article, "Real Estate Enterprise 2000," by the author, the statement in the article that received the greatest reader response was, "Have you ever seen a picture of a tenant on a developer's wall?"

Examples include energy, insurance, travel, day care, recreation facilities, and telecommunications. Some firms have been experimenting with "portfolio" lease arrangements in which the tenant is allowed to vacate a certain portion of the space each year at no or little cost penalty.

Still others are exploring the use of "branding" to create a readily recognizable image of the firm and thereby improve overall customer loyalty.

Internally, many real estate organizations have become leaner, with a new focus on building core competencies and outsourcing noncore functions. Greater teamwork has been encouraged, although it is still largely along functional rather than product or service lines.

In many cases compensation systems have been realigned to reward employees for having a strong customer orientation and contributing to the overall team effort.

The consolidation of much of the industry into larger operating units also has forced real estate managers to learn how to manage more complex organizations and seek ways to improve organizational leadership skills.

As these firms have grown, they have discovered and had to deal with the difference between building strong functional real estate skills such as negotiation, construction, leasing, building management, etc., and the more general management skills of strategic planning, market positioning, risk management, talent development, management succession, balance sheet management, corporate governance, and, in the case of public companies, investor relations.[2]

They also have come up against the most difficult question of all—the difference between good management and organizational leadership.

WHAT IS LEADERSHIP?

Leadership is somewhat like pornography—you can't always describe it but you know it when you see it. People just seem to be able to recognize a good leader, but often have a hard time identifying the qualities that comprise that person's leadership qualities.

In a real estate organization, it is not unusual to see bright, highly skilled managers with outstanding track records who, when promoted to positions of leadership, fail miserably.

Others, possessing much lesser skills and with a less extraordinary track record, often seem to be able to grow into effective leaders when promoted to similar positions.

---

2 This problem is even more complicated for those investment managers who have moved into international markets, where there is the additional complication of dealing with different cultures and business standards.

Is leadership the same as management? Some researchers have defined leadership as "the process whereby one individual influences other group members toward the attainment of defined group or organizational goals."[3]

Others have distinguished leaders from the general run of managers as being visionaries, as having a longer-term view of the organization than the immediate decision at hand.

Leaders are usually good communicators who understand the relationship between their organization and the world at large and who reach out to influence constituencies beyond their own area of responsibility. Leaders also tend to emphasize nontraditional approaches to decision making, leading the efforts to change and renew an organization in order to better adapt to external forces.[4]

Still other observers have focused on the degree of change that is effectuated by an individual. Managers are concerned primarily with the status quo through organizational order and stability. Often, it is thought that this is achieved through the planning, budgeting, staffing, and monitoring process.

In contrast, leaders are usually interested in transforming the organization to their vision of the future. They accomplish this through articulating their vision to others, building coalitions to achieve the vision, and motivating and inspiring people to overcome obstacles to achieving the vision.[5]

QUALITIES OF A GOOD LEADER

There is a growing body of academic research suggesting that while intelligence and technical skills are important, they are primarily "threshold capabilities" that allow leadership to spawn but that by themselves will not guarantee the emergence of an effective leader.

The most frequently recurring characteristic of good leadership is what some academics call "emotional intelligence," or the ability to work with others and be effective in leading change. The latter appears to be a dominant characteristic, particularly in a period of rapid change in the business and world environment.

Daniel Goleman, a researcher at Rutgers University's Graduate School of Applied and Professional Psychology, identifies emotional intelligence as contributing up to 90 percent of the difference between star performers and

3 R. A. Baron, R.A. and J. Greenberg. *Behavior in Organizations.* Allyn and Bacon, Needham Heights, Massachusetts, 1990.

4 J. W. Gardner. *On Leadership.* Free Press, New York, 1990.

5 J. P. Kotter. *A Force for Change.* Free Press, New York, 1990.

average senior managers. Goleman notes that managers possessing emotional intelligence generally have at least five qualities in common[6]:

Self-Awareness

This is the quality of a person to understand his or her own moods and emotions and its effect on others. These persons can be identified as having a high level of self-confidence without being arrogant, an ability to assess their own shortcomings, and a self-deprecating sense of humor.

These individuals are comfortable discussing their own strengths and limitations and often seek constructive criticism from others. They also are willing to admit failure and try to learn from the experience. Needless to say, they do not blame others.

Self-Regulation

A second characteristic of emotional intelligence is the ability of individuals to control or redirect their impulses or moods when they may be disruptive to the decision-making environment. These individuals have the ability to think before acting and to suspend judgment until the facts are known. In most cases they are able to avoid the "Ready, fire, aim" approach to decision making. This creates an environment of trust and fairness.

Self-regulated individuals are open to change, but are also comfortable with "ambiguity" in decision making. This characteristic is particularly important in today's real estate environment, where there are often different and perhaps conflicting paths to be taken and where the full nature of the trade-offs involved will not be known until all of the facts are assembled, if even then.

A hallmark of the self-regulated person is an aura of trust and integrity, where fellow workers are confident in the ability of the individual to hear all sides and then take the best course of action available. In this sense, individual integrity is not just a personal strength, but an organizational one as well.

Strong Motivation

Individuals with a high level of emotional intelligence generally have large amounts of energy and are highly motivated to achieve their goals.

---

6 Daniel Goleman, *Emotional Intelligence* (Bantam, 1995), and *Working with Emotional Intelligence* (Bantam, 1998).

They love to learn and seek out creative challenges, taking an enormous pride in doing things well. They are often very persistent in their questioning, which is due to their desire to explore new approaches in achieving their objectives.

In dealing with others, these individuals often ask subordinates to "stretch" to achieve common goals, and they are always willing to stretch themselves. They also like to keep score of their progress as well as that of others. Often, this "passion" goes beyond the normal goals of wealth or status.

These highly motivated people usually have a strong commitment to the work itself, a strong drive to achieve, and are generally optimistic, even when failure is obvious.

Empathy for Others

A fourth characteristic is empathy for those around them. This is the ability to understand the emotions of others and to take into consideration the emotional reaction that can be expected from a personal interaction or when a difficult decision has to be made.

People with empathy also are sensitive to social, economic, and cultural differences in others. This does not mean that they allow this understanding to dominate their actions, but rather, that it provides a foundation for listening and for sensitivity when decisions have to be made.

Individuals with this quality are generally good at building and retaining talent in the organization, a strong advantage in today's highly competitive and mobile real estate environment. Personal knowledge is often the major resource of most firms, and when good people leave, they take a part of the firm's knowledge resource with them, often to a competitor.

Social Skills

A final characteristic of emotional intelligence is the ability of an individual to find common ground with others and build personal rapport *before* tough decisions have to be made. Socially skilled people generally have many acquaintances both in and outside their real estate organization, regardless of age level or degree of business experience. They firmly believe that nothing important gets done alone, and they're willing to give credit to others when it is due.

People with these characteristics are good at managing relationships and building networks with others. They are also effective in building and managing project teams and in leading organizational change. In essence,

good social skills allow leaders to *utilize* their emotional intelligence in a work environment.

In a synergistic fashion, these personal qualities complement each other and are mutually reinforcing. Too much of any single quality without the support of the others will generally not produce the quality of leadership most real estate firms require in today's highly competitive environment.

HOW LEADERSHIP SKILLS CAN BE IMPROVED

Perhaps the best way to begin building leadership skills in others is to better understand an individual's own leadership skills. There are several ways to accomplish this.

Know What an Individual Is Good At

Most people have a misconception of their own personal strengths. One way to systematically learn more about their strengths and weaknesses is to keep track of decisions and subsequent events.

Peter Drucker suggested that every time a manager makes a key decision or proceeds with a key action, she or he should write down what they expect to happen and then review it a year or so later to better understand what actually happened.[7]

Over a period of time, this linkage between decision and results should lead to a better understanding of the areas of life where a person has few strengths, those areas where they are marginally competent, and those where they excel. It also will be a reality test between what they think their strengths are and what they actually are.

Work on Your Strengths, Not Weaknesses

With an understanding of an individual's strengths, the next step is to work on improving personal strengths; particularly those associated with excellence. This may involve acquiring new knowledge and skills to round out a special competency.

Or it may mean undertaking some tasks that in the past were delegated to others. This also helps in updating a manager's understanding of changes in technology and good business practice.

---

7 Peter F. Drucker. *Management Challenges for the 21st Century.* HarperCollins, New York, May 1999.

Gaining a better understanding of a person's strengths will also indicate those areas where they have little or no competence. Trying to improve in these areas generally will not be productive and should be avoided. As Drucker put it, "It takes far more energy to improve from incompetence to mediocrity than to improve from first-rate performance to excellence."[8]

Respect Others' Areas of Knowledge

Many people confuse "brightness" with knowledge, not fully realizing that knowledge can only come from thinking in considerable depth about a subject and then applying the resultant observations and conclusions to real world situations. This helps to calibrate theory and practice, translating data and information into true knowledge about a subject.

People with expertise in one area may not respect people with knowledge in other areas—the construction manager or financial whiz who takes pride in not wanting to know about how people behave, or the human resources person who never tries to understand accounting, finance, or other quantitative areas of expertise.

This lack of respect for other people's areas of knowledge makes it difficult to work with those who may be crucial to the success of a critical management initiative. One way to develop respect for others is to better understand what their area of expertise is all about.

It is also helpful in determining the personal skills and knowledge that make a person successful in other areas—a vital ingredient in selecting and promoting people in fields other than that of the manager.

Understand How an Individual Best Learns

Different people have different ways in which they learn. Some people learn best through reading, others through listening. The "reader" needs to digest large amounts of data before making a decision. This type of person also feels most comfortable taking copious notes in a meeting, to be reread at a later time.

The "listener" wants to discuss a problem with several other people in order to gain different perspectives. This person feels most comfortable, and gains the greatest knowledge, by focusing on the words and thoughts expressed by others.

In a group meeting, the listener also gains perspective from the body language of the speakers and the personal interchange between and among the individuals involved.

---

8 Ibid.

Generally, it is difficult for an individual to benefit equally from both reading and listening, and it's largely a waste of time and energy to even try. Drucker suggested that a manager use the method of learning that he or she utilizes best and with which they feel most comfortable.

This focus will help in sharpening a person's understanding and knowledge of a subject and of the individuals involved. It's another way to gain the greatest efficiency by building on a manager's strengths rather than trying to overcome personal weaknesses.

Determine How an Individual Best Performs

Generally there is a direct link between the way a person learns and the way they perform.

If they are a reader, they'll probably feel most comfortable communicating in writing, at least as the initial step in the process. In a meeting, they will probably perform better by reading from notes or by using a formal presentation.

If they're a listener, they probably will be most effective by speaking informally, gathering in the reaction from others as they proceed. In smaller groups or one-on-one situations, they may wish to utilize more of a Socratic method, utilizing questions as a way to focus discussion.

It's also important to establish the circumstances under which an individual best performs. Some individuals work best under stress, while others require a highly structured, predictable work environment. Some people work best in a small organization, others in a large one. Few are effective in all environments.

The central theme is not to try to change people, but to work on improving the things they do best, utilizing the way they learn and perform best, and in the environment in which they function best. A corollary is not to take on work that a person cannot perform or can only perform poorly.

Develop Personal and Organizational Value Congruency

Every organization has a value system within which it operates. The values may be explicit, as exemplified by the proverbial "mission statement," or implicit, to be discovered only by talking to managers and employees or observing the actions of the firm in the marketplace. In some cases the implied value system may differ sharply from the stated goals of the firm.

An organizational value system is more than ethical personal and business behavior. For example, the timing of a firm's expectation horizon

(short versus long term) is an overarching system that can influence all other organizational values.

The method of "getting there" can also significantly affect values: Does the firm grow by focusing on constant, small improvements or by risking a major "breakthrough" that may vault it into a significantly stronger market position?

Values also are influenced by the firm's method of hiring and promoting. Does the organization have a policy of looking outside to "bring in new blood" or does it try to promote from within? Or, preferably, does management have an open mind and try to deal with each situation on an individual basis?

If a person works in an organization with a significantly different value system then their own, they will not only be frustrated, but have great difficulty in maximizing their own personal performance. The value systems don't have to be exactly the same, but they need to be close.

A firm's value system also may change over time, through a change in management, from the effects of a merger or acquisition, or simply through strong organic growth. If so, a person should be certain that the firm's new value system is consistent with his or her own.

If it isn't, it will become evident to others who must then decide if they want to try to change the system or move on to an organization whose value system is more in line with their own.

As a senior manager, it's important to make certain that the firm's value system is fully understood by all concerned—employees, customers, suppliers, investors, etc.—and that the day-to-day operation of the firm is consistent with its stated values.

Taking Responsibility for Relationships

In most business (and life) situations, results are obtained through joint efforts. Working successfully with others requires reasonably good relationships between and among those involved.

While these relationships can evolve in a nonwork situation, most organizations work best when the ground rules for the working relationship are clearly understood. It is the role, indeed the obligation, of a senior real estate manager to take the responsibility to make sure this happens within his or her own organization.

This process begins with the personal relationship that an individual has with those members of management with whom they have the most frequent contact.

The first step is to understand that these individuals also have their own strengths, weaknesses, and preferred performance environments. To be most effective, they are entitled to a work environment that allows them to do their work in a way that they can do it best. Understanding their peculiarities and value systems makes it possible to establish and maintain such an environment.

Taking Responsibility for Communications

It's also important to take responsibility for communicating with other members of the management team.

This may involve no more than a voice or e-mail message of congratulations on a task well done, or a sit-down, in-depth discussion of a particular problem in the relationship that needs to be overcome. Or it may involve meeting with one or more individuals to work through a problem between (or among) them that as individuals they have not been able to deal with effectively.

If the management team has a good working relationship, this becomes well known to other employees and establishes a behavior norm that can permeate the organization, often more effectively than a more formal system of memos, decrees, employee directives, and, yes, mission statements.

A leader also needs to communicate directly with employees, either as individuals or in groups. This communication can be informal—"managing by walking around"—or through more formal means such as teleconferencing, voice or e-mails, or internal organization publications.

Given the contemporary means of communications, there is no excuse for a leader not to be in touch with everyone on the management team on a reasonably frequent basis.

ESTABLISHING A NURTURING WORK ENVIRONMENT

In today's highly competitive real estate environment, where people are often the most valuable resource, healthy organizations are built more on trust than through force.

Trust does not necessarily mean that people like each other, but rather, that they understand each other, generally share similar values, and are willing to work together to accomplish common goals. The senior manager's obligation is to make certain that an environment exists that not only allows this to happen, but encourages it to flourish.

Flat Organizational Structure

Modern communications technology makes it easier for real estate firms to have a much "flatter" organizational structure than in the past. Reducing or eliminating layers of middle management not only reduces operating costs, but allows senior managers to be closer to the customer and to better understand the dynamics of the firm's value proposition in the marketplace.

A flatter organization increases the number of direct reports to the senior manager, permitting more frequent interface with other members of management. It also forces senior managers to focus on strategic issues and rely more heavily on others to make and implement decisions.

In this environment, developing good leadership is not only good for the organization, but allows the senior manager to function more effectively.

The Right Mix for Influencing Changes in Individual Behavior

Changing individual behavior generally revolves around the question, "Do you change the people or change the environment?"

Changing the people means trying to influence individual behavior by changing attitudes, opinions, and value systems.

This can be accomplished through employee meetings, off-site conferences, newsletters, brochures, new physical surroundings, special training sessions, etc. While this approach can be used to support more substantive changes, it usually does not in itself result in affecting change.

A more direct approach is to change the environment in which people work. This can be accomplished through changes in personnel, management structure, reporting relationships, reward systems, etc. But though this approach can be much more effective, it involves significant risk if the change is inappropriate for the organization or not handled properly.

The solution that seems to work best is to try to change the person and the environment *simultaneously* in a manner in which each is supportive of the other.

If employees see actual changes around them that are consistent with what management said it would do, the impact is to create an environment in which employees believe that organizational change can improve their individual work environment. This provides a foundation for them to begin to develop their own leadership skills.

Dealing with a Multigenerational Workplace

As noted in Chapter 2, there are often significant differences between generations, particularly when it comes to skill levels associated with new technologies. Rather than assuming that all wisdom is associated with gray hair and "time in grade," it is better to develop a culture that permits different work styles to flourish so the entire organization benefits.

This is often accomplished by developing strong mentoring programs between generations, where, in appropriate situations, the mentor is the younger employee. Modifying work standards related to days and hours worked, working at home, scheduling vacation time, etc., are other ways in which the creative juices of younger employees can be harnessed for the benefit of not only the employee, but the organization as well.

The increasing role of women in the workplace also should be acknowledged by understanding and accommodating individual needs related to education, skills development, and child care, as well as meeting the general need to maintain a work environment in which there is no sexual harassment.

Dealing with Part-Time Employees

In many industries, including real estate, today's workplace is characterized by an increasing proportion of part-time employees. In some cases these employees (or "independent contractors," as they are often called) may be employed for many years and ultimately become an integral part of the organization.

From a leadership perspective, it is better to recognize these employees as a resource rather than a problem by treating them more as "interns" and mentoring them like other employees. This also means including them in management discussions, giving them the facts about the organization (to the extent that they are not confidential), and expecting the same level of work quality as a full-time employee.

ALLOW BROADER PARTICIPATION IN DECISION MAKING

One of the ways that senior management can change individual behavior is to allow broader participation in decision making. This approach not only improves the self-esteem of individual employees, but can also open up the firm to a much wider range of solutions to specific problems, a particular advantage in today's rapidly changing real estate environment.

To be effective, a more participative approach to firm decision making must consider several issues:

Which Decisions?

The range of decision making should be based on the responsibilities and work experiences of the employee. This not only improves the chances that the decisions will be good ones, but that they will carry more credibility with other employees, thereby enhancing individual leadership skills.

This range of experience doesn't have to be limited to an employee's current job; it can include experiences gained with other firms as well.

How Are They Made?

To the extent possible, employees should be encouraged to discuss problems on a peer level, exploring various alternative solutions within their range of decision making. This approach (somewhat similar to the "quality circles" approach used by the Japanese) encourages employees to talk more openly about how they would handle a particular problem. It also encourages individuals with leadership qualities to emerge as task leaders.

How Are They Implemented?

For participative decision making to be effective, senior management must fully support the process. This means being willing to support the implementation of decisions that "bubble up" from below.

Once approved, the same people making the decisions should be responsible for their implementation. This is only sensible, since the range of decision making involved their area of work responsibility, and because they are closest to the point of impact of the decision.

Handling Success (or Failure)

Senior management must be prepared to give full credit to those who suggest a particular course of action that turns out to be successful.

When failure is the result, senior managers should encourage (and participate in) a frank, constructive discussion as to why it didn't work out and the "lessons learned" for future decisions. Not all of senior management's decisions work out either.

Developing the right organizational environment to nurture leadership is not easy. In the short run it may involve giving up or reducing senior management prerogatives. It may mean that some decisions will turn out to be failures and perhaps expensive for the firm.

It also may mean that certain individuals who are unable to accept greater levels of decision-making responsibility will be asked to (or voluntarily) leave the firm. Or that management training, mentoring, and other investments of time in an individual may lead them to a point where they become so accomplished that they leave the firm to accept a better offer or start an organization of their own.

In today's turbulent real estate environment, however, the longer-term rewards appear to be well worth the risks. Establishing and nurturing organizational leadership is a proven way to build the resources necessary to beat the competition, capture market opportunities, attract investment capital, and create the kind of work environment that is fulfilling and financially rewarding to most, if not all, of those involved.

CHAPTER 17

Strategic Planning

The concept of enterprise strategic planning has been studied for over 50 years. During this period, management consultants and business school faculty have helped firms develop and implement wide-ranging strategic plans, to the point where strategic planning is now widely accepted in America's general business community.

Strategic planning has had a tougher time being accepted in the real estate industry. Part of the problem is the historic absence of firms in the industry large enough and sufficiently integrated to successfully implement organizational change on their own, to "control their own destiny," so to speak.

There are many reasons put forward to explain this situation. They include the historical local focus of the real estate industry, preoccupation of developers with new development rather than operations, the enormous influence of lenders due to the heavy debt needed to finance new projects, investor preoccupation with the tax benefits of real estate, and the unwillingness of building owners to recognize the tenant as the "customer" of a "bundle of services."

Whatever the reasons that explained the past, the industry is rapidly changing. Consider, for example, the emergence of major national and international real estate service firms in the fields of brokerage, mortgage finance, property management, maintenance, and telecommunications. For another example, we need only cite the growth of REITs to become a major force in real estate.

Most REITs have some similarities to general business firms: specialization (by property type), geographic focus, vertical integration as organizations, providing a wide range of customer services, compensation programs generally tied to the success of the enterprise. And most REITs are public, answerable to shareholders, and subject to often intensive analyst scrutiny.

In essence, they are true operating companies that can directly benefit from strategic planning and its successful implementation. Other real estate companies can benefit from the strategic planning process as well.

STRATEGIC PLANNING PROCESS

The strategic planning process provides a road map for strategic management and lays the groundwork for the action steps to follow. In its simplest terms, the process can be reduced to these fundamental questions:

- Where are we today? What does the future hold?
- What position in the marketplace will add the greatest value to our firm's customers, employees, and shareholders?
- What actions do we need to take to reach that position?

To put it even more simply: Where are we now? Where do we want to go? How do we get there?

Current Situation

"Where are we today?" The first step in the strategic planning process is to assess the current position of the firm. To be worthwhile, the research process must be fair, accurate, and, above all, objective in its approach as well as in the interpretation and dissemination of its findings.

This is not always an easy task since a wide variety of stakeholders—board members, management, employees, shareholders, partners, suppliers, financiers, etc.—may not like the answers that are forthcoming and may use the material to promote individual agendas that are not in the best interests of the firm.

A minimum threshold of success is the ability of a firm to *operate effectively* over the long term in a highly competitive world. This means providing the customer with better performance by creating greater value, or by delivering comparable value at a lower cost.

It could represent a change in the total organization or some of its business lines or products and/or services. It might even involve merging or dissolving the firm itself.

Identifying the Customer

A critical element in developing operational effectiveness is a thorough understanding of and identification with the increasingly demanding customer. Finding out who the customer really is and isolating the customer's needs, resources, and buying/use preferences is absolutely essential to a successful strategic plan.

We noted in Chapter 11 that many real estate firms today view the tenant as "the customer," although there are still some managers who view investors or lenders in this role. What many REITs have discovered, however, is that providing the tenant with a quality living or work environment and a high level of services generally results in lower occupancies, higher revenues, and greater profits for investors.

Value Proposition

Based on this understanding, a firm develops a mix of products and services to offer each customer, the prices it will charge, and the terms by which it will perform its obligations. This is the *value proposition* that defines the relationship between the firm (landlord) and its customers (tenants).

Core Competencies

In order to fulfill its value proposition, a firm must develop certain *competencies*. Hamel and Prahalad define a "competence" as "a bundle of skills and technologies rather than a single discrete skill or technology" representing the sum of learning across individual skill sets and individual organizational units."[1] In other words, competency is a methodology for doing the things the firm is "good at."

Unfortunately, in making "buy" decisions and developing long-term relationships, firms often spend vast sums of management time and money developing competencies that are largely irrelevant to the customer.

Part of this mismatch may be due to customers not being aware of their own needs. But more likely it is the result of firms proceeding to build competencies without fully understanding whether those competencies will assist in fulfilling the value proposition with the customer.

Therefore, it's important to focus on *core competencies* that represent a bundle of skills that will make an important contribution to the value of

---

1 Gary Hamel and C. K. Prahalad. *Competing for the Future.* Harvard Business School Press, 1994.

the firm *as perceived by the customer.* In other words, it must satisfy the value proposition equation.

Core competency also must be "competitively unique" within the industry, although not necessarily unique to one firm.

Finally, a core competency should be "extendable" to new products and services in the future, enhancing its value over time through continued development and use.

Which Competencies Are Core?

How does a firm determine which competencies should be considered "core" and avoid a customer/competency mismatch?

The answer is to *talk to the customer on an ongoing basis.*

As simple as this may sound, it's amazing how many times strategic decisions are made without sufficiently understanding the individual or organization making the buy decision or understanding what's important to them. Gaining this understanding requires more than a onetime customer survey or market research study.

But though such research is necessary, it is not sufficient. What is required is *customer intimacy*—an in-depth understanding of, and relationship with, those who rent the firm's buildings and purchase related services.

Building Customer Intimacy

To build customer intimacy, the firm must establish a continuing dialogue with its existing and potential customers. The goal of this dialogue is to clarify known needs, identify unmet needs, and better understand attitudes toward the firm's current and potential service or product offerings.

The first step in this process is to know more about the customer. Who are they and what are their requirements? It is also important to know the depth of the customer base, and how its size and activity patterns will change in the future. Is it vulnerable to new technology or business cycles? Is it vulnerable to demographic forces or lifestyle change? Who makes the leasing/service selection decisions? Who influences the process? (See Chapter 13 for a discussion of this.)

If a firm has a heterogeneous customer base, certain customers may perceive some but not all of the core competencies that the firm possesses. This forces the firm to segment its markets and focus its efforts on building core competencies that meet the needs of the majority of its tenant customers, and/or to determine that smaller customer groups will grow sufficiently to support the maintenance of each competency. Without this *market segmentation*, the firm is diluting its efforts by building competencies that are not economically viable.

This effort cannot be completely delegated. Senior asset managers, for example, must be involved on a personal basis in establishing ongoing relationships with key customers and potential customers.

This demonstrates to customers that senior management is concerned with their well-being. It also establishes a leadership model within the organization and eliminates any "noise" that might come from those with a personal stake in the outcome.

Competency Convergence

Over time, customers' perceptions of the importance of specific core competencies can change. Competitors may adopt similar bundles of skills and technology to the point where there is a *competency convergence*, with no one firm having a strategic advantage. In fact, a core competency may become an industry standard by which all firms are measured. This serves to intensify price competition until one of the firms comes up with a new competency.

Benchmarking the Competition

Defining the nature of the competition is closely related to and intertwined with understanding the customer. Who are the existing competitors, and how does the firm compare in the minds and actions of the customers? Who are the likely new competitors, and how will they change the competitive environment? How can the firm assume industry leadership in defining and establishing a new *competitive space* in which it can be a major player?

Meaningful continuing analysis of the customer and the competition requires establishment of benchmarks so that data produced from the interview/analytical process can be continuously compared to a standard.

The standard used might be the average of the competitive universe in order to gain an idea of the firm's general market position. It may be more useful to determine who the industry leaders are and how the firm compares to them. It also may be helpful to benchmark against other industries whose processes are more advanced.

The benchmarking process establishes a set of "best practices" against which the activities of the firm can be compared and measured.

This process should identify the optimal market position for the firm, as well as the competitive advantages that it has or can establish.

From this process, an understanding of a series of alternative courses of action begins to emerge.

EVALUATING ALTERNATIVES

The next step is to begin consolidating courses of action into alternative strategies. This *strategic issue analysis* contrasts the company profile with its external environment to identify a range of possible strategic alternatives.

Particular attention should be given to *critical success factors*—those areas in which high performance by the firm could result in an improved *competitive position*. These alternative growth strategies can be either externally or internally focused.

Externally Focused Strategies

Strategic alternatives that focus on external growth are generally directed at moving the firm to a more optimal competitive position, with a focus on revenue enhancement. Figure 17-1 is a graphic representation of some externally focused strategies.

Alternative strategies might involve introducing new building features or services, differentiating existing features or services, entering or leaving geographical markets, divesting existing operating units, or acquiring new operating units.

Since competitive marketplaces are seldom calm, the analysis of alternative growth strategies should also consider the potential *competitive reaction* to each alternative.

FIGURE 17-1

Externally Focused Strategies

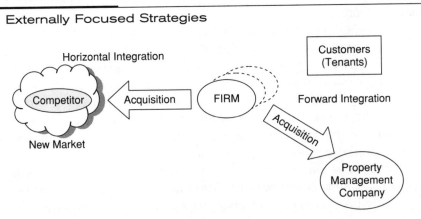

Source: McMahan Real Estate Services, LLC

Horizontal integration expands the firm through acquisition or internal growth without significantly changing its stage in the acquisition/development process. This strategy is utilized to enter new geographical markets or eliminate competition in existing markets.

Vertical integration, on the other hand, involves adding functions forward or backward in the production/marketing process. *Forward integration*, a form of vertical integration, attempts to move the firm closer to the customer, thereby improving market share and potentially reducing costs to the point of sale. Acquiring a property management firm is an example of forward integration.

Internally Focused Strategies

Internally focused growth strategies are usually associated with improving internal operations by lowering operating costs, improving procurement policies (*inbound logistics*), or improving the firm's overall work environment.

This may involve such initiatives as reorganizing the structure of the firm, reengineering the way the firm undertakes certain activities, outsourcing noncore functions, or recapitalizing the balance sheet.

It may also involve external actions, such as a merger or the acquisition of another firm. A shopping center REIT acquiring a retail merchandising firm, for example, could reduce costs to the consumer and/or improve retailer effectiveness. Figure 17-2 looks at various internally focused strategies.

FIGURE 17-2

Internally Focused Strategies

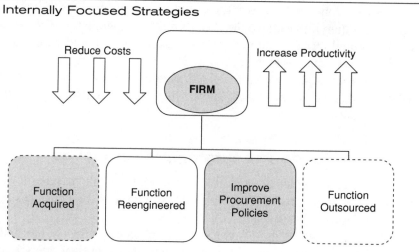

Source: McMahan Real Estate Services, LLC

Growth strategies also may reflect the presence or absence of synergies between consolidating firms. *Concentric diversification* reflects a strategy of acquiring firms similar to and synergistic with the acquiring firm in terms of markets, products, and/or technology. *Conglomerate diversification* is a strategy of acquiring firms for investment purposes only, with little or no anticipated synergy with the acquired firm.

Highly specialized firms are faced with the decision of whether to diversify or focus their operations even more. Diversification usually reduces the risk of a business being affected by a major adverse event (e.g., product/service obsolescence, market area deterioration, loss of key executives), but it may also lead to a decline in the firm's core business activity.

Given this choice, firms may decide it is better to "harden the silo" by developing a *defensible niche* in which margins improve and future competitive entry is made more difficult.

Dealing with Resource Constraints

In the course of evaluating strategic alternatives, management may reject alternatives that are unfeasible or not of sufficient economic value to the firm. The process of eliminating alternatives, while important, must be undertaken with some caution.

Too often strategic planning focuses on what a firm *can't do* rather than what it *must do* to gain a competitive advantage. It is certainly necessary to consider existing resources, particularly core competencies, but these should be viewed as a foundation, not a limitation.

Effective strategic planning first establishes what the firm must do to establish competitive advantage, and then concerns itself with the resources required to achieve the goal. It may turn out that in fact the firm will be limited by its resources, but this assumption should be put to the most rigorous tests possible.

Well-managed, creative firms are usually able to come up with the necessary resources, once they know what is required to achieve their strategic goals.

Valuation of Strategic Alternatives

As alternative strategies emerge, it is important to test them quantitatively against the baseline standards established during the current business evaluation previously discussed.

Each alternative should enhance shareholder/partner value and/or reduce downside risk when compared to the current level of operations.

If it does not, it should be rejected or modified to generate higher value. In some cases the firm might continue to consider a strategic alternative with certain desirable nonquantifiable characteristics, but the costs of doing so must be fully understood.

As previously noted, *strategic positioning means performing different activities than the competition or performing the same activities in a different way,* requiring that strategic trade-offs be made.

Selecting a strategic alternative from multiple options will limit what a company can do, because no firm can be all things to all people. This increases risk because the selected alternative may turn out to be wrong, and once this is discovered, it might be too late to go back and take a different route.

But making the "right" strategic decision(s) is what good management and industry leadership are all about, and if a correct strategic direction is chosen, it can distance the firm from its competitors and ensure successful corporate growth and long-term profitability.

The right decisions don't have to be optimal; they just have to be better than the competitors'.

FORMULATING THE FINAL PLAN

Once each of the strategic alternatives has been evaluated, management can begin the process of selecting desirable alternatives and formulating the final strategic plan.

Company Goals

The plan should first state the company goals that management expects to attain through implementation of the strategic plan.

Next, these goals should be translated into *measurable objectives,* projected over a multiyear period. These might include improvement in market share, profitability, return on investment, productivity improvements, employee relations, or investor relations.

Finally, company policies should be formulated, reflecting broad guidelines that will influence the thinking, decisions, and actions of managers and subordinates as the strategic plan is implemented.

Elimination of Noncore Activities

In order to force management to focus on establishing and maintaining core competencies, the strategic plan may identify and reduce or eliminate noncore activities by divesting or outsourcing them to other organizations.

It's tough enough for management to make critical decisions on the things that really matter without having to concentrate resources on those that are important but not essential. In many cases management discovers that the noncore activities weren't needed in the first place or can be performed better and less expensively by others.

Maintaining/Reorienting Core Competencies

Dealing with customers' changing perceptions of core competencies requires ongoing strategic planning and out-of-the-box thinking on the part of senior management. Given the high volatility of many real estate markets, improving core competencies may be almost as difficult as establishing them in the first place.

Management must have the ability to deal with changing reality—to face hard facts about customers, the effectiveness of the firm's products and services, and the strength and nature of the competition.

Establishing and/or Enhancing Competitive Advantage

If the firm is already operating effectively, in order to gain a strategic advantage it may choose to pursue a strategy of differentiating itself from the competition through its building products, tenant services, or operating processes.

Once a firm is operating effectively, the next and most crucial step is to differentiate itself by adding value through products and services that give it a *strategic advantage* over the competition.[2] A firm's long-term profitability will depend, in large measure, upon the degree to which this strategic positioning can be achieved and sustained over time.

As opposed to operational effectiveness, which involves performing the same activities better, faster, or cheaper than the competition, competitive advantage requires performing different activities than the competition, or performing the same activities in a different way.

This often requires management to make strategic trade-offs—for example, between higher value and lower cost, products offered, and customers served. Making these choices requires a high degree of personal and organizational discipline and integrity, clear lines of communication, and a willingness to say no.[3]

---

2 Michael E. Porter, "What is Strategy?" *Harvard Business Review,* November–December 1996.
3 Ibid.

Firms may establish competitive advantage in a highly focused niche or across a broad range of products and services, depending upon size, resources, established market position, and level of operating effectiveness.

In pursuing a strategy to establish or enhance competitive advantage, the goal should be to achieve a strong, sustainable advantage. Weak competitive advantages result in contestable positions, whether the scope of the advantage is narrow or broad.

For firms attempting a broad reach, moderate competitive advantages will allow the firm to participate in rivalry with other major firms but not establish clear-cut industry domination.

Niche firms with a moderate level of competitive advantage will be able to participate in one-off matches with other firms of comparable advantage. *It is only strong, sustainable competitive advantages that will lead to defensible niches or, for the firm with broad scope, industry domination.*

Competitive advantage can be established without developing core competencies, can be built on competencies, or can be achieved by creating an entirely new strategic initiative.

Independent of Core Competency

Some companies can gain strategic competitive advantage *without* developing core competencies, through legal control of monopolies such as patents or zoning; a market position resulting from a relationship with another firm (e.g., franchise or licensing agreement); or through an image inherited from years of market share dominance (e.g., strong historical brand identity).

Building on Existing Core Competencies

More commonly, and of much more importance to most firms, is utilizing existing core competencies to build strategic competitive advantage. Judging the sustainability of competitive advantages arising out of core competencies is not easy.

As previously noted, customer perceptions of what is expected from firms can change over time. Competitors also may improve their core competencies to the point where there is little differentiation between firms.

In today's highly competitive world it's generally a good idea to assume that most strategic advantages arising from existing core competencies will not be sustainable over extended periods of time unless they are redirected or combined with an entirely new strategic initiative.

As Michael Porter has observed, operational effectiveness is necessary but is not strategy. Porter argues that a firm can "outperform rivals only if it can establish a difference that it can preserve."

Establishing New Initiatives

Due to the time required to develop a competitive advantage, the rate of change in most industries, and corresponding competitor moves, it is often necessary to "leapfrog" the existing competitive environment. This may help the firm establish entirely new competitive space in which it is not only a leader but establishes most, if not all, of the standards by which all firms will be measured.

As previously noted, leapfrogging the competition requires a stretch in thinking about the future, not only in terms of customer preferences, but also of the firm's resources. In essence, new initiatives require the firm to say, "If we started from scratch, what would we do?" rather than be constrained by available resources.

IMPLEMENTATION

To be successfully implemented, a strategic plan must become an integral part of a firm's daily operations and culture. This is often the most difficult aspect of the strategic management process.

Institutionalization

Institutionalizing the plan—translating it into short-term action guidelines for all employees—is one of the most difficult challenges facing management. Not surprisingly, this is where many strategic plans fail.

The process of institutionalizing strategy requires the integration of a firm's structure, culture, leadership, and employee reward system. The seeds for success or failure may be sown in the planning process itself. A plan based on extensive senior management participation is more apt to receive the buy-in necessary for successful implementation.

Organizational Structure

Creating an organizational structure to support a strategic plan is a formidable problem. While firms may formulate a resourceful plan for their future, there is no single model for developing an organizational structure to successfully achieve the objectives of such plans. In many cases the plan is forced onto an existing organizational structure, which may or may not be appropriate.

For many years American business primarily relied on *functional* organizational structures. The functional structure stresses improving productivity by encouraging specialization by functions (e.g., marketing, production, financial reporting). This structure can pose significant problems, however, which become even more apparent in a highly competitive environment.

By focusing internally, the customer is given less attention, and numerous layers of costly middle management are created, increasing overhead and requiring higher levels of revenue to break even. It is also extremely difficult to establish responsibility for the success or failure of specific products or service lines.

As a result, over the years, several alternative organizational structures have emerged. The *matrix structure* delegates power to independent operating units, which then rely on centralized corporate facilities for functional support. Another approach is the *flat organization*, in which many middle management functions are eliminated. While this may reduce overhead and allow for more rapid decision making, information and communications are still largely centralized.

More recently, some firms have experimented with other forms of organization that are even less hierarchical in structure. Utilizing a *networked structure*, a firm is divided into units that operate independently of each other but within a framework consistent with broader corporate goals and objectives. Data and information are widely shared, largely through a telecommunication system linking all of the units to each other and to the corporate support group.

Unfortunately, the networked approach offers little opportunity to benefit from economies of scale and may lead to considerable duplication. It tends to work best in situations where local presence is critical and yet national information flow is needed to support local operations.

Figure 17-3 represents the networked and matrix organizational strategies.

With a *virtual organization*, the firm performs only its core competencies internally (perhaps just marketing), while outsourcing all other activities (potentially including all production activities). Similar to the networked firm, heavy reliance is placed on a state-of-the-art telecommunication system linking individual units.

The virtual organization also operates within an overall corporate strategic support structure, although there may be no formal corporate headquarters. This organizational structure is helpful in situations where being small aids in building customer intimacy but rapid access to other resources is required to perform larger tasks.

FIGURE 17-3

New Organizational Structures

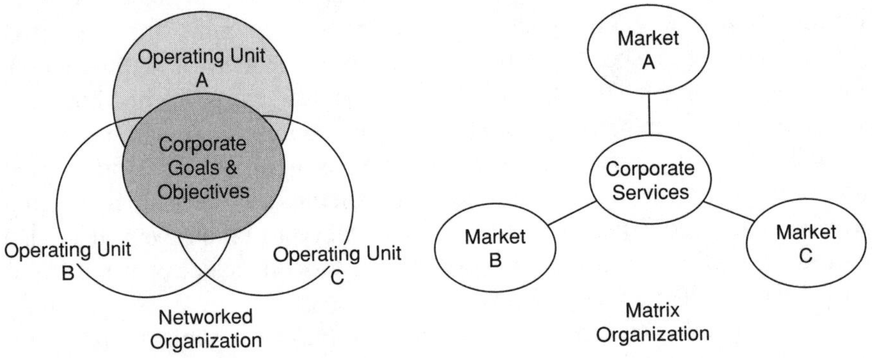

Source: McMahan Real Estate Services, LLC

Some firms are also linking together a series of *work teams*, each dedicated to developing and marketing one or more new products and services. Team members may be employees or external contractors.

The important thing is for team members to have the necessary complementary skills to bring new ideas to market or to determine that it is not feasible to do so. The life of any work team varies, depending upon the complexity of the task and the degree of market success.

The work team approach represents the most focused attack on aligning work skills and motivation with customer requirements. The bad news is that this approach may require periodic, often wrenching shifts in the organization and may be quite costly, as a result of resource duplication.

Each of these approaches to organizing the work effort has its advantages and drawbacks. Enterprises will have to experiment with various mixes and blends until the right combination is discovered—the one that works best for their markets, core competencies, and company culture.

The most important concern is that the organizational approach follows and is complementary with the strategic goals the firm has set. Any attempt to implement a new strategic initiative within an inappropriate structure is doomed to fail from the start.

Transition

A key element in making a final determination regarding strategic direction is the way in which the firm chooses to grow or "migrate" to its desired market position. Usually there are three choices: grow internally, consolidate with another firm, or partner with another firm.

Internal Growth

Most firms rely on internal resources to implement their strategic plan. This technique works well for firms that already have strong market share and significant resources.

The advantage of this approach is that it is less disruptive to the firm's internal organization, and as a result it may be more lasting as it is implemented. Disadvantages include the potential for the wrong person to be placed in a critical role, possible delays in implementation, and the possibility that insufficient organizational change will be achieved.

Consolidation

While getting bigger through consolidation is not an end in itself, mergers and acquisitions *do* have a place if they are well-thought-out and accomplish one or more key objectives of a broader strategic plan focused on attaining competitive advantage.

In fact, when the dust settles the merged firm may not be significantly larger than before, but better positioned to serve its customer base.

The objectives for consolidation may vary, depending upon the strategic plan. One goal may be to gain access to geographical markets not presently served. Another may be to add one or more product/service lines that will enhance the firm's value proposition with its existing customer base.

Still another objective may be to seek additional customers, spreading the same service/product mix over a larger base. In some cases consolidation may be undertaken to obtain or enhance a strong management team.

Of course, not all mergers are successful, particularly transactions involving weak firms. Without the resources to be an acquiring firm, the weak firm is truly adrift on the competitive seas. If it does nothing, it runs the risk of being scooped up by another firm and effectively dismantled for its remaining asset value.

Needless to say, not too many managers are interested in this outcome, so they often seek another weak firm as a merger partner, so that management prerogatives can be preserved, at least temporarily. Usually, the result is simply a larger weak firm, perhaps with more problems than the individual firms faced prior to the merger.

Strategic Alliance

Alliances between firms are gaining momentum, as firms seek to achieve strategic objectives without surrendering (or in some cases even sharing) operating control.

Partnering can take many forms. Firms may wish to expand into geographic markets or product/service lines where a single firm is dominant but doesn't wish to consolidate.

Two or more firms may wish to enter a new, uncharted market in which no one firm by itself has the resources required to succeed. Desiring to round out a product/service mix, a large firm might want to enter a highly specialized market where only small, "boutique" firms can operate successfully.

To be successful, such alliances must achieve an important strategic objective for both (or all) of the firms. In some cases the objectives may be different but complementary. It's important to clearly explain in writing the goals of both (or all) firms, and how the alliance will further these objectives.

The plan should also establish how the alliance will operate on a day-to-day basis, including a clear indication of management responsibilities and financial arrangements.

Although often underestimated, successful alliances require a lot of management involvement. It is generally a sound idea for each of the firms involved to dedicate (or hire) a senior manager to be responsible for the activities of the alliance. These individuals must be able to work well together if the alliance is to succeed.

Progress should be measured on a periodic basis, including benchmarking data similar to what management receives from their internal operations. Customer response to alliances may be negative and could require a change in direction or even termination.

It should be noted that a broad-based strategy might involve more than one implementation technique.

Monitoring

An ongoing *control and evaluation system* is important in order to assess the success of the repositioning effort and to establish a change in strategic direction, if required. *Milestone reviews* are established on the basis of time, critical events, or the use of a predetermined amount of resources.

Properly defined goals and performance measurement tools, such as the *balanced scorecard*, can keep management apprised of the strategy's success or failure on an ongoing basis.

Maintaining Flexibility

In an increasingly complex and rapidly changing business environment, it is critical that the strategic plan be continually reviewed to assess its continuing relevance.

A *premise control system* can be used to systematically determine if the premises on which a strategy is based are still valid. *Contingency plans* can be developed and activated if certain *trigger points* are reached (e.g., a competitor takes a predicted action).

During both planning and implementation, g*ame theory* can be useful in predicting the impact of certain changes on major premises, and in making changes to the strategy as new information (e.g., a competitor's response to your actions) becomes available.

SUMMARY

To summarize, operating effectiveness means having the requisite skills necessary to provide a successful value proposition to customers.

The successful firm's approach to providing value to customers and enhancing value over time is to develop and maintain a number of core competencies.

Each core competency represents a bundle of skills and technologies that transcend any one product or service, and in fact provide a platform for launching successful new products and services. Generally, the goal is to produce valued products and services as efficiently as possible.

In order to maintain and expand core competencies, successful companies continually benchmark their performance against that of the competition and perform to best practice levels for their industry.

In order to concentrate firm resources on establishing and maintaining core competencies, noncore activities should be eliminated or outsourced to others.

In today's highly competitive world, achieving operating effectiveness is equivalent to putting up the "table stakes" necessary to stay in the game. In fact, as more firms build core competencies, the competitive advantage enjoyed by early pioneers in an industry may largely evaporate.

To achieve the "winning hand" of long-term profitability, a firm must establish sustainable competitive advantage. This may be based on an extension and redirection of existing core competencies or created entirely from whole cloth, based on a reading of future trends and customer preferences.

Choosing among strategic alternatives requires an assessment of the assets and infrastructure required to implement the alternatives. It may involve trade-offs between objectives as well as pose substantial risk to the firm.

A key consideration in the ultimate success of any strategic plan is implementation. The first and often most critical implementation issue is the organizational structure that the firm will utilize, and its compatibility with the strategic plan.

Transition plans are also important, involving consideration of a variety of techniques, including internal growth, consolidation, and/or partnering with other firms.

Implementation must also involve some form of continual monitoring to determine the extent to which the repositioning effort is succeeding, and if it isn't, whether a change in direction would be desirable. Above all, the implementation process must be flexible and responsive to changes in major premises upon which the plan is based.

While by no means perfect, strategic planning may be the best (and perhaps only) approach to realizing a firm's growth objectives, and in some cases to ensuring its economic survival.

CHAPTER 18

Market Positioning

With strategic planning completed, a natural follow-on activity is working out a plan to position the firm in the marketplace in order to accomplish many of the goals of the strategic plan. This subject is addressed by reviewing a market positioning situation for a firm, disguised to avoid disclosing confidential material.

The firm in this situation is an investment advisor that is a highly regarded separate account manager for institutional investors with $8.7 billion currently under management. It order to diversify its client base and improve its competitive position, the firm wishes to sponsor a new enhanced-core equity fund in late 2006. The question facing the firm's management now is: "How to position this new fund in the marketplace?"

This market positioning process involves several basic steps: an identification of the target market, a detailed understanding of the competitive environment, formulation of a strategy for improving competitive position within this environment, establishing the features of the new fund, and development of a realistic program of implementation.

IDENTIFYING THE TARGET MARKET

Chapters 4 and 5 discussed the magnitude of institutional real estate investing and the investment strategies of its investors. In summarizing this material we can conclude that most institutional investors currently have a positive view of real estate. The largest segment in terms of real estate investment—pension plans—are aware of the lower volatility and diversification benefits of the asset class and also show an increasing preference for core and enhanced-core products.[1]

The only current factor constraining pension real estate investment appears to be the difficulty in increasing the target allocation to the asset class in light of strong opposition from other asset classes that would lose prospective capital (primarily those sponsoring financial security investments).

REFINING THE TARGET MARKET

The next task is to refine the target market to focus on the most probable type of pension funds that might invest in the new fund and what they are looking for in a fund sponsor.

In order to gain a better understanding of pension plan investment preferences,[2] a "blind" survey (sponsor not identified) was undertaken with the real estate officers of several pension plans that currently invest in real estate. Most of these funds could be considered candidates for investment in a fund similar to the proposed fund.

Based on this survey, the current attitudes of these investment officers can be summarized as follows:

Investment Vehicle

Most respondents indicated that both open- and closed-end commingled funds are acceptable vehicles for enhanced-core investing, with a very slight preference for closed-end funds. Overall, separate accounts were not popular vehicles for enhanced-core investments.

Size

Larger plans surveyed tended to prefer larger commingled funds so they can absorb a greater portion of their real estate allocation. Other reasons given were that "larger commingled funds offer broader diversification and enhancement at the portfolio management level," and "larger funds diversify risk and minimize fees."

---

1 An enhanced-core strategy, as defined in the glossary: "Core-quality properties with some type of problem that needs to be 'enhanced' before the properties can produce stabilized income at acceptable yield levels. This enhancement may take the form of redevelopment, retenanting, refinancing, or some other form of problem mitigation."

2 Although the proposed fund would appeal to other institutional investors, pension funds provide the major source of capital, and therefore were the focus of this survey.

For others, size didn't seem to matter: "Total fund capitalization doesn't matter, but I would feel more comfortable if other investors have shown an interest."

Pure Play

Respondents indicated a clear preference for "pure play" investment vehicles; that is, those that were either debt or equity but did not combine both. As one respondent put it, "Commingled funds should concentrate on either debt or equity."

Investment Risk

Most of the plans surveyed utilized enhanced-core investment strategies. The plans were asked what investment risks would be acceptable in order to get better-than-core investment returns. The answers, with all numerical responses rounded, were:

- 100 percent accepted some development risk
- 92 percent accepted some lease-up risk
- 74 percent accepted leverage (typically 50 to 65 percent Loan to Value, limited to 15 to 20 percent on entire portfolio)
- 75 percent accepted second-tier markets
- 50 percent accepted some geographical concentration

Of the risks listed, the two that are not commonly accepted in enhanced-core strategies are second-tier markets and geographic concentration. In practice, risk strategies are typically mitigated by limiting the percentage of total assets subject to these risks; for example, no more than 15 percent of a portfolio can include development projects.

Plans not currently considering enhanced-core strategies gave the following explanations:

- Risks of this nature are value-added rather than enhanced-core strategies.
- An investment strategy that includes building development cannot be considered "core."

Neither of these objections is correct in the commonly accepted definition of enhanced-core investing. This implies that an enhanced-core program may require further investor education regarding the risks and how they can be managed.

Preference Returns

A large majority of respondents would not require a preferred investment return as a condition of investing.

Quarterly Distributions

The majority of respondents indicated that quarterly cash distributions of income and sales proceeds would be required if they were to invest.

Withdrawals

Several respondents stated that they would require a withdrawal provision providing for liquidation of their interest in six to 12 months. One respondent mentioned the need for mechanisms to limit investor withdrawals in a poor real estate market.

Construction Financing

The majority of respondents would not invest in an enhanced-core fund that utilized construction financing provided by the fund. There appeared to be little objection to construction financing provided by third-party sources, as long as the assets of the fund were not at risk.

As one respondent put it, "Forward equity commitments are okay, but not through a construction loan program."

Joint Ventures

Half of the respondents chose joint ventures as a preferred way to undertake development projects. One respondent requires a 30-day notice for unwinding a joint venture agreement.

Manager Characteristics

Respondents considered the following investment manager characteristics as being desirable in their selection decision:

- Acceptable level of current assets under management
- Reputation
- Proven strategic vision
- Enhanced-core investment track record

- Firm growth and markets served
- Coinvestment by investment manager

The following characteristics were deemed less important:

- Full-service capability (okay to outsource)
- Current clients served
- Fees

Fees

As a general concept, most of the respondents believe that the investment manager should be reimbursed for ongoing costs, looking to the "back end" incentive fee to make its profit.

The respondents also stated that annual "all in" costs should be limited to 80 to 150 basis points (bps) of the value of the portfolio (excluding incentive fees).

If fees are to be disaggregated, they should be in the following ranges:

- Acquisition fees: 50 to 100 bps of property cost.
- Asset management fees: 50 to 150 bps of portfolio value.
- Disposition fees: 25 to 50 bps of sales proceeds.
- Incentive fees: Back-end incentive fees should be 15 to 20 percent of the disposition or liquidation proceeds, after a base or "hurdle" return to investors. These fees would result in disaggregated fees being in the lower portion of the ranges outlined above.

Seeking simplicity, one respondent said, "We will pay the industry standard for fees if our return requirement is met."

Governance

Generally, most of the respondents trust the manager to do the right thing. As one respondent put it, "A good manager will not put its investors in a conflicted position."

Most of the plans would not require an outside board of directors but would want to have an advisory board with investor participation. Those requiring an advisory board cited a desire to have a close interface with the fund's investment committee and the importance of monitoring potential conflicts.

If the manager fails to perform, the preferred removal feature would be 50 percent of the investors with "cause" and two-thirds if cause were not a factor.

COMPETITIVE ENVIRONMENT

The next step in the market positioning process is to better understand the competitive environment the fund will face in the marketplace. This is accomplished by developing a "competitive set" of firms that now offer similar products in the "enhanced core space" and are perceived to be attractive to institutional investors.

Developing the Competitive Set

Based on a review of the marketplace, the following criteria were selected in establishing the competitive set[3]:

- Open-end, commingled fund
- Core or enhanced-core investment strategy
- Equity real estate focus (not mortgages or "mixed")
- Over $1 billion in assets

Utilizing this sourcing approach, 10 competitive funds were selected for further examination. In order to retain confidentiality we will refer to them as Funds A-J.

General Fund Characteristics

The funds in this group are sponsored by eight investment managers with investment strategies targeted primarily to public and corporate pension plans; one marketing to union plans; and one fund with an investment strategy focusing on endowments and foundations.

All of the funds are open-end, commingled funds. Six are sponsored by insurance companies, two by banks, one by a public real estate firm, and one by a private real estate firm. Only one sponsor could be considered entrepreneurial.

The funds range in size from $325 million to $5.8 billion. The average number of investors per fund is 134. Most of the funds have been in existence for some time, several representing pioneering funds of the 1970s and 1980s.

---

3 Sources of data used in this selection process included annual reports; the National Council of Real Estate Investment Fiduciaries (NCREIF); Nelson's Directory of Institutional Real Estate; fund Web sites; and promotional material, news articles, and discussions with various pension real estate consultants.

Capital Activity

The average amount of capital raised by what we'll call the Competitive Set in 2004 was $470 million. This was offset by average fund withdrawals of $265 million and distributions of $44 million, resulting in an average net funds inflow of $161 million.[4]

Only three of the equity funds (A, F, and I) had cash distribution policies. In 2004 an average of $35 million was distributed by these funds to their investors, representing an average payout ratio of 18.4 percent of their operating income.

Investment Strategy

The only exclusively "core" fund is Fund B. All of the others assume some degree of additional risk to enhance investment returns and should be considered enhanced-core funds.

The most common form of enhancement is financial leverage, usually limited to 15–30 percent of the total portfolio. Many of the funds also take on development risk as a way to improve returns, usually through partnerships or joint ventures. Some of the funds utilize participating mortgage instruments as a quasi-equity form of investment.

Investment Returns

Figure 18-1 indicates the Competitive Set's investment returns as contrasted to NCREIF. The Competitive Set outperformed NCREIF slightly in 2004 and handily over longer time periods. Fund F had the best performance over the last three years, with Fund I the best in 2004 and over the last five years. Over 10 years, NCREIF had higher returns, largely due to the fact that many of the funds in the Competitive Set were still in formation and/or raising investment capital.

Portfolio Diversification

Figure 18-2 illustrates the portfolio diversification of the Competitive Set and NCREIF by property type, and Figure 18-3 by geographical area.

Note that the Competitive Set is overweighted in Industrial and Office, and underweighted in Retail and Apartments, two of the best performers over the last five years. Geographically, both the Competitive Set and NCREIF are heavily weighted toward the western United States.

---

4 It should be noted that some of the funds were not being actively marketed.

FIGURE 18-1

Investment Returns

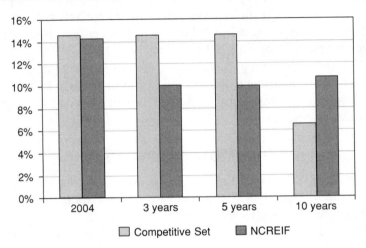

Source: NCREIF

FIGURE 18-2

Assets by Property Type

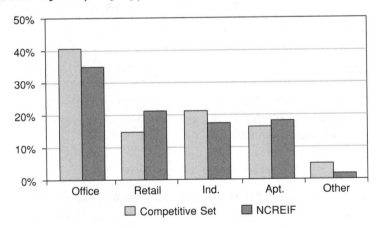

Source: NCREIF

Individual Funds

Some of the Competitive Set funds seek to enhance returns by actively managing the mix of assets in their portfolios, largely based on ongoing research concerning market trends.

FIGURE 18-3

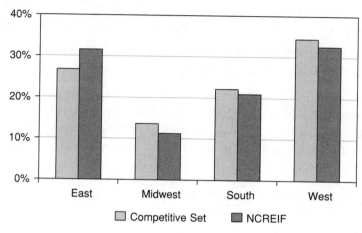

Assets by Geographical Area, 2004

Source: NCREIF

In recent years this approach has tended to overweight portfolios toward industrial and apartment investments located in the East and West regions. As an example, Fund C has 37 percent of its portfolio in industrial properties versus 21.5 percent for NCREIF, and 47.0 percent of its assets in the West versus 36.6 percent for NCREIF. Fund E has similar overweighting in Industrial, but has focused on the South rather than the West. Other examples: Fund H is overweighted in Office, Fund I in Apartments, and Fund D in Retail.

This approach has achieved mixed results. Funds E, C, and H have employed such a strategy, but are at the lower end of Competitive Set performance. On the other hand, one of the top investment return performers, Fund F, attributes a large part of its solid investment success in recent years to actively managing the mix of assets in its portfolio.

Fees

Annual management fees for the Competitive Set managers generally fall into one of three categories:

Fixed Asset Management Fee

A fixed percentage of the value of the portfolio, charged annually and paid quarterly. Generally, an "all-in" fee structure is one in which the manager is expected to recover all costs within a single fee.

In the Competitive Set, this fee ranges from 100 to 120 bps, with no distinction paid to the amount of funds a plan invests. Managers that utilize this approach include:

Fund A   Annual fee: 100 bps
Fund E   Annual fee: 120 bps
Fund G   Annual fee: 100 bps

Management Fee Scaled to Plan Investment

This approach utilizes a fixed percentage of funds invested, but scaled depending upon the amount of money each plan has invested. Funds that utilize this approach include:

Fund	Minimum	Maximum
Fund D	80 bps	115 bps
Fund F	130 bps	180 bps
Fund H	80 bps	125 bps
Fund I	75 bps	100 bps

Management Fee Scaled to Size of Fund

This approach reduces the amount of the management fee, based on the overall size of the fund. Each plan shares in any reduced fees. Only Fund C uses this approach.

	Fund Size	Management Fees
Fund C	First $1B	125 bps
	Next $1B	100 bps
	Over $2B	75 bps

Incentive Fees

Only two of the equity funds utilize incentive fees. Fund F charges an annual fee based on a percentage of the operating cash flow generated. This fee is scaled with the first $100 million of operating cash flow in an investor's account earning the sponsor a 6 percent fee, the next $50 million a 5 percent fee, and 3.5 percent in excess of $150 million.

Fund I has an incentive fee tied to a minimum annual real return. A fee of 7.5 bps is charged for every 100 bps of return over a 5 percent real return. The same fee is deducted from the fixed fee if the sponsor fails to achieve the target return.

Risk versus Return Comparison

Figure 18-4 compares risk and return for the Competitive Set. Return is measured by five-year annualized returns; risk by the standard deviation of returns over the time period.

Of the top three performers, Fund I dominates the five-year return numbers and delivers the returns with a median level of risk. Funds H and C deliver risk-adjusted returns most comparable to the NCREIF Index. Fund A provides above-medium returns with a lower risk profile.

BATTLEFIELD MAPPING

Selected pension real estate staff and consultants were asked to rank the Competitive Set sponsors, based on the following criteria:

- Performance
- Marketing success
- Historical investment program record/reputation
- Investment strategy
- Structure/terms
- Capabilities
- Volume

FIGURE 18-4

Risk vs. Return Comparison, 2000–2004

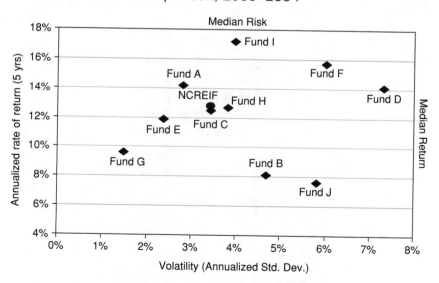

A key question was: "Do strong management capabilities and resources correlate to superior performance?" In order to answer this question, each respondent was asked to rate the fund sponsors on the basis of:

- Superior leadership at executive levels
- Superior acquisition staff and processes
- Superior due diligence function
- Superior research and analytical staff
- Proactive, experienced, and successful portfolio and asset managers
- State-of-the art information systems, models, and technology
- Incentives to recruit and motivate key personnel

The results of these interviews were then plotted to see if they could be good proxies for future performance (Figure 18-5).

Note that the correlations tend toward the mean, suggesting there is a high correlation from strong to weak for most of the criteria (those perceived as strong performers were generally perceived to be strong in marketing, strategy, etc.). Although scientific techniques were not utilized, the results do measure a degree of market perception.

Note that Funds F and I were rated high in virtually every criterion and the reality/perception among the respondents is that they are consis-

FIGURE   18-5

Battlefield Map

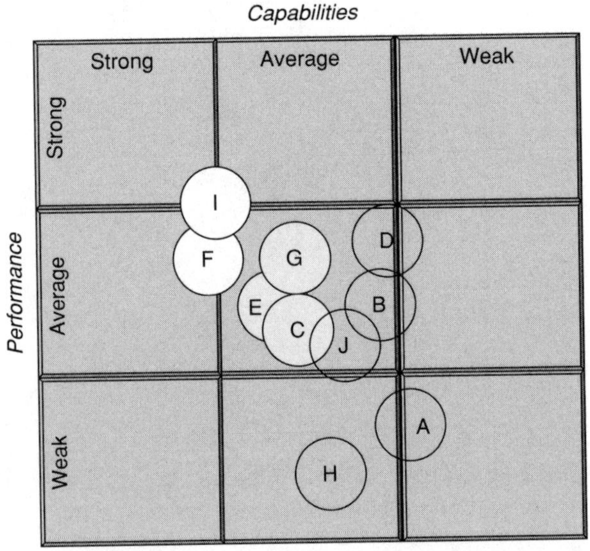

tently strong performers. Funds C, E, and G were also rated highly, although clearly in a secondary position to F and I.

PROPOSED FUND FEATURES

Figure 18-6 outlines the features of the proposed fund, based on research into the pension fund market and the Competitive Set. Comments on the logic behind each feature follow.

FIGURE 18-6

Proposed Features for Enhanced Core Fund (Draft)

Investment Strategy	Enhanced core investments
Fund Vehicle	Open-end fund
Size (maximum)	$350 million
Investment Focus	Equity or quasiequity investments
Property Types	Office, Retail, Industrial, Multifamily
Targeted Geographical Areas	National; focus on rapidly growing metro areas in the Western and Eastern regions
Risk Exposure	Property development; rehabilitation; lease-up
Cash Distributions	Quarterly
Participant Withdrawals	Paid within 12 months
Financing	Third party only; cannot exceed 20% of total portfolio
Joint Ventures	Only with experienced, financially strong developers; Not to exceed 25% of portfolio
Management Fees	1.2% of assets under management; paid annually
Incentive Fees	20% of appreciation in value after 12.0% annual return to investors; paid upon property sale
Advisory Board	Composed of six investor and two sponsor representatives

Investment strategy. Enhanced core was the original targeted strategy. The logic of this was supported by the research and surveys.

Fund vehicle. The survey of pension funds indicates a slight preference for closed-end funds; however, all of the Competitive Set funds are open-end and this will be the most likely comparison.

Size (maximum). Several of the pension funds surveyed indicated an interest in larger funds. The Competitive Set funds range from $325 million to $1.8 billion. Since this investment manager has, to date, been exclusively a separate account manager, it would be wise to keep the fund size small enough so it can be rapidly sold to create investor momentum. The size can be expanded later or a new fund created if there is sufficient market demand.

Investment focus. The pension funds surveyed were adamant they didn't want equity and debt in the same fund.

Property types. The proposed fund will be large enough so there is no reason to focus on any one property type. By having a broad charter, the mix of property types can be fine-tuned to the market on a somewhat opportunistic basis.

Targeted geographical areas. Again, the recommendation is to keep a broad charter but letting prospective investors know that areas popular with other pension funds will be the primary focus. Also, it's probably best to stay out of second-tier markets where it may be difficult to dispose of a property in a poor real estate market.

Risk exposure. The fund survey indicates broad support for accepting most revenue-enhancing activities, including property development and lease-up risks.

Cash distributions. Quarterly cash distributions will help differentiate the fund from most existing funds and make it competitive with Fund I, the strongest competitor.

Participant withdrawals. Twelve months is standard.

Financing. In light of the fact it will be an open-end fund with regular cash distributions, it's important to make it clear that the fund will only use third-party financing, including construction loans.

Joint ventures. Important to keep the door open, but limit the total exposure to 25 percent of the portfolio.

Management fees. From a simplicity viewpoint, an all-in fee is probably a good idea. The problem, however, is that some properties require more asset management attention than others, so there are some risks involved. The 1.2 percent of assets is pretty much in line with the competitive set, although Fund I has a sliding scale fee structure based on the amount of invested funds.

Incentive fees. Fund I also has a very competitive approach to the incentive fee. The major disadvantage to this approach, however, is that investment performance may not be realized until a property is sold or the participant withdraws from the fund, in which case it would be based on an appraisal.

A LEARNING PROCESS

It should be noted that the fund business is somewhat of a learning process in which an investment manager learns lessons from each fund that can be carried over to the next fund.

Unfortunately, it is a much more public process than separate account investing, so it's important to get as much right in the first fund, if possible. This is why research in advance of entering the public arena can often pay large dividends.

CHAPTER 19

Risk Management

Modern Portfolio Theory (MPT) distinguishes between systematic and unsystematic risk. Systematic risk represents overall market risk that cannot be diversified away; unsystematic risk refers to asset class and specific asset risks that can be reduced through portfolio diversification.

This chapter focuses on diversification of risk in a mixed asset portfolio and within the real estate portfolio itself. It concludes with a discussion on managing risks at the enterprise level.

MANAGING RISK IN A MIXED ASSET PORTFOLIO

Risk management of mixed asset investment portfolios is largely in the hands of institutional investors, their staffs, and outside consultants.

Most institutional investors fund future fiduciary liabilities (such as retirement benefits, annuity payments, etc.) through the earnings from investments in a portfolio of mixed assets usually consisting of bonds, stocks, and, increasingly, real estate.

The upside objective is to produce investment returns so a given asset portfolio can (1) fund escalating liability payments and/or (2) require a smaller asset base to fund the same level of payments.

Figure 19-1 illustrates the returns provided by the three major asset classes over the last seven years.

As noted in Chapter 5, another upside portfolio investment objective has emerged in the last few years, namely, the ability of an asset class to fund liability payments out of asset earnings and still continue to grow in

FIGURE 19-1

Mixed Asset Returns

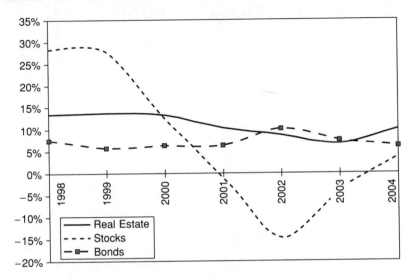

Source: NCREIF, S&P 500, Lehman Brothers Aggregate Bond Index

value.[1] This investment objective has increased interest in stocks paying dividends and/or real estate with reasonably dependable cash flows.

The downside objective of a mixed asset portfolio is to diversify portfolio risk by not relying excessively on a single asset class or individual assets within that class.

Fundamentally, this requires a determination of the level of "risk adjusted" investment returns that can be generated by varying the mix of assets in a portfolio.

Investment return therefore is usually measured by considering the risk of the asset class and how it interacts with other asset classes in the portfolio. Statistically, risk is measured by the historic standard deviation of the asset class.

This determination ultimately affects the amount of funds allocated to each asset class, the size of individual portfolios, and, to some extent, the level of risk diversification of individual assets within the asset class.

---

1 Bonds have historically provided a cash flow function, through dividends, but do not necessarily grow in value over time.

Role of Real Estate in a Mixed Asset Portfolio

Since the mid-1980s academicians and others have studied the impact of including real estate in a mixed asset portfolio.[2] Most of these studies have focused on the inverse relationship between real estate and financial assets and concluded that the inclusion of real estate can improve overall portfolio risk adjusted returns. These studies were a major factor in the entry and expansion of institutional investment in real estate. Today, most academicians and consultants recommend diversifying mixed asset portfolios that include real estate.

Figure 19-2 provides some common sense support for the academic studies reflecting the relationship between the investment returns of equities and real estate over a 30-year period. The figure represents the relationship between real estate and equity returns in years of negative equity returns.

While not statistically rigorous, this figure does provide a good indication of the general inverse relationship between these two major asset classes. Today, most researchers accept the proposition that real estate appears to be a good diversifier in a mixed asset portfolio.

FIGURE 19-2

Relationship Between Real Estate and Equity Returns

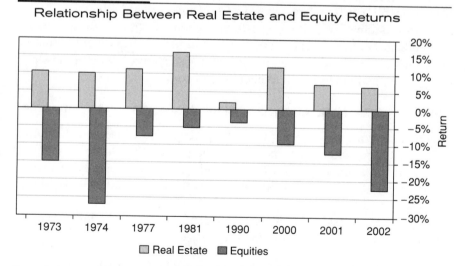

Source: Southern Company Master Retirement Trust; data for 1978–2002 based on S&P 500 and the NCREIF Property Index; data prior to 1978 based on Russell Open End Fund Universe

2 The pioneering effort was Hartzell, Hekman, and Miles (1986).

Investors' Perceptions

Acceptance by researchers does not mean necessarily that all investment professionals have come to the same conclusion. As we've noted several times, one of the major problems institutional real estate professionals face is the resistance on the part of many pension investors to increasing the allocation to the asset class.

In late 2004, PREA sponsored an interesting survey of institutional investors regarding their perception of risk and return for real estate as compared to other investments, particularly stocks and bonds. The study was conducted by Ravi Dhar and William N. Goetzmann, of the Yale School of Management, and published in May 2005.

The interview universe was made up of 202 investment officers for major institutional investors. Corporate pension plans were the largest in number, with 83; public plans the largest in terms of assets, with more than $1 trillion. Union pension plans, endowments, and foundations made up the remaining participants.

In terms of respondent experience with real estate, the sample was somewhat bimodal between those institutions with less than two years of experience and those with 11 or more years.[3]

Over half of the individuals responding to the survey had "a leading or at least a significant decision-making role in asset allocation policy." Twenty-two identified themselves as Chief Investment Officers.

Responding to written questions on an electronic questionnaire, respondents compared real estate returns and risks to five other alternative investments: fixed income, equity investments (stocks), hedge funds, private equity, and emerging markets (foreign countries).[4]

Perceptions of Comparable Investment Returns

Figure 19-3 considers the respondent's perception of investment returns, eliminating answers from respondents who replied they "didn't know," as well as those commenting on hedge funds, since the diversity of investment strategies associated with this investment alternative make direct comparisons difficult.

Note that considerably more respondents indicated a belief that equity investments had a higher return than real estate.

Perceptions of Comparable Risks

Figure 19-4 is a tabulation of responses to the risk portion of the survey. Most institutional real estate investors perceive real estate risk as

---

3 Of those participating in the survey, 60 institutions did not currently invest in real estate.
4 The participants responded to written questions on an electronic questionnaire.

FIGURE 19-3

Pension Investor Perceptions of Real Estate Return*

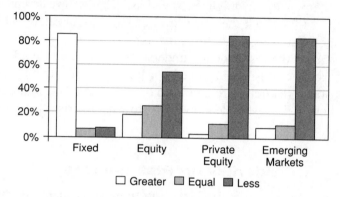

*Only those respondents expressing opinions; excludes hedge funds

Source: Ravi Dhar and William N. Goetzmann, Yale School of Management; Pension Real Estate Association; May 2005

FIGURE 19-4

Pension Investor Perceptions of Real Estate Risk*

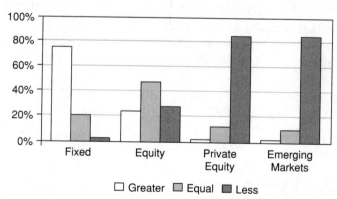

*Only those respondents expressing opinions; excludes hedge funds

Source: Ravi Dhar and William N. Goetzmann, Yale School of Management; Pension Real Estate Association; May 2005

considerably greater than fixed income and less than (or equal to) equity investments, but significantly less than private equity or emerging markets in foreign countries, two areas of recently popular investment strategies.

This contrasts to their views of comparable returns risks (Figure 19-5), in which equity returns were perceived to be greater than real estate.[5] Loosely interpreted, this might be stated as: "Equity investments produce higher returns for about the same level of risk as real estate, so why not allocate more funds to equity investments?"

Assuming the respondents' understanding of equity markets is reasonably accurate, this could indicate a lack of understanding regarding the comparable risk/return relationship of real estate. This requires a more detailed look at the respondents' view as to what the risks associated with real estate truly are.

Identifying Risk Factors

As can be seen in Figure 19-5, the top three risks identified by survey respondents—liquidity, lack of reliable data, and the risk of making a poor investment—indicate a possible lack of confidence in the underlying data associated with real estate.

The underlying assumption is that if real estate were a liquid investment similar to stocks or bonds, you should be able to get out of a "poor" investment.

The lack of faith in real estate data also reflects the fact that the asset class is less fungible (than financial assets) and that most real estate assets (except REITs) do not trade on a daily basis.

Figure 19-6 outlines the major risk factors that have influenced respondents' asset class allocation decisions. The first four responses also

FIGURE 19-5

Major Risk Factors Associated with Real Estate

- Liquidity risk
- Lack of reliable valuation data
- Risk of making a poor investment
- Macroeconomic uncertainty
- Hard to determine the best opportunities
- Risk of a crash (tie); risk of poor professional advice (tie)
- Asset volatility
- Legal and regulatory risk; moral hazard/operational risk; other (tie)

Source: Ravi Dhar and William N. Goetzmann, Yale School of Management; Pension Real Estate Association; May 2005.

FIGURE 19-6

Major Risk Factors Influencing Real Estate Allocation Decision

- Statistical estimates of risk and return; long-term historical performance (tie)
- Advice from external consultant
- Relative skill of external manager with this asset class
- Current market values of asset
- Recent trends in the market; expected changes in the economic outlook (tie)
- Economic forecasts; other (tie)
- Advice from internal staff
- Advice taken by industry peers; advice from other investors (tie)

Source: Ravi Dhar and William N. Goetzmann, Yale School of Management; Pension Real Estate Association; May 2005.

reflect a lack of confidence in the data underlying the asset allocation utilized in a Modern Portfolio Theory model.

Investment Strategies

Figure 19-7 illustrates the real estate investment strategies employed by the respondents. Commingled funds are the major investment vehicle utilized by the respondents, followed by partnerships, REITs, separate accounts, and solo investments in which the respondent is the only investor.

This figure reflects an investment spectrum that is consistent with respondents' apparent perception of the risks associated with real estate. This is characterized by a strong preference for liquidity and, apparently, some distrust of the data underlying the asset allocation process.

Survey Summary

The survey's general findings can be summarized as follows:

- The key factors utilized by institutional investors in allocating capital to potential investments are statistical estimates of risk and return, advice from external consultants, and long-term historical performance.

- Illiquidity and a lack of reliable data were the two major risks associated with investing in real estate. Respondents also mentioned the risk of "poor management," but this is not necessarily specific to the asset class.

FIGURE 19-7

Respondents Real Estate Investment Strategies*

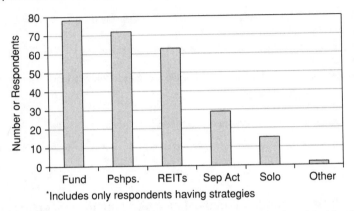

*Includes only respondents having strategies

Source: Ravi Dhar and William N. Goetzmann, Yale School of Management; Pension Real Estate Association; May 2005.

- Real estate's expected investment risk is perceived as greater than fixed income but less than or equal to equities.
- Investor experience in handling real estate risk-and-return data is much higher than other alternative investments such as private equity or emerging markets.
- There is a strong relationship between confidence in the ability to extrapolate investment risk-and-return numbers and the amount of investment capital the respondent is willing to target for real estate. Less confidence generally means less capital for real estate.
- Respondents who have invested in real estate in the past are more confident in extrapolating past return data than those who have not.

A major conclusion appears to be that some of the respondents' reluctance to invest in real estate was largely based on lack of confidence in the underlying data regarding the risk and return of the asset class.

As the authors point out in their paper, some of those participating in the study may be more concerned with the uncertainty of the data going into the investment model than in the results of the modeling itself,[5] or, in the vernacular, "garbage in—garbage out."

If greater confidence can be established in real estate data, it could result in a better understanding of how it compares to other asset classes;

---

5 Modern Portfolio Theory (MPT) can handle definable risk but has difficulty in dealing with users' lack of confidence in the quality of the data inputs.

and if perceptions are positive, it might mean more institutional money going into the asset class.

Role of REITs

In response to the concerns of the respondents, there is recent evidence that REITs may play an important role in providing liquidity as well as enhancing the returns of multiasset investment portfolios.

In a 2004 study, Stephen Lee and Simon Stevenson looked at the role of REITs in a mixed asset portfolio over both the short and long run and concluded:

> REITs effectively sit between the broad equity and fixed income sectors, with both risk and return measures in between stocks and bonds. This enables REITs to appear return enhancing to bonds, without the same degree of increased risk that would be seen with stocks, and also risk reducing to stocks.
>
> In the case of stocks, they provide diversification benefits due to their relative low risk measures and correlation coefficients, without the same level of return sacrifice that would occur if funds were switched into the fixed income market.[6]

MANAGING REAL ESTATE PORTFOLIO RISKS

Once the allocation decision has been made concerning asset classes, the next concern is how to properly diversify the investment portfolio to obtain the greatest amount of unsystematic risk reduction and/or investment return enhancement *within* the asset class; in this case, real estate.

Generally, managing these risks is the responsibility of real estate investment managers selected by institutional investors to make and manage their real estate investments.[7]

Criteria often utilized for portfolio diversification include geographical location, property type, tenants, lease terms, and investment vehicles selected to hold the investments.

Location

In the early years of institutional real estate investment, it was expected that portfolios would be reasonably balanced between eastern, southern,

---

6 Stephen Lee and Simon Stevenson, *Journal of Real Estate Portfolio Management,* vol. 11, no. 1, 2005, 55–67.

7 Pension real estate consultants also can play an important role in portfolio risk diversification, largely by measuring the degree of risk exposure in an investor's portfolio.

northern, and western regions. Academic studies in the early 1980s evaluated regional diversification strategies, however, and concluded that they were largely ineffective.[8]

Subsequent studies found that narrowing the definitions of geography to more clearly defined regions and metro areas helped somewhat, but the results were also somewhat marginal.[9]

In 1988 this approach was refined to focus on metro areas categorized by dominant industry and rate of employment growth.[10] This concept was tested further in 1992 and found to be more accurate than naive geographical diversification.[11] Most institutional investors today now measure portfolio diversification by metro areas rather than geographic regions.

As noted in Chapter 1, many investors have focused on distinguishing between the way in which metro area governments manage land use regulation powers to influence real estate values and, indirectly, the attraction or lack of attraction of their metro area to real estate investors.[12]

We termed these "commodity" and "constrained" markets, noting that the top 10 metro areas now targeted by pension funds all have "constrained" urban growth policies.

Figure 19-8 illustrates the risk and return characteristics for office building investments in major metro areas over the last 10 years. The bolded metro areas represent those on the preference lists of institutional investors as of 2005, all of which are supply-constrained markets.

Property Type

Balancing and rebalancing portfolios by varying mixes of office, retail, industrial, and apartment assets is often used as a method to reduce risks inherent in cyclical swings, technological change, consumer shopping trends, and lifestyle preferences.

As noted in Chapter 3, the annual investment returns from apartment and retail properties in pension fund portfolios over the last 20 years have tended to be less volatile and generally somewhat higher than office and industrial returns. The margin would not appear sufficient, however, to argue for a concentration in these property types alone.

---

8 Miles and McCue (1982, 1984), Hertzell (1986).
9 Corgel and Gay (1987); Hartzell, Shulman, and Wurtzbach (1987); Shulman and Hopkins (1988); Gilberto and Hopkins (1990); Malizia and Simons (1991).
10 Wurtzbach, 1988.
11 Mueller and Ziering (1992), Mueller (1993).
12 Johnson/Souza Group, 2005.

FIGURE 19-8

Metro Area Risk Matrix* for Office Buildings, 1996–2005

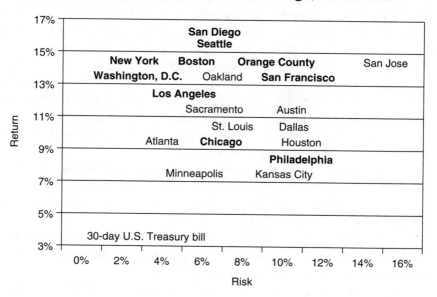

* Approximate position.
Source: NCREIF Federal Reserve. Based on an article by Mark Roberts, published in the PREA Quarterly, Fall 2005.

Instead, it argues for a balanced approach to property type selection, in an effort to maintain participation in both the household and business segments of the rapidly changing U.S. economy. Some observers would argue for retail and residential uses being at least half of investment portfolios.

Perhaps more important is the necessity to stay on top of structural changes in the economy that over time may have a considerable influence on real estate portfolio returns.

As an example, there are major demographic and technology changes occurring in the workplace (as noted in Chapter 2) that are now influencing the location and use of office and industrial properties. We also noted, as a result of many of these changes, the increasing use of industrial buildings for office purposes.

Both of these trends require investor attention to the response of both office and industrial properties to these fundamental trends. This may affect which type of future acquisitions to pursue and the decision as to which properties in the portfolio to put up for disposition.

Tenants

As noted in Chapter 2, real estate investments are, in reality, conduits for cash flows produced by businesses and households, which take the form of payments for building space and, increasingly, services. The level of these cash flows (after deducting operating expenses), when compared to the value of the investment, ultimately represents the level of periodic investment return.

In Chapter 8 we covered the importance of the tenant interview in the due diligence process in better understanding the tenant's business, financial condition (including their credit standing), and attitude toward the building and the space they occupy.[13]

In portfolios involving shopping centers and large multitenant office buildings, a certain amount of risk diversification can be undertaken at the property level, but it is difficult, if not impossible, with smaller buildings or those occupied by a single tenant.

At the portfolio level, however, a great deal of risk diversification can be accomplished through risk management, even in portfolios comprised entirely of single tenant buildings.

We noted earlier the importance of determining the "linkage" between tenants in terms of dependence upon a single firm or industry. This is even more critical at the portfolio level, since properties may be located in several metro areas and the linkage may be harder to trace.

A first step is to inventory all leases in all investment portfolios by tenant in order to establish the risk exposure posed by a tenant getting into financial difficulty or perhaps even declaring bankruptcy. Care should be taken to identify subsidiaries as well, since they may be influenced by adverse events at the parent company.

Tenants should be identified who, in the judgment of the asset management, comprise a "significant potential risk" to an investor's portfolio or to the investment manager's continuing operation. This decision should be confirmed by the Investment Committee.

A special credit and financial "watch" should be placed on this tenant, updated annually, and distributed to all asset managers and members of the transaction team (since it may influence future acquisitions). This watch should be established even if the tenant reportedly has a strong credit rating and is acknowledged to be in "good financial condition."

---

13 There is a corollary in apartment buildings, but with greater emphasis on the tenant's attitude toward the building, since they can move more readily. Unless this is accomplished, an asset manager may not find out until it is too late that the reason a desirable tenant left could have been easily remedied.

The issue is not the financial condition of the tenant, but rather the dependence of investors (and the investment manager) on the fate of a particular firm.

The goal is (1) for management to be forewarned of possible adverse events that could significantly impact one or more investor portfolios, and (2) not to compound the risk by continuing to concentrate investments in this particular risk exposure.

If the tenant's situation worsens, the watch should be moved to quarterly or even monthly, as necessary. The goal should be to reduce, over time, the dependency of investors and the investment management firm on this particular tenant.

If the tenant's situation improves or the impact of adverse events is reduced due to portfolio growth, the watch can be reduced in frequency and, over time, perhaps eliminated.

A second step is to establish linkages between this tenant and other tenants who are dependent upon the same set of factors for their operating success (customer base, type of technology, natural resource, etc.). As with the individual tenant, the goal is to have advance warning of events that might pose a major threat to the economic health of the portfolio.

Lease Terms

This is an area of concern at both the portfolio and individual property level. The most important objective is to stagger lease terms to avoid having a large percentage of leases turning over in the same year or in a combination of subsequent years.

The first step is to assemble lease information at the property level and then roll it up into the portfolio level. Key subjects include rental rates, lease beginning and ending dates, renewal options, and any other aspect of the lease that represents a potential risk to the portfolio. In the case of newly acquired assets, most of this information is available in the due diligence materials.

To the greatest extent possible, this information should be translated into positive and negative impacts on the cash flow of the property, the owning investor's portfolio, and the investment manager's internal financial projections. The time period is annual, through the anticipated holding period, which is generally 10 years.

This type of analysis should demonstrate key periods when investor portfolios will be under greater financial pressure, knowledge that can be utilized by the investment manager in anticipating talent and cost "pressure points" out beyond the current year. This information can be helpful in allocating resources, counseling investors, and planning preventive actions.

In soft markets, preventive actions may involve lowering current rental rates or making other concessions for tenants in exchange for longer lease terms ("blend and extend" arrangements). The goal is to continue to strive to reduce annual concentrations of lease turns as well as to retain desirable tenants.

Investment Vehicle

REITs provide several benefits for a real estate investment portfolio, particularly those that are relatively small or in the early stages of development. There are several reasons for this.

First, REITs generally focus on specific property types and geographical areas, making it possible to diversify a portfolio in the early stages of investment activity. With certain property types, such as regional shopping centers, REITs may be the only way to participate in investment opportunities.

Second, REITs can be sold quickly in order to exit investment positions that are perceived not to have future potential. They also can provide an exit alternative in case of a general real estate market downturn.

In addition, well-capitalized REITs have a diversified financial base, providing access to a wide arsenal of financial tools to pursue corporate growth strategies, specific investment opportunities, competitive threats, and the general state of local real estate markets.

Several public REITs also present an opportunity to participate in foreign real estate markets, which otherwise often pose significant obstacles to direct investing.

Further, since REIT portfolios and management teams are largely integrated, the case is often made (usually by REITs) that they attract and retain a higher quality of professional real estate manager.

And finally, commingled real estate funds and partnerships may also provide a risk-diversifying benefit for institutions desiring to participate in potentially volatile investments such as real estate, which are located in foreign countries.

MANAGING REAL ESTATE ENTERPRISE RISKS

Enterprise Risk Management (ERM) is a relatively new management concept involving a systematic look at all aspects and levels of an organization's operation in an attempt to identify and analyze risks (upside and downside) that it faces in its attempts to realize its strategic and financial objectives.[14]

ERM is comprehensive, requiring the identification of risks at all levels in the organization, from field managers to the CEO and the board. The risks identified include those associated with operations, financial, strategic, compliance, and the firm's culture and reputation.

The application of ERM has been accelerated by the Sarbanes-Oxley Act (Section 404), which requires a public corporation to annually prepare an internal control report. The accounting firm conducting the annual audit must also attest to the effectiveness of the company's internal control system.

Not that the process is easy; firms often find it difficult to gather information and measure the extent of enterprise risks, often because management and employees are unwilling to recognize that risks exist or that they are of a significant magnitude to merit concern. In some cases, identification of risks threatens a specific job or function within the organization.

There are also concerns about the management response to risks identified. How are they managed? Who will be responsible? What is the impact on the organization? On individual jobs?

Application to Real Estate

Corporate real estate managers have been in the vanguard of introducing ERM to real estate, largely because real estate occupancy costs are the second largest expense on a company's income statement and often an important item on the balance sheet as well.

Real estate issues important to corporate real estate mangers include:

- Highest and best use of owned properties
- Environmental issues
- Security issues
- Code compliance (for example, ADA)
- Property transactions (acquisitions and dispositions)
- International operations and ways in which they differ from the United States

---

14 ERM emerged as a result of a meeting held by the Committee of Sponsoring Organizations of the Treadway Commission (COSO). The commission was established to help American businesses cope with multiple enterprise risks following the terrorist acts of September 11, 2001.

- Accounting treatments
- Disclosures to shareholders

Another aspect of ERM is the determination of which risks to hold internally and which to "sell" to others (e.g., insurance). Because ERM involves both insurable and uninsurable risks, it requires collaboration between many disciplines within the organization.

It is only a matter of time before ERM spreads to real estate investment companies as well.

CHAPTER 20

Governance

The scandalous behavior of many of America's best-known companies has led to a series of reforms that directly impact public real estate companies such as REITs and indirectly impact virtually all other real estate businesses.

This final chapter reviews the governance reforms brought about by the collapse of Enron and other large firms rife with abuse, as well as the reaction of board members of public companies (including real estate) to the reform process three years after the major reform legislation was passed and implemented.

COLLAPSE OF ENRON

In 2000, Enron was the fifth largest company in the United States, hired the "best and brightest," possessed the most advanced technology, and operated in a state-of-the-art complex in Houston, Texas. What's more, Enron considered itself a model of modern management, a symbol of the "new economy firm" in which "virtual" assets (technology and people) were more important than hard assets in creating shareholder value.

In late December 2000, Enron was named one of the "100 Best Companies to Work for in America" by *Fortune* magazine, improving to number 22 from number 24 the prior year. Enron was the highest ranking global energy company on the *Fortune* list.

In reality, as events would subsequently reveal, Enron was a giant "Ponzi scheme," inflating revenue and profits, which increased the company's stock price, with lucrative executive bonuses tied to this inflated value.

This was accomplished by structuring off-balance-sheet, noneco-nomic energy deals arranged with partnerships and Special Purpose Entities (SPEs). Projected revenues were then discounted, and the resultant present value recognized in the current period, utilizing the "mark-to-market" method of accounting.

The increased capitalized value allowed Enron to maintain invest-ment grade credit and continue borrowing from its banks, which received above average interest payments (6.5 to 7.0 percent).

Figure 20-1 indicates the discrepancies between what was reported publicly and what was actually going on.

Unfortunately, Enron was only the tip of the iceberg, with several large firms involved in similar if less spectacular abuses. These included WorldCom, Global Crossing, Adelphia Communications, Tyco, HealthSouth Corporation, and Gemstar-TV Guide International Group Ltd.

During 2001, as the truth about Enron was finally understood, Enron's stock price collapsed (Figure 20-2).

Where Were the Gatekeepers?

A question many raised following the collapse of Enron was, "Where were the gatekeepers?" Where were those individuals and firms who were expected to keep this from happening to a major American public com-pany? The gatekeepers and their roles in the Enron disaster included:

Auditors. Arthur Andersen was alleged to have shredded docu-ments in violation of the law, and the resulting criminal indictment led to the rapid demise of one of America's oldest accounting firms.

Lawyers. The lawyers representing Enron were alleged to have responded inadequately to evidence that management may have been engaged in fraudulent conduct.

FIGURE 20-1

Enron by the Numbers

Year	Reported Income	Revised Income	True Debt	True Equity
1997	$105M	$77M	Up $771M	Down $258M
1998	733M	600M	Up 561M	Down 391M
1999	893M	645M	Up 685M	Down 710M
2000	979M	880M	Up 628M	Down 754M

Source: Enron/Powers Special Report

FIGURE 20-2

Enron's Stock Market Collapse

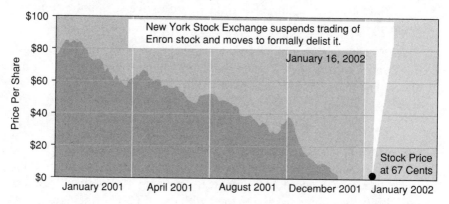

Bankers. JP Morgan, Bank of America, Barclays, Deutsche Bank, Canadian Imperial Bank of Commerce, Merrill Lynch, CS First Boston, and Lehman Brothers made short-term and takeout loans. Some of these bankers also sold SPE units to investors.

Board of Directors. The board waived Enron's Code of Ethics three times in 2000 and 2001 to accommodate management's participation in SPEs.

Ultimately, it was hard to avoid the logical conclusion that the gatekeepers who were supposed to protect shareholders were unable or unwilling to do so.

LEGISLATIVE AND REGULATORY REFORM

As the public became more outraged at the Enron and other corporate financial scandals, legislative and regulatory bodies reacted with a broad-based assault on public investment abuse.

The resulting reforms included:

- Congress: Sarbanes-Oxley Act of 2002 (SOX)
- NYSE and Nasdaq Exchanges: Regulatory reform[1]
- Securities and Exchange Commission (SEC): Regulatory reform

---

1 Much of the discussion that follows focuses on the new NYSE requirements, which as a general rule are more stringent than the Nasdaq requirements and can be viewed as fairly representing "best practices" in corporate governance.

- Selected state reform legislation
- Accounting profession: SOX required the formation of the Public Company Accounting Oversight Board to oversee public company auditors

As a result of the public outrage and ensuing reforms, by 2003 public corporations knew they were in for major changes in the way they did business. The major impact was in the following areas:

Financial Reporting

The Sarbanes-Oxley Act requires the Chief Executive Officer (CEO) and the Chief Financial Officer (CFO) to be held personally responsible for the ultimate accuracy of corporate financial reporting and to have primary responsibility for company reports filed with the SEC. This includes attesting to the "completeness and accuracy" of the information in the reports.

Other Reporting

SOX requires the SEC to implement a new disclosure system for public companies, one that is designed to produce more disclosure of higher quality information on a more frequent and timely basis.

Disclosure Controls and Procedures

As a result of SOX, management is responsible for developing, maintaining, and evaluating a system of disclosure controls and procedures that is designed to ensure the accuracy of publicly disclosed information.

Internal Controls

SOX mandates that management report annually on its assessment of the adequacy of the company's internal controls, and that the independent auditor attest to management's assessment of the effectiveness of the internal controls.

Code of Ethics

Under rules adopted by the SEC (in response to the mandate of SOX), a public company must now disclose whether it has adopted a written code of ethics applicable to the company's principal executive officer, principal financial officer, and principal accounting officer or controller, and if it has not, it must disclose why it has not done so.

If a company has a code of ethics, it must make it publicly available, which it may do by posting it on the company Web site. Any amendment or waiver of the code of ethics must be disclosed publicly within five days by making a filing with the SEC.

Management Compensation

Corporate compensation has been restructured to encourage better alignment with shareholders by restricting the utilization of stock options. Sarbanes-Oxley also banned most corporate loans to officers and directors.

Directors

The new governance regulations require boards to reorganize in order to gain greater independence from management. The majority of the members of boards of directors of NYSE companies are now required to be "independent." In essence, SOX resulted in the tightening of the definition of director "independence."

Under NYSE rules, the board must affirmatively determine that each director has no material relationship with the company. Among other things, the rules require that to be considered independent, a director:

- May not receive more than $100,000 in compensation annually from the company
- May not be an employee of the company
- May not be affiliated with the company's auditor
- May not be employed as an executive officer by a firm in which any of the company's senior executives serve on the compensation committee, or which contributes more than 2 percent of the company's revenues, or for which the company contributes more than the greater of 2 percent or $1 million of the firm's revenues

Under the NYSE rules, nonmanagement directors are now required to regularly schedule executive sessions without management present.

Board Committees

Under the NYSE rules, key-standing board committees (i.e., audit, compensation, and nominating/corporate governance committees) must be comprised exclusively of independent directors who meet regularly without management present. These committees must have direct access to individual managers, shareholders, and outside advisors.

Audit Committee

Public companies must disclose whether the audit committee includes a person who qualifies as an "audit committee financial expert" within the meaning of the SEC rules, and if not, why not.

If the audit committee includes a person who qualifies as an audit committee financial expert, the company must disclose the name of that person. The NYSE rules require that all audit committee members be "financially literate," and that at least one member have accounting or financial management expertise.

The audit committee directly hires and fires auditors and preapproves any nonaudit services provided by the auditing firm. Directors' fees are the sole remuneration for serving on the audit committee.

Compensation Committee

Under the new NYSE requirements, this committee was given an exclusive mandate to review and approve corporate goals for CEO compensation and to evaluate the CEO's performance against these goals.

The compensation committee also determines and approves—either as a committee or together with other independent directors—the CEO's compensation based on that evaluation. The compensation committee recommends to the board compensation for other senior managers. Finally, this committee produces an annual report on executive compensation for the proxy statement.

Nominating/Corporate Governance Committee

Although it has not been uncommon in the past for public company boards to have a nominating committee, the NYSE rules have expanded the role of this committee to encompass corporate governance matters.

With respect to this latter role, the committee must develop and recommend to the board a set of governance guidelines for the firm.[2]

Its responsibilities also include establishing director qualifications, identifying individuals qualified to become board members, selecting (or recommending that the board select) director nominees for election by the stockholders, developing and recommending to the board a set of corporate governance principles applicable to the company, overseeing the evaluation of the board and management of the company, and annually assessing the performance of the committee.

---

2 The responsibilities of the nominating/corporate governance committee can be allocated to any other committee of the board so long as it is comprised entirely of independent directors.

Corporate Governance Guidelines

The NYSE rules now require that each NYSE-listed company adopt and post on its Web site corporate governance guidelines that address, among other things, director qualifications, director responsibilities, director access to management, director compensation, director orientation and continuing education, management succession, and the annual performance evaluation of the board.

Shareholders

The NYSE and Nasdaq rules were amended in mid-2003 to require shareholder approval of substantially all stock option and equity compensation plans.

In addition, SEC rules now require extensive disclosure in a company's annual proxy statement of various matters relating to the access of shareholders to the company's board and the participation of shareholders in the director nomination process, including disclosure of the following:

- Whether the board has a process for shareholder communication with the board, and if it does not, why the board has determined that it is not appropriate to have such a process.
- If the board has a process by which shareholders may communicate with the board, a description of the process.
- Whether the nominating committee of the board has a policy for considering director candidates recommended by shareholders for election to the board, and if it does not, why the board has determined that it is not appropriate to have such a policy.
- If the nominating committee has a policy for considering director candidates recommended by shareholders, a description of the policy and the procedures shareholders must follow in submitting recommendations.
- A description of the minimum qualifications that the nominating committee believes must be met by a director nominee.
- If the nominating committee received a recommendation of a director nominee from a shareholder or group of shareholders owning more than 5 percent of the company's voting stock for at least one year, identification of the candidate and the shareholder or group recommending the candidate, and disclosure of whether the nominating committee chose to nominate that candidate.

Auditors

Under Sarbanes-Oxley, corporate auditing standards were strengthened to ensure greater independence from management.

The auditing firm must rotate the company's lead audit partner and concurring audit partner every five years, and must rotate other partners involved in certain capacities in the audit every seven years.

In addition, the mandatory rotation of audit firms, although not currently required, remains under consideration. Should the lead or concurring audit partner or certain other members of the audit team leave the auditing firm and become employed as the CEO, CFO, chief accounting officer, or controller of the company during the year following their departure, the auditing firm will cease to be independent with respect to the company.

Attorneys

Corporate attorneys are now held responsible for reporting evidence of possible violations of law to the company's general counsel (who has an obligation to investigate the possible violations), and under certain circumstances to the audit committee or the board.

Confidential Information

Regulations have been strengthened to prevent misuse of insider data and investor relationships.

Whistle-Blowers

Employees and outsiders now have increased protection from recrimination by the firm for "whistle-blowing" activities.

Enforcement

Sarbanes-Oxley imposed new criminal penalties for persons who fail to carry out the responsibilities imposed by SOX and related regulations.

REACTION TO GOVERNANCE REFORMS: PUBLIC FIRMS

In 2004, directors of 1,200 public companies were surveyed by PricewaterhouseCoopers (PWC) and *Corporate Board Member* magazine regarding their reaction to Sarbanes-Oxley following two years of attempting to implement this and other highly challenging governance reforms.[3]

General Response

The response of the directors surveyed was largely positive. Ninety-one percent found it easier to hire new directors, 85 percent expected the company image would be improved, and almost half (48 percent) expected the company's stock price to be positively affected.

Corporate Liability

When queried about corporate liability, 85 percent of the directors responded that the company would be exonerated if it faced shareholder or other litigation. Seventy-one percent believed that the company wouldn't be sued in the first place, and 62 percent said they expected their Directors and Officers (D&O) insurance to cost less as a result of the reforms.

Director Liability

When asked about their own personal liability, 68 percent responded that it had increased, with only 2 percent believing it had decreased. The remaining 30 percent believed it was "about the same."

D&O Insurance

When asked about the importance of D&O insurance in their decision to serve on a board, almost half (49 percent) replied "very important." Another 37 percent indicated it was "somewhat important," while the remaining 14 percent said it was "unimportant."

When queried further if they would pay personally for the insurance, 79 percent said no and 21 percent said they would. It's clear that most directors expect companies to have D&O coverage and to pay for it as an ongoing cost of operating a public company.

---

3 "What Directors Think," Corporate Board Member, 2004.

Sarbanes-Oxley Implementation

When asked if their company was ready to implement the internal controls requirement of Sarbanes-Oxley (Section 404), 82 percent of respondents replied yes and only 4 percent replied negatively. The remaining 14 percent felt they were "not sure yet."

One of the great concerns about SOX and other new governance regulations is the tremendous amount of time that companies have had to spend in putting the reforms in place, not to mention the higher auditing, legal, and other costs related to its implementation.

In the PWC survey, however, 44 percent of the directors felt that the time and costs were not so great as to adversely impact company financial performance. However, more than a third (36 percent) believed it was too early to tell.

Legislative Amendments

Despite their overall positive view of the new governance regulations, 77 percent of directors surveyed believed that Congress needed to "revisit" SOX to "eliminate some of the unintended consequences" of the act. Only 4 percent believed such an action wasn't necessary, with the remaining 19 percent "not sure yet."

Future Board Focus

Figure 20-3 indicates the directors' responses when queried about where they wanted to direct their focus, now that preparation for the major elements of SOX had been largely completed.

Not surprisingly, the majority of directors surveyed wanted to return to the traditional responsibilities of "strategic planning," "management succession," "analysis of the competition," and "risk management." The tasks they wanted to spend less time on, also not surprisingly, were "compliance issues" and "governance guidelines."

PUBLIC REAL ESTATE COMPANIES AND CORPORATE GOVERNANCE

Structural Obstacles to Improved Governance

Many REITs and other public real estate companies[4] were initially established as closely controlled private companies, with many built-in legal features that made implementing governance standards difficult.

---

4 Includes REITs, real estate operating companies (REOCs), publicly traded homebuilders, residential mortgage finance/insurance companies, and hospitality firms.

FIGURE 20-3

What Boards Want to Do More/Same/Less Of

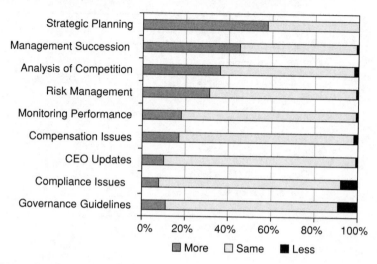

Source: PricewaterhouseCoopers, December 2004

For example, the articles of incorporation of many real estate companies established limitations connected to share ownership, as well as stringent antitakeover measures. Some of these companies went public with a large amount of the assets of the founders remaining in private hands, through various entities established for that purpose (e.g., UPREITs, SPEs, private partnerships).

Many boards also were closely held and controlled by the founders and their friends. And most REITs use unique, non–GAAP accounting and performance measures, such as Funds from Operations (FFO).

Shareholder Forces for Change

These structural obstacles were ultimately overcome, in most cases, by the makeup of the shareholder base of most public real estate companies.

A high percentage of shares are often held by institutions, for example, particularly pension funds. Many companies are listed on the New York Stock Exchange, which, as noted previously, developed new rules permitting large shareholders (those holding over 5 percent) to nominate their own directors.

And, finally, real estate is the only industry to have dedicated money managers who have a direct stake in how well REITs are governed. As an example, Figure 20-4 represents the firm-scoring criteria used by one of

F I G U R E 20-4

Greenstreet Advisors' Scorecard

Nonstaggered Board	20 points
Past Conduct/Reputation	15
Board Investment	12
Antitakeover Provisions	9
Ownership Limits	9
Insider Veto Rights	9
Shareholder Rights Plan	8
Independent Board	8
Dealings with Management	6
Investor Tax Basis	4
	100

Source: Greenstreet Advisors

the largest and most influential public real estate company advisors. Note that virtually all of the criteria are governance-related.

Ferguson Survey

In 2004, Ferguson Partners, a Chicago-based management search and compensation firm, interviewed over 200 public real estate company directors, CEOs, and institutional investors about governance and compensation issues.[5]

On a five-point scale, the respondents ranked corporate governance (4.27) second only to corporate performance (4.51) and ahead of corporate strategy (4.21).

BOARD OF DIRECTORS GOVERNANCE GUIDELINES

Today, there is no question that the board of directors of public real estate companies is responsible for the stewardship of the company.[6]

Generally, this takes the form of monitoring the activities of management, who are usually full-time employees of the organization. The

---

5 FPL Associates LP, Ferguson Partners Ltd., 2004 Board Practices and Compensation Survey.
6 Some or all of these also may apply to private real estate companies, depending upon the by-laws of the corporation and the particular state laws governing its operation.

scope of the authority of both the board and management are spelled out in the corporation's bylaws and board committee charters.

In response to Sarbanes-Oxley and other recent regulatory requirements, the boards of most public firms have developed corporate guidelines that they publish in their annual reports and post on their Web sites.

Although these guidelines are a work in progress, and therefore subject to change over time, the following discussion focuses on board governance guidelines for public real estate companies as of the summer of 2005. It is based on the author's experience with several public real estate companies, the Ferguson survey, as well as industry literature on the subject.

While there is little public record of private company governance, it is assumed that those that have developed guidelines would have gone through a somewhat similar process.

Director Responsibilities

Individual directors are now expected to spend the time and effort necessary to understand the issues associated with their decisions. Typically, their duties include:

- Reviewing and approving long-term strategy for future operations
- Evaluating whether the business is being properly managed in conformance with industry "best practices" and established company strategic and annual plans
- Reviewing and approving major changes in the company's auditing and accounting principles and practices
- Ensuring that the company's business is conducted with the highest standards of ethical conduct and in conformity with applicable laws and regulations
- Reviewing and, where appropriate, approving changes in the company's Corporate Governance Guidelines, Code of Business Conduct and Ethics, and other policies
- Reviewing and approving actions that would result in a material change in the control of the firm, the acquisition or disposition of any material company businesses or assets, or entry into any major new line of business and/or new geographical area
- Regularly evaluating the performance and approving the compensation of the CEO
- With the input of the CEO, regularly evaluating the performance and compensation of principal senior executives

- Planning for succession with respect to the position of CEO, and monitoring management's succession planning for other key executives

Increased media and regulatory emphasis on the performance of these responsibilities are new to most boards and are an indication of the impact of SOX and other new corporate governance regulations.

Director Qualifications

In evaluating the suitability of new candidates and current board members, most boards consider the following characteristics as being basic requirements:

- Character qualities of intelligence, honesty, good judgment, high ethics, and standards of integrity, fairness, and responsibility
- General understanding of marketing, finance, and other elements relevant to the success of a publicly traded real estate company in today's business environment
- General understanding of the firm's business
- Ability to make independent analytical inquiries
- Experience serving on other boards
- Educational and professional background
- Specific experience to fill needs or requests identified by the board

Boards are expected to evaluate each individual in the context of the board as a whole, with the objective of assembling a group that can best perpetuate the success of the business and represent shareholder interests.

In ranking important factors in selecting a new director, the Ferguson survey respondents ranked (out of five) "personal qualities" as being most important (4.96), followed by "time and commitment" (4.61), "public company experience" (4.18), and "prior board experience" (3.82).

Among the "least important" characteristics were "local community member" (2.08), "professors and academic administrators" (2.10), "government contacts" (2.12), and "legal experience" (2.46).

Female Directors

In the Ferguson survey, 54 percent of the respondents agreed with the statement that a public real estate company "needs a female director on the board," with only 10 percent disagreeing. Thirty-six percent were indifferent.

Minority Directors

Respondents were not quite as positive about ethnic minority representation on the board, with 46 percent agreeing this is important and 12 percent disagreeing. Forty-two percent were indifferent.

Director Independence

For firms listed on the NYSE, the majority of board members must qualify as "independent directors" as established under the exchange's listing standards. The board is required to annually review the relationship that each director has with the firm to determine if, in fact, they continue to be "independent."

Board Size

In most companies the size of the board is stated in the company's Articles of Incorporation or bylaws. Most boards range in size from three to 15 members. The exact number is usually determined from time to time by the board as proscribed in the firm's bylaws.

For most boards, an increasingly important problem is the annual cost of paying a director, particularly since the compensation is increasingly in cash and must come out of earnings. Directorships can cost upward of $100,000 per year.

When queried about the optimum size of a public real estate board, 42 percent of respondents to the Ferguson survey said nine was the optimum number, 25 percent said seven to eight, and 23 percent believed that 10 to 11 directors was the optimum size for a board.

Collectively, nine out of 10 respondents believed that a public real estate board should have between seven and 11 directors.

Frequency of Meetings

The frequency of board meetings each year ranges from six to as many as may be required to conduct the business of the board.

The minimum of six meetings results from the fact that most boards now require a minimum of four meetings per year of the independent directors. Assuming two additional meetings to review management proposals (e.g., strategic and operating plans as well as officer compensation), this would suggest a minimum of six regularly scheduled board meetings annually.

Election of Directors

Most public companies elect their entire board each year at the annual shareholders meeting. This allows shareholders to replace individual directors or an entire board if they are dissatisfied with their performance.

Several public real estate companies, however, continue to retain the concept of "staggered boards" in which only one-third of the directors stand for reelection each year. In the Ferguson survey, 44 percent of the directors of public real estate companies continue to support the concept of staggered boards.[7]

The major rationale for the staggered board concept is the importance of ensuring "institutional memory" as new members join and become acclimated to the firm and its operating history. The major reason is that staggered boards also serve as a deterrent to a hostile takeover of the company.

The investment community, however, sees staggered boards very differently, with many large public pension funds viewing the election of the entire board each year as a strong endorsement of good corporate governance.

Analysts and consultants also favor the elimination of staggered boards; some even penalize companies heavily for retaining them. As noted previously, Greenstreet, one of the most prestigious institutional consultants, penalizes firms 20 points (out of 100) for having a staggered board.

Maximum Term of Service and Age

Most public companies limit board service to 10 to 12 years or upon reaching a maximum age, usually 70 years old. Some public companies, however, have extended the age cap to 75, since people live longer and continue to be productive in their later years.

Service on Other Boards

Most boards do not prohibit its members from serving on boards of other organizations. This is an area of increasing concern to many companies, however, with some directors serving on as many as seven or eight boards.

While some experience with other public boards is desirable, the time commitment for being a conscientious director today has increased dramatically as a result of complying with Sarbanes-Oxley and other new

7 There was quite a split on this issue: 39 percent disagreed (14 percent "strongly"), and only 17 percent were indifferent.

governance requirements, as well as the greater complexity of modern business enterprises.

A director who serves on multiple boards may be in the process of retiring from general business and becoming somewhat of a "professional director." While there is something to be said for the "transfer of board experiences," many directors believe there is so much change in business today that it may be more desirable to have a majority of directors who still retain some linkage to the day-to-day pressures of being a corporate leader, perhaps as a CEO or other senior officer.

Directors' Compensation

Most boards are compensated through one or a combination of three major methods:

- Cash (directors fees)
- Mixed compensation including cash and stock
- Stock options

As noted previously, new legislation and increased regulations have placed an emphasis on cash compensation, deemphasizing the role of stock options. This has forced many boards to turn to mixed compensation as a way to compensate board members. For many boards, this is an exploratory process in which they find themselves trying to meet the new requirements without losing sight of the fact that an experienced business leader can bring unlimited value to the strategic process that fuels the future growth of the company.

Chairperson

Most companies envision a strong leader in the chairperson's role. A typical job description might include:

- Serving as leader of the board of directors
- Coordinating the activities of the independent directors and chairs of standing committees
- Facilitating communications between independent directors and management
- Mentoring individual directors and the CEO
- Serving as a member of the governance committee with primary responsibility for implementing the decisions of the committee as they relate to the board

- Meeting with the chair of the compensation committee and the chief executive officer to convey the results of the CEO's annual performance evaluations
- Approving the agenda for and chairing meetings of the board, executive committee, and annual shareholder's meeting

In performing these duties, the chairperson is expected to consult with the chairs of the appropriate board committees.

Note that the chairperson is responsible for governance issues facing the company. This places the final responsibility for compliance squarely at the board rather than the management level.

It would appear that this is where it should be placed since—as required by law, and in light of Enron and other public company litigation—the board is ultimately responsible to shareholders if good governance is not being pursued.

CEO as Chairperson

Most public company boards separate the duties of the CEO and chairperson. However, this is a continuing issue in the public real estate community, where many REITs still have a single person in both leadership roles.

But attitudes are changing, as reported in the Ferguson survey: 50 percent of respondents agreed that the position should be held by different individuals, and only 20 percent disagreed; 30 percent were indifferent.

Standing Committees

A major portion of the work of a board is accomplished through the use of standing committees. These committees are comprised entirely of independent directors, with the exception of the executive committee, on which the CEO serves.

The membership of each committee is approved by the independent directors, upon recommendation of the chairman of the board and the executive committee. Each committee usually has a minimum of three members.

The major standing committees include:

Audit Committee

The audit committee provides assistance to the board in fulfilling its responsibilities to its shareholders concerning the reliability and integrity of the firm's accounting policies, financial reporting, internal audit functions, internal accounting controls, and financial disclosure practices.

The audit committee now has sole responsibility to appoint and terminate the company's independent auditors and to approve any significant, nonaudit relationship with the auditing firm.

Compensation Committee

This committee reviews and approves the company's goals and objectives relevant to compensation, stays informed as to market levels of compensation, and based on evaluations submitted by management and outside consultants, recommends to the board compensation levels and systems for the board and the CEO that are aligned with the company's goals and objectives.

The compensation committee also produces an annual report on executive compensation for inclusion in the company's annual proxy statement, in accordance with applicable rules and regulations.

Governance Committee

For most boards, this is a new standing committee, responsible for developing, revising, and approving corporate governance guidelines, as well as reviewing and recommending revisions to these guidelines on a regular basis.

Nominating Committee

This committee recommends to the board individuals to be nominated as directors and committee members and prepares disclosure statements that may be required for inclusion in the annual proxy statement.

These responsibilities also may be undertaken by a combined governance-nominating committee, or in some cases established as a subcommittee of the compensation committee.

Executive Committee

Although circumstances may vary from firm to firm, the executive committee usually is comprised of the chairperson of the board and the chair of each of the standing board committees outlined above, plus the CEO.

The board may delegate to the executive committee full powers of the board, subject to limitations prescribed by the board and laws of the state of incorporation. The executive committee also may take an active role in broader company issues such as strategic planning, the company's capital structure, and management and board succession planning.

Each standing committee is expected to perform its duties as assigned by the board in compliance with the company's bylaws and the committee's charter, if applicable. From time to time the board may form a new committee or disband a current committee, depending upon circumstances.

Real Estate Committee

In addition to standing committees, the board also may appoint special committees reflecting the unique requirements of the firm's industry or a specific task that is too large or complex to be handled by one of the standing committees.

Many public real estate boards establish real estate committees to make final decisions regarding property transactions recommended by management. Some firms separate responsibility for approval based on the level of capital investment, project complexity, or location (new markets). In this situation, senior management approves smaller or less complex projects, with the board real estate committee approving the majority of projects that fall in the middle. For complex projects or those requiring a large commitment of capital, a vote of the full board may be required.

The real estate committee is also responsible for monitoring industry trends and real estate markets in which the company is active or anticipates being active.

Committee Agendas

The chairman of each committee, in consultation with the appropriate members of the committee, is responsible for developing the committee-meeting agenda.

Committee Self-Evaluation

Following the end of each fiscal year, each committee is expected to review its performance and charter and recommend to the board any changes it deems necessary.

Board Orientation and Continuing Education

Most firms provide new directors with a Director Orientation Program to familiarize them with, among other things: the firm's business; strategic plans; significant financial, accounting and management issues; compliance programs; conflict of interest policies; code of business conduct and ethics; corporate guidelines; principal officers; internal auditors; and independent auditors.

Most companies also make available to all directors continuing education programs at least every few years, as management or the board determines desirable.

Meeting Preparation and Attendance

Most boards expect a director to regularly prepare for and to attend meetings of the board and all committees on which the director serves (including separate meetings of independent directors). The law also requires that directors prepare for board meetings so that they are fully informed when taking action at the meetings.

It is, of course, usually understood that on occasion a director may be unable to attend a meeting. If so, he or she is expected to notify the chairman of the board or appropriate committee in advance and, whenever possible, participate in the meeting via teleconferencing.

Attendance of Outside Advisors

Many boards encourage the attendance of outside advisors, consultants, or company managers who are not on the board in order to provide additional insight into items being discussed by the board or committees. Attendance is usually at the discretion of the chairman or committee chairperson.

CONTINUING CORPORATE GOVERNANCE

Most boards believe that good corporate governance requires continuing vigilance and oversight if it is to be successful. The following guidelines represent efforts boards may use to accomplish this objective.

Conflicts of Interest

Directors are expected to avoid any action, position, or interest that conflicts with the interests of the company or gives the appearance of a conflict.

If an actual or potential conflict of interest develops, the director is expected to immediately report the matter to the chairman. Any significant conflict must be resolved or the director will be asked to resign.

If a director has a personal interest in a matter before the board, he or she is expected to disclose the interest and not participate in the discussion of or the vote on that matter

Meetings of Nonmanagement Directors in Executive Session

In most firms, nonmanagement directors are encouraged to meet in executive session (without management directors or management present) at least a minimum number of times per year (usually three to four).

At these meetings, the directors review the company's implementation of and compliance with its governance guidelines and consider whether the program is operating in conformance with applicable laws and the standards that the board believes desirable.

Shareholder Access to Independent Directors

If they have a concern about the company, shareholders are encouraged to pose written questions to independent directors and receive a written response.

Board Access to Independent Advisors

Board committees may hire independent advisors as set forth in their applicable charters. The board as a whole has access to these advisors and such other independent advisors that the company retains or that the board considers necessary to discharge its responsibilities.

Annual Self-Evaluation

Following the end of each fiscal year, the governance committee is expected to oversee an annual assessment of the board's performance during the prior year, as well as that of individual board members.

In most cases the committee will be responsible for establishing the evaluation criteria and implementing the process for this evaluation, as well as to consider other corporate governance principles that may merit consideration by the board.

The assessment should include a review of any areas in which the board or management believes the board can make a better contribution to the governance of the company, as well as a review of the committee structure and an assessment of the board's compliance with the principles set forth in the Corporate Governance Guidelines.

The purpose of the review is to improve the performance of the board as a unit and the performance of individual board members. The governance committee then utilizes the results of the board evaluation process in assessing and determining the characteristics and critical skills required of prospective candidates for election to the board.

Annual Review of CEO

The compensation committee, with input from the CEO, will annually establish the performance criteria (including both long-term and short-term goals) to be considered in connection with the CEO's annual performance evaluation.

At the end of each year, the CEO is required to make a presentation and/or furnish a written report to the committee indicating his or her progress against established performance goals.

Thereafter, the committee meets privately to independently review the performance report. The results of this review and evaluation will be communicated to the CEO by the committee chairman.

Succession Planning

The nominating committee is expected to work on a periodic basis with the CEO to review, maintain, and if necessary revise the company's senior management succession plan, including the position of CEO. The CEO is expected to report annually to the board on the status of this plan, including a discussion of assessments, leadership development plans, and other relevant factors.

CURRENT SITUATION

As of early 2006, most larger public companies, including real estate, had adjusted to the higher governance standards. Some even believed that many of the requirements, particularly Sarbanes-Oxley 404, had improved their internal control systems, and that as board members they knew much more about their firm's operation than ever before.

Many smaller firms complained about the high cost of complying with the new governance standards and about the drain of management time in getting the proper systems in place. As time passed, however, many managers and board members realized that most of the costs had been "start-up" costs and that the use of technology tended to lower continuing costs and provide real-time reporting on the company's operation.

Since many European and Japanese firms have operations in the United States, they have reportedly adopted many of the reforms to improve governance procedures as well.

Looking forward, senior managers have a major stake in making good governance standards work. Not only are many of them personally on the financial line for failing to accomplish governance goals, but they set the "tone at the top" that filters down throughout the organization and makes the difference between "conforming to" and "embracing" good governance.

As Susan Bies, a member of the Board of Governors of the Federal Reserve System put it:

> It is also important that a strong culture of compliance be established at the top of the organization and that a proper ethical tone be set for governing the conduct of business.
>
> The board and senior management are obligated to deliver a strong message to others in the firm about the importance of integrity, compliance with the law, fair treatment of customers, and overall good business ethics.
>
> Leaders should demonstrate their commitment through their individual conduct and their response to control failures.[8]

It now appears that what some considered an overreaction by Congress to the excesses of Enron and other corporate miscreants has turned out to be a long-term benefit to the business community, and the real estate industry as well.

---

8 Address to the Institute of Internal Auditors' Financial Services Conference, Washington, D.C., May 19, 2004.

Technology and the Due Diligence Process

By Craig Severance[1]

Over the last two decades, technology has been deployed disproportionately to support financial management components of the real estate investment process. The production components—sourcing, acquisition/development, and dispositions—have been largely ignored.

Today, financial management software still comprises 70 percent of the real estate industry's investment in new technology. This software includes spreadsheet analysis, customer relationship management (CRM), project management, discounted cash flow modeling, and document management applications.

This is hardly surprising since the real estate experience has tracked the software deployment pattern witnessed in other industries. As a result, real estate financial management accounting systems are simply more mature, having originally been developed for and deployed on computer mainframe systems long before the introduction of desktop computers.

BACKWARD VERSUS FORWARD FACING

Financial management systems are designed almost exclusively to manage quantitative data. Like the rearview mirror in a car, most financial management systems are backward facing. They are excellent tools for *describing where a firm has been and what has happened.*

---

1 Formerly Acquisition Director for AMB Properties, Inc., and now involved in applying technology to the due diligence process.

Financial management systems, however, have limited ability to address more qualitative decision-making information that can have a greater impact on the economic success of a real estate investment on a going-forward basis.

Furthermore, financial management components have a relatively limited ability to proactively impact investment returns generated by the investments themselves.

This situation is not limited to financial management systems exclusively—even excellent property and asset management cannot undo the cumulative harm of buying, developing, and/or disposing of the wrong property in the wrong market at the wrong time.

A corollary is that good real estate acquired, developed, and/or disposed of at the right time can magnify the returns generated by good management.

One of the most important goals of leveraging technology is to increase real estate investment returns. It just makes sense, therefore, to increase the allocation of technology expenditure to those elements of the process that have the greatest potential to impact real estate investment performance.

It also should be noted that an investment in technology should not be considered a zero sum game. Increasing technology investment in the production components of the process should not necessarily lead to a decrease in investment in the financial management component.

The reality for most investment managers is that, in order to remain competitive, more funds will have to be devoted to technology for all purposes. What is important is to be certain that an increasing portion of these expenditures is directed toward those systems that have the greatest potential to positively impact investment returns.

CURRENT TECHNOLOGY AND THE DUE DILIGENCE PROCESS

Faced with the reality of increasing expenditure levels, a logical question might be: "Can we convert existing financial management systems for use in the production elements of the investment process?"

Financial system technology, being generally quantitative, is optimal for tracking financial information. Unfortunately, the information needed to source, acquire/develop, and/or dispose of real estate is primarily qualitative in nature.

For example, assume that acquisition best practices require members of the due diligence team to interview planning and zoning personnel. In the course of this interview it is discovered that a governmental agency is planning to condemn a corner of the property to accommodate an expansion of the intersection. It is difficult, if not impossible, to capture this key information on a financial management system.

Another example: Assume that due diligence best practices suggest interviewing each tenant. During one tenant interview the tenant claims to have a special, undocumented "deal" with the landlord excusing the payment of the tenant's share of Common Area Maintenance (CAM) for the next three years.

Although this scenario can be modeled accurately in the cash flow analysis, a financial management system cannot track subsequent events so that this information doesn't fall between the cracks during the remainder of the diligence process.

The problem is that financial management systems are not designed to track qualitative information, nor can they be modified to effectively do so. New technology specifically designed to accomplish this objective is required.

ADDRESSING THE RIGHT PROBLEMS

Before considering an investment in new technology, however, it's important to be certain that the technology being considered addresses the real problem(s) that need to be resolved.

Imagine a process that attempts to harness the efforts of 20 or 30 people (many of whom don't even know each other), working in different locations, performing a complex set of tasks within an increasingly compressed period of time. This is the due diligence process most investment managers are now facing.

The underwriting team must validate the market, interview tenants, review building structure and systems, understand environmental issues, review leases and financials, decide on the property's value, estimate the investment return over time, confirm equity financial resources, and, if utilized, secure the appropriate debt financing for the property. Individual Investment Committee requirements must be considered as well.

To make all of this happen, a complex set of interwoven tasks must be completed, often under extreme time constraints. Just a few of the management tasks that need to be completed include:

- Draft and negotiate contracts
- Set and meet schedules
- Research and collect data
- Manage in-house staff
- Hire and coordinate consultants

- Abstract leases and manage documents
- Prepare and distribute reports
- Verify financial resources

The acquisition process can be slowed or even stopped if there isn't sufficient time or people available to do the job effectively. Important issues may be overlooked, or mistakes made, the most costly being to close a transaction without adequately answering, or perhaps even facing, the critical issues involved in the operation of the candidate property.

Unfortunately, the collaborative medium of choice for currently managing this type of qualitative information is a patchwork combination of legal pads, voice mail, and, increasingly, e-mail. Although ubiquitous and easy to use, each of these "technologies" has severe drawbacks and, most important, *is not integrated.*

The bottom line is that financial management systems are ill equipped to deal with the qualitative aspects of the due diligence process.

Stitching Together Disparate Software

Another solution that some investment managers have attempted is to stitch together several types of existing software such as Excel spreadsheets, word processing, e-mail, back-office accounting systems, etc.

Imagine a five-way telephone conference call where each participant can speak and understand only his or her own language. Now imagine if the telephone could magically translate words *and* grammar so that no matter what language anyone is speaking, each participant can hear what is being said in his or her native language.

Most companies employ multiple types of software and are required to work with due diligence data arriving from outside third parties who may use different software as well.

Similar to the translation issues described in the conference call above, most software does not "talk" to other software. As a result, inefficiencies exist because of the need to reenter data into multiple, disparate software applications. Even worse, the redundant entering of data creates opportunities for mistakes to be made; mistakes that are often difficult to discover, once they have been made.

Why Not Just Use E-mail?

When e-mail was first introduced, it provided managers instantaneous access to important time-sensitive information regarding a transaction. This represented a major improvement over the then existing technology of faxes and overnight mail.

Initially, receipt of five e-mails was considered a lot of activity. Each e-mail was an important, well-articulated message from someone familiar.

Now the e-mail environment has become polluted with spam, leaving many who rely on e-mail as a primary collaborative medium with two alternates:

- Use filtering mechanisms as a way to eliminate as much misinformation (spam) as possible and risk turning away or losing important information.
- Become resigned to looking for that informational needle in the spam haystack—a terribly inefficient way to operate.

Although e-mail obviously has its strengths, reliance on it to manage a company's due diligence collaborative environment appears to be a suboptimal strategy. Furthermore, e-mail cannot deliver any of the essential functionality described earlier. What is needed is a technology devoted exclusively to resolving the challenges of the due diligence process.

WHAT'S REQUIRED

What's required is a collaborative environment within which the due diligence team can organize in such a way that they become more productive and, at the same time, complete their work with greater care and accuracy.

Technology capable of creating this type of collaborative environment must be able to manage *multiple functions simultaneously* in an internally integrated system. The major objectives are:

Shared Involvement

Development of a process management checklist is a prerequisite to managing the due diligence process. Tasks must be clearly articulated with assigned responsibility and reasonably firm due dates.

Mere possession of a checklist, however, is simply not sufficient. For example, the real estate investment director for one of the country's largest pension funds indicated that a mistake made by an investment advisor cost the plan over $300,000.

"Not to worry," he said. "I have over $1 billion invested with this particular advisor and they do a great job for me. I know the individual in New York who made this mistake may make other mistakes, but he *will never repeat this mistake again.*"

The reply: "My concern is that his teammates in Los Angeles will make the same mistake because they don't share a common checklist."

In order to add value, the checklist must be rigorously used and dynamically updated to reflect a company's best practices as they evolve over time. The technology should be deployed over the Internet so changes in the checklist are automatically disseminated to the entire due diligence team, regardless of where they are located.

Privacy Concerns

Although much of the diligence information can and must be shared, the technology needs to be responsive to individual team member's privacy concerns.

For example, attorneys may be reticent to use the technology if it does not safeguard "attorney-client" privileges. The technology must empower Role Base Access Control (RBAC), which provides control over read/write privileges based on the teammate's role in the diligence process.

It is important to enable outside third-party service providers to see work assigned to them, but to be precluded from seeing work assigned to other people.

Managing Documents

The due diligence technology also needs to address document management requirements. At a minimum, the technology should be able to handle any type of electronic file of *unlimited* size.

The document management system should be seamlessly linked to the process roles and tasks, and in addition enable "version control." By doing so, a group of five revisions to a purchase agreement can be sequentially reviewed in the order in which they were uploaded into the application.

The technology also should contain excellent query capabilities so that any file is always at a team member's fingertips no matter where they are located.

Managing Content

A basic requirement of effective technology is the inventorying of factual information about the acquisition property for ease of access not only during the due diligence period, but also for later retrieval during asset management and disposition phases.

Examples of content include:

- Sources and uses of cash
- Rates of return

- Size parameters (automatically calculated ratios such as coverage ratios, parking ratios, etc.)
- Tenant interviews
- Lease abstracts
- Credit analysis
- Replacement cost analysis
- Strengths and weaknesses
- Opportunities and risks
- Major due diligence findings
- Exit strategy considerations

Essentially, the goal of due diligence technology should be to provide immediate access to any information related to any property via the Internet, without having to resort to paper files back in the home office.

Managing Time

Inclusion of a centralized Web-based calendar in the language of due diligence technology is of critical importance to enable the effective management of the dozens of date-critical issues that reveal themselves during the due diligence period. Deadlines should be assignable to any task or work item in the application.

Furthermore, exposing the number of past due items related to a given individual can provide corrective action on behalf of the tardy individual. It is beneficial for senior management to have overview capabilities; that management can know, at any time, who's behind schedule, and, as a result, request justification.

ADVANTAGES OF NEW TECHNOLOGY

Today there are several firms offering technology devoted exclusively to meeting the needs of due diligence management. Some of the advantages of these new technologies are:

Reducing Mistakes

In the last several years, institutional investors have become more involved in real estate, increasing allocation levels, broadening the spectrum of investments they will consider, and generally accepting higher investment risks.

This, in turn, has forced many investment managers to accept higher risks as well. While not always apparent, these can take the form of investing in phases of the cycle the industry has historically avoided, accepting yields that provide little cushion for cycle downturns, investing in markets and products not previously considered, and agreeing to shorter diligence times than are realistically required.

In any type of time-constrained, complex endeavor it is inevitable that some mistakes will be made, but the concern is how the same mistake can be prevented in some other office at some other time. If using due diligence technology keeps the investor or the developer from repeating just one big mistake, it can easily pay for itself, many times over.

Metaphorically speaking, due diligence technology should be the "seat belt" for a company's real estate transactions. You don't get into an accident every time you get behind the wheel of your car. You do, however, buckle up because auto accidents, when they do occur, can be very costly, or worse. The same logic should follow in dealing with real estate investments.

Enhancing Reputation with Sellers

Without the detailed scheduling possible with due diligence technology, important architectural and environmental reports are often delivered just days before the removal of conditions. Last minute, brinkmanship negotiations often ensue.

These last minute negotiations strain, often to the breaking point, a vital asset of any real estate manager: its credibility and its reputation. Who wants to deal with a buyer who appears to be withholding information until the last minute and then "retrades" the deal on last minute information?

With due diligence technology, service providers can deliver critical information in real time, often weeks in advance of their final written reports. With time, creative solutions can be devised. For example, a missing roof warranty certificate can be recovered in time to avoid costly replacement costs.

Using Resources More Effectively

By utilizing due diligence technology, the acquisition team can work as effectively from their homes or hotel rooms as they can from their offices because everything they need is available at their fingertips wherever they log in and bring up the application.

Senior management can "virtually" walk the halls and at a glance see who is falling behind. Younger employees have unparalleled access to the mind-set of a company's most experienced deal makers.

Since all of the tasks are spelled out in detail, work can be allocated down to less expensive resources, freeing up the time of more senior people to focus on value-added work.

Outsourcing clerical work offshore has the potential to make a company more productive, allowing its workforce to focus increasingly on value-added work (versus clerical input work).

Without due diligence technology, however, issues created by poor communication over multiple time zones can dilute the productivity gains being sought. When an outsourced service provider can adopt a company's best practices and communicate in real time, the potential productivity gains are locked in.

Reducing Employee Turnover

A common (and extremely costly) problem in any investment manager operation is employee turnover and its associated impact on employee morale.

Frequently, the culprit is the perception that performance reviews are arbitrary and/or politically based, notwithstanding concerted efforts by senior management to create a fair and nonarbitrary review process.

Due diligence technology also can help measure an employee's productivity and the quality of the employee's work. Now, perhaps for the first time, management will be able to inject a degree of objectivity into the performance review process.

As a result, more productive employees can be identified and rewarded through the establishment of a meritocratic culture.

Reducing Litigation Costs

Legal proceedings between investors and investment managers regrettably are occurring with increasing frequency. With few exceptions, cases are settled for large sums of money (seven figure amounts are not uncommon) because the investment manager could not demonstrate either: possession of a transaction checklist or, in the event they possessed one, proof they actually used it.

Avoidance of potential litigation and its concomitant bad publicity could be sufficient reason in itself to make due diligence technology a good investment.

Improving Employee Training

Many companies give "lip service" to training. In reality, these efforts often fall short, particularly in the transaction area where the subject is best taught by experienced transaction people. Unfortunately, this may not happen because it takes valuable time away from the transaction flow that the firm depends upon. This issue is exacerbated in large companies with multiple offices and/or a global presence. There is also the cost of removing from productivity the trainees who must attend the training sessions.

Effective due diligence technology can help reduce these costs though the use of a checklist that informs a company's employees (and the professionals to whom they outsource work) how to do each and every task.

With due diligence technology, everyone knows exactly what to do, when to do it, and how to do it. As a result of lessons learned, improvements can continually be made to the checklist.

With due diligence technology, these best practices are automatically disseminated to employees on the front line no matter where they are located: in the office, at home, or while on the road.

Achieving a Competitive Advantage

There also may be some positive competitive advantages as well. When it comes down to the final decision between one company and its competition, demonstrating the degree to which the company can reduce potential errors in the diligence process and thereby save its client untold dollars in potential loss may make a considerable difference.

In a more general sense, by using due diligence technology to manage its acquisitions, an investment manager can prove that it not only possesses a best practices checklist, but that it actually uses it.

TECHNOLOGY OPTIONS

Real estate companies have three broad options available to them.

Do Nothing

By far the most prevalent approach is to "do nothing." After all, "we've bought a lot of real estate without resorting to the use of technology." Doing nothing has the advantage of apparent cost savings and can be an internally popular nondecision.

On the other hand, even the most technophobic skeptics are likely to admit that the introduction of calculators, personal computers, e-mail, and the Internet have had positive impacts on their businesses.

There may be legal problems, however, if a serious problem develops with an investment asset that can be traced to faulty due diligence on the part of the investment management firm.

Managers are expected to use "best practice" standards in executing their fiduciary duties on behalf of their clients. "Best practices" doesn't mean what all of the firms in an industry are doing—only the leading firms. If it can be proven that an error could have been avoided by employing new technology and the leading firms are using it, the defendant manager has an uphill battle proving that its nontechnology approach is better or at least would have been "adequate" in avoiding the problem,

Internal Development

The second most popular approach is to "build it yourself" (otherwise known as the "full employment act for internal IT departments"). In fact, unless a company is very large, with millions of dollars budgeted to IT, it can't afford the cost and it shouldn't assume the risks inherent in software development.

It is largely a question of a company's core competency: Is the firm a real estate company or a software company? There are good reasons why legal work and engineering work are often outsourced to experts. Why, then, should an investment manager attempt to develop technological applications internally, particularly applications so critical to its professional reputation and financial well-being?

Outsource

The third option is licensing or acquiring the due diligence technology from a software company. This approach has several benefits. Good software is available from well-known, well-capitalized software providers that can provide the level of functionality described in this appendix. Why not let them assume the risk and cost of developing the software and providing customer support?

WIDE AND SHALLOW VERSUS NARROW AND DEEP

Generally speaking, the best-known, best-capitalized software companies sell "wide and shallow" software. From their perspective, the software can be used by companies in many different industries. By keeping their software "general," they can amortize its cost over a much larger universe of customers.

Unfortunately, the "wide and shallow" approach has certain limitations. An acquisition professional may be able to abstract leases into an Excel spreadsheet; however, he or she may find they cannot access these lease abstracts over the Internet from any computer, nor automatically export their content to discounted cash flow modeling software.

In other words, "wide and shallow" software also requires the using firm to bear the cost of entering data into multiple software systems. This takes time and money and risks the mistakes caused by redundant data inputs.

On the other hand, several companies focus exclusively on the specific needs of commercial real estate companies. These firms can design, develop, and deploy software that is focused on the specific needs of the real estate industry and currently represents the best approach for most firms seeking a solution to adopting due diligence technology.

ADOPTING THE NEW TECHNOLOGY

The successful adoption of any new technology is a formidable management challenge. Due diligence software is of no value unless it is adopted into the culture of a company and used by its employees in conducting their day-to-day activities.

It is critical, therefore, to successfully address the "adoption" issue, which in some ways is more critical to the successful use of due diligence technology than any of the other decisions discussed above.

To successfully adopt new software, top management must be 100 percent behind the decision to use it. Early adopters should be rewarded and technophobic employees appropriately trained and motivated.

CONCLUSION

Leveraging technology to better facilitate the production components of the real estate investment process makes common sense. By doing so, an investment manager can benefit from increased productivity and mitigation of avoidable risks.

Because there are no perfect solutions, real estate managers need to weigh the pros and cons of the issues outlined in this appendix.

However, the effort can be very worthwhile. The increasingly competitive nature of the real estate industry should motivate consideration of every possible competitive advantage.

The issues discussed in this appendix also should stimulate thinking about the benefits of a successful adoption of technology to due diligence activities as well, and the advantages and disadvantages from various alternatives, providing a framework from which a final decision can be made.

A final word of caution: If a company's culture is not open to beneficial change, consideration of adopting due diligence technology should be postponed.

Legal Documents

B-1 LETTER OF INTENT

_____, 200____

[Name]
[Company]
[Address]

Re: _____

Dear _____:

The purpose of this letter is to define the business terms under which _____ ("Seller") is prepared to sell its 100% fee simple interest in _____ (the "Property") to _____ _____("Buyer").

1. **Property.** The Property consists of three two-story office buildings, containing approximately _____ rentable square feet of office space situated on approximately _____ acres of land located at _____ in ____ _____.

2. **Purchase Price.** The Purchase Price shall be_____ _____ Dollars ($_____), all cash.

3. **Deposit.** A deposit (the "Deposit") in the amount of _____Dollars ($_____) shall be paid into escrow by Buyer upon the full execution of and subject to the Contract and shall be refundable (i) for any reason whatsoever prior to the expiration of the Due Diligence Period (as defined below) and (ii) if the transaction fails to close after the expiration of the Due Diligence Period for any reason other than a default by Buyer under the Contract. At Closing, the Deposit (plus any and

all accrued interest) shall be credited to Buyer against the Purchase Price.

4. **Due Diligence Period.** Buyer shall have Thirty (30) days from the receipt of due diligence materials ("Due Diligence Period") to inspect (i) any documents related to the Property including, without limitation, any and all leases (including leases or extensions out for signature), operating statements and other financial information deemed necessary to verify the financial status of the Property, (ii) the site plans, "as-built" plans, zoning approvals, building permits, management agreements, development agreements and any other agreements pertaining to the management of the Property; and (iii) examine and/or update surveys, obtain engineering and environmental inspections, and otherwise do that which, in the opinion of Buyer, is necessary.

5. **Escrow and Title Company.** Upon execution of a Purchase Agreement, Seller shall open an escrow with the San Francisco office of Chicago Title Company (the "Title Company") and a copy of said Purchase Agreement, along with Buyer's Deposit, as set out below, shall be forwarded to the Title Company.

6. **Closing Date.** The closing date of the Purchase and Sale of the Property shall occur fifteen (15) days after the expiration of the Due Diligence Period, or as mutually agreed upon by Buyer and Seller.

7. **Closing Costs.** Closing costs for the sale contemplated herein shall be apportioned as follows: Seller shall pay one-half (1/2) of the escrow fee and the title insurance premium applicable to the standard coverage portion of the title policy. Buyer shall pay the costs of obtaining the extended coverage portion of the title policy, the cost of any endorsements, and one-half (1/2) of the escrow fee. Any real estate excise taxes, recording charges and any other escrow expenses applicable to the sale of the Property shall be paid by Buyer and Seller per local custom. Buyer and Seller shall pay the fees and expenses of their own counsel and advisers.

8. **Certain Warranties.** Buyer shall receive (i) an ALTA title insurance policy insuring its fee simple ownership of the Property subject to such exceptions as are acceptable to Buyer,

[Addressee]   **B-1 Letter of Intent**
_____, 200____
Page 3

and (ii) reasonable representations, warranties, indemnities or other satisfactory assurances from Seller.

9. **Prorations.** Buyer will receive a credit against the Purchase Price to be paid at Close of Escrow in an amount equal to the security deposits, prepaid rents, property taxes and assessments, and other items of income and expense as of midnight of the day preceding closing.

10. **Sales Commission.** Seller shall be responsible for all sales commissions and will indemnify Buyer for payment of any sales commissions paid in connection with this transaction.

11. **Purchase Agreement.** Seller shall provide Buyer with Seller's standard purchase agreement within ten (10) days of acceptance of the terms and conditions of this offer.

12. **Confidentiality.** The parties agree that the terms of this document are confidential and shall not be released to third parties (other than the parties' attorneys, consultants, partners, accountants, lenders, and advisors) without the approval of Buyer and Seller.

   Other than as required by law, the parties further agree that there shall be no public announcement of the proposed transaction unless agreed to in writing by Buyer and Seller.

13. **Acceptance.** This offer remains valid until 5:00 p.m. on _____, 200__.

   Buyer and Seller each acknowledge that (i) a transaction of this type involves many essential and nonessential terms and conditions and that there has not yet been a definitive statement of all the terms and conditions of the proposed transaction, and (ii) this letter is not intended to constitute an agreement to execute a Purchase Agreement or any real estate agreement in the future. It is the intention and understanding of Buyer and Seller that the only instrument executed between Buyer and Seller with respect to the Property shall be the Purchase Agreement and that the Purchase Agreement, if executed, will contain all of the terms and conditions deemed essential by Buyer and Seller with respect to the purchase and sale of the Property as contemplated by this letter. It is understood that, except for the obligations set forth in section 12

[Addressee]   **B-1 Letter of Intent**
_____, 200____
Page 4

"Confidentiality," neither Buyer nor Seller shall be legally bound in any manner unless and until the Purchase Agreement has been prepared, executed, and delivered by both Buyer and Seller.

If you are in agreement with the terms and conditions as generally set forth in this letter would you please indicate your acceptance of said terms and conditions by signing below and returning a fully executed copy of this letter to our attention. We look forward to working with you on the purchase of this Property.

Sincerely,

_____

_____

By: _____
Name: _____
Title: _____

Agreed and Accepted this _____ day of _____, 200___.

By: _____
Name: _____
Title: _____

B-2 PURCHASE AGREEMENT

This Purchase Agreement is made and entered into as of this _____ day of _____, 200___ (the "Effective Date"), by and between _____ _____("Purchaser"), and_____ _____, a _____ ("Seller").

In consideration of the respective agreements hereinafter set forth, Seller and Purchaser hereby agree as follows:

1. Purchase and Sale

Seller agrees to sell and convey to Purchaser, and Purchaser agrees to purchase from Seller, on the terms and conditions set forth in this Agreement, the Property. As used herein, the term the "Property" shall mean, collectively: (a) that certain parcel of land located in_____, _____ and containing approximately _____ acres of land and more particularly described on *Exhibit A* attached hereto (the "Land"), together with all of Seller's right, title, and interest in all rights, easements, and interests appurtenant thereto, including, but not limited to, any streets or other public ways adjacent to the Land and any development rights, water or mineral rights, owned by, or leased to, Seller; (b) all improvements located on the Land, including, but not limited to, _____ _____ rentable square feet (the "Building"), and all other structures, systems, and utilities associated with, and utilized by, Seller in the ownership and operation of the Building (all such improvements, together with the Building, being referred to herein as the "Improvements"); (c) all personal property owned by Seller, located on or in the Land or Improvements and used in connection with the operation and maintenance of the Property (the "Personal Property"), including, without limitation, any personal property listed on *Exhibit B* attached hereto; (d) all buildings materials, supplies, hardware, carpeting, and other inventory located on or in the Land or Improvements and maintained in connection with Seller's ownership and operation of the Property (the "Inventory"); (e) all trademarks, trade names,

B-2 Purchase Agreement

permits, approvals, and entitlements and other intangible property used in connection with the foregoing, including, without limitation, all of Seller's right, title, and interest in any and all warranties and guaranties relating to the Property (the "Intangible Personal Property"); and (f) Seller's interest in all leases and other agreements to occupy all or any portion of the Property that are in effect on the Effective Date (defined below) or into which Seller enters prior to Closing (defined below), but pursuant to the terms of this Agreement (the "Leases").

2. **Purchase Price**

    (a) The Purchase Price of the Property shall be _____ Dollars ($_____) (the "Purchase Price"). The Purchase Price shall be paid to Seller at Closing, plus or minus prorations and other adjustments hereunder, in the manner set forth in Paragraph 2(b) below.

    (b) The Purchase Price shall be paid as follows:

        (i) Within three (3) business days after the mutual execution and delivery hereof, Purchaser shall deposit the sum of _____ Dollars ($_____) with a title company designated by Purchaser ("Escrow Holder"), to secure Purchaser's performance hereunder (the "Deposit"). Interest on the Deposit shall belong to Purchaser. Prior to the expiration of the Due Diligence Period, Escrow Holder shall return the Deposit to Purchaser on Purchaser's notification that this Agreement has terminated. Thereafter, if Purchaser instructs Escrow Holder to return the Deposit, then Escrow Holder shall notify Seller of Purchaser's demand, and, unless Escrow Holder receives within seven (7) days of the date of Escrow Holder's notice an affidavit from Seller stating that there is a genuine dispute as to which party is entitled to the proceeds of the Deposit and describing the basis of Seller's claim thereto, Escrow Holder shall return the Deposit to Purchaser, without any further instructions or authorizations from Seller. Except as provided to the contrary hereinbelow, if Purchaser makes a demand for return of the Deposit and Escrow Holder does receive such an affidavit from Seller within seven (7) days after Escrow Holder's notice, then Escrow Holder shall hold the Deposit in escrow in an interest bearing account until the dispute as to which party is entitled to the proceeds of the Deposit is resolved. In the event the sale of the Property as contemplated hereunder is

2

consummated, the Deposit shall be delivered to Seller at the closing of the purchase and sale contemplated hereunder (the "Closing") and credited against the Purchase Price.

(ii) The balance of the Purchase Price shall be paid to Seller at the Closing in immediately available funds.

3. **Title to the Property**

(a) At Closing, _____ Title Company (the "Title Company") shall issue to Purchaser an ALTA Owner's Policy of Title Insurance (Form B, rev. 10/17/70) in the amount of the Purchase Price, insuring fee simple title to the Land and the Improvements in Purchaser, subject only to the Permitted Exceptions (as hereinafter defined the "Title Policy"). The Title Policy shall provide full coverage against mechanics' and material men's liens arising out of the construction, repair, or alteration of any of the Improvements, including any tenant improvements therein, and shall contain such special endorsements as Purchaser may require (the "Endorsements"). Seller shall execute and deliver to Title Company an owner's affidavit sufficient to support the issuance of the Title Policy. As used herein, the term "Permitted Exceptions" shall mean, collectively: (i) interests of tenants in possession under the existing Leases or any new Leases entered into in accordance with the terms of this Agreement, as tenants only without any right of first refusal or option to purchase all or any part of the Property or interest therein; (ii) the standard printed exceptions on an ALTA Owner's Policy of Title Insurance (Form B, rev. 10/17/70); (iii) nondelinquent liens for general real estate taxes and assessments; (iv) matters disclosed by a current survey of the Property and approved by Purchaser hereunder; and (v) any exceptions disclosed by the Preliminary Reports (as defined below) or any Supplements (as defined below) and approved by Purchaser hereunder. Notwithstanding the foregoing, the term "Permitted Exceptions" shall not include (x) any monetary liens, including, without limitation, the liens of any deeds of trust or other loan documents secured by the Property; or (y) any mechanics' liens.

4. **Due Diligence and Time for Satisfaction of Conditions**

Purchaser shall have the right to commence due diligence with respect to the Property following the Effective Date, and the due diligence period ("Due Diligence Period") shall expire on the

B-2 Purchase Agreement

date that is sixty (60) days after the Effective Date. Purchaser hereby acknowledges that it has received all of the items identified on *Exhibit G* attached hereto and identified with an asterisk. In addition to the foregoing, Seller shall make available to Purchaser and its employees, representatives, counsel, and consultants access to all of its books, records, and files relating to the Property in Purchaser's possession or reasonable control, including, without limitation, all of the items set form on said *Exhibit G* other than the Delivery Items (collectively, the "Due Diligence Items"); and Seller agrees, to the extent reasonably feasible, to allow Purchaser to make copies at Seller's office or the property management office of such items as Purchaser reasonably requests.

5. Diligence Period Conditions

The following conditions are precedent to Purchaser's obligation to purchase the Property and to deliver the Purchase Price (the "Diligence Period Conditions"):

(a) Purchaser's review and approval of title to the Property, as follows. Seller shall deliver to Purchaser at Seller's sole cost and expense, within five (5) days after the Effective Date, the following:

(i) a current standard coverage preliminary title report with respect to all of the Land, issued by Title Company, accompanied by copies of all documents referred to in the report (the "Preliminary Report");

(ii) copies of all existing and proposed easements, covenants, restrictions, agreements or other documents which affect title to the Property that are actually known by Seller and that are not disclosed by the Preliminary Reports;

(iii) a current ALTA survey of the Land and Improvements certified by a duly licensed surveyor or surveyors showing all physical conditions affecting the Property sufficient for deletion of the survey exception from the Title Policy;

(iv) copies of the most recent property tax bills for the Property;

(v) copies of all documents relating to actions, suits, and legal or administrative proceedings affecting the Property;

4

B-2 Purchase Agreement

(vi) financial information concerning income and expenses relating to the ownership and operation of the Property; and

(vii) copies of the Leases and financial information pertaining to the tenants under the Leases.

Purchaser shall deliver written notice (the "Objection Notice") to Seller, prior to the end of the Due Diligence Period, if any of the exceptions to title disclosed by the Preliminary Report, any surveys provided by Seller or any surveys obtained by Purchaser during the Due Diligence Period are objectionable to Purchaser ("Objections"). Seller shall have three (3) days after receipt of the Objection Notice to give Purchaser: (i) written notice that Seller shall use all reasonable efforts to remove all Objections from title on or before the Closing Date, or (ii) written notice that Seller elects not to cause the Objections to be removed. If Seller gives Purchaser notice under clause (ii), Purchaser shall have ten (10) days to elect to proceed with the purchase or terminate this Agreement. If Purchaser shall fail to give Seller written notice of its election within said ten (10) days, Purchaser shall be deemed to have elected to terminate this Agreement. If Seller gives notice under clause (i) above and fails to remove all the Objections prior to the Closing Date and Purchaser is unwilling to accept title subject to such Objections in its sole and absolute discretion, Purchaser shall have, as its sole right and remedy on account of such failure by Seller, the right to terminate this Agreement. In the event that Purchaser terminates this Agreement pursuant to this paragraph, the Deposit shall be immediately returned to Purchaser and neither party shall have any further obligations hereunder except to the extent set forth in Paragraphs 12(a), 15(b), 15(g), 15(k), and 15(l) hereof.

In the event the Title Company issues any supplement ("Supplement") to the Preliminary Report during the term of this Agreement, Purchaser shall have until the later of the end of the Due Diligence Period and ten (10) days following delivery of such Supplement to Purchaser to deliver an Objection Notice to Seller setting forth any Objections to any exceptions contained therein and not disclosed in the Preliminary Report, or any prior Supplement thereto. Thereafter, Seller shall have three (3) days after receipt of such Objection Notice to give Purchaser: (x) written notice that Seller shall use all reasonable efforts to remove all Objections from

5

B-2 Purchase Agreement

title on or before the Closing Date, or (y) written notice that Seller elects not to cause the Objections to be removed. If Seller gives Purchaser notice under clause (y), Purchaser shall have five (5) days to elect to proceed with the purchase or terminate this Agreement. If Purchaser shall fail to give Seller written notice of its election within said five (5) days, Purchaser shall be deemed to have elected to terminate this Agreement. If Seller gives notice under clause (x) above and fails to remove all the Objections prior to the Closing Date and Purchaser is unwilling to accept title subject to such Objections in its sole and absolute discretion, Purchaser shall have, as its sole right and remedy on account of such failure by Seller, the right to terminate this Agreement. In the event that Purchaser terminates this Agreement pursuant to this paragraph, the Deposit shall be immediately returned to Purchaser and neither party shall have any further obligations hereunder except to the extent set forth in Paragraphs 12(a), 15(b), 15(g), 15(k), and 15(l) hereof.

Notwithstanding anything to the contrary provided herein, Seller shall be obligated to remove from title prior to the Closing (a) any delinquent taxes and assessments, (b) any mechanics' liens, (c) any other monetary liens, and (d) any exceptions caused by Seller's voluntary acts after the Effective Date and not approved by Purchaser hereunder.

(b) Purchaser's review and approval in its sole and absolute discretion, prior to the end of the Due Diligence Period, of all aspects of the Property, including, without limitation, all of the Due Diligence Items, and the results of Purchaser's examinations, inspections, testing, and/or investigations of the Property and the Due Diligence Items (collectively, "Purchaser's Due Diligence Investigations"). Purchaser's Due Diligence Investigations shall include an examination for the presence or absence of Hazardous Material (as defined below) on, under, or in the Property. Notwithstanding anything to the contrary contained herein, Purchaser shall not engage in or otherwise conduct any additional environmental studies or environmental testing or sampling of any kind with respect to the Property or with respect to the soils or groundwater, or other studies which would require test boring or which testing would otherwise damage or disturb any portion of the Property, without obtaining Seller's prior written consent thereto, which consent Seller shall not unreasonably withhold, delay, or condition. Seller or its representative may be present to observe

6

any testing performed on the Property by Purchaser or its representatives. As used herein, the term "Hazardous Material" shall mean any substance, chemical, waste, or other material which is listed, defined, or otherwise identified as "hazardous" or "toxic" under any federal, state, local, or administrative agency ordinance or law, including, without limitation, the Comprehensive Environmental Response, Compensation and Liability Act, 42 U.S.C. §§ 9601 *et seq.*; and the Resource Conservation and Recovery Act, 42 U.S.C. §§ 6901 *et seq.*; or any regulation, order, rule, or requirement adopted thereunder, as well as any formaldehyde, urea, polychlorinated biphenyls, petroleum, petroleum product or by-product, crude oil, natural gas, natural gas liquids, liquefied natural gas, or synthetic gas usable for fuel or mixture thereof, radon, asbestos, and "source," "special nuclear" and "by-product" material as defined in the Atomic Energy Act of 1985, 42 U.S.C. §§ 3011 *et seq.*

(c) Purchaser's review and approval, prior to the expiration of the Due Diligence Period, of a schedule prepared by Seller and delivered to Purchaser on or before the Effective Date, identifying all of the service contracts and similar agreements that Seller intends to assign to Purchaser at Closing (the "Schedule of Agreements"). Purchaser shall have the right, in its sole discretion, to require the termination of any service contract or other agreement identified on the Schedule of Agreements effective as of the Closing Date, by delivering to Seller written notice (the "Contract Termination Notice") on or before the expiration of the Due Diligence Period, provided that such contract or agreement is terminable by Seller without the payment of any fee or penalty and Purchaser provides to Seller adequate notice that Purchaser shall require the termination of such contract or agreement (collectively "Terminable Agreements"). If Purchaser fails to deliver the Contract Termination Notice within such time period, Purchaser shall be deemed to have elected to assume all of the agreements identified on the Schedule of Agreements. Under all circumstances, Seller shall cause to be terminated as of the Closing all property management agreements and leasing agreements with respect to the Property. Those service contracts and agreements identified on the Schedule of Agreements that are not terminated by Purchaser pursuant to this Paragraph 5(c) are referred to herein as the "Assumed Contracts."

7

B-2 Purchase Agreement

(d) Purchaser's review and approval of reports by engineers and/or architects selected by Purchaser to inspect the Property.

(e) Purchaser's review and approval of evidence satisfactory to Purchaser and its legal counsel that the Property complies with all applicable zoning, subdivision, land use, redevelopment, energy, environmental, building, and other governmental requirements applicable to the use, maintenance, and occupancy of the Property.

(f) Review and approval by Purchaser and its legal counsel of all documentation relating to leases, contracts, service agreements, closing documentation, title, certificates of occupancy, and all other legal matters related to the Property and its acquisition by Purchaser.

(g) Receipt by Purchaser of a certificate, in form satisfactory to Purchaser, confirming that all state and local real property and business taxes pertaining to the Property (including, without limitation, all corporate, sales, and withholding taxes) have been paid in full by Seller.

Prior to the end of the Due Diligence Period, Purchaser shall deliver written notice (the "Approval Notice") to Seller informing Seller whether or not Purchaser has approved or waived all of the Diligence Period Conditions. Notwithstanding anything in this Agreement to the contrary, Purchaser shall have the right to terminate this Agreement at any time prior to the end of the Due Diligence Period in its sole and absolute discretion and for any or for no reason whatsoever. If, by the end of the Due Diligence Period, Purchaser shall not have delivered the Approval Notice to Seller approving or waiving all of the Diligence Period Conditions, then this Agreement shall automatically terminate. In the event that this Agreement is terminated pursuant to this paragraph, the Deposit shall be immediately returned to Purchaser and neither party shall have any further obligations hereunder except to the extent set forth in Paragraphs 12(a), 15(b), 15(g), 15(k), and 15(l) hereof.

6. **Conditions to Closing**

The following conditions are precedent to Purchaser's obligation to acquire the Property and to deliver the Purchase Price

DOCSSF1:843643.1
1-3150 NWN

B-2 Purchase Agreement

(the "Conditions Precedent"). If any Conditions Precedent are not satisfied as determined by Purchaser in Purchaser's sole discretion, Purchaser may elect by written notice to Seller to terminate the Agreement and receive a refund of the Deposit. Upon such termination, neither party shall have any further obligations hereunder except as provided in Paragraphs 12(a), 15(b), 15(g), 15(k) and 15(l) hereof.

(a) This Agreement shall not have terminated pursuant to any other provision hereof, including, without limitation, Paragraph 5 above.

(b) Seller's obtaining and delivering to Purchaser tenant estoppel certificates from all of the tenants ("Tenants") of the Property in the form attached hereto as *Exhibit H*, as revised by Seller to reflect the terms of the respective Leases, and modified to address specific concerns arising as a result of Purchaser's review of the Leases that are conveyed to Seller in writing prior to the expiration of the Due Diligence Period (the "Estoppel Form"). Seller shall deliver to each of the Tenants of the Property, and shall use its reasonable efforts to obtain from each of the Tenants, a tenant estoppel certificate in the Estoppel Form.

(c) The physical condition of the Property shall be substantially the same on the day of Closing as on the date of Purchaser's execution of this Agreement, reasonable wear and tear and loss by casualty excepted (subject to the provisions of Paragraph 11 below), and, as of the day of Closing, there shall be no litigation or administrative agency or other governmental proceeding of any kind whatsoever, pending or threatened, which after Closing would materially adversely affect the value of the Property or the ability of Purchaser to operate the Property in the manner in which it is currently being operated, and no proceedings shall be pending or threatened which could or would cause the redesignation or other modification of the zoning classification of, or of any, buildings code requirements applicable to the Property or any portion thereof, which after Closing would materially adversely affect the value of the Property or the ability of Purchaser to operate the Property in the manner in which it is currently being operated.

(d) As of the Closing Date, there shall be no increase in the rentable area of the Building with respect to which (i) a Lease is not in full force and effect, (ii) a Lease default exists by either Tenant or

9

B-2 Purchase Agreement

Seller, or (iii) a Tenant is the subject of a pending bankruptcy or insolvency proceeding, from that which existed and was disclosed to or otherwise known by Purchaser at the end of the Due Diligence Period.

(e) Title Company shall be irrevocably and unconditionally committed to issue to Purchaser the Title Policy as described in Paragraph 3(a) above (subject only to payment of its premiums therefor).

(f) All of Seller's representations and warranties contained herein shall be true and correct on the Closing Date.

7. **Remedies**

(a) In the event the sale of the Property is not consummated because of the failure of any condition or any other reason except a default under this Agreement solely on the part of Purchaser, the Deposit shall immediately be returned to Purchaser. If said sale is not consummated solely because of a default under this Agreement on the part of Purchaser, Seller shall be excused from further performance hereunder and the Deposit shall be paid to and retained by Seller as liquidated damages. The parties have agreed that Seller's actual damages, in the event of a default by Purchaser, would be extremely difficult or impracticable to determine. THEREFORE, BY PLACING THEIR INITIALS BELOW, THE PARTIES ACKNOWLEDGE THAT THE DEPOSIT HAS BEEN AGREED UPON, AFTER NEGOTIATION, AS THE PARTIES' REASONABLE ESTIMATE OF SELLER'S DAMAGES AND AS SELLER'S EXCLUSIVE REMEDY AGAINST PURCHASER, AT LAW OR IN EQUITY, IN THE EVENT OF A DEFAULT UNDER THIS AGREEMENT ON THE PART OF PURCHASER. THE PARTIES ACKNOWLEDGE THAT THE PAYMENT OF SUCH LIQUIDATED DAMAGES IS NOT INTENDED AS A FORFEITURE OR PENALTY, BUT IS INTENDED TO CONSTITUTE LIQUIDATED DAMAGES TO SELLER.

INITIALS: Seller _____
                 Purchaser _____

(b) In the event the sale of the Property is not consummated because of a default under this Agreement on the part of Seller, Purchaser may either (1) terminate this Agreement by delivery of

10

B-2 Purchase Agreement

written notice of termination to Seller, whereupon (A) the Deposit shall be immediately returned to Purchaser, and (B) Seller shall pay to Purchaser any out-of-pocket title, escrow, legal and inspection fees, costs and expenses actually incurred by Purchaser and any other out-of-pocket fees, costs, and expenses actually incurred by Purchaser in connection with the performance of its due diligence review of the Property and the negotiation and performance of this Agreement, including, without limitation, environmental and engineering consultants' fees and expenses, and neither party shall have any further rights or obligations hereunder except to the extent set forth in Paragraphs 12(a), 15(b), 15(g), 15(k), and 15(l) hereof; or (2) continue this Agreement and bring an action for specific performance hereof.

8. Closing and Escrow

(a) Upon mutual execution of this Agreement, the parties hereto shall deposit an executed counterpart of this Agreement with Title Company and this Agreement shall serve as instructions to Title Company for consummation of the purchase and sale contemplated hereby. Seller and Purchaser agree to execute such additional escrow instructions as may be appropriate to enable the Title Company to comply with the terms of this Agreement; provided, however, that in the event of any conflict between the provisions of this Agreement and any supplementary escrow instructions (other than joint escrow instructions), the terms of this Agreement shall control.

(b) The parties shall conduct an escrow Closing pursuant to this Paragraph 8 on the date that is the date that is fifteen (15) days after the expiration of the Due Diligence Period, or on such other date as Purchaser and Seller may agree in their sole and absolute discretion (the "Closing Date"). In the event the Closing does not occur on or before the Closing Date, the Title Company shall, unless it is notified by both parties to the contrary within five (5) days after the Closing Date, return to the depositor thereof items which were deposited hereunder. Any such return shall not, however, relieve either party of any liability it may have for its wrongful failure to close.

(c) At or before the Closing, Seller shall deliver to Title Company (for delivery to Purchaser upon Closing) the following (other than the materials described in clause [xi] below, which shall

11

B-2 Purchase Agreement

be delivered directly to Purchaser by Seller substantially concurrent with the Closing):

(i) a duly executed and acknowledged _____ deed in the form attached hereto as *Exhibit C* (the "Deed");

(ii) a bill of sale in the form attached hereto as *Exhibit D* (the "Bill of Sale");

(iii) an assignment of service contracts, warranties, and guaranties and other intangible property in the form attached hereto as *Exhibit E* (the "Assignment of Intangible Property");

(iv) an assignment of leases in the form attached hereto as *Exhibit F* (the "Assignment of Leases");

(v) duly executed estoppel certificates as required pursuant to Paragraph 6(b) above to the extent such estoppel certificates have not previously been delivered to Purchaser as provided in Paragraph 6(b) above;

(vi) originals of all Leases, Assumed Contracts, and, to the extent in Seller's possession or reasonable control, buildings permits, certificates of occupancy, plans and specifications for the Improvements and all tenant-occupied space included within the Improvements, and all other material documents, agreements, and correspondence and items relating to the ownership, operation, maintenance, or management of the Property;

(vii) notices to the Tenants in form reasonably satisfactory to Purchaser and Seller, duly executed by Seller, which notices, shall, among other matters, inform the Tenants that their security deposits have been transferred to Purchaser;

(viii) a "FIRPTA Affidavit" pursuant to Section 1445 (b)(2) of the Internal Revenue Code, duly executed by Seller;

(ix) a duly executed and acknowledged excise tax affidavit with respect to the Property in a form reasonably acceptable to Purchaser;

(x) such resolutions, authorizations, bylaws, or other corporate and/or partnership documents relating to Seller as shall be required by Title Company;

12

B-2 Purchase Agreement

(xi) the certificate certifying as to Seller's representations and warranties as required by Paragraph 9(b) below;

(xii) a duly executed and acknowledged affidavit of real property value with respect to the Property;

(xiii) keys to all locks located in or about any portion of the Property and all personal property described in the Bill of Sale to the extent in Seller's possession or reasonable control; and

(xiv) any other closing documents reasonably requested by Title Company or Purchaser. Purchaser may waive compliance on Seller's part under any of the foregoing items by an instrument in writing.

(d) At or before the Closing, Purchaser shall deliver to Title Company (for delivery to Seller upon Closing) the following:

(i) the duly executed Assignment of Leases and Assignment of Intangible Property; such resolutions, authorizations, bylaws, or other corporate and/or partnership documents or agreements relating to Purchaser as shall be required by Title Company;

(ii) the duly executed and acknowledged affidavit of real property value;

(iii) any other customary and/or reasonable closing documents requested by Title Company or Seller (provided that in no event shall any such documents increase the liability of Purchaser); and

(iv) the balance of the Purchase Price in cash or other immediately available funds, subject to prorations and adjustments as set forth herein.

(e) Seller and Purchaser shall each deposit such other instruments as are reasonably required by the Title Company or otherwise required to close the escrow and consummate the acquisition of the Property in accordance with the terms hereof (provided that in no event shall any such documents increase the liability of Purchaser or Seller). Seller and Purchaser hereby designate Title Company as the "Reporting Person" for the transaction pursuant to Section 6045(e) of the Internal Revenue

13

B-2 Purchase Agreement

Code and the regulations promulgated thereunder and agree to execute such documentation as is reasonably necessary to effectuate such designation.

(f) The following are to be apportioned as of the Closing Date as follows, with Purchaser being deemed to be the owner of the Property during the entire day on which the Deed is recorded and being entitled to receive all income of the Property, and being obligated to pay all expenses of the Property, with respect to such day:

(i) *Rent.* Rent for the current month under the Leases shall be apportioned as of the Closing Date, regardless of whether or not such rent has been paid to Seller. With respect to any rent arrearages arising under the Leases (as well as any interest earned thereon or any late charges imposed thereon), after Closing Purchaser shall pay to Seller any rent actually collected which is applicable to the period preceding the Closing Date; provided, however, that all rent collected by Purchaser shall be applied first to all unpaid rent accruing after the Closing Date, and then to unpaid rent accruing prior to the Closing Date. Purchaser shall use good faith efforts for a period of twelve (12) months after Closing to recover rent arrearages, provided that Purchaser shall not be obligated to sue any Tenant, evict any Tenant, terminate any Tenant's lease or institute any other legal or quasilegal proceeding against any Tenant. Seller shall not be permitted to take any steps to recover any rent arrearages after Closing, provided that Seller shall have the right to commence suit against a Tenant to recover rent arrearages (as well as any interest earned thereon or any late charges imposed thereon) for a period of twelve (12) months after the Closing and prosecute such suit to completion, and Seller shall have the right to sue a Tenant at any time after such Tenant's Lease has expired or otherwise terminated, provided that in no event shall Seller have the right to bring either an unlawful detainer action, terminate any Tenant's lease, or seek recourse to a Tenant's security deposit transferred to Purchaser.

(ii) *Leasing Costs, Tenant Inducements.* Seller shall pay all leasing commissions and Tenant improvement costs arising under or in connection with any Lease executed on or before the Effective Date.

14

(iii) *Security Deposits, Prepaid Rent.* Purchaser shall be entitled to a credit against the Purchase Price for the total sum of all security deposits that are required to be returned to the Tenants under their respective Leases (including any interest earned thereon to the extent such interest is to be repaid to any Tenant), and Purchaser shall assume at the Closing the obligation under the Leases with respect to all security deposits credited to Purchaser.

(iv) *Other Tenant Charges.* For all items subject to proration for which the landlord receives reimbursement from the Tenants as common area maintenance charges ("CAM Charges"), it is acknowledged that Seller has prepaid certain CAM Charges and already received reimbursement on account of certain estimated CAM Charges for the period prior to Closing and Purchaser will similarly make certain payments and receive reimbursements on account of CAM Charges for the period after Closing. Seller shall be responsible for collection of all estimated CAM Charges, including all delinquent amounts, payable by the Tenants prior to Closing, and Purchaser shall be responsible for collection of all estimated CAM Charges, including delinquent amounts, payable by the Tenants after Closing, and the parties agree to cooperate with each other to the extent reasonably necessary to enable a party to collect such CAM Charges. Consistent with the foregoing sentence, Purchaser and Seller shall prorate the expense items which are subject to reimbursement pursuant to the CAM Charges in such a way that Seller shall be responsible for the payment of all costs and expenses which are intended to be reimbursed by such CAM Charges for the period prior to Closing, and Purchaser shall be responsible for all such costs and expenses after Closing. At the end of the fiscal year applicable to the CAM Charges described in the preceding sentences of this subparagraph, to the extent that the landlord has received excess CAM Charges and is obligated to reimburse to the Tenants any portion of the excess CAM charges collected by Seller, Seller shall, within ten (10) days of written demand therefor (together with reasonably satisfactory supporting evidence), reimburse to Purchaser the portion of such excess CAM Charges which have been paid to and retained by Seller, and Purchaser shall thereafter assume the obligation under the Leases to return such amounts to the Tenants. In the event that at the end of the fiscal year applicable to such CAM Charges, Tenants on the Property are obligated to pay to the landlord any sums on account of an underpayment of CAM Charges, Purchaser shall pay to Seller

15

B-2 Purchase Agreement

promptly after receipt thereof Seller's portion of such reimbursement by the Tenants that relates to the period prior to the Closing Date. Purchaser shall deliver to Seller at the same time that such notices are delivered to the Tenants any accounting or reconciliation of the CAM Charges for the fiscal year in which the Closing occurs.

(v) *Utility Charges.* Seller shall be responsible for the cost of all utilities used prior to the Closing Date, except to the extent such utility charges are billed to and paid by Tenants directly.

(vi) *Other Apportionments, Closing Costs.* Amounts payable under the Assumed Contracts, annual or periodic permit and/or inspection fees (calculated on the basis of the period covered), and liability for other Property operation and maintenance expenses and other recurring costs, shall be apportioned as of the Closing Date. Seller shall pay all transfer taxes and excise taxes with respect to the Property and sales tax (if any) on the Personal Property. Seller shall pay the premium for the Title Policy that is properly allocable to the CLTA or standard coverage portion thereof and all endorsements, and Purchaser shall pay the portion for such premium that is properly allocable to the ALTA or extended coverage portion. Seller shall be responsible for all costs incurred in connection with the prepayment or satisfaction of any loan secured by the Property, including, without limitation, any prepayment fees, penalties, or charges. Seller shall pay the costs and fees payable in connection with the assignment to Purchaser of any warranties and guaranties with respect to the Property. All other costs and charges of the escrow for the sale not otherwise provided for in this Subparagraph 8(f)(vi) or elsewhere in this Agreement shall be allocated in accordance with the applicable closing customs for the county in which the Property is located as determined by the Title Company.

(vii) *Real Estate Taxes and Special Assessments.* All delinquent real estate taxes and assessments shall be paid by Seller at or before Closing. Nondelinquent real estate taxes and assessments shall be prorated between Purchaser and Seller as of the Closing Date using the actual current tax bill, but if such tax bill is not available at Closing, then such proration shall use an estimate calculated to be 102% of the amount of the previous year's tax bill, subject to a post-Closing reconciliation using the actual current tax bill when received pursuant to Subparagraph 8(f)(ix)

16

below. In the proration(s), Purchaser shall be credited with an amount equal to the real estate taxes and assessments applicable to the period prior to the Closing Date, to the extent such amount has not been actually paid by Seller. In the event that Seller has paid prior to Closing any real estate taxes or assessments applicable to the period after the Closing Date, Seller shall be entitled to a credit for such amount. If, after Closing, any additional real estate taxes or assessments applicable to the period prior to the Closing Date are levied for any reason, including back assessments, escape assessments or any assessments under, then Seller shall pay all such additional amounts.

(viii) *Preliminary Closing Adjustment.* Seller and Purchaser shall jointly prepare a preliminary Closing adjustment on the basis of the Leases and other sources of income and expenses, and shall endeavor to deliver such computation to Title Company at least two (2) days prior to Closing.

(ix) *Post-Closing Reconciliation.* If any of the aforesaid prorations cannot be calculated accurately on the Closing Date, then they shall be calculated as soon after the Closing Date as feasible. Either party owing the other party a sum of money based on such subsequent proration(s) shall promptly pay said sum to the other party, from the Closing Date to the date of payment, if payment is not made within ten (10) days after delivery of a bill therefor.

(x) *Survival.* The provisions of this Paragraph 8(f) shall survive the Closing.

9. **Representations and Warranties of Seller**

(a) Seller hereby represents and warrants to Purchaser as follows:

(i) Seller has not, and as of the Closing Seller shall not, have (A) made a general assignment for the benefit of creditors; (B) filed any voluntary petition in bankruptcy or suffered the filing of any involuntary petition by Seller's creditors; (C) suffered the appointment of a receiver to take possession of all, or substantially all, of Seller's assets, which remains pending as of such time; (D) suffered the attachment or other judicial seizure of all, or substantially all, of Seller's assets, which remains pending as of

17

B-2 Purchase Agreement

such time; (E) admitted in writing its inability to pay its debts as they come due; or (F) made an offer of settlement, extension, or composition to its creditors generally.

(ii) Seller is not, and as of the Closing shall not be, a "foreign person" as defined in Section 1445 of the Internal Revenue Code of 1986, as amended (the "Code"), and any related regulations.

(iii) This Agreement (A) has been duly authorized, executed, and delivered by Seller; and (B) does not, and as of the Closing shall not, violate any provision of any agreement or judicial order to which Seller is a party or to which Seller or the Property is subject.

(iv) Seller has full and complete power and authority to enter into this Agreement and to perform its obligations hereunder, subject to the terms and conditions of this Agreement.

(v) The copies of the Leases delivered to Purchaser by Seller are true, correct, and complete copies of the Leases. The only Tenants or other persons possessing contractual rights to occupy a portion of the Property as of the Effective Date are set forth on *Schedule 1* attached hereto (the "Rent Roll") or are permitted assignees or subtenants under the Leases. The Rent Roll is true and correct in all material respects as of the Effective Date.

(vi) To Seller's knowledge, there is no litigation pending or threatened with respect to the Property or the transactions contemplated hereby.

(vii) To Seller's knowledge, there are no violations of any applicable buildings codes or any applicable environmental, zoning, or land use law, or any other applicable local, state, or federal law or regulation relating to the Property, including, without limitation, the Americans with Disabilities Act of 1990.

(viii) To Seller's knowledge, Seller has not failed to obtain any material governmental permit necessary for the operation of the Improvements in the manner in which they are presently being operated.

(ix) To Seller's knowledge, Seller is not in default under any of the Leases.

18

(x) To Seller's knowledge, no Tenant is in default under the terms of its respective Lease.

(xi) To Seller's knowledge, there are no condemnation proceedings pending or threatened that would result in the taking of any portion of the Property. Seller has not received any written notice of any special assessment proceedings affecting the Property that is not disclosed on the Preliminary Reports.

(xii) Seller has not granted any option or right of first refusal or first opportunity to any party to acquire any fee or ground leasehold interest in any portion of the Property.

(xiii) To the best of Seller's knowledge, there are no physical, structural, or mechanical defects applicable to the Property.

(xiv) The Due Diligence Items and documents delivered to Purchaser pursuant to this Agreement will be all of the relevant documents, materials, reports, and other items pertaining to the condition and operation of the Property, will be true and correct copies, and will be in full force and effect, without default by any party and without any right of set-off except as disclosed in writing at the time of such delivery.

(xv) Neither Seller nor any of its affiliates or partners is a "disqualified person" under Section 4975(e) of the Code or a "party in interest" within the meaning of Section 3(14) of the Employee Retirement Income Security Act of 1974, as amended ("ERISA"), with respect to Purchaser or any investor therein.

(xvi) Neither Seller, nor to the best of Seller's knowledge, any third party, has used, manufactured, stored, or disposed of, on under or about the Property, or transported to or from the Property, any Hazardous Materials.

(xvii) Seller is in compliance with all laws, statutes, rules, and regulations or any federal, state, or local governmental authority in the United States of America applicable to Seller and all beneficial owners of Seller, including, without limitation, the requirements of Executive Order No. 133224, 66 Fed Reg. 49079 (September 25, 2001) (the "Order") and other similar requirements contained in the rules and regulations of the Office of Foreign Asset

19

B-2 Purchase Agreement

Control, Department of the Treasury ("OFAC") and in any enabling legislation or other Executive Orders in respect thereof (the Order and such other rules, regulations, legislation, or orders are collectively called the "Orders"). Neither Seller nor any beneficial owner of Seller:

(1) is listed on the Specially Designated Nationals and Blocked Persons List maintained by OFAC pursuant to the Order and/or on any other list of terrorists or terrorist organizations maintained pursuant to any of the rules and regulations of OFAC or pursuant to any other applicable Orders (such lists are collectively referred to as the "Lists");

(2) has been determined by competent authority to be subject to the prohibitions contained in the Orders;

(3) is owned or controlled by, nor acts for or on behalf of, any person or entity on the Lists or any other person or entity who has been determined by competent authority to be subject to the prohibitions contained in the Orders; or

(4) shall transfer or permit the transfer of any interest in Seller or any beneficial owner in Seller to any person who is or whose beneficial owners are listed on the Lists.

(b) It shall be a condition precedent to Purchaser's obligation to purchase the Property and to deliver the Purchase Price that all of Seller's representations and warranties contained in or made pursuant to this Agreement shall have been true and correct when made and shall be true and correct as of the Closing Date. At the Closing, Seller shall deliver to Purchaser a certificate certifying that each of Seller's representations and warranties contained in Paragraph 9(a) above are true and correct as of the Closing Date.

(c) All representations and warranties by the respective parties contained herein or made in writing pursuant to this Agreement shall be deemed to be material and shall survive the execution and delivery of this Agreement and the Closing for a period of twelve (12) months. In the event that a claim is not made with respect to a breach of a representation or warranty set forth herein or made in writing pursuant to this Agreement within such twelve (12) month period, such claim shall be deemed waived.

DOCSSF1:843643.1
1-3150 NWN

(d) Purchaser understands and agrees that the phrase "to Seller's knowledge" or "receipt of notice" or in either case words of similar import, as used in this Agreement, means only the actual knowledge of, without investigation, or the receipt of notice by, ___ _____.

10. **Representations and Warranties of Purchaser**

Purchaser hereby represents and warrants to Seller as follows:

(a) Purchaser is a duly organized and validly existing limited liability company in good standing under the laws of the State of _____; this Agreement and all documents executed by Purchaser which are to be delivered to Seller at the Closing are or at the time of Closing will be duly authorized, executed, and delivered by Purchaser, and do not and at the time of Closing will not violate any provisions of any agreement or judicial order to which Purchaser is subject.

(b) Purchaser has not, and as of the Closing Purchaser shall not have (i) made a general assignment for the benefit of creditors, (ii) filed any voluntary petition in bankruptcy or suffered the filing of any involuntary petition by Purchaser's creditors, (iii) suffered the appointment of a receiver to take possession of all, or substantially all, of Purchaser's assets, which remains pending as of such time, (iv) suffered the attachment or other judicial seizure of all, or substantially all, of Purchaser's assets, which remains pending as of such time, (v) admitted in writing its inability to pay its debts as they come due, or (vi) made an offer of settlement, extension, or composition to its creditors generally.

(1) (c) Buyer is in compliance with all laws, statutes, rules, and regulations or any federal, state, or local governmental authority in the United States of America applicable to Buyer and all beneficial owners of Buyer, including, without limitation, the requirements of Executive Order No. 133224, 66 Fed Reg. 49079 (September 25, 2001) (the "Order") and other similar requirements contained in the rules and regulations of the Office of Foreign Asset Control. Department of the Treasury ("OFAC") and in any enabling legislation or other Executive Orders in respect thereof (the Order and such other rules, regulations, legislation, or orders are collectively called the "Orders"). Buyer agrees to make its policies,

21

B-2 Purchase Agreement

procedures, and practices regarding compliance with the Orders available to Seller for its review and inspection during normal business hours and upon reasonable prior notice. Neither Buyer nor any beneficial owner of Buyer is listed on the Specially Designated Nationals and Blocked Persons List maintained by OFAC pursuant to the Order and/or on any other list of terrorists or terrorist organizations maintained pursuant to any of the rules and regulations of OFAC or pursuant to any other applicable Orders (such lists are collectively referred to as the "Lists");

      (2) has been determined by competent authority to be subject to the prohibitions contained in the Orders;

      (3) is owned or controlled by, nor acts for or on behalf of, any person or entity on the Lists or any other person or entity who has been determined by competent authority to be subject to the prohibitions contained in the Orders; or

      (4) shall transfer or permit the transfer of any interest in Buyer or any beneficial owner in Buyer to any person who is or whose beneficial owners are listed on the Lists.

11. Risk of Loss

      (a) Purchaser shall be bound to purchase the Property for the full Purchase Price as required by the terms hereof, without regard to the occurrence or effect of any damage to the Property or destruction of any improvements thereon or condemnation of any portion of the Property, provided that (i) the cost to repair any such damage or destruction, or the diminution in the value of the remaining Property as a result of a partial condemnation, does not exceed $100,000, (ii) in the case of any such damage or destruction, the repair can be completed within ninety (90) days and no Tenant shall be entitled to terminate its Lease or abate its rent as a result of such occurrence, and (iii) upon the Closing, there shall be a credit against the Purchase Price due hereunder equal to the amount of any insurance proceeds or condemnation awards collected by Seller as a result of any such damage or destruction or condemnation, less any sums reasonably expended by Seller toward the restoration or repair of the Property, and, if all of the proceeds or awards have not been collected as of the Closing, then such proceeds or awards shall be assigned to Purchaser, and

DOCSSF1:843643.1
1-3150 NWN

B-2 Purchase Agreement

Purchaser shall also be entitled to a credit against the Purchase Price in the amount of any deductible or uninsured loss.

(b) If the amount of the damage or destruction or con-demnation as specified in Paragraph 11(a) above exceeds $_____, or, in the case of any such damage or destruction, the repair cannot be completed within ninety (90) days or one or more Tenants is be entitled to terminate its Lease or abate its rent as a result of such occurrence, then Purchaser may, at its option to be exercised within twenty (20) days of Seller's written notice of the occurrence of the damage or destruction or the commencement of condemnation proceedings, either terminate this Agreement or consummate the purchase for the full Purchase Price as required by the terms hereof. If Purchaser elects to terminate this Agreement or fails to give Seller written notice within such 20-day period that Purchaser will proceed with the purchase, then the Deposit shall be immediately returned to Purchaser and neither party shall have any further rights or obligations hereunder except to the extent set forth in Paragraphs 12(a), 15(b), 15(g), 15(k), and 15(l) hereof. If Purchaser elects to proceed with the purchase, then upon the Closing there shall be a credit against the Purchase Price due hereunder equal to the amount of any insurance proceeds or condemnation awards collected by Seller as a result of any such damage or destruction or condemnation, less any sums reasonably expended by Seller toward the restoration or repair of the Property, and, if all of the proceeds or awards have not been collected as of the Closing, then such proceeds or awards shall be assigned to Purchaser, and Purchaser shall also be entitled to a credit against the Purchase Price in the amount of any deductible or uninsured loss.

12. **Access, Indemnity, Possession**

(a) Commencing on the Effective Date and through the Closing Date or the earlier termination of this Agreement, Seller shall afford authorized representatives of Purchaser reasonable access to the Property for purposes of satisfying Purchaser with respect to the representations, warranties and covenants of Seller contained herein and with respect to satisfaction of any Diligence Period Condition or any Condition Precedent, including, without limitation, for the purpose of conducting Tenant interviews, provided (i) such access does not interfere in any material respect with the operation of the Property or the rights of the Tenants, (ii) Purchaser

23

B-2 Purchase Agreement

shall not contact any Tenant without providing Seller with at least one (1) business day's prior written notice, and (iii) Seller shall have the right to preapprove in its reasonable discretion and be present during any physical testing of the Property or interviews of Tenants. Purchaser hereby agrees to indemnify, defend, and hold Seller and Lender harmless from and against any and all claims, judgments, damages, losses, penalties, fines, demands, liabilities, encumbrances, liens, costs, and expenses (including reasonable attorneys' fees, court costs, and costs of appeal) actually suffered or incurred by Seller and to the extent arising out of or resulting from damage or injury to persons or property caused by Purchaser or its authorized representatives during their investigation of, entry onto, and/or inspections of the Property prior to the Closing. If this Agreement is terminated, Purchaser shall repair the damage caused by Purchaser's entry onto and/or inspections of the Property, provided the foregoing shall not require Purchaser to repair or remediate any conditions that are discovered by Purchaser. The foregoing indemnity shall survive the Closing, or in the event that the Closing does not occur, the termination of this Agreement.

(b) Possession of the Property shall be delivered to Purchaser on the Closing Date, subject to the rights of Tenants under the Leases.

13. Seller Covenants

(a) At the time of Closing, Seller shall cause to be paid in full all obligations under any outstanding written or oral contracts made by Seller for any improvements to the Property, and Seller shall cause to be discharged all mechanics' and material men's liens arising from any labor or materials furnished to the Property prior to the time of Closing (other than obligations that are properly the obligation of the Tenants under the Leases or any third party).

(b) Between the Effective Date and the Closing, Seller shall perform all of the landlord's obligations under the Leases in the same manner as historically performed and shall and otherwise operate and maintain the Property in the same manner as before the making of this Agreement, as if Seller were retaining the Property. Between the Effective Date and the Closing, Seller shall promptly notify Purchaser of any condemnation, environmental, zoning, or other land-use regulation proceedings of which Seller

24

B-2 Purchase Agreement

obtains knowledge, between the Effective Date and the Closing, as well as any notices of violations of any Laws relating to the Property of which Seller obtains knowledge, and any litigation of which Seller obtains knowledge, between the Effective Date and the Closing, that arises out of the ownership of the Property.

(c) Through the Closing Date, Seller shall maintain or cause to be maintained, at Seller's sole cost and expense, all policies of insurance currently in effect with respect to the Property (or comparable replacements thereof).

(d) Seller shall deliver to Purchaser copies of all Operating Statements (as defined in *Exhibit G* below) prepared in the ordinary course of business within fifteen (15) days after Seller's preparation thereof relating to periods prior to Closing, even if prepared after Closing. Seller shall also deliver to Purchaser copies of any bills for real estate taxes and personal property taxes and copies of any notices pertaining to real estate taxes or assessments applicable to the Property that are received by Seller after the Effective Date, even if received after Closing. The obligations set forth in this Paragraph 13(d) shall survive the Closing.

14. **Purchaser's Consent to New Contracts Affecting the Property, Termination of Existing Contracts**

(a) Seller shall not, after the Effective Date, enter into any Lease or contract, or any amendment thereof, or permit any Tenant to enter into any sublease, assignment, or agreement pertaining to the Property (where the consent of Seller is required under the applicable Lease), or waive any rights of Seller under any contract or Lease, without in each case obtaining Purchaser's prior written consent thereto, which consent in the case of any Lease shall include approval of the financial condition of the proposed tenant, the configuration of the space to be leased, and the terms of such Lease (including, without limitation, the rent and any concessions provided under such proposed Lease), and which consent shall not be unreasonably withheld by Purchaser (provided that Purchaser may withhold or condition its consent in its sole and absolute discretion following the end of the Due Diligence Period). Seller shall be entitled, without the consent of Purchaser, to enter into, amend, or otherwise deal with service contracts and similar agreements that are not Assumed Contracts in the ordinary course of business that are terminable on not more than thirty (30) days'

25

B-2 Purchase Agreement

prior notice and which shall not be binding on Purchaser after the Closing Date. Seller shall deliver to Purchaser, together with any request for approval of a new Lease, a copy of the proposed Lease, a description of the proposed Tenant and its proposed use of the premises and whatever financial information on the proposed Tenant Seller has received, as well as any additional information reasonably requested by Purchaser (including, without limitation, if applicable, an environmental questionnaire). Notwithstanding anything to the contrary provided in this Paragraph 14(a), if Purchaser fails to disapprove in writing any such new Lease or other action requiring Purchaser's consent under this Paragraph 14(a) within five (5) business days after Purchaser's receipt of such request and information, Purchaser shall be deemed to have approved such new Lease or other action. If Purchaser disapproves of any such new Lease or other action, Purchaser shall provide to Seller, along with such written notice of disapproval, the reasons for Purchaser's disapproval.

(b) Seller shall terminate prior to the Closing, at no cost or expense to Purchaser, any and all management agreements, service contracts or similar agreements affecting the Property that are not Assumed Contracts (other than such contracts or agreements that Seller is not obligated to terminate pursuant to Paragraph 5[c] above) and all employees, if any, of the Property.

(c) Seller shall not, after the Effective Date, create any new encumbrance or lien affecting the Property other than liens and encumbrances (i) that are reasonably capable of being discharged prior to the Closing and (ii) that in fact will be and are discharged prior to the Closing. The obligations set forth in this Paragraph 14(c) shall survive the Closing to the extent such obligations are violated prior to the Closing.

15. Miscellaneous

(a) *Notices.* Any notice, consent, or approval required or permitted to be given under this Agreement shall be in writing and shall be deemed to have been given upon (i) hand delivery, (ii) one (1) business day after being deposited with Federal Express or another reliable overnight courier service, with receipt acknowledgment requested, (iii) upon receipt if transmitted by facsimile telecopy, with a copy sent on the same day by one of the other permitted methods of delivery, or (iv) upon receipt or refused

26

delivery deposited in the United States mail, registered or certified mail, postage prepaid, return receipt required, and addressed as follows:

IF TO SELLER: _____

_____

_____

Attn: _____

Fax No. _____

WITH A COPY TO: _____

_____

_____

_____

Fax No.: _____

IF TO PURCHASER: _____

_____

_____

Fax No.: _____

_____

_____

_____

Fax No.: _____

WITH A COPY TO: _____

_____

_____

_____

_____

Fax No.: _____

or such other address as either party may from time to time specify in writing to the other.

(b) *Brokers and Finders.* Neither party has had any contact or dealings regarding the Property, or any communication in connection with the subject matter of this transaction, through any real estate broker or other person who can claim a right to a commission or finder's fee in connection with the sale contemplated

27

B-2 Purchase Agreement

herein except for _____ ("Seller's Broker"), whose commission and fees shall be paid by Seller. In the event that any other broker or finder makes a claim for a commission or finder's fee based upon any contact, dealings, or communication, the party whose conduct is the basis for the broker or finder making its claim shall indemnify, defend, and hold harmless the other party against and from any commission, fee, liability, damage, cost, and expense, including without limitation attorneys' fees, arising out of or resulting from any such claim. The provisions of this Paragraph 15(b) shall survive the Closing, or in the event that the Closing does not occur, the termination of this Agreement.

(c) *Successors and Assigns.* Purchaser reserves the right to take title to the Property in the name of a nominee or assignee, or in the name of one of the institutional investors for which Purchaser is then acting as investment manager (a "Separate Account") or a nominee or assignee of a Separate Account. In the event the rights and obligations of Purchaser hereunder shall be assigned by Purchaser to a Separate Account, the assignor shall be released from any obligation or liability hereunder, and such Separate Account shall be substituted as Purchaser hereunder and shall be entitled to the benefit of and may enforce Seller's covenants, representations, and warranties hereunder as if such Separate Account were the original Purchaser hereunder, and shall assume all obligations and liabilities of Purchaser hereunder, subject to any limitations of such liabilities and obligations hereunder or provided by law. Upon notification to Seller of any such assignment, Seller's representations and warranties hereunder shall be deemed remade to such assignee as of the date of such assignment. This Agreement shall be binding upon the successors and assigns of the parties hereto. Without limiting the foregoing, if Seller liquidates prior to satisfying all of Seller's obligations hereunder, Purchaser shall have recourse against the proceeds distributed in such liquidation to the extent of any unsatisfied obligations of Seller hereunder.

(d) *Amendments.* Except as otherwise provided herein, this Agreement may be amended or modified only by a written instrument executed by Seller and Purchaser.

(e) *Governing Law.* This Agreement shall be governed by and construed in accordance with the laws of the State of _____.

28

B-2 Purchase Agreement

(f) *Merger of Prior Agreements.* This Agreement, and the exhibits and schedules hereto, constitutes the entire agreement between the parties and supersede all prior agreements and understandings between the parties relating to the subject matter hereof.

(g) *Enforcement.* If either party hereto fails to perform any of its obligations under this Agreement or if a dispute arises between the parties hereto concerning the meaning or interpretation of any provision of this Agreement, then the defaulting party or the party not prevailing in such dispute shall pay any and all costs and expenses incurred by the other party on account of such default and/or in enforcing or establishing its rights hereunder, including, without limitation, court costs and attorneys' fees and disbursements. Any such attorneys' fees and other expenses incurred by either party in enforcing a judgment in its favor under this Agreement shall be recoverable separately from and in addition to any other amount included in such judgment, and such attorneys' fees obligation is intended to be severable from the other provisions of this Agreement and to survive and not be merged into any such judgment. The provisions of this Paragraph 15(g) shall survive the Closing, or in the event that the Closing does not occur, the termination of this Agreement.

(h) *Time of the Essence.* Time is of the essence of this Agreement.

(i) *Severability.* If any provision of this Agreement, or the application thereof to any person, place, or circumstance, shall be held by a court of competent jurisdiction to be invalid, unenforce-able, or void, the remainder of this Agreement and such provisions as applied to other persons, places, and circumstances shall remain in full force and effect.

(j) *Marketing.* During the term of this Agreement, Seller shall not list the Property with any broker or otherwise solicit or make or accept any offers to sell the Property, engage in any discussions or negotiations with any third party with respect to the sale or other disposition or financing of the Property, or enter into any contracts or agreements (whether binding or not) regarding any disposition or financing of the Property.

DOCSSF1:843643.1
1-3150 NWN

B-2 Purchase Agreement

(k) *Confidentiality.* Each party agrees to maintain in confidence, and not to disclose to any third party, the information contained in this Agreement or pertaining to the sale contemplated hereby and the information and data furnished or made available by Seller to Purchaser, its agents, and representatives in connection with Purchaser's investigation of the Property and the transactions contemplated by the Agreement; provided, however, that each party, its agents, and representatives may disclose such information and data (a) to such party's accountants, attorneys, prospective lenders, accountants, partners, consultants, and other advisors in connection with the transactions contemplated by this Agreement (collectively called "Representatives") to the extent that such Representatives reasonably need to know (in Purchaser's or Seller's reasonable discretion) such information and data in order to assist, and perform services on behalf of, Purchaser or Seller; (b) to the extent required by any applicable statute, law, regulation, governmental authority, or court order; (c) in connection with any securities filings, registration statements, or similar filings undertaken by Purchaser; and (d) in connection with any litigation that may arise between the parties in connection with the transactions contemplated by this Agreement. Purchaser shall consult with Seller prior to making any press release intended for general circulation regarding the transactions contemplated hereunder. The provisions of this Paragraph 15(k) shall survive the Closing, or in the event that the Closing does not occur, the termination of this Agreement.

(l) *Return of Documents.* In the event that this Agreement terminates, Purchaser shall return to Seller all due diligence materials and all copies thereof delivered by Seller to Purchaser hereunder. The provisions of this Paragraph 15(l) shall survive the termination of this Agreement.

(m) *Counterparts and Facsimile Signatures.* This Agreement may be executed in one or more counterparts, each of which shall be deemed an original and all of which, when taken together, shall be deemed to be one agreement. This Agreement may be executed pursuant to original or facsimile copies of signatures, with the same effect as if the parties had signed the document pursuant to original signature.

(n) *Limited Liability.* The obligations of Purchaser are intended to be binding only on Purchaser and the property of

30

B-2 Purchase Agreement

Purchaser, and shall not be personally binding upon, nor shall any resort be had to, the private properties of any of its trustees, officers, beneficiaries, directors, members, or shareholders, or of its investment manager, the general partners, officers, directors, members, or shareholders thereof, or any employees or agents of Purchaser or its investment manager.

IN WITNESS WHEREOF, the parties hereto have executed this Agreement as of the date first above written.

PURCHASER: _____

a _____

Please initial Paragraph 7(a) above

By: _____

Name: _____

_____

Title: _____

SELLER: _____,

a _____

Please initial Paragraph 7(a) above

By: _____

Name: _____

Title: _____

31

B-2 Purchase Agreement

COUNTERPART SIGNATURE PAGE TO
PURCHASE AGREEMENT

DATED AS OF _____, 200___

(TITLE COMPANY)

        Title Company agrees to act as escrow holder and title
company in accordance with the terms of this Agreement and to act
as the Reporting Person in accordance with Section 6045(e) of the
Internal Revenue Code and the regulations promulgated
thereunder.

                              _____TITLE COMPANY

                              By: _____

                              Its: _____

                              Date: _____ , 200__

Exhibit A: Legal Description Of Land [SEE ATTACHED]

Exhibit B: List Of Personal Property [SEE ATTACHED]

Exhibit C: Form of Special Warranty Deed [SEE ATTACHED]

        EXHIBIT A TO SPECIAL WARRANTY DEED: LEGAL DESCRIPTION

Exhibit D: Form of Bill of Sale

        EXHIBIT A TO BILL OF SALE: LIST OF PERSONAL PROPERTY

Exhibit E: Form of Assignment of Intangible Property

        SCHEDULE A TO ASSIGNMENT OF SERVICE CONTRACTS
        WARRANTIES AND GUARANTIES AND OTHER INTANGIBLE
        PROPERTY: REAL PROPERTY

B-2 Purchase Agreement

SCHEDULE 1 TO ASSIGNMENT OF SERVICE CONTRACTS WARRANTIES AND GUARANTIES AND OTHER INTANGIBLE PROPERTY: LIST OF WARRANTIES

SCHEDULE 2 TO ASSIGNMENT OF SERVICE CONTRACTS WARRANTIES AND GUARANTIES AND OTHER INTANGIBLE PROPERTY: LIST OF CONTRACTS

Exhibit F: Form of Assignment of Leases

EXHIBIT A TO ASSIGNMENT OF LEASES: REAL PROPERTY SCHEDULE 1 TO ASSIGNMENT OF LEASES

Exhibit G: Seller's Deliveries

Exhibit H: Tenant Estoppel Certificate (OFFICE PROPERTY)

SCHEDULE 1 RENT ROLL [SEE ATTACHED]

B-3 TENANT ESTOPPEL CERTIFICATE

(Office Property)

[Purchaser and/or Lender]

Attn: _____

Re: _____   **Suite:** _____
                                           Tenant: _____

Gentlemen:

You are hereby advised that the undersigned is the Tenant and present occupant of a portion (the "Premises") of that certain real property and improvements thereon known as _____, in the City of _____, State of _____ (the "Property"). The undersigned hereby warrants:

1. The Premises are leased under the provisions of a lease agreement dated _____, 200__. The lease agreement is valid and in existence as executed, except as amended by document(s) dated _____, copy(ies) of which is (are) attached hereto, which contain all of the understandings and agreements between Landlord and Tenant (herein collectively referred to as the "Lease"). Tenant's leased Premises occupy _____ square feet.

2. The commencement date of the term of the Lease is _____, 200__, and the expiration date is _____, 20__; and the undersigned's obligation to pay rent has commenced.

3. The Lease provides for an option to renew the Lease term as follows: _____
   _____
   _____,
   at a rental rate of $_____.

4. The Lease provides for rent payable as follows:

B-3 Tenant Estoppel Certificate

    (a)   Current minimum fixed monthly rent: $_____ with future escalations as follows:

    (b)   No rent has been paid by Tenant in advance under the Lease except for the minimum monthly rent that became due for the current month. The minimum monthly rent has been paid through _____, 200_.

    (c)   The Lease provides for the Tenant to pay ____% of any increase in property operating expenses including but not limited to insurance and real property taxes in excess of the 20__ base year operating expenses of $_____.

5.   The Lease contains no first right of refusal, option to expand, option to terminate, or exclusive business rights, except as follows: _____

_____.

6.   The Lease contains no option to purchase or preferential right to purchase all or any part of the Property or all or any part of the building or project of which the Premises are a part.

7.   Landlord is holding a security deposit of $_____.

8.   The undersigned is not in default under the Lease and is current in the payment of any taxes, utilities, common area maintenance payments, or other charges required to be paid by the undersigned.

9.   The improvements and space required to be furnished according to the Lease have been duly delivered by the Landlord and accepted by the Tenant. Landlord's obligations to pay for tenant improvements, if any, have been satisfied.

10. The undersigned has no set-offs against the Landlord, nor does the undersigned assert any claim against the Landlord for any failure of performance of any of the terms of said Lease, and there are no defaults by the Landlord, including, without limitation, defaults relating to the design, condition, and tenant uses of the building of which the Premises are a part.

B-3 Tenant Estoppel Certificate

11. The undersigned has not entered into any sublease, assignment, or any other agreement transferring any of its interest in the Lease or the Premises except as follows: _____
_____.

12. Tenant has not generated, used, stored, spilled, disposed of, or released any hazardous substances at, on, or in the Premises. "Hazardous Substances" means any flammable, explosive, toxic, carcinogenic, mutagenic, or corrosive substance or waste, including volatile petroleum products and derivatives. To the best of Tenant's knowledge, no asbestos or polychlorinated biphenyl ("PCB") is located at, on, or in the Premises. "Hazardous Substances" shall not include those materials which are technically within the definition set forth above but which are contained in prepackaged office supplies, cleaning materials, or personal grooming items or other items which are sold for consumer or commercial use and typically used in other similar buildings or space.

The undersigned makes this statement for your benefit and protection with the understanding that you (and any assignee of your right to purchase the Property) intend to rely upon this statement in connection with your intended purchase of the above described Property from Landlord. The undersigned agrees that it will, upon receipt of written notice from Landlord, commence to pay all rents to you (or your assignee) or to any agent acting on behalf of you (or your assignee).

Dated: _____, 200__.

_____
"TENANT"

_____
(Signature)

_____
(Title)

B-4 LEASE ABSTRACT

Property Information

Building Name:

Building Address:

Property Type:

Property Square
Footage:

Tenant Information

Tenant Name:

Trade Name:

Suite Number:

Tenant Billing
Address:

Tenant Type:

Type of Business:

Guarantor:

Contact Name:

Lease Terms

Lease Date:

Amendment Dates:

B-4 Lease Abstract

Lease Term: Years
                     :
                     Start   End Date:
                     Date:

Opening
Requirements:
Square Feet: Pro Rata Share:

Deposits: Security: Interest:
                                             Yes / No
                     Other:

Financial Terms

Current Base Rent   Annual: Per S.F.:

  Base Rent Schedule   Period   Rent/SF   Annual   Monthly

Annual Rent Increase: CPI   Fixed   Other

Free Rent:

Percentage Rent: Breakpoint:

Other Concessions:

Expense Responsibility
  Real Estate   *LL / Tenant*   Structural   *LL / Tenant*
Taxes: Repairs:
  Utilities: *LL / Tenant*   Parking Lot   *LL / Tenant*
                                             Repairs:

B-4 Lease Abstract

CAM:	*LL / Tenant*	Roof Repairs:	*LL / Tenant*
Landscaping:	*LL / Tenant*	Management:	*LL / Tenant*
HVAC:	*LL / Tenant*	Overhead:	*LL / Tenant*
Other ( ):	*LL / Tenant*	Admin. Fee:	% *C - T - I*

Base Year Information

	Base Year	Base Year Amount	Base Stop/SF; Net
CAM:			
Tax:			
Insurance:			

Additional Comments:

Parking:	Spaces	Rent:
Storage:	Square Feet	Rent:

Additional Lease Terms

Renewal Options	Term:	Rent:

Required Notice:

Expansion Options	Suite	Square Feet	Date	Rent

Required Notice:

Assignment/Sublet	LL Approval:	Recapture:

Cancellation/Termination	Date:	Penalty:

Required Notice:

First Right of Refusal:

B-4 Lease Abstract

First Refusal to
Purchase:
Building Planning:

Tenant Exclusives:

Subordination:

Holding Over:

Estoppel Provision: Required:

Miscellaneous Terms & Provisions:

B-5 CLOSING STATEMENT

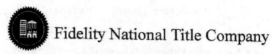 Fidelity National Title Company

3100 Oak Road, Suite 100, Walnut Creek, CA 94597
925 935-3210 • FAX 925 934-4182

DATE:
ESCROW NO.:   **TIME:**
LOCATE NO.:
ESCROW OFFICER: **CLOSING DATE:**

BUYER FINAL CLOSING STATEMENT

SELLER:
BUYER:
PROPERTY:

	$ DEBITS	$ CREDITS
FINANCIAL:		
Total Consideration	645,000.00	
Deposit -		75,000.00
Deposit -		600,000.00
PRORATIONS/ADJUSTMENTS:		
Prepaid County Taxes at $1,939.52 Semi-Annual from 7/1/2005 to 10/4/2005		1,002.08
Rents at $1,250.00 Monthly from 10/4/2005 to 10/31/2005		1,125.00
Rents at $945.00 Monthly from 10/4/2005 to 10/31/2005		850.50
Rents at $975.00 Monthly from 10/4/2005 to 10/31/2005		877.50
fixed expense reimbrusement of $100.00		251.61
last months rents		2,675.00
Security Deposit		2,375.00
TITLE CHARGES:		
04-ALTA Owners - 1992 for $645,000.00	2,439.00	
Endorsement Fee(s)	736.38	
Inspection Fee(s)	40.00	
Recording Deed	16.00	
ESCROW CHARGES:		
Escrow Fee to Fidelity National Title	950.00	
Overnight Delivery Fee	4.60	
MISCELLANEOUS:		
Civil Engineers & Surveyors, Inc. for invoice	5,893.54	
BUYERS REFUND	$29,077.17	
TOTALS	$684,156.69	$684,156.69

SAVE THIS STATEMENT FOR INCOME TAX PURPOSES

B-6 LISTING AGREEMENT

Exclusive Listing Agreement

This Exclusive Listing Agreement (the "Agreement") is made as of _____, 200__, between _____ _____ ("Owner"), and _____ ("Broker"). Owner hereby grants to Broker the exclusive right to solicit offers from parties interested in purchasing its interest in the real property described below (the "Property"). This exclusive right to solicit offers will extend for a period (the "Listing Period") commencing as of the date hereof as noted above and ending at midnight on the date that is six (6) months from the approval by the Owner of the marketing plan described in Section 2(a), below, unless this Agreement is sooner terminated in accordance with the terms hereof. Notwithstanding anything to the contrary contained herein, Owner may elect, in Owner's sole and absolute discretion, to withdraw the Property from the market at any time upon written notice to Broker. Upon such withdrawal, the Listing Period shall automatically end. The Property is located in the City of _____, County of _____, State of _____, and is more particularly described in Exhibit A.

1. All purchase offers obtained by Broker will be presented to Owner and will be subject to the approval and acceptance by Owner. The terms and conditions of any purchase offer and the proposed purchaser thereunder must be acceptable to Owner in Owner's sole and absolute discretion. Owner reserves the right to accept or reject any offer for any reason or for no reason whatsoever. Broker will not have the authority to accept any offer or proposal or to enter into any commitment on behalf of Owner.

2. Broker's services pursuant to this Agreement will include the following:

(a) No later than thirty (30) business days after the date hereof, preparing for Owner's approval, in Owner's sole discretion, descriptive offering materials and a detailed marketing plan for the Property at Broker's expense. Marketing of the Property shall at all times be conducted by Broker pursuant to a marketing plan approved by Owner. If any Owner elects to withdraw the Property from the market during the Listing Period, such Owner shall reimburse Broker for its out-of-pocket marketing expenses up to a maximum amount of _____Dollars ($_____).

(b) Providing advice and assistance in structuring the offering price and terms as required by Owner.

(c) Screening inquiries from prospective purchasers and/or other brokers.

(d) Showing the Property to prospective purchasers.

(e) Negotiating, in coordination with Owner representatives and to the extent required by Owner, the terms and conditions of the sale of the Property.

(f) Assisting Owner and its counsel in coordinating efforts to achieve timely and efficient documentation and closing of the transaction.

(g) To the extent required by Owner, assisting Owner in providing due diligence materials to prospective purchasers and providing assistance in addressing due diligence issues raised by prospective purchasers.

(h) Distribute marketing materials to prospective purchasers, provided that Broker shall first obtain Owner's consent and approval of the persons to whom marketing material may be delivered ("Approved Prospective Purchasers") before distributing marketing materials to any prospective purchasers.

3. In consideration of this authorization and Broker's agreement to diligently pursue the procurement of a purchaser for the Property and subject to the provisions of this Agreement, Owner agrees to pay Broker a commission equal to _____% of the final purchase price of the Property obtained by Owner at the close of escrow. Such fee shall be earned and payable only in the event that during the Listing Period the Property is conveyed to a purchaser, or in the event that during the Listing Period Owner enters into a contract to sell the Property to a purchaser and the Property is subsequently conveyed to such purchaser

B-6 Listing Agreement

pursuant to said contract, as extended by Owner and such purchaser. No fee or other compensation will be payable to Broker if the sale of the Property pursuant to a contract entered into by Owner and a purchaser during the Listing Period fails to close for any reason whatsoever or for no reason whatsoever in Owner's sole and absolute discretion. Owner will not reimburse Broker for any expenses incurred in connection with the sale of the Property, except as provided in Subsection 2(a) above. No Owner shall receive any real estate commission, finder's fee, or other such commission or fee with respect to the sale of the Property.

4. Subject to the provision of Paragraph 9 below, Owner agrees that during the Listing Period it will refer all further inquiries of any such parties concerning the Property to Broker so that all further negotiations between Owner and such parties will be conducted pursuant to this Agreement.

5. Notwithstanding any other provision of this Agreement, Broker understands that any and all decisions on whether to sell the Property and the timing (e.g., whether within the term of this Agreement or later) shall be made by Owner, in its sole and absolute discretion and for any reason or for no reason at all. Therefore, Broker acknowledges that it may not receive a commission, whether it be for any reason or no reason at all.

6. Owner shall also pay said commission to Broker if within three (3) months after the expiration of the Listing Period Owner enters into a contract for the sale of the Property, and such sale pursuant thereto is ultimately consummated within six (6) months after the expiration of the Listing Period, with any person or entity, (i) provided that during the term of the Listing Period either (a) such person or entity made a written offer to purchase the Property, or (b) at the expiration of the Listing Period such person or entity was actively negotiating with Owner concerning the sale of the Property and had submitted a letter of intent to purchase the Property during the Listing Period, which was countersigned by Owner; and (ii) provided further that the name of such person or entity appears on a list of persons and entities meeting the criteria set forth in clauses (a) and (b) above, which list Broker shall have delivered to Owner at the addresses stated below within seven (7) business days following the expiration of the Listing Period.

7. No signs shall be placed on the Property without the prior written consent of Owner, which consent may be withheld in Owner's sole and absolute discretion.

8. Any commission payable to Broker under this Agreement shall be paid by Owner only upon the close of escrow.

9. Owner agrees to cooperate with Broker in effecting a sale of the Property and to refer to Broker all inquiries of any person or entity interested in purchasing the Property. At any time during the terms of this Agreement, Owner may notify Broker that it wishes to conduct negotiations directly with any party or parties, and thereafter such negotiations shall be conducted by Owner without the participation of Broker. Owner shall keep Broker reasonably updated as to progress of the transaction in such event.

10. After Owner's approval of the offering materials, Broker shall submit to Owner every two (2) weeks a written status report concerning Broker's marketing efforts and any sales activity. Broker shall include in such reports the names and addresses of prospective purchasers, Broker's assessment of each prospect's level of interest, and any other information about the prospect which would be of interest to a sophisticated seller of commercial real estate or which otherwise is reasonably required by Owner.

11. At all times during the term of this Agreement, Broker shall present to Owner any and all offers or letters of intent presented to Broker with respect to the Property and shall promptly inform Owner of any other expressions of interest in the Property by potential purchasers. At all times, Broker shall provide descriptive offering materials to Approved Prospective Purchasers. Broker agrees that in the event that any other person or entity brings a claim for a portion of the commission or any other compensation based on such other person's or entity's dealings with Broker, Broker shall indemnify Owner and its partners, members, managers, shareholders, beneficiaries, trustees, officers, and directors (collectively, the "Owner Related Parties") against, and hold Owner and the Owner Related Parties harmless from, any and all claims, losses, damages, liabilities, costs, and expenses, including, without limitation,

B-6 Listing Agreement

attorneys' fees and costs, incurred by Owner in connection with such claim and its defense.

12. Broker shall indemnify, hold harmless, and defend Owner and the Owner Related Parties from any and all claims, losses, damages, liabilities, costs, and expenses, including, without limitation, attorneys' fees and costs, arising out of Broker's negligence, willful misconduct, or breach in the performance of its obligations hereunder. All indemnification obligations contained in this Agreement shall survive the expiration of the Listing Period.

13. Except for information which Owner approves for release in the offering materials for the Property or such other information Owner agrees to disclose to prospective purchasers, Broker agrees to keep all information disclosed to it by Owner regarding the Property or Owner's business, the terms of any sale of the Property and the terms of this Agreement, strictly confidential, except to the extent required by law. In making any disclosure of information authorized by Owner, Broker shall clearly state and inform all parties receiving such information that such information is provided without representation or warranty of any kind or nature, express or implied.

14. If either party (including, without limitation, any individual Owner) hereto fails to perform any of its obligations under this Agreement, or if any dispute arises between the parties hereto concerning the meaning or interpretation of any provision of this Agreement, then the defaulting party or the party not prevailing in such dispute, as the case may be, shall pay any and all costs and expenses incurred by the other party on account of such default and/or in enforcing or establishing its rights hereunder, including, without limitation, court costs and reasonable attorneys' fees and disbursements. Any such attorneys' fees and other expenses incurred by either party in enforcing a judgment in its favor under this Agreement shall be recoverable separately from and in addition to any other amount included in such judgment, and such attorneys' fees obligation is intended to be severable from the other provisions of this Agreement and to survive and not be merged into any such judgment.

15. The heirs, transferees, successors, and assigns of the parties hereto shall be duly bound by the provisions hereof, provided

B-6 Listing Agreement

Broker may not assign or otherwise transfer its right of obligations hereunder without the written consent of Owner, which may be given or withheld in Owner's sole and absolute discretion.

16. This Agreement shall be governed by the laws of the State of _____.

17. Broker hereby represents and warrants to Owner that:

    a. All persons acting on behalf of Broker hereunder are properly licensed to practice in the State of _____;

    b. Broker will use its best efforts, skill, judgment, and abilities to show the Property, offer the Property for sale, and procure a purchaser;

    c. There are no obligations, commitments or impediments of any kind that will limit or prevent performance of Broker's duties hereunder; and

    d. Broker will not use or employ any other broker to offer the Property for sale without Owner's prior written consent.

18. The parties intend that the terms of this Agreement shall be the final expression of their agreement with respect to the subject matter hereof and may not be contradicted by evidence of any prior or contemporaneous agreement. No amendments to or modifications of this Agreement shall be valid or binding unless made in writing and signed by both Owner and Broker.

19. Broker is authorized to inform potential purchasers that Owner intends to sell the Property in "As Is" condition and does not intend to make any representations with respect to the physical or environmental condition of the Property and that potential purchasers should undertake their own investigations with respect to such matters. Owner acknowledges that Broker has no specific expertise with respect to the environmental assessment or physical condition of the Property. Owner acknowledges that Broker has not made an independent investigation or determination of the physical or environmental condition of the Property.

B-6 Listing Agreement

20. The parties acknowledge that it is illegal for either Owner or Broker to refuse to show or sell the Property to any person because of race, color, religion, regional origin, sex, sexual orientation, marital status, or disability.

    IN WITNESS WHEREOF, the parties hereby execute this Agreement as of the date first listed above.

Owner:

_____
a _____

By: _____
Name: _____
Title: _____

Broker:

_____
a _____

By:_____
Name:_____
Title:_____

B-7 CONFIDENTIALITY AGREEMENT

_____, 200___

Private and Confidential

[Name]
[Company]
[Address]

Ladies and Gentlemen:

In connection with your consideration of a possible trans-action (a "Transaction") with_____
(collectively with its subsidiaries and affiliates, the "Company"), the Company is prepared to make available to you certain information concerning the business, financial condition, operations, assets and liabilities of the Company. As a condition to such information being furnished to you, you agree to treat such information in accordance with the provisions of this letter agreement and to take or abstain from taking certain other actions hereinafter set forth.

1. _Definition of Evaluation Material._ The term "Evaluation Material" means all information concerning the Company and its business (whether prepared by the Company, its advisors, or otherwise, and irrespective of the form of communication) that is furnished to you or to your Representatives (as defined below) by or on behalf of the Company at any time prior to the 15th day following notice of a decision not to proceed with a Transaction given in accordance with Section 2(d) hereof. "Evaluation Material" also shall be deemed to include all notes, analyses, compilations, studies, interpretations, or other documents prepared by you or your Representatives which contain, reflect, or are based upon, in whole or in part, the information furnished to you or your Representatives pursuant hereto. The term "Evaluation Material" does not include information which (i) is or becomes generally available to the public other than as a result of a disclosure by you or your Representatives, (ii) was within your possession prior to its

B-7 Confidentiality Agreement

[Addressee]

_____, 200____

Page 2

being furnished to you by or on behalf of the Company, provided that the source of such information is not known by you to be bound by a confidentiality agreement with or other contractual, legal, or fiduciary obligation of confidentiality to the Company or any other party with respect to such information, or (iii) becomes available to you on a nonconfidential basis from a source other than the Company or any of its representatives, provided that such source is not known by you to be bound by a confidentiality agreement with, or other contractual, legal, or fiduciary obligation of confidentiality to, the Company or any other party with respect to such information.

2. *Use of Evaluation Material and Confidentiality*

(a) You hereby agree that the Evaluation Material will be used for the purpose of evaluating a Transaction, that the Evaluation Material will be kept confidential, and that you and your Representatives will not disclose any of the Evaluation Material in any manner whatsoever except as permitted by this agreement. Further, you agree that any of such Evaluation Material may be disclosed or made available only to such of your managers, directors, officers, employees, affiliates, agents, or advisors, in-cluding, without limitation, attorneys, accountants, financial ad-visors, and prospective financing or equity sources (collectively, the "Representatives") who need to know such information for the purpose of evaluating a Transaction; provided, however, that such Representatives, prior to receipt of any Evaluation Material, shall be informed by you of (i) the confidential nature of such information and (ii) the terms of this agreement and the obligations of confidentiality undertaken by you under this agreement. You agree, at your sole expense, to take all commercially reasonable measures to restrain your Representatives from prohibited or unauthorized disclosure or use of the Evaluation Material.

(b) You agree that, without the prior written consent of the Company, you will not disclose to any other person the fact that the Evaluation Material has been made available to you, the fact that discussions or negotiations are taking place concerning a Transaction, or any of the terms, conditions, or other matters then being discussed with respect thereto (including the status thereof), provided that you may make such disclosure as required by law or legal proceedings (in which event you will consult with the Company regarding the nature, extent, and form of such disclosure prior to

[Addressee]

_____, 200____

Page 3

making any such disclosure, except to the extent there is a reasonable likelihood that the making of such efforts may cause you to stand liable for contempt or suffer other censure or penalty, in which case you may make such disclosure to such extent). The term "person" as used in this letter agreement shall be broadly interpreted to include the media and any corporation, partnership, group, individual, or other entity.

(c) In the event that you or any of your Representatives are requested or required (by oral questions, interrogatories, requests for information or documents in legal proceedings, subpoena, civil investigative demand, or other similar process) to disclose any of the Evaluation Material, you shall provide the Company with prompt written notice of any such request or requirement so that the Company may seek a protective order or other appropriate remedy. If, in the absence of a protective order or other remedy, or the receipt of a waiver by the Company, you or any of your Representatives are nonetheless legally compelled to disclose Evaluation Material to any tribunal or else stand liable for contempt or suffer other censure or penalty, you or your Representatives may, without liability hereunder, disclose to such tribunal only that portion of the Evaluation Material which counsel advises you is legally required to be disclosed, provided that you exercise your reasonable efforts to preserve the confidentiality of the Evaluation Material, including, without limitation, by reasonably cooperating with the Company to obtain an appropriate protective order or other reliable assurance that confidential treatment will be accorded the Evaluation Material by such tribunal.

(d) If one of us decides not to proceed with a Transaction, such party will promptly inform the other party in writing of that decision, which notice shall state that it is being given pursuant to this Confidentiality Agreement. In that case, upon the request of the Company, you will promptly deliver to the Company all Evaluation Material (and all copies thereof) furnished to you or your Representatives by or on behalf of the Company pursuant hereto. In the event of such a decision or request, all other Evaluation Material furnished to you or your Representatives and any other written materials containing or reflecting any information in the Evaluation Material shall be destroyed and no copy thereof shall be retained. Notwithstanding the foregoing provisions, you shall not be required to deliver to the Company the materials which you generate internally,

B-7 Confidentiality Agreement

[Addressee]
_____, 200____

Page 4

including, but not limited to, financial analyses prepared for your management and reports made to your Investment Committee, provided that such materials shall be held by you and kept subject to the terms of this agreement or destroyed. Notwithstanding the return or destruction of the Evaluation Material, you will continue to be bound by your obligations of confidentiality hereunder.

   3. *Accuracy of Evaluation Material.* You understand and acknowledge that neither the Company nor any of its representatives (including, without limitation, any of the Company's directors, officers, employees, or agents) makes any representation or warranty, express or implied, as to the accuracy or completeness of the Evaluation Material. You agree that neither the Company nor any of such representatives shall have any liability to you or to any of your Representatives relating to or resulting from the use of the Evaluation Material or any errors therein or omissions therefrom. Only those representations or warranties which are made in a final definitive agreement regarding any Transaction, when, as, and if executed, and subject to such limitations and restrictions as may be specified therein, will have any legal effect.

   4. *Remedies.* It is understood and agreed that money damages would not be a sufficient remedy for any breach of this letter agreement by you or any of your Representatives and that the Company shall be entitled to equitable relief, including injunctions and specific performance, as a remedy for any such breach. Such remedies shall not be deemed to be the exclusive remedies for a breach by you of this letter agreement, but shall be in addition to all other remedies available at law or equity to the Company.

   5. *Waivers and Amendments.* No failure or delay by the Company in exercising any right, power, or privilege hereunder shall operate as a waiver thereof, nor shall any single or partial exercise thereof preclude any other or future exercise thereof or the exercise of any other right, power, or privilege hereunder. This letter agreement may only be amended with the written consent of you and the Company.

   6. *Effect of Agreement.* Neither the Company nor you nor any of your affiliates are under any legal obligation of any kind whatsoever with respect to conducting negotiations relating to or consummating a Transaction by virtue of this letter agreement. We

each understand and agree that no contract or agreement providing for a Transaction with the Company shall be deemed to exist between you and the Company unless and until you and the Company execute and deliver a definitive agreement (a "Transaction Agreement") acceptable to each party hereto in its sole discretion. We each also agree that unless and until a Transaction Agreement between the Company and you has been executed and delivered, there is no legal obligation of any kind whatsoever with respect to any such Transaction by virtue of this letter agreement or any other written or oral expression with respect to any such Transaction except, in the case of this letter agreement, for the matters specifically agreed to herein. The Company reserves the right, in its sole discretion, to reject any and all proposals made by you with regard to a Transaction.

7. _Miscellaneous._ This agreement shall be governed by, and construed in accordance with, the laws of the State of California without regard to any conflicts of law principles thereof. This agreement may be executed in counterparts. This agreement shall remain in effect for two (2) years from the date first above written, unless sooner terminated by mutual written agreement of the parties or as otherwise provided herein.

8. _Mutuality._ During the course of evaluating the possibility of a Transaction, you may make available to the Company certain information regarding your or your affiliates' business, financial condition, operations, assets and liabilities. In such event, all of the terms and conditions of this letter agreement shall be enforceable against the Company by you as if you or your affiliates were the Company hereunder and this letter agreement were addressed to the Company.

Please confirm your agreement with the foregoing by signing and returning one copy of this letter agreement to the undersigned, whereupon this letter agreement shall become a binding agreement between you and the Company.

Very truly yours,

_____,

a _____

B-7 Confidentiality Agreement

[Addressee]

_____, 200_____

Page 6

                              By: _____
                              Name: _____
                              Title: _____

Accepted and agreed as of the date
first written above.

[Addressee],
a _____

By: _____
Name: _____
Title: _____

GLOSSARY

Acquisition Report Combines all information collected during the due diligence and analytical processes. Constitutes an official record of the transaction.

American Congress on Surveying and Mapping (ACSM) A national association of surveying and mapping professionals.

American Institute of Real Estate Appraisers (AIREA) A national professional and trade association of appraisers. Designations include: MAI (Member, Appraisal Institute) and SRA (Senior Residential Appraiser).

American Land Title Association (ALTA) A national trade association of title insurance companies, abstracters, and title insurance agents.

Anchor Tenant The main (and usually largest) tenant in a shopping center; attracts customers and other tenants to the center. Also called "magnet tenant" and "puller tenant." Sometimes used to describe the dominant lessee in an office building.

Asset management A system that directs and measures the performance of asset groups (in this case, real estate assets) and produces a flow of information needed by ownership to make investment decisions. (Source: Institute of Real Estate Management.)

Baby Boomers Generation which, as of 2005, included people aged 41-62. The largest generation in American History, influenced by the Vietnam War, Watergate, TV, and the Pill.

Benchmark A measurement that forms the standard for comparison; used to measure management "best practices" of individual firms. In property surveys, physical permanent mark that establishes elevation of a property

Best Practices Establishment of industry "benchmarks" (standards) against which the management of individual firms is measured. Generally, the benchmarks reflect what "the best firms are doing."

B2B firms Technology firms linking business firms with other business firms.

B2C firms Technology firms linking business firms with retail customers.

Cash Flow Analysis Cash received during a certain time period from an investment after deducting all cash operating expenses, debt service, and, in the case of taxable investor, an allowance for income taxes.

Category Killers   Major "in depth" (usually discount) retailers, specializing in bulk foods, drugs, toys, home furnishings, sporting goods, consumer electronics, computers, office supplies, and home improvement goods and services. Generally associated with Power Shopping Centers.

CCIM Institute (Certified Commercial Investment Member Institute)   Professional real estate association offering networking, conference, educational, and training resources; confers the CCIM designation denoting "A recognized expert in disciplines of commercial and investment real estate."

CCIM (Certified Commercial Investment Member)   Professional designation conferred by the Commercial Investment Real Estate Institute.

CC&Rs   Public and/or private covenants, conditions, and restrictions affecting the ownership of real property.

Central Business District (CBD)   Traditional center of a city's principal retail, office, service, and government functions. Often called "downtown."

Closed-End Funds   In real estate, a fund with a fixed number of units issued to investors. Also characterized by limited fund life (usually 10 years) and return of invested capital at fund termination or upon property sale or refinancing.

Closing Statement   An accounting of funds involved in a real estate transaction. Also called "settlement statement."

Commercial Real Estate   Real estate owned and operated with the objective of receiving rental income from tenants. Traditional forms of commercial real estate include office buildings, shopping centers, industrial buildings, apartments, and hotels.

Commodity Markets   Markets where real estate is viewed largely as a factor of production. Public policy is to keep land costs and building rents low in order to appeal to new firms and remain attractive to existing firms.

Community Shopping Center   Serves customers within a market radius of approximately 30 minutes driving time. In addition to providing the same goods and services as neighborhood centers, also features tenants selling hard goods such as appliances and hardware as well as soft goods merchants handling apparel. Size ranges from 100,000 to 250,000 SF or larger.

Competence   "A bundle of skills and technologies rather than a single discrete skill or technology; represents the sum of learning across individual skill sets and organizational units; methodology for doing things a firm is "good at." Source: Gary Hamel & C.K. Prahalad, *Competing for the Future*, Harvard Business School Press, 1994.

Competency Convergence   Competitive firms developing the same set of skills to the point where no one firm has a strategic advantage. Serves to intensify price competition until one of the firms comes up with a new competency.

Competitive Properties Survey   Survey of properties in a market area directly competing with a potential or existing property in an investment portfolio.

Concentric Diversification   A strategy of acquiring firms which are similar to, and synergistic with, the acquiring firm in terms of markets, products, and/or technology.

Confidentiality Agreement (C/A)   Agreement designed to protect against misuse of sensitive information. Often used in situations involving properties sold through the competitive bidding process.

Conglomerate Diversification   A diversification strategy of acquiring firms for investment purposes only, with little or no anticipated synergy with the acquired firm.

Constrained Markets   Markets where the supply of real estate is restricted as an integral part of public land use policy. New projects usually undergo a rigorous approval process including compliance with environmental, economic, social, and construction quality standards. Building users, particularly those involved in technology and other high growth industries, are attracted to these areas because the "quality of life" of the area helps them attract and retain high value employees. Real estate investors often target these markets because it is believed that constrained supply allows rent prices to increase, ultimately resulting in greater appreciation in rents and real property values.

Core Investments   Investment Strategy featuring investments in office, industrial, retail, and apartment properties built with quality construction and located in major metropolitan areas. Most properties have a stabilized income stream at the time of purchase with total investment return expectations generally in the 8–10% IRR range.

Council of Commercial Investment Managers (CCIM)   Professional real estate association offering networking, conference, educational, and training resources; confers the CCIM designation denoting "A recognized expert in disciplines of commercial and investment real estate."

Deal Approval Sheet   Final step in the underwriting of a lease transaction. Compares the proposed deal to underwriting projections.

Debt Service Coverage Ratio (DSCR)   Ratio of the Net Operating Income (NOI) to Annual Debt Service (ADS) measuring the times the debt service is covered by the NOI. Used as underwriting criteria for income property mortgage loans. Inverse of Loan To Value Ratio (LTV) which is expressed as a percentage.

Directors and Officers (D&O) Insurance   Insurance that covers legal defense expenses and a portion of possible adverse litigation awards resulting from claims of negligent conduct by a corporate director or officer.

Discounted Cash Flow Analysis (DCF)   A method of analyzing investment opportunities in which future cash flows are discounted and cumulated to arrive at their Net Present Value (NPV) or Internal Rate of Return (IRR).

Due Diligence   In prospective property acquisitions, making a concerted effort to verify previously disclosed information and by uncovering additional problems that may adversely impact property ownership. If problems are uncovered, renegotiation is involved to establish seller legal and monetary responsibility and/or development of a mitigation plan for buyer resolution following close of the transaction.

Earnest Money Deposit (EMD)   A deposit placed in escrow by the buyer of a property to demonstrate intention to complete the transaction. Also called "good faith deposit."

Easement   A right or privilege to enter or use real property which is owned by another party.

"Echo Boomers"   See "Generation Y."

Emotional Intelligence   The ability to work with others and be effective in leading change. People with emotional intelligence are characterized by: self-awareness, self-regulation, strong motivation, empathy for others, and social skills. (Source: Daniel Goleman, Rutgers University.)

Employment Retirement Income Security Act (ERISA)   Legislation passed by congress in 1974 establishing tough new fiduciary standards for the management of pension plans including personal, criminal liability for proven violations. Directed primarily at preventing a repeat of pension abuses related to corporate bankruptcy (Studebaker) and union graft and corruption (Teamster's Union).

Enhanced-Core Investments Generally, core-quality properties to be acquired for an institutional investment portfolio having some type of problem that needs to be "enhanced" before the properties can produce stabilized income at acceptable yield levels. Enhancement strategies may involve redevelopment, retenanting, refinancing, or some other form of problem resolution. This category also includes the development of new core properties as well as the use of above-average leverage to enhance returns. Investment returns are generally in the 10–12% IRR range.

Enterprise Risk Management (ERM) Management concept involving a systematic look at all aspects and levels of an organization's operation in an attempt to identify and analyze risks that it faces in its attempts to realize its strategic and financial objectives.

Escrow A legal arrangement, often connected with the sale of real property, whereby all funds, contracts, mortgages, and deeds are deposited by the buyer and the seller with a third party (an escrow holder). When all conditions have been met, the escrow holder will pay out all funds and deliver all papers as directed by terms of the escrow agreement.

Exit Strategy A series of assumptions made during the acquisition process with respect to when a property should be sold and at what anticipated price.

Externally Focused Strategies Strategic alternatives that focus on external growth and are directed at moving the firm to a more optimal competitive position, with an emphasis on revenue enhancement.

Extranet Major technology interface in the B2B sector providing communication between firms.

Fiduciary A person in a position of confidence or trust, such as an agent, trustee, administrator, or attorney-in-fact (includes a firm or individual investing pension plan assets governed by ERISA).

Final Underwriting Following due diligence, the final management recommendation about whether or not to acquire a property and, if so, a strategy for its ownership and operation; future sale; anticipated investor returns; and remediation of any postclosing problems identified in due diligence. Provides the foundation for approval by the Investment Committee.

Financing Memorandum A document used by lenders for reviewing potential acquisitions. Usually includes property description, pro-forma operating statement, market analysis, and lease comparables.

Flat Organization Organizational structure wherein some middle-management functions are reduced or eliminated.

Floor/Area Ratio (FAR) The ratio of the bulk area of a building to the land on which it is situated. Calculated by dividing the total square footage in the building by the square footage of land area. For example, a 500,000-square-foot building on a 50,000-square-foot land parcel would have an FAR of 10X. Often used by public agencies in regulating building development.

Forward Integration A corporate strategy which attempts to move the firm closer to the customer, thereby potentially reducing costs and improving market share.

Functional Organizational Structure Organizational structure which involves specialization by functions (e.g., marketing, production, financial reporting, etc.).

Funds from Operations (FFO) Method in which periodic earnings from REITs are measured. Noncash items such as building depreciation and amortization of deferred charges are added back to net income to determine FFO.

Game Theory   An analysis of interactive decision problems involving conflicting interests with assumptions of rational behavior by opposing players.

Generation X   The generation which, as of 2005, includes 29–40-year-olds. The first generation of indviduals typically growing up with both parents working full time. "X'ers" seek to integrate family life into career; often embrace entrepreneurial tendencies, and treasure independence above organizational structure.

Generation Y   The generation which, as of 2005, includes most Americans under 28 years old. Major influences include: the first Gulf war; the stock market boom/bust of the late 1990s; September 11 and the war on terrorism; and the Iraq war. Also known as the "echo boomers."

Gross Leasable Area (GLA)   The total area of a building on which the tenant pays rent. Measured from the face of outside walls and the center of joint walls; expressed in square feet. Used primarily in connection with shopping centers.

Growth Corridor   Geographical area which contains certain infrastructure which tends to induce economic growth (e.g., new transportation systems, sewer lines, urban renewal projects etc.). Influences the path of urban growth over the medium term and may create opportunities for real estate investment.

Hard Assets   Assets that are fixed in location.

High Net Worth Individual (HNW)   Term used to describe individuals who have sufficient discretionary income to invest in real estate opportunities.

Historical Cost Basis of Accounting   Traditional accounting model used by most operating companies. Under this method, rental revenues are recognized when earned and operating expenses are accrued as they are incurred. Depreciation expense is also recognized over the useful lives of related assets. Appreciation is not recognized until a sale occurs.

Hold-Sell Analysis   The process of evaluating property disposition decisions (including unsolicited offers) against the original investment strategy, the business plan, and the local market in which the building is located.

Horizontal Integration   Process of firm expansion through acquisition or internal growth without significantly altering the firm's business strategy.

Hoteling   A concept in which employees do not have a personal office but rather a "locker" in which they store their personal effects. They are then assigned a workspace for as long as they will be in that location. Used primarily by accounting and other professional firms with multioffice locations.

Independent Director   Under NYSE rules, a director who has no material relationship with the company. Among other things, regulations require that independent directors: may not receive over $100,000 in compensation directly from the company; an independent director may not be an employee of the company; may not be affiliated with the company's auditor; and may not be an executive officer of a firm with significant financial ties to the company.

Individual Investor   Investors investing directly in a property rather than through an intermediary.

In-Line Tenant   In a shopping center, merchants who occupy space in multitenant buildings.

Institute of Real Estate Management (IREM)   A professional and trade association of real property managers. Affiliated with the National Association of REALTORS. Designations include: CPM Certified Property Manager (individuals) and AMO Accredited Management Organization (firms).

Institutional Investor Financial intermediaries that invest on behalf of depositors, policyholders, or beneficiaries. Generally, investment activities are regulated by laws to limit investor risk.

Institutional Partnership The process of coinvesting by institutional investors (such as pension funds) and real estate operating companies such as REITs, REOCs, or general partnerships. Usually accomplished through a joint-venture limited partnership agreement.

Internal Rate of Return (IRR) A discounted cash flow technique in which investment outlays and future cash flows are discounted by a series of present-value factors, in a trial-and-error process, to arrive at that discount rate (internal rate) which most nearly reduces the current value of future cash flows to zero. Also called the "yield method."

Internally Focused Strategies Strategic alternatives associated with improving internal operations by lowering operating costs, improving procurement policies, or improving the firm's overall work environment.

Internet Worldwide electronic linking of individual, enterprise, institutional, and community Web sites.

Intranet Structured technology interface providing a firm with internal communications and/or with suppliers and contractors.

Investment Committee Formal or informal group of the firm's owners and managers who establish and monitor a firm's investment policy and the investments it makes.

Investment Criteria Sheet List of property criteria consistent with the investment objectives of the firm's investors and approved by the Investment Committee. Used in property acquisition activities.

Investment Discretion Situations in which an investment manager has investor's prior approval to invest in properties which meet established criteria.

Investment Log A daily record of property submissions.

Investment Management Agreement (IMA) An agreement between an institutional investor and an investment manager encapsulating the investor's strategic approach to real estate investing, allowing the manager to acquire, manage, and dispose of properties that fulfill the investor's investment requirements.

Investment Risk Analysis A summary of anticipated risks associated with a prospective investment, including the magnitude of each risk and its potential negative impact on the success of the investment.

Investor Memorandum A document used by investors to review a potential acquisition. Usually includes a property description, pro-forma cash flow, market analysis, lease comparables, management comments regarding possible areas of risk mitigation, and a final investment return analysis.

Landlord The owner of land or a building who leases space to an individual, partnership, corporation, nonprofit organization, or other entity.

Lease Abstract A shorter document that summarizes the key elements of a lease.

Lease Spreading Strategy of spreading tenant lease terms in order to reduce "bunching" of lease terms.

Legal Due Diligence Part of the due diligence process involving legal considerations such as survey and title review, entitlements, Tenant Estoppel Certificates, warranties, and any other legal agreements.

Letter of Credit (LOC) An instrument, usually issued by a bank, authorizing a named person or firm to draw a specified amount of money on the issuer bank.

Letter of Intent (LOI)   A nonlegal document which sets forth certain basic business parameters regarding a potential property acquisition. Generally used by a potential buyer to make an offer to purchase a property.

Leverage   The use of another's money (usually a financial institution) for a portion of the costs of purchasing or developing a real estate investment. Such use may increase equity return.

Limited Liability Corporation (LLC)   A type of business ownership that combines features of a partnership and a corporation.

Listing Agreement   A formal contract appointing a broker as the agent with the right to market a property on behalf of a property owner.

Loan-to-Value Ratio (LTV)   The percentage a loan represents of the cost or value of a property.

Local Improvement District (LID)   Improvement districts organized to provide public improvements or services within an area of a public jurisdiction established and administered by the jurisdiction or an independent board.

London Inter-Bank Offered Rate (LIBOR)   The interest rate at which banks borrow funds from each other in the international overnight market.

Market Timing   Investment strategy based on the real estate cycle, where the investor buys or sells shortly before the trough (low point) or peak of the cycle.

Matrix Organization   Organizational structure where power is concentrated in independent operating units, which then rely on centralized corporate facilities for functional support.

Member Appraisal Institute (MAI)   Professional designation granted by the American Institute of Real Estate Appraisers.

Metropolitan Statistical Area (MSA)   One or more counties having a combined population of at least 50,000, as designated by the U.S. Bureau of the Census.

Modern Portfolio Theory (MPT)   Investment strategy or methodology that seeks to construct an optimal portfolio by considering the relationship between risk and return of individual asset classes. MPT seeks to maximize the risk-adjusted return for the total portfolio. Also called "modern investment theory."

Multifamily REIT   A real estate investment trust that invests primarily in apartment properties.

National Association of Real Estate Investment Managers (NAREIM)   Founded in 1990, a professional association of real estate investment managers. Members represent both domestic and foreign capital, and include real estate advisors, financial institutions, REITs, opportunity funds, and private investors. In aggregate, NAREIM members manage over $300 billion in real estate assets.

National Association of Real Estate Investment Trusts (NAREIT)   A trade association of Real Estate Investment Trusts (REITs) and other publicly traded real estate firms as well as corporations, partnerships, or individuals who advise, study, or service these businesses.

National Council of Real Estate Investment Fiduciaries (NCREIF)   Nonprofit organization that collects, processes, validates, and publishes historical data on real estate performance. Publishes NCREIF Property Index (NPI).

Neighborhood Centers   One of the most common types of shopping centers, usually located within 15 minutes' driving time from the majority of its shoppers. Provides "necessities" such as food, drugs, personal services, etc., primarily through large food and drug chains. Size ranges from 30,000 to 100,000 SF of gross leasable area.

Neighborhood revitalization programs   Programs aimed at revitalizing and restoring deteriorating neighborhoods.

Net Operating Income (NOI)   The gross income from a real estate project, less operating costs and an allowance for anticipated vacancy. Also called "free and clear income" and "project income."

Net Present Value (NPV)   A discounted cash flow technique in which investment outlays and future cash flows are discounted by a predetermined discount rate to arrive at a property's current value. The present-value factor may reflect a "riskless" rate of return (government bonds), the cost of internal capital (opportunity rate), or a "target" or "hurdle" rate which incorporates some assessment of risk.

Net Rentable Area   The amount of space in a building or buildings available for rent to prospective tenants, measured in square feet. Generally excludes elevator shafts, duct shafts, stairways, and smoke towers, and includes rest rooms and janitorial, telephone, and electrical ducts, or a pro-rata share of such space for tenants on multitenant floors. Used primarily in connection with office buildings. Also called "net leased area."

Networked Organizational Structure   A method of organization whereby a firm is divided into units which operate independently of each other but within a framework that is consistent with broader corporate goals and objectives. Data and information are shared through a telecommunications system linking all of the units to each other and to the corporate support group.

Offering Memorandum (OM)   A formal description of a property being offered for sale and the terms of the prospective transaction. Most commonly used in a competitive bidding situation.

Open Listing   A listing given a broker on a nonexclusive basis; i.e., the same listing can be given to other brokers at the same time.

Open-End Fund   In real estate, a fund with a varying number of investors, of differing amounts, who enter or leave the fund periodically (usually quarterly or annually) based on their pro-rata share of the appraised value of all of the properties in the fund.

Opportunistic Investments   High-risk investments which involve some form of value arbitrage arising from disequilibrium in real estate markets.

Other Comprehensive Basis of Accounting (OCBOA)   A modification in the pure cash basis of accounting in which the costs of real estate assets are capitalized and periodic depreciation is charged against these assets.

Perfect Storm   Refers to a combination of location factors contributing to increases in property value. An example would be a parcel or improved property situated in or near a transportation growth corridor, located in a constrained growth local jurisdiction, which is also part of a rapidly growing regional market.

Physical Due Diligence   The process of investigating physical characteristics of a property including but not limited to structural analysis, mechanical systems, electrical systems, environmental review, etc.

Power Shopping Center   A collection of "big box" buildings containing at least 20,000 square feet each and leased to major (mostly discount) retailers specializing in bulk foods, drugs, toys, home furnishings, home improvement, etc. Usually requires at least four of these retailers to provide critical mass. In some situations, anchors may occupy 80–90% of the total center.

Preliminary Underwriting In the investment process, preliminary analysis of investment potential of a property; usually in preparation for submittal to an investment committee for preliminary approval.

Private Placement Memoranda (PPM) A contract between individual investor(s) and the investment manager regarding the investment strategy and level of discretion to acquire, dispose, and manage properties that fulfill an investor's investment requirements. Similar to the Investment Management Agreement (IMA) used primarily for institutional investors.

Pro Forma Cash Flow Analysis (Pro Forma Statement) A projection of the annual income, expenses, and resulting cash flows expected from the operation of an investment.

Project Organization An organizational structure in which employees are organized into a series of high-performance "project" teams focused on product/service tasks. Each project contains its own marketing and financial personnel reporting to the project manager directly and the corporate marketing and the centralized functional managers indirectly.

Propensity to Rent Inclination of market participants to rent rather than own housing.

Property Management Day-to-day management of individual properties, generally involving responsibility for on-site tenant relations, custodial services, maintenance, supply procurement, security, and disaster plan execution. Services may be provided internally or by contact with one or more independent firms.

Property Screening Evaluation process comparing potential acquisitions against criteria "screens" to determine which opportunities best measure up to a set of pre-established investment criteria. Process assists investment managers in continuing to focus on acquiring properties that are consistent with investor's investment strategy.

Property Sourcing First phase of the acquisition process during which potential sources of investment opportunities are researched and identified.

Pro Rations The allocation of taxes, insurance, and other costs among tenants, usually in proportion to the amount of physical space occupied, time of property ownership, or frequency of use.

Public Real Estate Companies Real estate companies with shares traded in public security markets. Includes REITS, real estate operating companies (REOCs), publicly traded homebuilders, mortgage/finance/insurance companies, hospitality firms, property management firms, and legal and real estate service companies.

Purchase Agreement A written document in which the seller and the purchaser set forth their agreement on the terms and conditions of a sale. Also called purchase and sale agreement," "contract of sale," or "agreement of sale."

Qualified Plan Asset Manager (QPAM) Legislation passed by Congress in 1980 as a clarification of ERISA standards for hiring of real estate managers. Establishes the role of a QPAM whose use allows plan sponsors to escape direct liability for the management of real estate assets in their portfolios.

Real Estate Investment Trust (REIT) An unincorporated trust or association managed by one or more trustees, with beneficial ownership in 100 or more persons. Provided 90% of annual income is distributed to beneficial owners, the income is taxed directly to the owners and not to the trust. Sometimes defined as a "real estate mutual fund."

Real Estate Operating Company (REOC)   Company which owns, operates, and/or services real estate assets. Usually organized as a corporation without the special income tax treatment available to real estate investment trusts (REITs). Examples include homebuilders, mortgage/finance companies, hospitality firms, property management firms, and legal and real estate service organizations.

Regional Shopping Centers   A shopping center that serves a market area of up to 45 minutes' driving time, usually used for "big purchase" needs such as appliances, furniture, and apparel. Ranges in size from 500,000 to 900,000 square feet. Most regional centers are anchored by one or more major department stores. May also have tenants such as travel agencies, home services, entertainment, banks, and other personal and business services.

Resolution Trust Corporation (RTC)   A federal agency created by Congress in 1989 to manage and resolve insolvent savings and loan associations placed into its conservatorship or forced into receivership. In 1995 its duties, including insurance of deposits in thrift institutions, were transferred to the Savings Association Insurance Fund.

Right of Survivorship   The automatic succession by a surviving owner to a deceased owner's interest.

Risk Diversification   An investment portfolio strategy designed to spread potential risk by not concentrating investments in a single property type, geographical submarket, or tenant business. Since most portfolios are built "one property at a time," they are difficult to diversify until several properties have been acquired.

Sarbanes-Oxley Act (SOX)   Federal legislation enacted in 2002 in order to protect public company shareholders from financial malpractice, accounting errors, and poor corporate governance practices. Also known as the Public Company Accounting Reform and Investor Protection Act.

Securities and Exchange Commission (SEC)   The federal regulatory agency for the securities industry. Created in 1934 to enforce the Securities Exchange Act. Its main purpose is to protect investors against malpractice in the financial markets and to promote full disclosure; now also acts as one of the enforcers of the Sarbanes-Oxley Act of 2002.

Senior Residential Appraiser (SRA)   A professional designation granted by the American Institute of Real Estate Appraisers.

Sensitivity Analysis   A method of analysis which evaluates several different outcomes critical to a project's success and tests the impact of each event on the overall rate of return.

Silent Generation   The generation which, as of 2005, included people ages 63–80. Heavily influenced by the Great Depression and World War II, resulting in respect for security and centralized authority.

Silo Organization   Traditional hierarchical organizational structure with well-defined marketing, finance, and production functions, each centered on specific tasks.

Special Purpose Entity (SPE)   A business entity formed solely for the purpose of accomplishing a specific task. Also referred to as "off-balance sheet arrangements."

Standard Industrial Classification Codes (SIC)   A method of classifying industries in accordance with the structure and composition of the economy; used to assess the comparability of statistics.

Strategic Planning   A planning process that provides a roadmap to achieving strategic objectives and lays the groundwork for action steps to follow.

Strategic Positioning   A strategy in which a firm performs different activities than its competitors or performs the same activities in a different way in order to obtain better positioning in a market(s).

Subtenant   An individual, partnership, corporation, nonprofit organization, or other entity which leases space in a building in accordance with a written legal sublease agreement, provided that approval of the landlord has been granted.

Super Regional Shopping Center   The largest of all shopping centers, providing a merchandise mix similar to a regional center, but in greater quantity and diversity. Anchored by three or more department stores, it ranges in size from 500,000 to 1,500,000 square feet and serves a market of up to 60 minutes' driving time. May also have an office employment center and entertainment complex on or adjacent to its site. More similar to CBD than any other shopping center.

Synergy   The interaction of two or more parts of a system so that the combined effect is greater than the sum of the parts. In business, synergy describes a hoped-for or real effect resulting from different individuals, departments, or companies working together and stimulating new ideas that result in greater productivity.

Systematic Risk   In an investment portfolio, overall market risk that cannot be diversified.

Tax Basis of Accounting   Method of accounting under which books and records are maintained in a manner consistent with the appropriate provisions of the Internal Revenue Code; supports the reporting an entity uses or expects to use to file its federal income tax return.

Tenant   An individual, partnership, corporation, nonprofit organization, or other entity which leases space in a building in accordance with a written legal lease agreement.

Tenant Estoppel Certificate   A written statement by a tenant identifying that a lease is in effect and certifying that no rent has been prepaid and that there are no outstanding defaults by the landlord, except as specified; relied upon by a prospective lender or purchaser.

Tenants in Common (TIC)   An ownership or a partial interest in property without individual legal title or rights of survivorship.

Transitional Neighborhoods   Neighborhoods going through a revitalization process.

Unrelated Business Income Tax (UBIT)   Income from a trade or business owned by a tax-exempt organization that is not substantially related to its exempt purpose. UBIT applies to all organizations exempt from tax under section 501(a) except certain U.S. instrumentalities.

Unsystematic Risk   Asset class and specific asset risks that can be reduced through portfolio diversification.

Urban Growth   Increase in the intensity of land resource uses in an urban area; may or may not entail an increase in population. Usually includes higher capital investment per unit of land employed and increased productivity associated with urban economic processes.

Urban Land Institute (ULI)   A nonprofit organization dedicated to providing information on development and use of land resources and building operations.

Urban Renewal   The redevelopment of a deteriorated urban area in which one or more governmental agencies assume a leadership role in organizing and implementing the process. Usually includes restructuring of land ownership parcels; oversight of physical planning activities; financing, construction, and operation of public improvements; and oversight of development and operation of private development within the project area.

UST   Abandoned underground storage tanks.

Valuation   An estimate of value of a property by means of an appraisal.

Value-Added Investments   Properties not meeting core quality standards, but which can add value to the overall portfolio. These investments generally involve a higher level of risk and include properties such as raw land, hotels, restaurants, entertainment complexes, factory outlets, and business showrooms. These investments may also involve a higher level of financial leverage. Expected investment returns are generally in the 12–15% IRR range.

Vertical Integration   Process of firm expansion through addition of functions forward or backward in the production/marketing process.

Virtual Organization   Organizational structure in which the firm performs internally only its core competencies, while outsourcing all other activities (which may include production activities). Heavy reliance placed on state-of-the-art telecommunication system linking individual units.

Zoning   Governmental process by which the character and use of real property is regulated and controlled.

Index

Acquisition process
  asset manager's role in, 173–182
  closing in, 142–145, 160, 176–179, 359
  due diligence in, 111–135, 137–138,
      175–176, 303–314
  final approvals in, 140, 142
  final underwriting in, 137–140, 141
  flow chart for, 86
  negotiations during, 105–109
  preliminary approvals in, 103–105
  preliminary underwriting in, 91, 93–102
  property screening in, 88–91, 92, 174–175
  property sourcing in, 85–88, 173–174
Acquisition Report, 143
  asset manager's role with, 177
Acquisition timeline, 105, 113
Apartment facilities, 38–43
  demographics' influence on, 39–41
  investment returns for, 42–43
  location factors for, 41–42
  other market demand criteria for, 42
  population growth's impact on, 38–39
Appraisals, in due diligence, 134
Approvals, investment
  final, 140, 142
  preliminary, 103–105
Asbestos, 126n9
Assembly facilities, 51
Asset managers
  building operations through, 169–170,
      191–200
  business plan development by, 167–168
  definition of, 163–164
  financial reporting through, 171–172
  investment transactions through, 173–182
  investor relations with, 172
  project management by, 170–171
  property insurance negotiation by, 169
  property managers v., 164–166
  responsibilities of, 166–172
  risk diversification monitored by, 168–169
  tenant relations with, 18–20, 167, 183–189
Asset manager-tenant relations
  importance of, 18–20, 167, 183–184
  lease renewal strategies in, 185–188
  new lease process in, 188–189

Audit committees
  governance reforms' impact on, 284, 286
  role of, 296–297

Baby Boomers, 27, 28–29, 39, 40, 72
Board of directors. *See also* Governance,
      enterprise
  governance guidelines for, 285, 290–301
  governance reforms' impact on, 283–286
  role of, 290–291
Boomers. *See* Baby Boomers
Brokers, 91
  acquisition process influenced by, 87
  property screening by, 174–175
  selection of, 149–152, 182
Budgets, due diligence, 104, 113
Building development, in value cycle, 7
Building operations
  asset manager's role in, 169–170, 191–200
  construction management in, 170–171, 194
  disaster planning in, 197–200
  maintenance for, 191–194
  security for, 194–197
Business organizations
  as market demand drivers, 31–33
  silo *v.* project formats in, 32–33
Business travelers, hotels influenced by, 57
Buyers, potential
  broker's role with, 149–152, 182
  property criteria for, 149
  targeted geographical areas for, 148–149
  tenant criteria for, 149
  types of, 148

C/A. *See* Confidentiality Agreement
Cash flow analysis, 97, 99
  discounted, 99, 100, 138, 139
Central Business Districts, office locations in, 49
CEOs
  annual review of, 301
  chairpersons as, 296
  succession planning of, 301
Chairpersons
  CEOs *v.*, 296
  role of, 295–296
Closed-end funds, 67

Closing process
  documents for, 142–143, 359
  transition to buyer in, 144–145, 160, 176–179
  waiving contingencies in, 143–144
Closing Statement, 144
  asset manager's role with, 176
  description of, 160
  sample of, 359
Code of ethics, company, 282–283
Coldwell Banker, 67
Commercial banks, 59n2, 60
Commercial real estate
  asset management in, 163–210
  decline in, 23–25
  definition of, 1, 5n
  enterprise management in, 213–302
  investment process in, 3–81
  legal documents in, 315–376
  subsets of, 37
  transaction management in, 85–160
Commodity markets, 12–13, 272
Community centers, 44
Company-Tenant Interview Questionnaire, 133,
  134, 135
Compensation committees
  governance reforms' impact on, 284
  role of, 297
Competency convergence, 233
Competitive advantage, in strategic planning,
  238–240
Competitive bidding, in property disposition,
  156–157
Competitive properties survey, 96–97, 98
Concentric diversification, 236
Confidentiality Agreement (C/A), 105
  purpose of, 153
  sample of, 367–372
Conglomerate diversification, 236
Consolidations, 243
Constrained markets, 13–14, 48, 272
Construction management
  new buildings in, 194
  space build-outs in, 170, 194
  space remodeling in, 170
  space repairs in, 170–171, 194
Contractors, for due diligence, 113, 114
Conventioneers, hotels influenced by, 57
Core competencies, 245
  convergence of, 233
  definition of, 231–232
  improvement of, 239–240
  maintaining/reorienting of, 238
Core investment strategies, 76, 248, 249
Customers, as tenants, 214–215, 231–233

DCF analysis. See Discounted cash flow analysis
Decision making, employee participation in,
  225–227
Demographics, 26–31, 40–41
  absolute population change in, 27
  apartments influenced by, 39–41
  Baby Boomer, 27, 28–29, 39, 40, 72
  Echo Boomer, 31, 39, 40
  generation cohorts in, 27–31
  Generation X, 29–31
  silent generation, 27–28
Developers
  leadership role of, 213–214
  value creation influenced by, 7, 8–9
Dhar, Ravi, 266
Directors. See Board of directors
Directors and Officers (D&O) insurance, 287
Disaster planning, lessons from, 197–200
Disaster planning checklist, 200
Discounted cash flow (DCF) analysis, 99, 100
  final, 138, 139
Disposition process, 147–160
  alternatives in, 156–157
  asset manager's role in, 179–182
  broker selection in, 149–152, 182
  buyer due diligence in, 159–160
  importance of, 147
  property reports in, 156
  targeting buyers in, 148–149
  transaction documents in, 157–159
  transition to buyer in, 144–145, 160, 176–179
Distribution facilities, 51–52
  technology's impact on, 52
Diversification risk. See Risk diversification
D&O insurance. See Directors and Officers
    insurance
Dot-com boom, 31
Downtown areas. See Central Business Districts
Drucker, Peter, 219, 220
Due diligence process, 111–135. See also Legal
    due diligence; Physical due diligence
  asset manager's role in, 175–176
  best practices checklist for, 307–308
  budget for, 104, 113
  business, 132–135
  buyer, 159–160
  checklist for, 113, 115–118
  contractors for, 113, 114
  environmental review in, 125–127
  financial review in, 133
  insurance review in, 134
  legal, 127–132
  management of, 112–118
  physical, 118–127

Due diligence process (*Cont.*):
reconciliations in, 137–138
role of, 112
steps prior to, 113–115
tasks in, 305–306
technology applied to, 124–125,
303–314
tenant interviews in, 132–133, 134–135

Earnest money deposit (EMD), 108, 159
Echo Boomers, 31, 39, 40
E-commerce, components of, 24–26
Economic growth, as market demand driver, 23,
24, 25
EMD. *See* Earnest money deposit
Emotional intelligence, 216–219
Empathy, as leadership quality, 218
Employment Retirement Income Security Act
(ERISA)
issues in, 131, 178
pension plan managers influenced by, 66
Enhanced-core investment strategies, 76–77,
248, 249
Enron, 279–281
Enterprise management
governance in, 279–302
leadership in, 213–227
market positioning process in, 247–261
risk management in, 263–278
strategic planning in, 229–246
Enterprise Risk Management (ERM),
276–278
real estate companies influenced by,
277–278
Entrepreneurs, 12
Generation X as, 30
technology's role with, 214
Environmental review, in due diligence process,
125–127
Environmental Site Assessment (ESA), 126
ERISA. *See* Employment Retirement Income
Security Act
ERISA/UBIT issues, 131
asset manager's role with, 178
ERM. *See* Enterprise Risk Management
ESA. *See* Environmental Site Assessment
Escrow, 108
Estoppel certificate. *See* Tenant Estoppel
Certificate
Executive committees, 297–298
Exit strategy, role of, 179
Expansion, in real estate cycle, 16, 17
Externally focused strategies, 234–235
Extranet, 26

Fiber-optic system, 125
Final Investment Underwriting, copy of, 138,
140, 141
Financial reporting, 201–210
asset manager's role in, 171–172
comparative analysis in, 205–210
fair value basis in, 202–203
federal tax requirements in, 203–205
governance reform's impact on, 282
historical cost basis in, 203
modified cash basis in, 201–203
tax basis in, 202
Financing Memorandum, 142
5/50 rule, 62
501C(25) corporation, 143
Flat organizational structures, 224, 241
Foreign investors, 61
direct representation of, 79–80
equity investment of, 60
intermediary investing by, 79
U.S. real estate assets of, 62
Forward integration, 234, 235

Generation cohorts, 27–31
Generation X, 29–31
Goetzman, William N., 266
Goleman, Daniel, 216
Governance, enterprise, 279–302. *See also*
Reforms, enterprise governance
board of directors guidelines for, 285,
290–301
current situation in, 301–302
Enron's influence on, 279–281
legislative and regulatory reforms in,
281–288
public real estate companies influenced by,
288–290
Governance guidelines, corporate, 285,
290–301
annual review of CEO in, 301
board access to independent advisors in, 300
board meeting frequency in, 293
board orientation and continuing education
in, 298–299
board self-evaluation in, 300–301
board size in, 293
board term of service in, 294
CEO as chairperson in, 296
chairperson's job description in, 295–296
conflicts of interest in, 299
director qualifications in, 292
director responsibilities in, 291–292
directors' compensation in, 295
election of directors in, 294

Governance guidelines, corporate (*Cont.*):
    female directors in, 292
    independent directors in, 293
    meeting preparation and attendance in, 299
    minority directors in, 293
    nonmanagement directors' role, 300
    outside advisor attendance in, 299
    service on other boards in, 294–295
    shareholder access in, 300
    standing committees in, 296–299
    succession planning in, 301

Heating, ventilation, and air-conditioning
        (HVAC), 123–124
High net worth (HNW), 78
HNW. *See* High net worth
HNW investors, 78–79
Hold-sell analysis, asset manager's role in,
        180–182
Horizontal integration, 234, 235
Hotel facilities, 55–58
    demand sources for, 55–57
    investment returns for, 58
    management of, 55–56
    types of, 57–58
"Hoteling," 34n
HVAC. *See* Heating, ventilation, and
        air-conditioning
Hypersupply, in real estate cycle, 16, 17

Immigration, 26, 32, 39
Individual investors, 59n1
    federal tax reporting by, 203
    financial reporting analysis of, 205–210
    objectives of, 78–79
    partnerships of, 78, 177–178
Industrial facilities, 51–55
    building factors for, 53–54
    investment returns for, 55
    location factors for, 53
    office space in, 36
    types of, 51
    warehouse layouts in, 54
Information Technology (IT)
    due diligence influenced by, 124–125, 303–314
Institutional investors, 59–69
    foreign, 60, 61, 62, 79–80
    life insurance, 59, 60
    pension fund, 60, 64–69, 71–78
    real estate's importance to, 247–248
    REIT, 1, 14, 60, 61–64, 65, 73–74
Insurance
    D&O, 287
    due diligence review of, 134

Insurance (*Cont.*):
    environmental, 127
    property, 169
Internal rate of return (IRR), 99, 100, 101
Internally focused strategies, 235–236
Internet, 26
    maintenance issues impacted by, 193
Intranet, 26
    disposition property marketed through, 155
Investment Committee, 89, 101
    asset manager's influence on, 175
    definition of, 89n3
    final approvals by, 140, 142
    preliminary approvals by, 103–105
    purpose and functions of, 103–104
Investment criteria sheets, 89, 90
Investment log entries, 92
Investment Management Agreement, 81
Investment managers. *See also* Acquisition
        process; Disposition process
    investor objectives represented by, 71–81
    role of, 1, 68, 182
Investment partnership agreement
    asset manager's role in, 177–178
Investment portfolios. *See* Portfolios, real estate
        investment
Investment process. *See* Real estate investment
        process
Investment strategies
    core, 76
    enhanced-core, 76–77, 248, 249
    pension fund, 76–78, 269, 270
    real estate cycle's role in, 18, 19
Investor Memorandum, 142–143
Investor objectives, 71–81
    differences in, 80
    foreign, 79–80
    individual, 78–79
    pension fund, 71–78
    portfolio diversification reconciled with, 80–81
IPOs, of REITs, 63–64
IRR. *See* Internal rate of return
IT. *See* Information Technology

KB Home, 6, 7

Land use regulation, 12–14
    commodity markets impacted by, 12–13
    constrained markets impacted by, 13–14
Landlord-tenant relations. *See* Asset manager-
        tenant relations
Leadership, enterprise, 213–227
    changing roles of, 214–215
    decision making influenced by, 225–227

Leadership, enterprise (*Cont.*):
  manager's role in, 215–216
  qualities of, 216–219
  skills developed in, 219–223
  work environment nurtured through,
    223–225
Leadership development skills
  communication's role in, 223
  expertise acknowledged through, 220
  learning differences recognized in, 220–221
  performance recognized in, 221
  personal *v.* organizational values in, 221–222
  relationship's importance in, 222–223
  strengths emphasized in, 219–220
Leasing process, 188–189
  abstracts for, 130–131, 355–358
  investor portfolios influenced by, 275–276
  renewal strategies in, 185–188
  spreading strategy for, 20
Lee, Stephen, 271
Legal documents, sample
  Closing Statement, 359
  Confidentiality Agreement, 367–376
  Lease Abstract, 355–358
  Letter of Intent, 315–318
  Listing Agreement, 360–366
  Purchase Agreement, 319–351
  Tenant Estoppel Certificate, 352–354
Legal due diligence, 127–132
  consent decrees and court orders in, 132
  contractors for, 113, 114
  entitlements in, 128–129
  ERISA / UBIT issues in, 131, 178
  lease abstracts in, 130–131, 355–358
  other agreements in, 132
  service contracts in, 131–132
  survey and title in, 127–128
  warranties in, 131
Letter of Credit (LOC), 108, 159
Letter of Intent (LOI), 101, 105–107, 108, 109
  asset manager's role in, 175
  purpose of, 157–158
  sample of, 315–318
Life insurance companies, 59
  equity investment of, 60
Limited Liability Corporations (LLCs), 143
  federal tax reporting of, 203, 207
Listing Agreement
  provisions of, 152–153
  sample of, 360–366
LLCs. *See* Limited Liability Corporations
LOC. *See* Letter of Credit
Location, of property, 11–12
LOI. *See* Letter of Intent

Maintenance process, 191–194
  building supplies procurement in, 193–194
  corrective, 193
  custodial, 192
  preventative, 192
Major players. *See* Institutional investors
Manufacturing facilities, 51
Market demand driver(s), 23–36
  business organizations as, 31–33
  demographics as, 26–31, 39–41, 72
  economic growth as, 23, 24, 25
  firm dependent, 37–38
  household dependent, 37–38
  physical workplace as, 33–36
  population growth as, 26–27, 38–39
  technology as, 23–26, 35
  workplace location as, 35
Market positioning process, enterprise, 247–261
  battlefield mapping in, 257–259
  competitive environment in, 252–257
  investment preferences survey in, 248–251
  proposed fund features in, 259–261
  target market identified in, 247–248
  target market refined in, 248–251
Market timing, 15–18, 19
Matrix organizational structure, 241, 242
Mergers, 243
Metro areas
  analysis of, 94–96
  apartment facilities in, 41–42
  entrepreneur's influence on, 12
  industrial facilities in, 53
  land use regulation in, 12–14
  office facilities in, 48, 271–272, 273
  office investment in, 48–49
  property factors of, 15
  rankings of, 11–12
  selection of markets in, 48
  submarket location factors in, 14–15
Milken Index, 11–12
Mitigation action plan, asset manager's role in,
    179
Mixed asset portfolios, 75, 80–81
  real estate's role in, 265
  returns in, 264
  risk diversification of, 263–271
Modern Portfolio Theory (MPT), 72
  systematic *v.* unsystematic risk, 263
Motels, 58
Motivation, as leadership quality, 217–218
Motor hotels, 58
MPT. *See* Modern Portfolio Theory
Mueller, Glenn, 16
Multigenerational workplace, 225

Nasdaq regulatory reforms
    corporate areas influenced by, 281–286
    public companies reaction to, 287–288
Negotiated sales, in property disposition, 157
Negotiations, with seller, 105–109
    escrow in, 108
    LOI in, 105–107, 108, 109
    Purchase Agreement in, 105, 107
    strategies in, 108–109
Neighborhood centers, 43–44
Net present value (NPV) analysis, 99, 100,
    180–182
Networked organizational structure, 241, 242
New York Stock Exchange reforms. *See* NYSE
    reforms
Nodes, business/community, 49–50
Nominating/corporate governance committees
    governance reforms' impact on, 284
    role of, 297
NPV analysis. *See* Net present value analysis
NYSE (New York Stock Exchange) reforms
    corporate areas influenced by, 281–286
    public companies' reaction to, 287–288

Offering Memorandum (O/M), 89n4
    description of, 153–155
Office facilities, 46–51
    investment returns for, 50–51
    location factors for, 49–50
    metro area risk matrix for, 273
    metro area's impact on, 48–49, 271–272,
    273
Office parks, 50
Office space
    demand for, 46–48
    in industrial facilities, 36, 51
    technology's impact on, 34–35, 47–48
O/M. *See* Offering Memorandum
Open-end funds, 66–67
Opportunistic investment strategies, 77
Organizational structure, 33, 224
    types of, 240–242
Ownership transition
    asset manager's role in, 176–179
    importance of, 144–145, 160

Partnership investors, 78, 243–244
    asset manager's role with, 177–178
    federal income tax requirements for, 204
    financial reporting analysis of, 205–210
Part-time employees, 225
Pension funds, 64–69
    cash generation by, 72–73
    closed-end, 67

Pension funds (*Cont.*):
    concentration of capital and management in,
        68–69
    early history of, 65
    equity investment of, 60
    ERISA standards for, 66
    federal income tax requirements of, 204–205
    financial reporting analysis of, 205–210
    investment characteristics of, 74–75
    investment preferences survey of, 248–251
    investment strategies for, 76–78, 269, 270
    investment vehicles for, 73–74
    open-end, 66–67
    plan funding obligations in, 71–72
    portfolio risk diversification in, 72
    QPAM legislation's impact on, 68
    real estate avoided by, 65–66
    risk and return survey of, 266–271
Pension Real Estate Association (PREA)
    portfolio survey by, 74–75
    risk and return survey by, 266–271
"Perfect storm," 15
Phase I Environmental Site Assessment, 126
Phase II Environmental Analysis, 126–127
Physical due diligence, 118–127
    architectural systems in, 122
    contractors for, 113, 114
    electrical systems in, 124
    electronic systems in, 124–125
    environmental insurance in, 127
    environmental review in, 125–127
    governmental approvals in, 120–122
    maps, specialized in, 119–120
    mechanical systems in, 123–124
    plans and specifications in, 120, 121
    property photos in, 118–119
    structural systems in, 122–123
    vertical transportation in, 124
Physical workplace, 33–36
    horizontal *v.* vertical structures in, 33
    office space decline in, 34–35, 47–48
    technology's impact on, 34–35
Pleasure travelers, hotels influenced by, 56–57
Population growth, 26–27
    apartments impacted by, 38–39
Porter, Michael, 240
Portfolio diversification. *See* Multiasset portfolios
Portfolio risk diversification, 72
Portfolios, multiasset. *See* Multiasset portfolios
Portfolios, real estate investment
    lease terms' influence on, 275–276
    managing risk in, 271–276
    property types' influence on, 272–273
    tenants influence on, 274–275

Power centers, 44–45
PPM. *See* Private Placement Memoranda
PREA. *See* Pension Real Estate Association
Preliminary Investment Underwriting, copy of, 101–102
Preliminary title report, 93–94, 95
Premarketing activities, 147–149
  asset manager's role in, 182
Private Placement Memoranda (PPM), 81
Project management, asset manager's role in, 170–171
Project organizations, 32–33
"Propensity to rent," 39
Property factors, in value creation, 15
Property life cycle, 6
Property managers
  asset managers *v.,* 164–166
  building operation responsibilities of, 169, 170, 191–200
Property owners, as source for acquisitions, 86–87
Property screening, 88–91
  asset manager's role in, 174–175
  broker's role in, 174–175
  investment criteria sheets in, 89, 90
  investment log entry in, 92
  property submittals in, 89, 91, 92
  pursuit costs in, 91
Property sourcing, 85–88
  asset manager's role in, 173–174
  broker's importance in, 87
  other leads for, 88
  property owner's role in, 86–87
  tenant's role in, 88
Property types, 37–58
  apartment, 38–43
  hotel, 55–58
  industrial facility, 36, 51–55
  investor portfolios influenced by, 272–273
  office facility, 46–51
  retail facility, 43–46
Pro-rations, 144, 160
Public real estate companies
  corporate governance for, 288–290
  governance guidelines for, 290–301
  shareholders influence on, 289–290
Purchase Agreement, 105, 107
  asset manager's role in, 175
  description of, 158
  sample of, 319–351

QPAM. *See* Qualified Plan Asset Manager
Qualified Plan Asset Manager (QPAM), 68

Real estate. *See* Commercial real estate
Real estate committees, 298
Real estate cycle, 16–18
  expansion in, 16, 17
  hypersupply in, 16, 17
  as investment strategy, 19
  recession in, 16, 18
  recovery in, 16, 17
Real estate investment process
  institutional investors in, 59–69, 71–78, 79–80
  investor objectives in, 71–81
  market demand drivers in, 23–36, 37–38, 38–39, 42, 72
  property types in, 37–58
  value creation in, 5–20
Real estate investment trusts (REITs), 1, 14, 61, 68, 73–74, 78, 86
  business firms similar to, 229–230
  equity investment of, 60
  federal income tax requirements for, 205
  financial reporting analysis of, 205–210
  governance reforms' impact on, 279
  history of, 62–64
  multiasset portfolios enhanced by, 271
  old *v.* new, 64
  portfolio benefits from, 276
  property type investments of, 65
Real estate operating companies (REOCs), 63
Recession, in real estate cycle, 16, 18
Recovery, in real estate cycle, 16, 17
Reforms, enterprise governance, 281–288
  attorneys influenced by, 286
  auditing standards strengthened by, 284, 286
  code of ethics in, 282–283
  corporate governance guidelines required by, 285
  directors influenced by, 283
  disclosure controls and procedures impacted by, 282
  enforcement of, 286
  financial reporting impacted by, 282
  firm security impacted by, 286
  internal controls impacted by, 282
  management compensation impacted by, 283
  other reporting impacted by, 282
  public companies' reaction to, 287–288
  shareholders influenced by, 285
  standing board committees impacted by, 283–284
  whistleblowers protected by, 286
Regional centers, 45
REITs. *See* Real estate investment trusts
REOCs. *See* Real estate operating companies

Resort hotels, 58
Resource constraints, 236
Retail facilities, 43–46
  investment returns for, 46, 47
  location factors for, 45–46
Risk and return, in value creation, 8–9
Risk diversification, 77–78
  asset manager's role in, 168–169
  in mixed asset portfolios, 263–271
  in real estate investment portfolios, 271–276
Risk management, 263–278
  enterprise, 276–278
Rural land conversion, 6–7

Sarbanes-Oxley Act (SOX), 282
  ERM influenced by, 277
  public companies impacted by, 281–286
  public companies' reaction to, 287–288
Savings associations, 59n2, 60
Screening. See Property screening
Securities and Exchange Commission (SEC),
    regulatory reforms of, 281–286
Security, building
  modification options in, 195–197
  redesign options in, 194–195
Self-awareness, 217
Shareholders
  governance reforms' impact on, 285
  public real estate companies influenced by,
    289–290
Shopping centers. See Retail facilities
Silent generation, 27–28
Silo organizations, 32
Single family housing, 1n, 23, 38
Social skills, as leadership quality, 218–219
Software, due diligence. See Technology, due
    diligence
Sourcing. See Property sourcing
SOX. See Sarbanes-Oxley Act
Specialized nodes, 50
Standing committees
  governance guidelines for, 296–299
  governance reforms' impact on, 283–284
Stevenson, Simon, 271
Strategic planning process, enterprise, 240–245
  alliance between firms in, 243–244
  alternative strategies in, 234–237
  assessment of firm in, 230
  company goals in, 237
  competition benchmarking in, 233–234
  competitive advantage in, 238–239
  consolidations in, 243
  core competencies in, 231–232, 233, 238,
    239–240, 245

Strategic planning process, enterprise (Cont.):
  customer identification in, 231
  customer intimacy in, 232–233
  final plan formulation in, 237–240
  flexibility in, 244–245
  implementation of, 240–245
  institutionalization of, 240
  internal resources in, 243
  monitoring of, 244
  new initiatives in, 240
  noncore activities in, 237–238
  organizational structure support of, 240–242
  real estate industries impacted by, 229–230
  summary of, 245–246
  value proposition in, 231
Submarket location factors, 14–15
Succession planning, 301
Super regional centers, 45
Survey and title review, 127–128
Synergy, in value creation, 9–10

Technology, 23–26, 47, 214
  business organizations impacted by, 32
  distribution facilities impacted by, 52
  Echo Boomer's role with, 31
  e-commerce's role in, 24–26
  employment impacted by, 23
  Generation X's role with, 30–31
  office space impacted by, 34–35, 47–48
  productivity increased by, 25
  workplace location impacted by, 35
Technology, due diligence, 303–314
  best practices checklist in, 307–308
  competitive advantage through, 312
  content managed by, 308–309
  critical information delivered by, 310
  documents managed by, 308
  e-mail's limitation in, 306–307
  employee training improved by, 311–312
  employee turnover reduced through, 311
  litigation costs reduced through, 311
  management support of, 314
  mistakes reduced through, 309–310
  other approaches v., 312–313
  privacy concerns addressed by, 308
  problems addressed by, 305–306
  qualitative v. quantitative software in, 303–306
  time managed by, 309
Tenant Estoppel Certificate, 129–130
  sample of, 352–354
  seller's role with, 159
Tenants
  asset manager's role with, 18–20, 167, 179,
    183–189

Tenants (*Cont.*):
  as customers, 214–215, 231–233
  due diligence interviews with, 132–135
  estoppel certificates for, 129–130, 159,
      352–354
  investor portfolios influenced by, 274–275
  potential buyers' interest in, 149
  as property source leads, 88
Title holding entity, 143
  asset manager's role with, 178
Tour groups, hotels influenced by, 57
Transaction management. *See* Acquisition
      process; Disposition process

UBIT. *See* Unrelated Business Income Tax
UBTI. *See* Unrelated business taxable income
Umbrella Partnership REITs (UPREITs), 63
Underground storage tanks (UST), 126
Underwriting, final, 137–140, 141
  asset manager's role in, 176, 179
  discounted cash flow analysis in, 138, 139
  due diligence reconciliations in, 137–138
Underwriting, preliminary, 91, 93–102
  asset manager's role in, 175
  cash flow analysis in, 97, 99
  competitive properties survey in, 96–97, 98
  discounted cash flow analysis in, 99, 100
  metro area analysis in, 94–96
  sensitivity analysis in, 99, 101
  site visit in, 93
  submarket data in, 96
  title report in, 93–94, 95
Unrelated Business Income Tax (UBIT)
  issues with, 131, 178
Unrelated business taxable income (UBTI),
      204–205
Unsolicited offers, asset manager's role with,
      180–182
UPREITs. *See* Umbrella Partnership REITs

Uptown commercial nodes, 50
Urban growth process, 5–8
UST. *See* Underground storage tanks

Value creation, 5–20
  asset manager's role in, 18–20
  investor participation in, 8–9
  land use regulation in, 12–14
  location's importance in, 11–12
  market timing in, 15–18, 19
  property factors in, 15
  risk and return in, 8–9
  stocks *v.* real estate in, 9–10
  submarket location factors in, 14–15
  synergy's role in, 9–10
  value cycle's role in, 5–8
Value cycle, real estate, 5–8
  building development in, 7
  decline and renewal process in, 5–8
  property life in, 6
  rural land conversion in, 6–7
Value proposition, 231
Value-added investment strategies, 77, 249
Value-added properties, 77
Vertical integration, 234, 235
Virtual organization, 241

Waivers, 143–144
  asset manager's role in, 176
Warehouse layouts, 53–54
Work environment
  flat organizational structure in, 224, 241
  multigenerational influence on, 225
  value of trust in, 223
Work teams, 242
Workplace location, technology's impact on, 35

Y Generation. *See* Echo Boomers
Yuppies. *See* Baby Boomers